THE PAWNEE INDIANS

THE CIVILIZATION OF THE AMERICAN INDIAN SERIES

THE PAWNEE INDIANS

By

GEORGE E. HYDE

FOREWORD BY SAVOIE LOTTINVILLE

UNIVERSITY OF OKLAHOMA PRESS

NORMAN

By George E. Hyde

Corn Among the Indians of the Upper Missouri (with George F. Will)
(Cedar Rapids, Iowa, 1917)
The Early Blackfeet and Their Neighbors (Denver, 1933)
Rangers and Regulars (Denver, 1933; Columbus, 1953)
Red Cloud's Folk: A History of the Oglala Sioux Indians (Norman, 1937, 1957)
The Pawnee Indians (Denver, 1951; Norman, 1973)
A Sioux Chronicle (Norman, 1956)
Indians of the High Plains: From the Prehistoric Period to the Coming of Europeans (Norman, 1959)
Spotted Tail's Folk: A History of the Brulé Sioux (Norman, 1961)
Indians of the Woodlands: From Prehistoric Times to 1725 (Norman, 1962)
Life of George Bent: Written from His Letters (Norman, 1968)

Dedicated
to
THE TWO DOCTORS GIFFORD (FATHER AND SON)
AND TO DOCTOR WILLIAM H. STOKES
in gratitude

Library of Congress Cataloging in Publication Data

Hyde, George E.   1882–1968.
    The Pawnee Indians.

    (The Civilization of the American Indian series)
    1. Pawnee Indians.   I. Title.   II. Series.
E99.P3H93   1974   970.3   72–9260
ISBN 0–8061–1065–1

Foreword

WHEN YOUNG George Bird Grinnell, just graduated from Yale College, went out to the Platte and the Loup rivers in the summer of 1872 to see the Pawnees and go with them on their summer buffalo hunt, he was beginning a career that would prove to be highly fruitful for western history and Indian anthropology. There, among the Chaui, the Skidis, Pitahauerats, and Kitkehahkis, he heard absorbing recitals of Pawnee deeds in battle, on horse raiding expeditions, and in the age-old pursuit of the Plains buffalo herds.

In subsequent travels among the Pawnees and other Plains tribes he forged a method for the future development of Indian history. It would combine oral accounts from Indian informants, the use of white documents, and, in developing a picture antedating both, reliance upon archaeological findings. Grinnell's first book was *Pawnee Hero Stories and Folk Tales* (1889). His method, utilized in a succession of books, would find its highest expression in *The Fighting Cheyennes* (1915) and *The Cheyenne Indians* (1923). After Grinnell, the art of Indian history would never again be the same.

Nor, for that matter, would the life of young George E. Hyde, whom Grinnell met and employed as his research assistant sometime after the turn of the century. A Nebraskan living in Omaha, Hyde in his youth had looked westward from the Missouri River upon the panorama of Plains life and history stretching to the Rocky Mountains. He was at the very doorstep of the historic Council Bluffs, trading center of the first half of the nineteenth century for the Missouri River tribes—Missourias, Kansa, Kickapoos, Otos, Pawnees, Iowas, and even the Osages, ranging northwestward towards the buffalo ranges of the upper Plains. Although most of the tribes of Nebraska and Kansas had by 1900 been relocated in Indian Territory (now Oklahoma), the history of these peoples was never far away in such an environment. The opportunity to assist Grinnell simply made it more real.

George Hyde's early professional tasks were to seek out Cheyenne informants and collect from them the oral history and eye-witness testimony which Grinnell needed but couldn't always get. He carried out his duties well for his employer, and he gained for himself a schooling in method which, for the Cheyennes, is best demonstrated in *Life of George Bent,* which he assembled at the end of his life and I edited in 1968. In between, Hyde worked on his own very much as Grinnell had done, on various tribes: the Blackfeet; the Brulé Sioux, with whom the Southern Cheyennes and their northern kinsmen were closely allied after the Sand Creek Massacre of 1864; the Oglala Sioux; the Southern Arapahos; the life and work of intermarried western figures like William Bent of Bent's Fort and his half-Cheyenne son George; peripherally the Kiowas and Comanches; and, not least of all, the Padoucas or Patokas, powerful but shadowy figures, whether Apaches, as he believed, or Comanches, as many European observers in the early period variously asserted. Through all of his work (a complete list of his books appears on the copyright page of this book) runs the fine line of historical balance between what primitive men saw or recited from the tribal memory and the records kept by more sophisticated men.

In many ways, *Pawnee Indians* is the best synthesis Hyde ever wrote. It looks far back in tribal history, assessing cautiously the values in oral history extending for as long as a century and a half. It looks critically not only at white motives but at Pawnee cultural characteristics and military patterns. All—or almost all—of the relevant historical sources are implicit in the account. (Hyde never quite developed an acceptance, much less a fondness, for precise scholarly forms; but the searcher who retraces his steps will usually find him accurate in his management of government and other documents.) And his impatience with historical figures who were stupid or venal, and his amusement in telling about the Pawnee Scouts who threw off their splendid U.S. Army uniforms before engaging the Sioux, are the bold and human stuff of historical interpretation. To the tears of the Pawnee women over the repeated losses of their men, their children, and their corn crops on Loup River to the savage Sioux there is added more than a hint of his own tears.

The Pawnees were of Caddoan linguistic and cultural stock, kinsmen of the Wichitas, Tawakonis, Iscanis, Kichais, and Wacos, located historically on and south of Red River. They were also kinsmen of the Arikaras, the tribe living farthest north of all these semisedentary peoples, in the present Dakotas. Producers of corn, the Pawnees attracted a whole complex of enemies bent on plundering their fields and vast horse herds.

Not always friendly to whites, they nevertheless attracted also some of the best observers traveling in the West in the nineteenth century: Edwin James of the Long Expedition of 1819–20; Duke Paul Wilhelm of Württemberg in 1823; John Treat Irving in 1833; John Dunbar in 1834; Charles Augustus Murray in 1835; Major Frank North beginning in 1860 and his brother Captain Luther H. North in 1870; John Brown Dunbar immediately after the Civil War; and George Bird Grinnell beginning in 1872. After 1900 and to the present, George A. Dorsey, John R. Swanton, Waldo R. Wedel, and Miss Gene Weltfish have fixed many aspects of Pawnee history and material and non-material culture.

In the life of every people, from the Classical Greeks to the inhabitants of today's democracies, there are certain imperatives, socially captivating and seemingly inexorable. With the Pawnees it was the notion that other people's horses were the means to their own fulfillment. In raiding parties entirely afoot, they would go as far south as Mexico and silently dispossess the Comanches and other tribes of their herds. Back in Nebraska with their plunder, they would sooner or later be dispossessed of it in turn by the Sioux. Separated into four great bands, they could not live together, and in the end they could not live alone. By 1875 their corn-growing, buffalo-hunting, horse-raiding culture had run its course, and they were asking the government to provide for their removal far to the south, in Oklahoma, from whence they had come in centuries past. This was the katabasis of the proud and once numerous Pawnees.

The story, as George E. Hyde constructed it in 1951, is vivid and memorable. Its essential elements and his handling of them are unlikely to be displaced in this century.

SAVOIE LOTTINVILLE

Norman, Oklahoma
January 5, 1974

Contents

Pitalesharo (from McKenney and Hall)

Illustrations

MAPS

THE PAWNEE INDIANS

Introduction

FOR MANY YEARS MEN WHOSE WORK LAY AMONG THE INDIANS OF
the Plains area have felt the need for an extended history of the Pawnees, a work dealing with this tribe not only in the 19th century but
going back to the dawn period in the 16th century, when the first
Spanish explorers ventured into the Plains. The present volume has
been written in the hope that it might in some degree fill this need;
but it cannot be regarded as the final word on some of the obscure
phases of early Pawnee, Caddoan, and Plains Apache movements:
dim events of an ancient day, historical mysteries that still remain
unsolved secrets of the Plains.

In writing of the Pawnees and their Caddoan kindred of the
South, one is impressed by the wide divergence of these Indians from
the type, spirit, and way of life of such northern Plains tribes as the
Teton Sioux and Cheyennes. Although there are indications that
both the Sioux and Cheyennes led a settled life before coming into
the Plains, from the period of their appearance in that region they
were wanderers, living by war, and generally making a success of it,
keeping their people together and coming through two centuries of
fighting with their spirit high and their numbers probably increased.
The Pawnee and Caddoan tribes normally led a semi-sedentary life,
dwelling in fixed villages and cultivating the soil. Culturally they had
in every way reached a higher stage of development than the Sioux
or Cheyennes; yet in the same centuries and in the same region that
witnessed the growing strength of these tribes the Caddoans lost their
people and their land, many of their tribes vanishing. The rather
highly-developed political and religious organization of the Caddoans
apparently was not a source of power when they engaged in war, but
was rather a cause of division and weakness. Dwelling in permanent
villages and cultivating crops, the Caddoans had become used to a
standard of living higher than anything known among the wandering
tribes of the Plains; but when war came the Caddoan villages often
proved to be mere death-traps for their inhabitants. They were fixed
targets, places at which the wandering tribes knew that they would

find the Caddoan people at certain seasons of the year, and off their guard. The ancient Caddoan custom of setting their big grass-lodges widely spaced apart among the patches of cultivation on low valley-land made it impossible to defend the settlements against the attacks of bands of mounted Plains Apaches or war parties of Osages and other eastern enemies equipped with firearms; yet, so strong was the bond of old custom that most of the Caddoans scorned to adopt the simple expedient of forming compact villages on high ground and surrounding them with ditch and earth wall defenses. The people of the Pawnee groups (the Pawnees, Arikaras, and Wichitas) learned at an early period the wisdom of forming strong villages on high ground that could be defended; and today these tribes are the only considerable groups of Caddoan Indians that are left. Smallpox and other diseases introduced by the whites caused dreadful havoc among the Pawnee villages; but to the last these tribes were able to keep their people together and to hold out against all enemy attempts to destroy them.

In the turmoil of war and the sudden shock of great losses through pestilence that they had suffered in earlier centuries, the Pawnees seem to have lost much of the offensive spirit that was characteristic among the wandering Plains tribes, and in the 19th century they rarely went to war with the purpose of fighting the enemy in their own country. To the Pawnees a war expedition commonly meant for a party of from five to one hundred warriors to set out on foot, to cross hundreds of miles of plains, to approach enemy camps in the night, to sweep off the horse herds, and to drive the animals night and day until all danger of pursuit was over. Sometimes these Pawnee horse-lifting expeditions were caught in the Plains by great mounted bands of Comanches, Kiowas, or Cheyennes; and then the Pawnees, all afoot and surrounded, fought like heroes. But they fought a losing fight; and it was the same in the Pawnee homelands, when the warriors went out to hold off an assault by hundreds of well-armed Sioux or Cheyennes who had come to attack the Pawnee villages or hunting-camps. The Pawnees can speak as proudly as any tribe of their heroes; but how did these heroes die? What was the fate of the brave men of the Knife Lance, the Fighting Lance, and the *Raris Kahut* or Red Warriors? The Pawnees know. They have forgotten the year, they do not remember the name of the tribe that attacked them; but they know that these men of their warrior brotherhoods were destroyed, one group after another, fighting to the last to beat off enemy attacks on the Pawnee villages on Loup Fork, or holding off some overwhelming force of mounted foes in the buffalo plains of Nebraska, to give the Pawnee hunters time to draw together to defend the women and children in the camp.

The Pawnees destroyed a Spanish expedition that ventured into their lands in Nebraska in 1720; and in later times they occasionally sent a war party into New Mexico and brought home rich plunder, taken from some Spanish caravan they had captured on the road. But the tribe had little success in its attempts to resist American encroachments on its territory; and, unlike the Sioux and some other Plains tribes, the Pawnees did not carry their opposition to the Americans to the point of open war. In the 1860's their warriors enlisted with enthusiasm in the Pawnee Scouts, to aid the troops in fighting the Sioux and Cheyennes; and with proper arms and good leadership, the Pawnees never lost a fight and made a fine reputation for courage and skill.

With the war ended, the Pawnees, like all the other friendly tribes, were neglected by the government, and they were massacred by the Sioux, who were equipped with firearms, given to them as peace gifts by an absurd and wicked government peace policy that armed hostile Indians and left friendly tribes to shift for themselves. The Pawnees, indeed, were put under the control of Quaker agents, who preached peace and brotherhood while the Pawnees were left exposed to constant enemy aggression. The final blow fell when the tribe was removed from a well-improved reservation in Nebraska to a tract of wild land in Indian Territory, where the Osages and other tribes promptly began to raid the Pawnee horse herds. Prevented by their Quaker agent from striking back, the Pawnees lost all their horses; and with a general loss of spirits and health produced by a change of climate and environment, the tribe came near to perishing. It is only in the past decade that the Pawnee birth rate has risen once more above the dreadful rate of deaths. The population roll is increasing now; but there are almost no full-blood Pawnees left today.

The story of the Pawnees may seem to be one of failure; but there are features in the history of the tribe that offset this apparent defeat. After all, every Indian tribe was defeated in the end; and in the summing up we must take into account other matters than simple fighting. It was the Pawnees who gave to the Indian race that beautiful ceremony of the Calumet of Peace, and this tribe contributed abundantly to the growth of social institutions and religious ritual that formed so important a part in the life of the Indians of the Plains. Drifting northward through the slow centuries, the Pawnees broke the ground for planting and built the first large settlements, all the way from eastern Oklahoma up through Kansas and Nebraska and on into Dakota. They supplied wandering tribes, and even the white fur-traders and pioneer settlers, with maize, dried vegetables, and tobacco; and some of the hardy Pawnee varieties of seed, specially suitable for semi-arid regions, are still found useful by farmers of today.

During the quarter century in which the materials for the present volume were being gathered the writer has received valuable aid from many men, both Indians and whites. Most of these old friends are gone now; but here I wish to record the names of George Bird Grinnell, of Captain L. H. North of the Pawnee Scouts, of John W. Williamson, trail-agent for the Pawnees during the disastrous buffalo hunt of 1873, and of F. M. Osborne of Genoa, Nebraska, who has given me valuable information concerning the Pawnee Agency that was located on the present site of Genoa from 1859 to 1875. George H. Roberts, the son of Rush Roberts, who was at one time the head of the Nasharo or Pawnee Council of Chiefs, has also given me much assistance during the many years I have known him.

I

Pawnee Origins

FROM THE MOST DISTANT TIMES DOWN TO THE MIDDLE OF THE 19th century the Pawnees, and those kindred Caddoan tribes that were in closest touch with them, dwelt remote in the plains, away from the usual routes of travel and so distant from any European settlements that they were rarely visited by white men, with the exception of a few traders of the type that kept no written records and made no reports as to what they had seen or heard. For three centuries after their first appearance in history we have hardly one clear statement as to the location, numbers, and condition of the Pawnee tribes, and through the same long period of time one may count on the fingers of one hand the individual Pawnees who are mentioned by name.

This obscuration of Pawnee origins has attracted scholars to the study of the early history of this interesting people; yet to the present only two men have put into print any extended study of the early history and condition of the Pawnees. These men were John Brown Dunbar and George Bird Grinnell.[1] To them we are indebted for the preservation of the Pawnee migration traditions and considerable other material on the history of the tribe. Dunbar was born in the Pawnee country, the son of the Reverend John Dunbar, who came among these Indians as a missionary in 1834. The younger Dunbar began his study of the Pawnees after the close of the Civil War. He visited the tribe and set down what he was told by the old people; he also utilized references to the tribe in the early American, French, and Spanish records that were available in print at that date; and in 1880-1882 his papers on the Pawnees were published in the *Magazine of American History*.

Grinnell first came among the Pawnees in 1872. A young man just out of Yale, he went on a summer buffalo hunt with the tribe and became greatly interested in the people. He paid several more visits to the Pawnees, both in Nebraska and after their removal to Indian

Territory, and in 1889 his book, *Pawnee Hero Stories*, was published.

In these studies by Dunbar and Grinnell all that the Pawnees of the third quarter of the 19th century knew of their early history was set forth. This was not much; but these fragments of information have proved invaluable to later scholars.

Dunbar made it clear in his work that the Skidi Pawnees and their Arikara cousins were the first to migrate northward, but he made no attempt to give a definite date to this movement, merely expressing the opinion that these tribes preceeded the other Pawnees by about one century. He then quoted the latter group of three Pawnee tribes as stating emphatically that the Skidis were the remnant of a once separate people who had been conquered by the Pawnees and incorporated into the tribe. Dunbar referred to the coming into Nebraska of the three Pawnee tribes and the conquest of the Skidis as events of ancient times, for he was not familiar with the fact that Indian memory for early events goes back only about ninety years and that even their traditions, which are vaguer than their historical tales, do not refer to a time more remote than a century and a half.

Knowing as we do today that the Skidi Pawnees were in Nebraska as early at least as 1600 (the new archeology suggests that the tribe was there at least two centuries earlier), we need not be surprised at Dunbar's failure, after 1870, to obtain a migration tradition from the tribe. At that date the other three Pawnee tribes had a detailed memory of their defeat of the Skidis, and this fact would lead one to suppose (even though Dunbar termed the event one of ancient times) that the so-called Pawnee conquest of the Skidis dates after the middle of the 18th century. A study of the historical materials supports such a view. As late as 1760 the three southern Pawnee tribes were evidently not in Nebraska, and the Skidis were still the dominant people of that region. Historical documents also disclose that when these Pawnees informed Dunbar that after defeating the Skidis they conquered several Siouan tribes in eastern Nebraska, they were indulging in a form of boasting that most Indians were guilty of at times. It is true that there are some faint hints that early in the 18th century a group of southern Pawnees made their way northward into Nebraska and even penetrated to the Missouri River in South Dakota; but there is no evidence that they conquered any Siouan tribes. But Dunbar accepted these Pawnee stories unquestioningly, and Grinnell repeated them after Dunbar.

Dunbar's tradition is that the Pawnees came from the south. When Grinnell took up the story a few years later he asserted that there were two traditions, one known only to very old men, telling of a migration from the southwest; and a second which many younger men knew, recounting a migration from the southeast. These tales were common to both the Pawnees and Skidis; which may mean that the latter tribe had forgotten their own migration and adopted that of the Pawnees. That the Pawnees in 1875-1885 believed these migration tales is evident; but Dunbar was certainly correct in stating that these people had no true memory as to when or how they came into Nebraska.

Secret Pipe Chief, a very old Chaui Pawnee and head-priest of the tribe, told Grinnell that "after languages were confused" the Pawnees and Wichitas moved from the southwest across two ranges of mountains and came to the Missouri, where they planted (*i.e.*, built villages and settled). Bear Chief, a very old Skidi, said that long ago the people were in the southwest, beyond the Rio Grande. They migrated to near the Wichita Mountains and planted; then moved north to the Arkansas and planted; then to the mouth of the Missouri, and there his father was born. His father being born about 1765, we are expected to believe that the Skidi Pawnees, then a very numerous nation, were dwelling in the immediate vicinity of French settlements on the Mississippi, and that this was quite unknown to the French. As a fact the French had been trading with the Skidis in Nebraska, hundreds of miles up the Missouri, for fifty years prior to the birth of Bear Chief's father.

We must not be too critical of these fragments of migration traditions. If we strike out the reference to the mouth of the Missouri and simply say "to the Missouri," Bear Chief's tradition agrees with that of Secret Pipe Chief, and they both indicate a belief in an original home beyond the Rio Grande, a movement to Red River near the Wichita Mountains, a second movement to the Arkansas (the second mountain range being perhaps the Ozarks), and a final movement northward into Nebraska. Some of the Pawnees told Grinnell that when they lived in the southwest they had houses of stone. These tales were known only to very old men.

The second set of migration traditions, known to most of the younger men in 1875-1885, stated that the Pawnees came from the southeast, from a land where cane grew. Grinnell suggested that this land was in the lower Mississippi valley, for he was not familiar with the fact that in early times dense canebrakes were found in Oklahoma, along the Arkansas River as far north as the Canadian River and the Verdigris. These tales recounted that the people left their home in the southeast and moved north to obtain sinew (*i.e.*, buffalo). The Wichitas joined in this migration, but presently grew discouraged

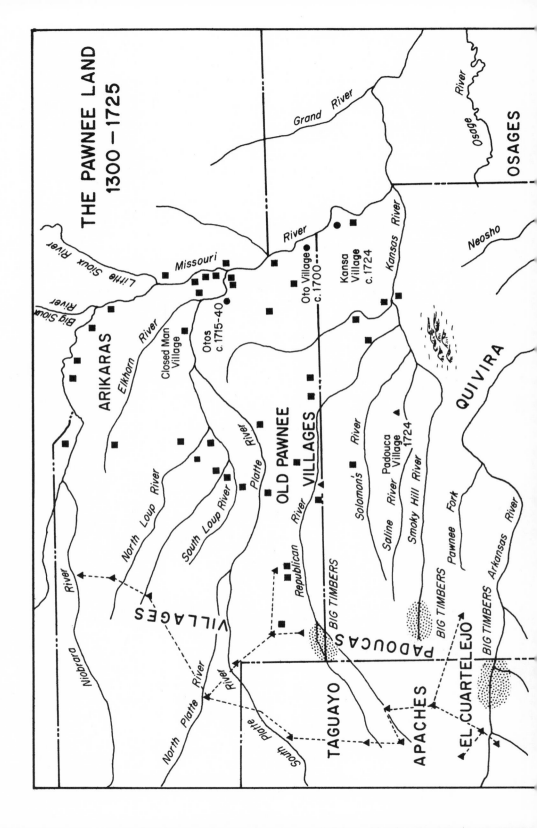

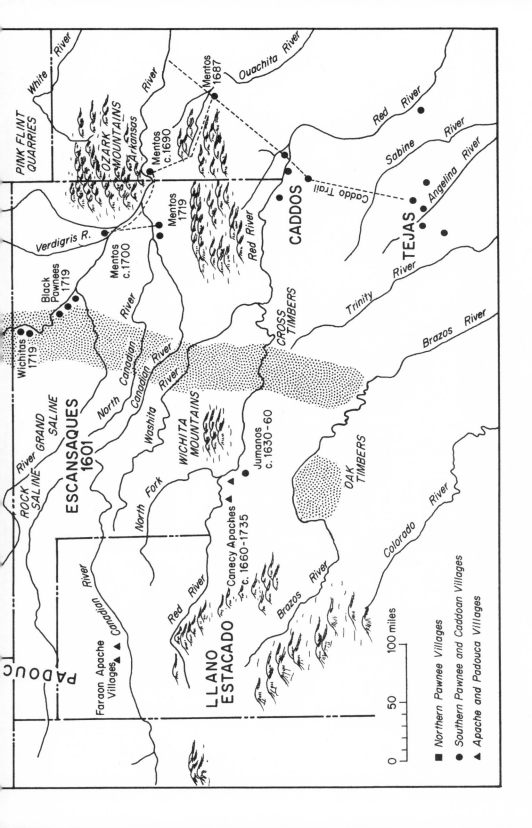

PADOUC

PINK FLINT QUARRIES

White River

River

OZARK MOUNTAINS

Arkansas River

Ouachita River

Red River

Sabine River

Angelina River

Mentos 1687

Mentos c.1690

Mentos 1719

Mentos 1700

Verdigris R.

Black Pawnees 1719

Wichitas 1719

ROCK River GRAND SALINE

SALINE

ESCANSAQUES 1601

North Canadian River

Canadian River

Washita River

North Fork

Red River

Arkansas River

CADDOS

Caddo Trail

TEJAS

River

Trinity River

CROSS TIMBERS

Brazos River

Colorado River

WICHITA MOUNTAINS

Jumanos c.1630-60

Canecy Apaches c.1660-1735

OAK TIMBERS

Faraon Apache Villages ▲ ▲

Canadian River

LLANO ESTACADO

Red River

Brazos River

■ Northern Pawnee Villages

● Southern Pawnee and Caddoan Villages

▲ Apache and Padouca Villages

0   50   100 miles

and turned back. The Pawnees went on northward into Kansas, and after remaining for some time continued their migration, establishing themselves on the Platte in Nebraska. This version clearly refers to the movements of three Pawnee tribes: the Chauis or Grand Pawnees, the Kitkehahkis, and the Pitahauerats. Everyone seems to agree that the Skidi Pawnees had preceded the other tribes, reaching Nebraska a century or more in advance.

Like Dunbar, Grinnell regarded this migration tradition as referring to events of very early times, and he pointed to the marked differences in the Pawnee and Wichita dialects as proof of the long period of time that had elapsed since the two peoples had separated. This argument seemed strong when it was made, but in recent years evidence has been found which enables us to date the Wichita and Pawnee migration northward. These tribes left their old home on Red River perhaps after 1650, dwelt on the Arkansas River in northeast Oklahoma until after 1750, and then moved, the Wichitas back to Red River, the Pawnees northward into Kansas. We have also learned that the people known to Grinnell as the Wichitas after 1870 were a group made up of fragments of several Caddoan tribes, people speaking different dialects, the mingling of which produced the Wichita language of the 19th century. John T. Irving stated that in 1835 the Pawnees could not understand what a Wichita Indian said to them. In 1939 George H. Roberts, a Skidi Pawnee, stated that the Pawnees cannot understand the Wichita speech, although it does contain a few words which are the same as in Pawnee. He added that some Wichita and Pawnee personal names are the same.

Later attempts than those of Dunbar and Grinnell have failed to obtain additional information from the Pawnees as to their migrations. When, after 1900, George A. Dorsey collected the Pawnee traditions with great care, he was informed by the oldest living Skidis that Arisa, one of their priests who had died at a great age in 1878, had told them that none of the old men he had known in his younger days knew where the Skidi tribe came from. The best information that Dorsey could obtain on this subject was to the effect that there was a girl and a boy, that these two dwelt in a grass-lodge, and that they were aided by four gods, who gave them buffalo and corn and taught them to plant and to make earth-lodges. These young people taught all the Pawnees; then languages were changed and the people became scattered. Long after that they came together again on the Loup Fork of the Platte in Nebraska. It was probably a tale of this type that induced Dunbar to state emphatically that the Skidis did not know where they had come from, except that they had moved northward to their historic location.

As for the Arikaras, the most northerly group of Pawnees, they believed that they were an off-shoot from the Skidis in Nebraska; they often visited the Skidis, and at times some of their men went, usually on foot through one thousand miles of hostile plains, to visit their Caddoan kindred on the Red River of Texas; yet the tribe had no tradition to explain how it had come to wander so far away toward the north. The earliest memories of this people centered about their ruined villages near the present city of Pierre in South Dakota, a district which they occupied until about 1790.

Turning to the south, it is not difficult to locate the homeland from which these Pawnee tribes originally came. At the dawn of the historic period in the south, in the middle of the 16th century, the Caddoan tribes, from whom the Pawnees had separated at an earlier date, held a vast tract of land in Louisiana, Arkansas, Oklahoma, and Texas. Toward the east, along the Mississippi, were tribes of a different stock: mound-builders, ruled by priest-kings, worshippers of the sun and of sacred fire; and it was from these tribes apparently that many of the Caddoan religious and social practices came, including that curious custom of artificial head-flattening, which some of the Caddoan Indians had adopted.

The large number of tribes once included under the name Pawnee and in the kindred Caddoan stock has often caused confusion, and particularly so because many of these tribes were little known and are now extinct. To avoid such confusion here it may be as well to tabulate the principal tribes in the Caddoan stock, beginning with the Caddo group in the south and concluding with the Arikaras in Dakota:

Caddo group:

Cadohadachos (Real Caddo or Grand Caddo) always on Red River, in the district where Caddoan culture reached its highest stage.

Hasinais (Cenis or Tejas) occupying east Texas in the Angelina and Trinity River district.

The Nasonis, Anadarkos, Nabedaches, Nacagdoches, and many other tribes belonged to this southern Caddo group but are now extinct or nearly so.

Tawehash or Mento group:

Tawehash or Mentos, first noted in Arkansas but moved westward into Oklahoma and then to upper Red River. The Tawehash are now merged into the modern Wichita tribe.

Tawakonis, said to have been an off-shoot from the Wichitas, but they were a principal group in the Tawehash villages in 1719. They are now merged into the Wichitas.

Wichita group:

Wichitas, first noted by the French on the Arkansas River in north Oklahoma about the year 1700. Later fled to west Texas and then joined the Tawehash.

Iscanis, were on the Arkansas with the Wichitas early in the 18th century and today are merged into the Wichita tribe.

Panis Noirs or Black Pawnees, were on the Arkansas near the Wichitas and Iscanis until after the middle of the 18th century; then moved northward and joined the Skidi Pawnees in Nebraska, where they remained until removed to Oklahoma by the government in 1874-5.

Skidi or Awahi group:

Skidi Pawnees (Panimahas, Loup, or Wolf Pawnees). Were in Nebraska from prehistoric times until removed to Oklahoma in 1874-5.

Arikaras, the most powerful tribe in South Dakota early in the 18th century. Almost destroyed by smallpox and Sioux attacks, the Arikaras retired up the Missouri, where today a remnant of the tribe is living in North Dakota.

When De Soto's Spanish expedition crossed west of the Mississippi in 1541 they came among the towns of the mound-building tribes of east Arkansas and Louisiana. The armored and mounted Spaniards had little difficulty in subduing these Indians; but here there was no gold, and the rumor that tribes farther toward the west had yellow metal persuaded De Soto and his captains to push in that direction. The little army marched through flooded lowlands covered with forest, wading all day long through mud and water and sleeping on mud banks at night; but presently they came out on prairies and found themselves among Indians of a type very different from the mound-builders near the Mississippi. They had come now into the borders of the Caddoan tribes, a land of prairies and hills with Indian towns, usually small and scattered, placed at wide intervals, with great stretches of empty land between one village and the next. The villages were made up of groups of big grass-thatched lodges, each lodge standing in its own small field of maize and vegetables. Here there were no great stores of maize such as had been found in the towns farther toward the east; and some of the Caddoans had the custom of going to considerable distances from their villages on communal deer hunts, or even out among the buffalo herds, to obtain a supply of meat to add to their diet of maize, vegetables, and fish.

Unlike the people of the great mound-builder towns, these Caddoans were not easily overawed by the bearded white invaders with their terrible weapons and galloping horses. When De Soto's men seized a village and began the work of plunder, the Indians rushed back among the grass-lodges and fought like tigers. When the Spaniards ventured out on a foraging expedition they were ambushed by bands of naked warriors, who boldly charged in on them, armed with sharpened sticks (small lances) with which they attacked the horses and armored men. Many women fought at the side of their men. De Soto was losing too many horses and having too many men put out of action. These Indians had no gold; and the discouraged general led his army back toward the Mississippi, where he presently died.

It is impossible from the Spanish narratives to learn the exact location of the several Caddoan groups in 1541. The fierce mounted Spaniards marched through the land, killing and destroying, and then a curtain was drawn across the stage, to hide the scene until the time of Marquette's and Joliet's canoe voyage down the Mississippi (1673) and La Salle's landing on the Texas coast (1685), when the curtain was drawn aside to disclose the Caddoan tribes of the south in their historic locations. Perhaps they had moved from the districts in which De Soto's men had found them; a drift toward the south and west seems possible;[2] but the tribes had not moved far, and they had now reached the positions in which the main groups were to remain for many years to come. There were three of these main groups: the Cadohadacho or Grand Caddo, whose villages stood on Red River in that great bend where the town of Texarkana is now located; the Hasinai group of tribes in east Texas, south of the Cadohadacho, in the Angelina River country; and the Natchitoches group along Red River, below the Cadohadachos and east of the Hasinai villages.

Of these three groups the Hasinais were the strongest in the number of people and warriors; but the Cadohadachos were recognized as the leading group. They were termed *fathers* by the other Caddoans who looked up to them as the elder and leading group of their people. When visited by La Salle's men in 1687 the Cadohadachos had four tribes: Grand Caddo or Real Caddo, Nasonis, Nanatsohos, and Upper Natchitoches. These tribes were numerous when the French came among them in 1687; but by 1700 enemy attacks and diseases introduced by the whites had reduced them to 2,000 or 2,400

Date			Northwestern Plains	Central Plains	Southern Plains	Middle Missouri	Northeastern Periphery	Age
1850	Nomadic Bison Hunters (W. Pl.)	Plains Village Pattern (E. Pl.)	BLACKFEET CROW SHOSHONE HAGEN	DAKOTA, PAWNEE CHEYENNE, OMAHA ETC.	COMANCHE KIOWA SPANISH FORT DEER CR.	MANDAN ARIKARA STANLEY	ASSINIBOIN YANKTON SANTEE	100
			PICTOGRAPH–GHOST CAVES	DISMAL RIVER UPPER REPUBLICAN LOWER LOUP SMOKY HILL GREAT BEND ONEOTA NEBRASKA	ANTELOPE CR. APACHE CUSTER WASHITA R. HENRIETTA NEOSHO	MIDDLE MANDAN HUFF ARZBERGER LA ROCHE BENNETT		500
1500								
1000						T. RIGGS F. ANDERSON F. MONROE F. OVER F.	MILL CREEK	1000
				PLAINS WOODLAND ASH HOLLOW CAVE WHITE RIVER TERRACE SITES LOSEKE Cr. KEITH Focus VALLEY Focus K.C. HOPEWELL				1500
A.D. / B.C.	Hunters & Gatherers		Wyoming Basin Foragers MUDDY Cr. McKEAN Upper SHOSHONE BASIN KEYHOLE Res.		EDWARDS PLATEAU ASPECT "BURNT ROCK MIDDENS"	PLAINS WOODLAND	SANDY CR.	
1000			McKEAN LOWER	SIGNAL BUTTE I		PRECERAMIC MISSOURI RIVER TERRACE SITES		2500
	ALTITHERMAL			Bison bison			THUNDER CR.	3500
2500								5000
							OXBOW	
4500				LOGAN CREEK B				7000
			HORNER FINLEY		PORTALES COMPLEX		?	
6500	Early Big Game Hunters		EDEN PLAINVIEW SCOTTSBLUFF ANGOSTURA	SIMONSEN				9000
				Bison occidentalis	PLAINVIEW			
8500			FOLSOM	FOLSOM	FOLSOM	?	?	
10000 B.C.				DENT	CLOVIS LLANO COMPLEX	?	?	12000

Northwestern Plains vertical labels: LATE PREHISTORIC / MIDDLE PREHISTORIC / EARLY PREHISTORIC / LIME CREEK SITES

Northeastern Periphery vertical labels: WHITESHELL F. / LARTER F. / ANDERSON F. / NUTIMIK F. / MANITOBA F. / SELKIRK F. (CREE) / DAKOTA MOUNDS

Columbian Mammoth

Provisional chart showing approximate time relationships of certain archaeological sites and complexes in the Plains area. (From *Prehistoric Man on the Great Plains,* by Waldo R. Wedel, Norman, 1961)

people, who could muster 600 to 700 warriors. The Hasinais in east Texas were called Cenis by the French and Tejas or Texas (from *techis* meaning *friends*) by the Spaniards. Late in the 17th century they had nine tribes, each in its own village, with a total of 2,400 to 2,800 people; but they had lost 3,000 people, more than half of their population, in an epidemic in the spring of 1691.[3]

The third Caddoan group lived in villages near the present town of Natchitoches, to which they gave their name. These Natchitoches Indians were unfortunate in being located in the borderland between the Spanish missions in east Texas and the French settlements in Louisiana, and their population dwindled away with dreadful rapidity. The Natchitoches and, indeed, all of these southern Caddoans, wished to be friends with the whites, in the hope that the newcomers would aid them against their Indian enemies; but the introduction of new diseases injured them more than the weapons of hostile tribes could have done, and their once great population was soon destroyed.

Dwelling in rich lands and in a warm and humid climate, where crop-growing was an easy and very productive pursuit, and where wild fruits and nuts, deer, wild turkeys, and fish abounded, the Caddoans had the opportunity to lead a comfortable and rather lazy life, if their enemies would permit them to do so. The very character of the villages they built seems to indicate that up to perhaps the middle of the 17th century the Caddoans had no enemies near enough or strong enough to cause them serious injury. Apparently for this reason the Caddoan villages were in open land with the lodges scattered here and there in small groups. To anyone familiar with the compact, easily defended, and sometimes fortified villages of the northern Pawnees and Arikaras, it cannot but seem strange to read the French and Spanish descriptions of the southern Caddoan villages of the 17th century, set in open stream valleys, the big dome-shaped grass-lodges scattered here and there, each surrounded by its small maize and vegetable patches, and all wide open to enemy attack. There must have been a Golden Age, sometime prior to 1650, which had convinced these Indians that such open settlements were safe. By 1687 they were not safe at all; but old habit caused the Caddoan people to cling to the way of life of their ancestors; and when La Harpe in 1719 warned them that if they did not form close villages in positions that could be defended they would be destroyed by their enemies, most of the people paid no heed.

Father Douay, who came into Texas with La Salle in 1685, stated that at that date the Cenis or Hasinai villages extended for twenty leagues (fifty miles) along the valley of Trinity River, the big grass-lodges set in groups, with long stretches of vacant land between one group and the next. Joutel, another of La Salle's followers, termed these groups *cantons.* Espinosa stated that each group of lodges was occupied by one division of a particular tribe.[4] The grass-lodges were circular and dome-shaped, from forty to sixty feet in diameter, each accommodating from fifteen to twenty persons. The beaten clay floors were at the natural ground level, and a covered vestibule several yards in length extended out from the doorway of each lodge. Father Massanet described one of these grass-lodges in east Texas in these words:

> In the middle of the house is the fire which is never extinguished by day or night, and over the door on the inner side there is a little mound of pebbles very prettily arranged. Ranged around one-half of the house, inside, are ten beds, which consist of a rug made of reeds laid on four forked stakes. Over the rug they spread buffalo skins, on which they sleep. At the head and foot of the bed is attached another carpet, forming a sort of arch, which, lined with a very brilliantly colored piece of reed matting, makes what bears some resemblance to a very pretty alcove. In the other half of the house, where there are no beds, there are some shelves about two varas high, and on them they range large round baskets made of reeds (in which they keep their corn, nuts, acorns, beans, etc.), a row of very large earthen pots. . . and six wooden mortars for pounding corn in rainy weather (for when it is fair they grind it in the courtyard).

The Caddoans of the south made splendid pottery in many forms, their black polished ware, decorated with incised designs, being really beautiful. The women made this pottery indoors in winter; but the stone and shell work (weapons, tools, and ornaments), which were mostly the work of the men, have been described by W. K. Moorehead as not abundant and of a rather poor quality.[5]

These southern Caddoans had two crops of maize each season through their practice of planting two varieties, a small corn that matured in forty-five days, and a larger variety that required ninety days. They also grew several kinds of beans, squashes, melons, and great sunflowers, from the pounded seeds of which they made a kind of meal which was mingled with maize flour. They also collected great quantities of nuts, acorns, and wild fruits. Deer and bear were the principal big game, though some of the tribes went on extended hunts for buffalo. The French and Spanish accounts give a pleasing picture of the happy life in these villages in the 17th century. The men did not have the absorbing interest that Pawnee men in the north had in war and distant hunts for buffalo, but did their hunting and fishing near the villages, leading a rather leisurely and care-free existence. In many communities the men helped with the field work; but this was more of a social pleasure than real labor. The custom was for the neighbors to gather to help one family, at planting-time, at harvest, or when a new grass-lodge was to be built; and with many hands to help and much joking and laughter, the work was quickly done. At the end of the day they betook themselves to the big communal lodge, where feasting and dancing followed.

At the head of each tribe was a *xinesi* or hereditary priest-chief, who was keeper of the sacred fire in the temple. He led in all tribal religious ceremonies and held the highest rank in the tribe. Below him in rank were the *caddis* or village chiefs; and according to Father Massanet some communities had chiefs of a higher rank termed *deszas*. These names for chiefs were taken to the north by the Pawnees and Arikaras in very early times; and among them *caddi* was still used occasionally in the 19th century in some personal names; while *desza*, turned in the Pawnee dialect into *lesha* and in Arikara into *nesha*, was always the common name for chief; but these northern tribes usually added *ro*, making the word *lesharo* and *nesharo*.

Each village caddi among the Caddoans had from three to seven *canahas*, officers who attended him on ceremonial occasions, who bore his messages and brought him news. They were what Grinnell termed *servants* among the Nebraska Pawnees. They brought the chief's food, lighted his pipe for him, and performed other personal services. The warriors as well as the chiefs seem to have had such servants, whom the Spaniards in Texas termed pages. This type of personal service rendered by one Pawnee to another was a thing that set the tribe apart from all the other northern Indians, who had no such custom. In the south the system seems to have been elaborated, for the *caddi* had *canahas* to wait on him, the *canahas* had *chayas* to wait on them, and also had *tammas* (a kind of Indian soldier) to execute their orders and whip offenders.

Like the Pawnees and Arikaras in the north, the southern Caddoans had a system of matrilineal clans. Descent was in the female line; and in 1690 Tonti found that a woman was ruling as the chief of the Grand Caddo. Little information has survived concerning the clan system of these southern tribes, but a list of clan names obtained at a very late date shows that the clans were all named for animals and birds.

The religious practices of the southern Caddoans had ugly features, such as the keeping of enemy heads at the tribal temple and the practice of human sacrifice and cannibalism. That this condition was

quite general among Caddoan Indians there can be little doubt; for
the human sacrifices among the tribes on Red River and in Texas
are duplicated by similar practices among the Skidi Pawnees in Nebraska, and archeology has recently uncovered indications of cannibalism in Caddoan village ruins in both Kansas and Nebraska.[6]

The southern Caddoan religion was sun worship, featuring the
keeping of sacred fire in temples. Swanton regards this religion as a
link connecting the Caddoans with tribes toward the southeast, particularly with the Natchez; indeed, the Caddoan chief-priest or *xinesi*
seems to be a modification of the priest-king of the Natchez and
Taensas tribes, and the Caddoan fire temples were probably copied
from those of the tribes named. The star cult features and human
sacrifice of the Caddoan religion form clear connections with the Skidi
Pawnee religious customs.

The Caddoan temples held the sacred fire and images of gods, kept
in wooden coffers. These images, as the French and Spanish chroniclers inform us, were in the shapes of animals, birds, serpents, and in
one case a toad god is mentioned. All of this reminds one of the
northern Pawnee and Arikara priests and medicine-men, who had
large medicine-lodges filled with stuffed birds, animals, and similar
sacred articles, which were used both in religious and conjuring practices. In the south the Caddoans had a great forecasting ceremony in
February, when the priests (by consulting the stars, as the Spanish
friars stated) foretold the year to come, predicting crop-growing conditions and other important matters. These Indians could not perform the simplest task without the supervisory aid of their priests,
who had charge at the time of seed planting, watched the skies during
the growing season, pretended by conjuring feats to drive away tem-
pests and other dangers to the crops, and took a leading part in the
harvest ceremonies.

The harvest festival was in September at the time of the full moon,
and the ceremonies were begun about midnight, when the Pleiades
were directly overhead. These stars were called in the south *Sanates,
The Women;* in the north the Skidi name for the same constellation
was *Chaka,* and they said that the seven stars had been set in the heav-
ens by their god, to travel from east to west and form a guide to the
Skidis, so that their people would not wander off and become lost.
In the south the Caddoan harvest ceremonies seem to have been of a
solemn religious character; but among the Pawnees, judging from the
statements of white men who observed the harvest ceremonies, the
performing of feats of magic was the important matter. The Pawnees
called this festival Big-Sleight-of-Hand. It lasted for twenty evenings,

just after harvest; and Tabeau (c.1804) describes a similar festival at harvest among the Arikaras in Dakota, lasting for fifteen or twenty evenings.[7] In later years the whites sometimes referred to these performances as *the opera*. Chanting and the music of drums and other instruments accompanied the continuous performance of feats of conjuring and clowning; for there were clowns as well as magicians in every performance. Unlike the Caddoans in the south, who had priests to direct the harvest ceremonies, the Pawnees had *kurau* or doctors in charge. The doctors from each village performed in turn; and there was great rivalry among the villages, each of which wished to demonstate that its own doctors had more power than those of the other villages. The feats performed were often really amazing, as most of the white witnesses have testified. Bears and other savage animals appeared suddenly in the big medicine-lodge where the performances were held; they pursued and mangled people; and then the doctors cured what seemed to be fatal wounds in a brief period. Men were shot or stabbed and apparently fell dead, only to be quickly revived and cured; seeds, such as maize, were planted, sprouted, and reached maturity within a few minutes, under the watchful eyes of the wondering Indians and white men.

No real migration tradition was ever recorded among the southern Caddoans; but they had an origin myth which told of their people coming out from under the ground in the district in which they lived when the whites first came among them. Old-Home-in-the-Darkness was the name they gave to their first home under the ground; and the myth tells how the people selected the Moon as a leader and followed her toward the west, eventually coming out on the surface of the earth. Morfi in 1763 recorded one form of this myth, connected directly with the Grand Caddo. They pointed to a hill near one of their old villages as the place of origin, and they spoke of a woman, Zacado, their first divinity, who helped the people in the beginning. This Caddoan myth concerned with an underground origin, a journey, and the final emergence into the light of day, is quite similar to the origin myth of the Arikaras of Dakota.

From the material set down on the preceding pages the kinship of the southern Caddoan tribes with the northern Pawnees and Arikaras, in language, beliefs, social organization, and culture, is strikingly apparent; but when a search is made for traces of Pawnee residence in the south prior to the 18th century, the results are negative. In the long lists of Caddoan tribes recorded by the French and Spaniards after 1685, there is no tribe with a name resembling Pawnee, Wichita, or Tawehash, which are the names for the principal Pawnee groups after the year 1700; but the reason for this is fairly clear. The Caddoans of Red River and Texas must have known these Pawnee tribes under other names.

Like nearly everything else connected with the Pawnees and of really early date, the tribal name is a mystery. Among themselves the Pawnees did not use this name until a late date, when the whites and neighboring tribes had generally adopted it, and the Pawnees found it convenient to identify themselves by that appellation when speaking to outsiders. Grinnell stated that their own tribal name was *Chahiksichahiks,* meaning *Men of Men;* but the Pawnees have persistently denied that this was the name for their tribe, and there is no evidence to support a contrary opinion. The fact is that the Pawnees in Nebraska never achieved the unity necessary to regard themselves as one people. They were not one tribe, but four; and they spoke of themselves as Skidis, Chauis, Kitkehahkis, and Pitahauerats.

John B. Dunbar, after 1870, was the first to attempt to explain the name *Pawnee* as of Pawnee origin. His attempt to obtain confirmation of this view from the Indians was a failure. He then searched in the Pawnee dictionary he was compiling and hit on the word *pariki* (*horn*) as the possible origin of the name Pawnee. Grinnell, some years later, failing to find among the Pawnees any evidence as to the origin of the name, accepted Dunbar's guess; and in later years he made his opinion standard authority by inserting it in *The Handbook of American Indians North of Mexico,* edited by Dr. F. W. Hodge and published by the government Bureau of Ethnology. Under the heading *Pawnee* Grinnell stated:

> The name is probably derived from *pariki,* a horn, a term used to designate the peculiar manner of dressing the scalp-lock, by which the hair was stiffened with paint and fat, and made to stand erect curved like a horn. This marked feature of the Pawnee gave currency to the name and to its application to cognate tribes.[8]

It seems strange that an opinion advanced by Dunbar as little more than a conjecture should have developed into the standard explanation of the name's origin; and this is all the more surprising when we learn that Grinnell, after questioning most of the older Pawnees, some of them born before the year 1800, could obtain no evidence that the method of dressing the scalplock in the form of a horn had been generally practiced by Pawnee warriors. In recent years Lesser and Weltfish looked carefully into the *pariki* matter and expressed doubts of the validity of Dunbar's view; but these linguists permitted the present generation of Pawnees to hand them a tale explaining the origin of the name Pawnee: the usual idle talk about the first white man meeting Pawnees, no one knows where or when, but the exact words of the conversation are remembered. The white man asked who they were, and the Pawnees, who were hunting, replied, *Parisu*: hunters. Why did not the grandfathers of these modern Pawnees tell this to Grinnell, when he was inquiring anxiously into the origin of the name *Pawnee*? It seems obvious that they did not because the tale had not been invented in their time.

The name *Pawnee* (French *pani, pana;* Spanish, *Panana;* Sioux, *Panani*) appears to have been in use only among the northern and eastern neighbors of the Pawnees in the 17th century. The French picked up the name from the northeastern tribes; and as the spread of the name in the lands east of the upper Mississippi seems to have been due to early Siouan contacts with the Pawnees, we might suppose that the name was either a Pawnee one adopted by the Siouan Indians or that it was of Siouan invention. By tradition it was with the Siouans of the Chiwere dialect (the Otos, Missouris, Iowas, and Winnebagos) that the Pawnees had early and friendly contacts; and it is interesting to note that in this dialect the name is *Pani*, but with a palatalized *n,* making the word *Panyi*. In the Dhegiah Siouan dialect (that of the Osages, Quapaws, Kansa, Omahas, and Poncas) the name is hardly recognizable, as it turned into *Bpari, Bparin,* and *Pathi*.[9] It is curious to observe that among these Siouan tribes the names of some birds and animals that peck or delve in the earth have *panyi* added, and so also have the names of some birds with red marks or red heads. Thus one form of the name *Pawnee* (*Panani*) is added to the name for the hairy woodpecker, *zongpanani,* and among the Omahas the robin with his red marking is the Pawnee-bird. Here are hints that, among these Siouan tribes, at least, the name *Pawnee* may have referred to delving in the soil (not digging gardens, for all these tribes gardened, but perhaps excavating the ground in building earthlodges) , or that the name indicated red feathers or a red crest. And this last brings us back to Dunbar's conjecture, but in a somewhat different form; for he was attempting to derive a red crest name from a Pawnee word, while here we have a slender hint that, back in the 16th or 17th century, at a date far beyond the reach of Pawnee memory in Dunbar's day, the Siouans saw Pawnees with red crests or red feather head ornaments, and for that reason called them *Panyis*.

We might remark that all Indians used bright-colored feathers on their heads, and that red crests for warriors may have been common to several tribes; but by adopting such a view we would be leaving out of account the well-known fact that the Pawnees and other Caddoans were specially fond of beautiful feathers. The temples of the southern Caddoans were filled with wonderful feather crowns and great rolls of lovely feather work, which were for use in tribal ceremonies. And there is that splendid Pawnee ceremony, the *Hako* or calumet of peace, an elaborate performance, lasting for days, with endless pageantry and singing. This is primarily a bird ritual; the birds represent the gods and the people; one sees the flocks afar off, flying and calling; they come sweeping across the sky, circling, alighting; and at the center of the great ceremony are the calumet stems, adorned from end to end with feathers and bird heads. This great Pawnee ceremony of peace and friendship impressed all the tribes of the east and north very strongly, and they all adopted the calumet in one form or another. Nicolas Perrot describes one of these calumets among the Wisconsin Indians in the middle of the 17th century as a great red stone pipe with a very long stem, ornamented along its entire length with red bird heads, and at the middle of the stem a large fan of red feathers.

Curiously, the only word recorded among the southern Caddoans at an early date that might be turned into *Pawnee* is a bird name. There were birds called *banit* that migrated in flocks across Red River and over east Texas; and the Caddoan priests made use of the flight of these birds as omens. When a war party had been absent from the village for a considerable time and the relatives of the warriors were growing anxious, the priests would watch, and when they saw a flight of *banit* they would pretend to the people that these birds had brought a message from the warriors, who were returning in safety.[10]

In the middle of the 17th century the Pawnees were being savagely raided by eastern tribes that had obtained metal weapons from the French, which gave them a terrible advantage over Indians who had only weapons of wood, flint, and bone. The raiders carried off such great numbers of Pawnees into slavery that in the country on and east of the upper Mississippi the name *Pani* developed a new meaning: *slave*. The French adopted this meaning, and Indian slaves, no matter from which tribe they had been taken, were presently being termed *Panis*. It was at this period, after the middle of the 17th century, that the name was introduced into New Mexico in the form *Panana* by bands of mounted Apaches who brought large numbers of Pawnee slaves to trade to the Spaniards and Pueblo Indians.

From these notes, which seem to be about all we have on the problem of the origin and meaning of the name *Pawnee*, we must admit

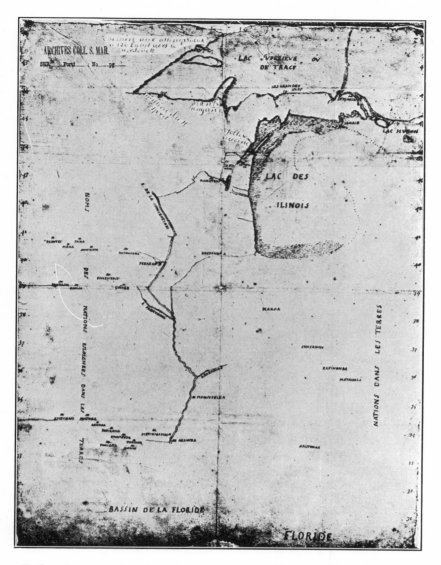

Father Jacques Marquette's Map, 1673–74. (From *An Introduction to Pawnee Archaeology*, by Waldo R. Wedel, BAE *Bulletin 112*, from the *Jesuit Relations*, Vol. LIX)

that the mystery is still a mystery. The conjecture made by Dunbar
before 1880 is as good today as the most recent opinions.

The old Caddoan name for their Pawnee kinsmen was *Awahi,* written by modern linguists as *Awahu,* and recorded by the French as far
back as 1673 as *Ouace* (*Waci*) and in compound form as *Paniouasse*
(*Pani-awasi*). The Arikaras of North Dakota still have today a tribal
division called *Awahu,* and this tribe sometimes termed all the Skidi
Pawnees of Nebraska *Awahu,* which they explain as meaning *Left Behind,* as their view is that when they separated from the Skidis and
moved north into Dakota the Skidis were left behind. But in Pawnee
this name *awahi* seems to have the meaning *here and there, hither and
yon, scattering;* and considering the scattered small villages in which
the northern Pawnees dwelt in very early times, such an interpretation of the name would fit perfectly.

The earliest locations of the northern Awahi or Pawnees can only
be conjectured from archeological discoveries, which make it certain
that some of these Indians were scattered in tiny earth-lodge settlements in southwest Nebraska, and that other groups were presumably
in Kansas, and still others possibly on and near the Missouri River
in east Nebraska and west Iowa. At a considerably later date, late in
the 17th century, the French usually located the Paniouce or Paniassa
villages near the Arkansas River, apparently in southern Kansas, with
the Panimahas or Skidi Pawnees on or near the Platte in Nebraska,
and the Pana (evidently the Arikaras) on or east of the Missouri in
the region of the present Sioux City. The Marquette autograph map
(1673), which does not show rivers west of the Mississippi, has the
Pana in west Iowa with the Omahas and some other Siouan tribes
near them; and it shows two groups of Paniassa villages, one apparently near the Arkansas River or upper Neosho in southern Kansas,
and a second group farther toward the north.

No account of Pawnee origins would be complete without reference
to the Quivira episode, which has been built up, elaborated, and discussed until it has assumed a false importance in early Pawnee history.
When Coronado and his little Spanish force crossed the plains from
New Mexico in the summer of 1541, they certainly found a large
Caddoan settlement in the eastern edge of the buffalo range, evidently
in the district of south Kansas, on or near the Arkansas River. In the
last decade of the 19th century Judge J. V. Brower announced that he
had rediscovered Quivira, and he pointed out a ridge with some bluish
chert deposits in it, on the south side of Kansas River near Junction
City, as the exact site of Quivira and of Coronado's camp. He wrote

two books on the subject, formed a Quivira Historical Society in Kansas, put up a granite monument on the site of Quivira, and obtained some support for his claims from the Bureau of Ethnology in Washington. All of this he accomplished, mainly by persuasive talk, without doing any real excavation.

W. K. Moorehead and certain other archeologists were from the first a little critical of the Brower claims; and even in Kansas some men refused to accept his location of Quivira. One Kansas man, P. H. Jones, carried his opposition to the point of printing pamphlets at his own expense, in which he claimed persistently that Quivira was not in the Brower location but farther south, on the Little Arkansas and Cow Creek. The argument grew, and the numerous partisans now engaged in the contest became embittered. Quivira was a political issue in Kansas; but the Brower faction (with a granite monument to add solid support to their claims) fought off all proposals to pick up Quivira and move it bodily to a more likely site.

The Brower party had the granite monument, but they had no Indian village ruins near it. P. H. Jones had no monument, but he could point out extensive remains of ruined Indian villages, clearly of Caddoan type, in the Little Arkansas and Cow Creek districts. And even before Brower had come into Kansas, J. A. Udden had excavated a Caddoan village site at Paint Creek, quite far west of Brower's site of Quivira, finding bits of Spanish chain armor of the Coronado period. As the years passed the evidence against the Brower location piled up, and in 1929 W. E. Connelly, the secretary of the Kansas State Historical Society, deserted the Brower faction, stating that the land along the north side of the Arkansas River was Quivira and that the Wichita Indians were the people of Quivira.

What was needed was a thorough examination of this Kansas field by trained archeologists; and at last, in 1937, the way was opened for the U. S. National Museum to undertake this task. After some preliminary work, in 1940 a party led by Dr. W. R. Wedel went into the Arkansas Valley and started excavation. The results came quickly and were better than anyone could have hoped for. In the district to the east of the great bend in the Arkansas River, in Rice, McPherson, Marion, and neighboring counties, the party found the remains of six or seven large Caddoan Indian villages; while farther south, in Cowley County on Walnut River, they came on extensive settlements of the old Red River scattered village type, extending for at least three miles along both sides of the river. Before these lands had been plowed up they had been thickly dotted with low mounds, the surface cluttered with broken Indian pottery, stone arrowheads, knives, and

other Indian material. Local archeologists had always supposed that
these mounds were ruined Indian lodges; but excavation now proved
that the lodges (some semi-permanent type, in all probability grass-
lodges) had stood between these mounds, which were simply refuse
heaps. In one of the villages on the Little Arkansas more pieces of
Spanish chain armor, pointing back to Coronado's time, were dug
up; a few bits of iron and some glass beads indicated slight contact
with the whites or with tribes that traded with the whites; and from
the mass of broken native pottery were recovered some bits of Pueblo
ware from New Mexico, which can be dated. Some of these potsherds
have been given the dating 1500-1650, and a second type is termed
1525-1650. A few turquoise beads also point to slight trade relations
with the Pueblos of New Mexico; and as the Pueblo dated pottery
is found in all sections of these Indian settlements, the inference is that
they date back to Coronado's time.

That these villages were grass-lodge Caddoan settlements seems
certain. In four settlements in Rice and McPherson counties there
were circular remains, one in each village, from ninety to one hundred
twenty feet in diameter—about three times the size of ordinary Caddoan lodges. When excavated these proved to be the ruins of very
large lodges of a peculiar construction, for there was considerable
burnt clay plaster, such as the Caddoans of Red River employed only
in the walls of their temples. There can be no doubt that these Kansas
structures were such temples. On one of the floors a quantity of
human bones hinted at cannibalism, a well-known feature of southern
Caddoan life.

Considering that only one season's work was expended on these
Kansas ruins, the results achieved were surprising. Dr. Wedel's report
is a fine piece of work. Its tone is moderate and sensible, making no
claims to finality until further excavations have extended the knowledge of the Caddoan remains, especially in the Neosho and Verdigris
river districts and southward into Oklahoma. Still, the report does
suggest, and with every justification, that these Kansas remains are
what is left of Quivira; and the further suggestion is made that
Coronado in 1541 entered Quivira in the north, in Rice County,
while Oñate in 1601 came in farther to the south, among the settlements on Walnut River, near the town of Arkansas City.

Of even more interest than the question as to just where the Spaniards found Quivira is the extent and nature of these Caddoan remains in Kansas. In the northern section, in Rice, McPherson, and
neighboring counties, the villages seem to be mainly large ones, some
with temples. As the southern Caddoans usually had but one temple

to each tribe, even if the tribe had more than one village, the four Kansas temples so far found would seem to indicate four tribes in the northern section. The southern settlements, along lower Walnut River, seem on the contrary to be loosely scattered, like Red River and Texas Caddoan settlements of the period 1685; but unlike those southern villages part of the Walnut River settlements are on the bluffs, in defensible positions. This hints at enemy attacks; and Oñate in 1601 found the powerful Escansaque tribe, evidently Apaches, in the plains very close to Quivira and engaged in a savage war on these Caddoan settlements. Moreover, the native pottery in this Walnut River district is largely shell-tempered, while that in Rice and McPherson counties is grit-tempered; and if this condition is established firmly by later excavations it would indicate a real division in these Kansas settlements, either in culture or in date.

The matter of time is of prime importance; for there is reason to suspect that Caddoan tribes occupied this Kansas district more than once, at widely separate dates. The Pueblo pottery dating of these villages is interesting; but further evidence of this nature seems desirable; for in 1940 the Pueblo pottery found at Cow Creek was said to date late 17th and early 18th century, but in 1942 this was changed to 1500-1650, throwing the date back about a century.[11] And are the grooved stone mauls, found in all these ruins, as early as 1541? Such tools are usually given a much later date.

The attempts that have been made, over a period of nearly fifty years, to identify the Quiviras as Wichitas, are not convincing. The effort to twist the name Quivira into Kidikwius (an old name for the Wichitas) , made in Hodge's *Handbook of Indians North of Mexico*, and the recent suggestion of the linguists, Lesser and Weltfish, that Quivira is a perfectly good Pawnee word with the meaning *strange*, are fair examples of the many conjectures that have been published. The old belief that Quivira was the name of the village is blocked by Jaramillo, one of Coronado's captains, who states explicitly that the Indians called their settlements *Teucarea. Tuh* is the old Pawnee prefix, meaning *village*. It is not a Wichita name; but it is strikingly like the name *Touacara* which La Harpe in 1719 applied to the settlement and leading tribe in a Caddoan group on lower Canadian River in Oklahoma. That tribe was known in later times as the Tawakonis.

There is some slender excuse for connecting the Wichitas with Quivira by conjecture; but the men who have insisted that the Wichitas were the Quiviras have not troubled to collect this evidence. The Pawnee migration tradition, known about 1870 to all the younger

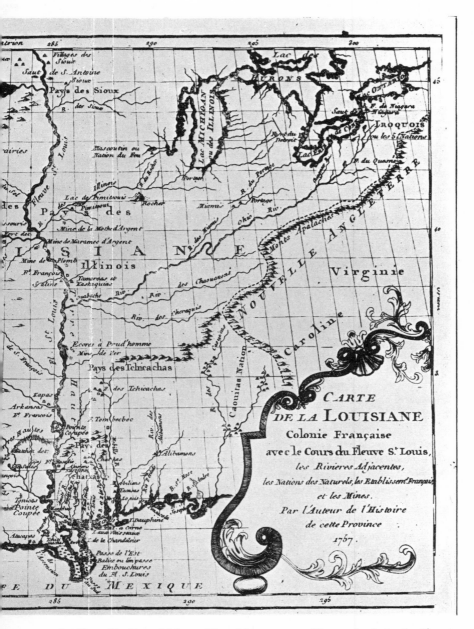

Le Page Du Pratz' Map of Louisiana, 1757. (From *An Introduction to Pawnee Archaeology*, by Waldo R. Wedel, BAE *Bulletin 112*, from *Histoire de la Louisiane*, tome premiere)

men, stated that their tribe (evidently the three Southern or Black
Pawnee tribes) and the Wichitas formerly dwelt on lower Red River
and migrated northward together in quest of buffalo; but the Wichitas became discouraged and turned back southward. This tradition
cannot possibly refer to a time previous to 1541 as these Indians did
not have a real memory for events farther back than about ninety
years; but they could retain a memory of an old home for perhaps
as long as a century and one half. The migration referred to here was
therefore one that took place in the late 17th century or early 18th
century; and it is certainly the one Lewis and Clark heard about in
1804. In their version the Wichitas are termed Panis Blancs, and the
Du Pratz map of 1757 places that tribe in Kansas, near the head of
the Neosho River, and right in the eastern edge of the Kansas Quivira
ruins. A map in the *Gentleman's Magazine,* June, 1763, also marks a
Panis Blancs village at the head of Neosho River, and so does the
Smith map of 1722.

The Wichitas, when driven from home by danger, had the quite
human trait of wishing to seek safety in an earlier home. When the
Civil War came in 1861 they were Union Indians; and, finding Red
River a dangerous location for Union people, they fled northward
and established themselves on the site of Wichita, Kansas, in the very
heart of the Quivira district. We may therefore state with fairness
that this tribe regarded that district in Kansas as their early home;
that they fled there about 1861; that they had lived there (as French
documents and maps indicate) from late in the 17th century to about
the year 1770, when they fled to Texas, evidently after being defeated
by the Osages. The Wichita and Pawnee migration north into Kansas
would therefore seem to be a 17th-century event; and this movement
northward may not have been the first. These tribes may have gone
northward at an earlier period; they may have been at or near Quivira
in 1541, and they may have been driven down to Red River by the
advance of the Apaches into central Kansas and Oklahoma, around
the date 1600-50. The Wichitas told Colonel W. S. Nye that their
name is made up of two archaic words, meaning Men of the North.
Here we have a little evidence connecting this tribe with the Kansas
region, perhaps with Quivira. The men who have insisted since 1898
that the Wichitas were Quiviras had no evidence. They picked the
Wichitas for the roll of Quiviras because in 1898 the very mixed
Caddoan group known as Wichitas was the only surviving tribe of
any size that still built grass-lodges of the type Coronado had found
at Quivira. But when the Wichitas fled south into Texas and made
their first clear appearance in history, in 1772, De Mézières visited

them and found to his astonishment that they had built a village of some type of northern earth-lodges. This grass-lodge tribe *par excellence* of 1898 did not know how to build grass-lodges when they made their first appearance from the north, in the late 18th century.

The Coronado narratives record the names of two Indian tribes or provinces to the north and east of Quivira: Harahey (Arahei or Arche in the Spanish texts) and Guas. The Harahey Indians are supposed to have been Pawnees, Harahey or Awahi being the old Caddoan name for the tribe. Guas seems to be the Spanish form of Ouace, another Caddoan name for the northern Pawnees. Dr. Wedel (1942) suggested that Harahey was in the Junction City area, east of the supposed location of Quivira, as the ground in that district is often littered with broken pottery of a type similar to the so-called Upper Republican ware found farther northward. As the Upper Republican folk seem to have been prehistoric Pawnees, probably of the Skidi tribe, the name Harahey would be appropriate for them. If the Arikaras are finally proved to have been an off-shoot from the Skidis, as the Indians themselves have always claimed, they would also properly come under the tribal name of Harahey. As for the Guas or Ouace, are they not the people whose villages were placed in the plains west of the Osages, under the name of Paniouace, by the French map-makers from 1673 onward?

Only in further archeological work in ruined villages can we hope for more enlightenment concerning the early movements of these Pawnee groups in the region south of Kansas River. Dr. Wedel seems inclined to the belief that it may be ultimately demonstrated that these tribes came northward by way of the valleys of the Verdigris and Neosho. Today there is nothing known concerning the archeology of that district further than the fact that Washington Irving while riding along the Neosho in September, 1832, noted in his journal that some holes in the ground were pointed out by an old Osage Indian, who said that they were *caches* in which the Pawnees used to hide their property when they left their village there to go on buffalo hunts. J. B. Thoburn, in a note for the Irving entry, stated that when excavations were made here on the Neosho, in northeastern Mayes County, Oklahoma, in 1924-25 to obtain gravel for roads, a number of these Indian *caches* were then uncovered, and Thoburn states explicitly that they were Wichita remains.[12] A Pawnee or Wichita village here on the Neosho must have been early in date; for before 1700 the Osages seem to have driven all Caddoan Indians out of the district. To this we may add the curious statement of the Wichita agent in the *Report of the Commissioner of Indian Affairs* for 1877 (p. 112) to the effect that the Wichitas, Wacos, and Tawakonis speak the same language and that the names Waco and Tawakoni were given to the descendants of "two bands of Wichitas who, about one hundred years ago, left the main tribe on the Neosho River in Kansas, one taking up a residence on the Arkansas River near the present town of Wichita and the other pushing on to Texas." Here we have a definite statement that the Wichitas lived on the Neosho River, evidently in the 18th century, and that one band went to live at the site of the town of Wichita, while the other group (Tawakonis?) removed southward into Texas.

NOTES TO CHAPTER 1

[1] Guy Rowley Moore prepared a master's thesis on Pawnee history in 1925, a typewritten copy of which is in the Oklahoma University Library. The paper is good for the period after 1835, but rather sketchy for the earlier years.

[2] The map in the U.S. De Soto Commission's report, p. 348, indicates that four tribes of the *Na* group: Nasonis, Nadaco, Nacao, Nabiti, retired in a southwestward direction after De Soto's time and established themselves near Angelina River, in east Texas.

[3] Father Casanas, quoted by Swanton, 1942, p. 17.

[4] Espinosa, quoted by Swanton, 1942, p. 163.

[5] Swanton, 1942, p. 162; Moorehead, 1931, p. vi.

[6] Wedel, 1942, p. 4, reports human bones scattered on the floor of a ruined temple in Kansas. In Nebraska indications of cannibalism are confined to the Missouri valley (and across the river in Iowa), with one instance on the Elkhorn River, a little to the west. It is useless to make phrases about the mere eating of a tiny sliver of human flesh in a purely ceremonial manner. These Indians cut up entire bodies, cooked and ate them, roasting and cracking the bones to obtain the marrow. The Iroquois, supposed to be kindred to the Caddoan Indians, were seen by the early French, indulging in similar cannibal feasts.

[7] Abe I: *Tabeau's Narrative of Loisel's Expedition,* 1939, p. 187.

[8] *Handbook of Indians,* v. II, p. 213.

[9] The Kansa tribe, in close contact with the Skidi Pawnees at an early date, used the form *Panin,* sometimes saying *Pa'i.*

[10] Father Espinosa, quoted by Swanton, 1942, p. 27.

[11] Wedel, 1940, p. 333; Wedel, 1942, p. 20 and various pages.

[12] Irving: *Tour of the Prairies,* Oklahoma City edition, 1926, p. xxxix.

A Pawnee earth lodge. (Western History Collections, University of Oklahoma Library)

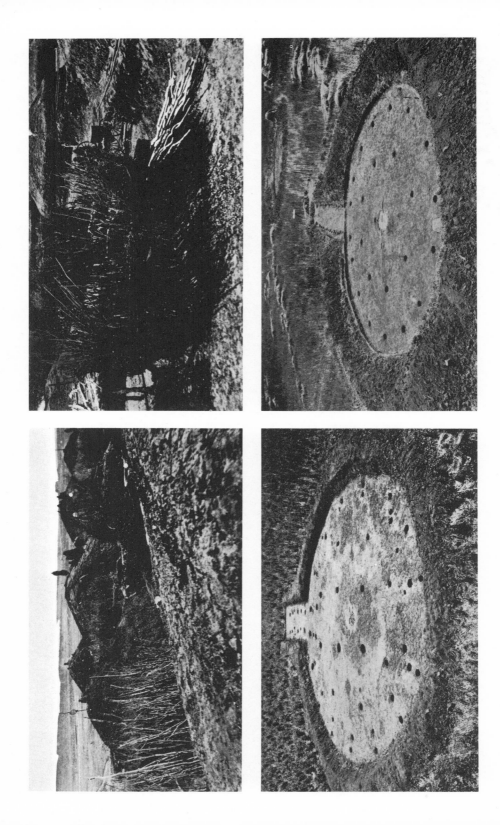

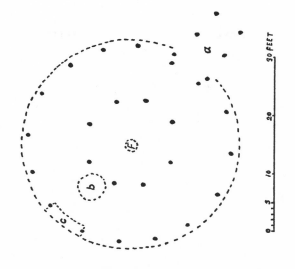

Upper left: Scenes in a Pawnee village on the Loup River near Genoa, Nebraska, 1871, the last northern settlement of the tribe before removal to Indian Territory. (Photographs by W. H. Jackson)

Top right: Excavated floor of protohistoric Pawnee earth lodge at Larsen site on Looking-glass Creek, showing central firepit, surrounded by four primary and three circles of secondary post molds. (Nebraska State Historical Society)

Middle right: Excavated floor of late historical Pawnee earth lodge near Leshara, occupied probably after 1850. This lodge had eight central roof supports, a raised altar platform at the rear directly opposite the doorway, and a sill of baked clay across the inner end of the entrance passage. Another house floor can be seen in the background. (Nebraska State Historical Society)

Right: Ground plan of historic Pawnee earth lodge: *a* = entrance passage, *b* = interior cache, *c* = raised platform altar, *F* = firepit. (From *An Introduction to Pawnee Archaeology*, by Waldo R. Wedel, BAE Bulletin *112*, and *The Direct-Historical Approach in Pawnee Archaeology*, by Waldo R. Wedel, Smithsonian Misc. Coll., Vol. 97, No. 7)

A Pawnee earth lodge of the post-removal 1880's in Indian Territory. (From *Indian Territory: A Frontier Photographic Record*, by W. S. Prettyman and Robert E. Cunningham, Norman, 1957)

II

The Pawnees and the Padoucas

WHEN WE ATTEMPT TO FOLLOW THE MIGRATION OF THE FIRST PAWNEES
northward into Kansas and Nebraska we find at once that we are dealing with prehistoric events and that the only evidence is in the form
of archeology. By means of tree-ring studies and other tests, the
archeologists have dated these events back to 1400, possibly to 1300;
which explains why the Pawnees, depending on oral tradition, had no
knowledge of this first migration when they talked to Dunbar and
Grinnell, late in the 19th century.

The slow movement northward of these primitive Pawnees was
up the Arkansas River and, perhaps, up that stream's eastern branches,
the Neosho and Verdigris. Here they were outside the eastern borders
of the buffalo range, and deer and wild turkeys were apparently the
main sources of meat supply. In the 19th century the Pawnees had
a faint memory of this; for they stated that in ancient times when a
man of the Skidi Pawnee tribe wished to gratify the gods and gain
their goodwill for the benefit of his family and tribe, he made a vow
to consecrate a deer, whereas in later times a buffalo was consecrated
for such a sacrifice. They also recalled that in early times the wild
turkey held the position of honor in the sacred rites that was in later
days assigned to the eagle.

Moving up into Kansas, these Pawnees came into the district which
the Spanish explorers later called Quivira, and into the lands to the
north, along Kansas River. Here the archeological evidence indicates
that they divided, one group going westward into the buffalo plains,
while the second division spread toward the northeast, establishing
many small villages in eastern Nebraska and along the east bank of
the Missouri River in western Iowa. The western division formed
similar small villages of rectangular earth-lodges, mainly along the
branches of Republican River in southwestern Nebraska. Basically
the simple cultures of both these Pawnee groups were very similar at

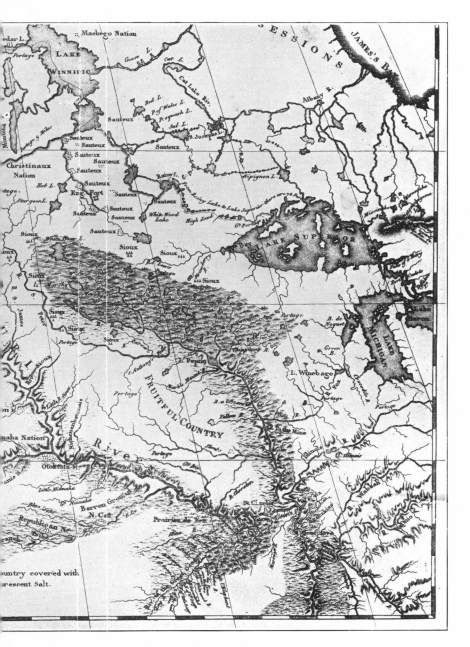

Victor Collot's Map, 1796. (From *An Introduction to Pawnee Arch-aeology*, by Waldo R. Wedel, BAE *Bulletin 112*, from a *Journey in North America*, Vol. I)

first. They lived by hunting and by growing small crops. Their villages were small, containing from four to five and at times up to as many as twenty little earth-lodges set out widely apart on open valley-land: little communities fairly typical of the old-time Caddoan scattered and undefended villages, far to the south along Red River. The environment of these first Pawnee villages in Nebraska clearly suggests an era of peace, with no near neighbors of alien stock from whom hostile acts might have been expected. The Pawnees on the Republican River seem to have been for a long time almost completely isolated. Perhaps they exchanged visits and had a little barter trade with their Caddoan kinsmen in the south, as well as with the other Pawnee group along the Missouri in eastern Nebraska. This second group differed from the Republican River Pawnees in one respect; for they were big river people, while their kinsmen on the Republican were creek valley people; thus the Pawnees along the Missouri gained a considerable part of their food by fishing, while the Pawnees of the Republican substituted buffalo meat for fish. Moreover, the Missouri River Pawnees were not isolated as those along the Republican were; for they were in contact with powerful Indian groups of alien stock that dwelt to the eastward, on or near the Mississippi; and through their intercourse with these tribes the Pawnees in eastern Nebraska were induced to alter their simple ways of life to such an extent that some archeologists have attempted to rule them out, by declaring that they were not Pawnees, not of Caddoan stock. But such a view is not in conformity with what slight historical evidence we have, or with Indian tradition; and even from the archeological angle the argument is weak. The pottery and some other features in the eastern Nebraska villages were much altered through intercourse with other tribes; but the type of earth-lodges, the stone work (knives, arrow and lance heads, skin-scrapers), were kept true to the old Pawnee forms; and the evidence of the Caddoan origin of these Indians is clear. Dr. W. R. Wedel has connected one of their village ruins on the lower Elkhorn River with the culture of the Spiro village in eastern Oklahoma, which is a fine type of early Caddoan remains.[13] Again, these eastern Nebraska Indians practiced cannibalism, which was in early times a feature of Caddoan Indian life in the south. Along the Republican in western Nebraska, the land of the primitive Skidi Pawnees, no traces of cannibalism were found by the archeologists.

At an unknown date during their occupation of the Republican River country the Skidi Pawnees came into contact with an alien tribe in the plains, who must have been the Indians known to the Spaniards of New Mexico as Apaches and termed by the French

Padoucas. During the past twenty years the early camps and village ruins of this tribe have been discovered, extending from northern Nebraska southward across the heads of Loup Fork to the district above the forks of the Platte, and on southward through western Nebraska, eastern Colorado, and western Kansas. The veteran Nebraska archeologist, A. T. Hill, discovered the first of these Padouca remains, on the Dismal River fork of the Loup, and in 1939 he and George Metcalf carefully excavated an extensive village ruin in Chase County, western Nebraska, and identified it as Padouca.[14] Dr. Wedel in 1947 termed this Indian culture Apache, which confirmed the matter from a different angle; for the Apaches and Padoucas were undoubtedly the same Indians.[15]

This bringing of the Apaches or Padoucas on the scene is a most important matter; for it supplies us with a reasonable explanation as to why the Pawnees abandoned their little villages on the Republican River and moved north of the Platte, to form new settlements on the upper Loup River. That this was the course they took is indicated by the facts that their village ruins on the Republican are deeply buried under top soil and the pottery in these ruins seems to be of the oldest period; the first little villages on the Loup River are not deeply buried; the pottery seems to be of later type; and it was in these villages that the old type of rectangular earth-lodges began to shift over into the form of circular lodges, which were the only kind known to the Pawnees in 18th and 19th centuries.[16]

This meeting of the Pawnees and Apaches in the Nebraska plains is paralleled by similar events in the southern plains; and in that region we have Spanish evidence to indicate just how the situation developed. Moreover, in the south we have yet another group of Pawnees: the Southern Pawnees, Panis Noirs, or Black Pawnees; and by following their experiences with the Apaches we may judge fairly well what conditions were among the Nebraska Pawnees at the same period.

The Southern Pawnees were apparently either a part of the population of the province of Quivira, as the Spaniards termed it, or close neighbors of Quivira. In 1541 Coronado did not report any enemy tribe in the plains near Quivira, nor did he say anything about war; but when Oñate's Spaniards marched across the plains to Quivira in 1601 they found in the plains close to the Caddoan villages a warlike tribe called Escansaques, who were evidently Apaches.[17] These Indians followed Oñate into Quivira and attempted to induce the Spaniards to assist them in setting the villages afire and plundering them. After leaving Quivira, Oñate had a hard fight with the Escansaques. Fifty

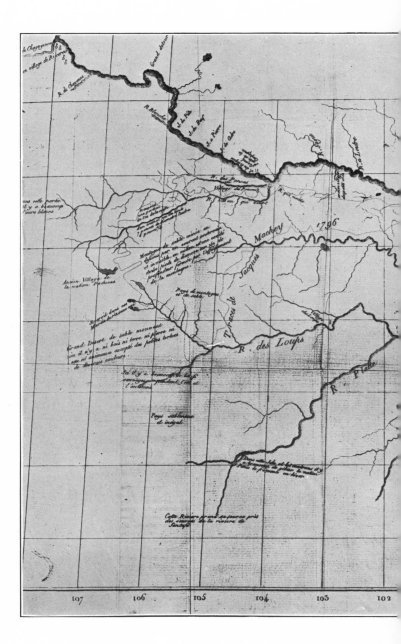

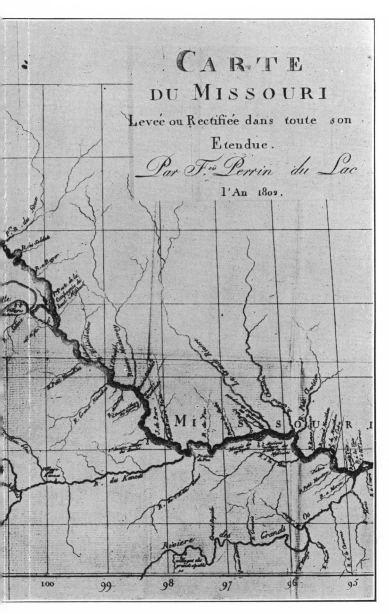

Perrin Du Lac's Map of the Missouri, 1802. (From *An Introduction to Pawnee Archaeology,* by Waldo R. Wedel, BAE *Bulletin 112,* from *Travels Through the Two Louisianas*)

years later they appeared farther to the south, on the head of Red River; and from that time until after 1720 the lands near the upper Red River were regarded by the Caddoan tribes as the country of their bitter enemies, the Canecy Apaches. These same Caddoans, in eastern Oklahoma, told the French explorer La Harpe in 1719 that they had formerly crossed the plains to trade in New Mexico, but that the Padoucas had then moved into these plains and blocked their way.

It was apparently about the date 1670 that the Apaches in the southern plains obtained horses and metal weapons in sufficient quantities to make them the dread of all neighbor tribes; and the Apaches in the south must have traded horses and weapons to their Padouca kinsmen in the north; for in 1679 La Salle in the Illinois country heard stories of mounted warriors fighting in the plains to the west, and he met an Oto chief who had a horse's hoof—evidently a war trophy—dangling from his belt. He saw Padouca slaves that had been brought from the plains to the Mississippi.

The carrying off of women and children into slavery was a feature of this war between the Apaches of the plains and the Pawnees and other Caddoan tribes farther toward the east. Both in New Mexico and on the Mississippi the slave trade was brisk. A New Mexican Spanish account of the Apache method of raiding the Caddoan villages at the period 1692 is enlightening. These Apaches were now mounted and equipped with long metal-pointed lances and Spanish knives and hatchets, which gave them an immense advantage over the "Quiviras" and other Caddoan tribes, who had to fight on foot with primitive weapons. The Apaches waited until the bad weather of February confined the Caddoan Indians to their villages; they then set out in great mounted parties, approached some small village by stealth and took the Caddoans by surprise, killing as many men as they could, capturing women and children, and setting the village aflame. In a single expedition they often destroyed several villages. The Apaches then rode home triumphant; and in the following May they went to New Mexico to trade their slaves to the Spaniards and Pueblo Indians, obtaining for Caddoan women and children more horses and metal weapons, to be used in future raids. In 1694 the Apaches (said to have been of the Navaho group) brought a large number of "Quivira" children to the trading-fair in New Mexico; but for some reason there were no buyers; and finding that they could not obtain what they desired for the children the enraged Apaches beheaded all of the little slaves before the eyes of the horrified Spaniards.[18]

There is some reason for the belief that during this period of destructive Apache raids, between 1680 and 1695, the Caddoan Indians known in New Mexico as the Quiviras were forced to abandon their old lands on the Arkansas River in southern Kansas and to retire southward, to join the other Caddoan groups.[19] At this period the Caddoans in the south were being raided by large bands of mounted Apaches from the west, while from the east they were being assailed by war parties of fierce Chickasaws and Choctaws from the Mississippi, who were equipped with metal weapons and even firearms. These eastern raiders were carrying off great numbers of Caddoan slaves; and, thus attacked from both the west and east, the Caddoans seem to have retired from some of the most exposed positions, of which Quivira may have been one, to consolidate their forces in new settlements on the Arkansas, at or near the mouth of the Canadian River. Presently they began to obtain horses and metal weapons; and by the time La Harpe visited them in 1719 these Pawnees and other Caddoans of the Arkansas River were returning the Apache raids with interest, destroying Apache camps, and carrying off Apache women and children. The hatred engendered by these raids was so intense that—as the French reported—both the Caddoan Indians and the Padoucas were cooking and eating many of the captives they brought back from the enemy camps.

That this war of the Apaches or Padoucas on the Caddoan Indians in the south extended up into the Pawnee country in Nebraska seems obvious, for the Apache groups held all the plains country, and the groups were probably in constant touch with one another and acting together. At this period in the 17th century the Spaniards, who loved to set down reports of rich Indian provinces beyond their frontiers, had some information concerning what they termed the Province of Taguayo, lying in the plains to the north of New Mexico, a land which was inhabited in part by the Apaches of the Tagui group, who seem to have been included by the French among the Indians they termed Padoucas.[20] This Province of Taguayo seems to have embraced the plains country of Colorado: the lands east of the mountains and north of the Arkansas River; for some Pueblo Indians who had been held as slaves there, having escaped and returned to New Mexico, reported that Taguayo lay sixty leagues to the northeast of the Utes, who were in the mountains near the present southern border of Colorado. Father Posadas, who was in New Mexico at this time, depicted Taguayo as a province similar to Quivira; Taguayo was on the western edge of the high plains, Quivira on the eastern borders; while the plains between the two provinces were filled with roving herds of buffalo and bands of wandering Indians.

In the Colorado plains north of the Arkansas, where the Spaniards

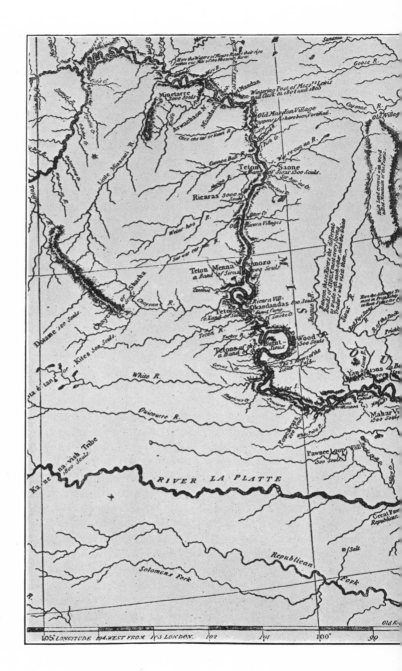

Meriwether Lewis and William Clark's Map, 1804. (From *An Introduction to Pawnee Archaeology*, by Waldo R. Wedel, BAE *Bulletin 112*, from *Travels to the Source of the Missouri River*, Vol. I)

located Taguayo, Dr. E. B. Renaud, then of the University of Denver, made an archeological survey; and in a region where it was always supposed that there were no Indian village ruins or camp sites containing evidence of the use of pottery, he has found an unbroken series of such sites with the surface dotted with pieces of broken pottery. He has found such remains north of the Arkansas in the district where in the 17th and 18th centuries the Apache rancherias known as El Cuartelejo were located. He has found other groups of camp sites farther north, on the heads of the Smoky Hill and Republican rivers in eastern Colorado; and many more still farther north, along the South Platte in northeast Colorado, and on both forks of the Platte in Nebraska. The pottery fragments scattered over all of these Renaud sites in the Colorado plains compare nicely with the Padouca type of pottery from sites in Nebraska; moreover, both in Colorado and in western Nebraska finds have been made of broken Pueblo pottery from New Mexico, mingled with the local ware, the rude pottery of the Apaches or Padoucas.[21]

In the Nebraska region we do not have the historical advantage of Spanish reports, which in the country farther south enlighten us as to the course of events all through the 17th century and on into the 18th. In the north we have no evidence beyond the colorless and often hazy records of archeology; but even so we observe a retirement of the Skidi Pawnees from the upper Republican River valley northward to the Loup Fork; the occupation of the old Pawnee lands near the Republican by the Padoucas; and the appearance of the villages of this tribe in the lands immediately west of the Pawnees, on the Loup and Platte. These clues point to a condition similar to that in the southern region, where in the 17th century the Apaches were persistently pressing against the Caddoans and forcing them to combine for purposes of defense. In the south this period dates 1680-1700; but what appears to be the same period in Nebraska is dated by the archeologists about 1541-1682. To the historian this dating seems arbitrary and—as far as the Nebraska Pawnees are concerned—misleading. Here the archeologists have taken the date of Coronado's visit to Quivira (1541) as the beginning of the vague period between prehistory and history, and they have given the year of La Salle's second expedition into Illinois (1682) as the time this period closed. In doing this they seem to ignore the significance of the presence of the Apaches or Padoucas in the plains and the evidence in the south of the habitual hostility of the Apaches toward the Pawnees and other Caddoan tribes, mainly from 1650 to after 1700. In Nebraska the Pawnees removed from the Republican River district, seemingly because of Apache pressure; for the Apaches then occupied these Pawnee lands. The Pawnees went north to Loup Fork; and after living in small undefended villages for a long time they formed large and strong villages, the archeologists dating this last event about 1541. Yet they have their own tree-ring dating, which shows that one Apache (Padouca) village in the Republican River district, after the Pawnee left that land, was built about 1667 and was still in use until after 1709, while a second village dates from about 1674 until after 1704.

The Pawnees in the 19th century had no knowledge of their history in the 17th and early 18th centuries, and they clearly had never heard of a time when their people dwelt in rectangular earth-lodges, which were in use on the Republican and during the early period on the Loup Fork. Even the older of the later type villages, with circular lodges, were a mystery to the people in the 19th century; and they could do no more than guess that their ancestors had once dwelt in these villages. It is only in the story of Closed Man—a Skidi Pawnee tale, half tradition, half religious myth—that we obtain a glimpse through the mists of Time of the change from the primitive Pawnee life in the little villages of rectangular earth-lodges to the big and compact villages of circular lodges.

This curious tale opens with the activities of the Skidi star-deities. Morning Star and Evening Star had a daughter; Sun and Moon had a son; a wolf, who bore the name of the old Wolf Clan of the southern Caddoan Indians of Red River and who seems to have symbolized war, was prowling through the land, destroying the Pawnees. Presently the son of Sun and Moon, who was called Closed Man, was placed on earth by the gods, and with him was placed the daughter of the two star-deities. They married and were instructed by four gods, who taught them how to build earth-lodges (not the small rectangular lodges of early times, but the big circular ones of the later historic period), and other useful arts. All this happened, the tale relates, before the Pawnees had horses, which may mean sometime before 1700. Closed Man and his wife, after being instructed, moved northward into Nebraska and formed a new village on Loup Fork, called Center Village. Nothing is said of their bringing any people with them except one errand man—a kind of servant such as Pawnee chiefs maintained in later times. They found numerous small Pawnee villages in every direction from Center Village; and the errand man was sent out to call all the people to a great ceremony. His journeyings are recorded in detail; the villages he visited are named and their location given; and the curious fact is that in each district in which the errand man found a Pawnee village the archeologists in recent

years have found ruins of the old rectangular-lodge type. As for Center
Village, it is the large Pawnee ruin on the north bank of the Loup
at the mouth of Beaver Creek. Unlike the older rectangular-lodge
ruins, which are in undefended sites on low ground, Center Village
is strongly set on a high tableland; it is a big village with lodges of
the more recent circular type, and there are indications that it was
fortified.

All the Pawnee groups visited by the errand man were evidently
independent; for every village had its sacred bundle, usually given
to it by one of the star-deities. The Closed Man plan for helping the
people was to form all these villages into a united tribe, in which
each village and its sacred bundle would have an assigned position
and certain privileges. The people from the villages to the west,
south, and north all obeyed the summons and came to Center Village
for the great ceremony; but toward the east, on or near the Elkhorn
River, the errand man found Pawnees of a different mind, perhaps
of a separate division of the tribe. They refused to obey the summons
to Center Village, telling the errand man bluntly that they had gods
of their own and magic power of their own. They were not interested
in Closed Man and his doings. Here archeology assists us in the inter-
petation of this story; for the lower Elkhorn River district is inside
the territory of the second Pawnee group, the one that on leaving
Kansas turned toward the northeast and built villages along the Missouri, extending westward to the Elkhorn. Archeologically these
people of eastern Nebraska were related to the Skidi Pawnees who
were now assembling at Center Village on the Loup to attend the
ceremony; historically the only group in the north thus related to
the Skidis were the Arikaras, whose tradition was that they left the
Skidis in Nebraska and moved up the Missouri into Dakota. Now, in
the Closed Man story we learn that on or near the Elkhorn the errand
man found two villages with Arikara names: *Arikaraikuchu* (Big
Antlered Elks Standing) and *Arikaraikih* (Little Antlered Elks Standing). Taking into account that the Pawnees interpret these village
names as meaning Antlered Elks Standing and explain the tribal
name Arikara as meaning Elkhorn or Antler, we have here in the
Closed Man story an implication that at least part of the Arikara
tribe was still in eastern Nebraska, on or near the Elkhorn, in Closed
Man's day. As we know that the French traders often gave the name
of a tribe to the river that tribe dwelt on, and as the French gave the
name Elkhorn to this river prior to 1723, we have here another
possible connection of the Arikara tribe with the Elkhorn River in
the early years of the 18th century. Unknown French woodrunners

Pierre Charles Le Seuer's Map, 1701. (From *An Introduction to Pawnee Archaeology*, by Waldo R. Wedel, BAE *Bulletin 112*, from the South Dakota Historical Collections, Vol. I, page 49)

might have wandered into eastern Nebraska some years prior to 1700, and finding villages of the Arikaras or Antlered Elk Indians may have named the river Elkhorn for that reason.[22]

With the Arikaras refusing to join them, all the little Skidi villages assembled at Closed Man's village on Beaver Creek; and there in a solemn ceremony they formed themselves into a united tribe. This Closed Man story is a faint memory of that far-off time, of which the Skidi Pawnees in the 19th century had no definite knowledge. When this tale was printed in English many years ago it had little meaning; but taken in connection with the recent archeological discovery of all the little Pawnee village ruins of the old rectangular-lodge type, it assumes a new importance; for it states quite clearly what the archeologists have been too cautious to assert: that the Skidis were living in nearly a score of little independent and exposed villages; that they were being warred upon; that some Pawnees from the south came and induced them to form a compact settlement and united tribe for defense; and that the Arikaras were still in the Elkhorn district at this date but refused to unite with the Skidis.[23]

The assertion that Southern Pawnees induced the Skidis to form a united tribe is interesting; for when the French traders first came into Nebraska early in the 18th century they found not only the Skidi tribe on the Loup Fork but one village of Panis, evidently Southern Pawnees, on the south bank of the Platte, south of the Skidi villages. Moreover, the French map-makers placed from two to five villages of Panis Noirs (Black Pawnees from the south) with the Arikara tribe, on the Missouri in the district near the mouth of the Niobrara River, in northeastern Nebraska and in South Dakota. Some event in the Oklahoma region must have caused these Black Pawnees to move up into Nebraska; but whether they came of their own volition or were driven northward by enemies we do not know.

It was at this same period that the first of the Siouan tribes, the Otos, came into eastern Nebraska from their older home in Iowa. They built a village on the Great Nemaha in southeastern Nebraska; and pottery and other articles from this Oto village have been found in the Skidi village ruins on Loup Fork, clearly indicating that there was a trade between the two tribes and that the villages were contemporary. The exact date of this Oto village is not known; but Marquette and La Salle locate the Otos east of the Missouri in 1673-83, and the French trader Le Sueur, who was in southern Minnesota at the time, states that it was in 1700 that the Otos moved westward across Iowa to the Missouri. The Oto tradition is definite. This states that the tribe crossed the Missouri and lived on the Great Nemaha;

and later they moved to the Platte and built a village at the mouth of Salt Creek, a southern tributary of that river; and here the French traders found the tribe about the year 1715. On the whole the clues we obtain from the Closed Man tale and from the location and movements of the Arikaras and Otos, seem to cast doubt on the archeologists' dictum that the forming of the big Skidi villages on Loup Fork was an event of the early 17th or even the middle 16th century. This seems much too early, and a date around 1680 would seem more reasonable for the uniting of the Skidi tribe.

The coming of the Siouan tribes into the country west of the Missouri at this period, late in the 17th century, was an event that affected the Pawnees and other Caddoan tribes as profoundly as the operations of the Apaches or Padoucas in the plains did. Curiously, that war-loving tribe, the Iroquois, who were related by blood and language to the Pawnees, appear to have been mainly responsible for the driving of the Siouan Indians westward. At about the date at which the Apaches in the plains acquired horses and metal weapons, the Iroquois obtained metal weapons and firearms and began to terrorize the tribes that dwelt to the west of them.

The Quapaws were a far-fled tribe of Siouans, whose old home was apparently on the Wabash. They and their kindred tribes, the Osages, Omahas, Poncas, and the Kansa tribe, seem to have fled westward down the Ohio. The Quapaws continued their flight, down the Mississippi to the mouth of the Arkansas, where Marquette found them in 1673. The Osages went to the river in Missouri that still bears their name; while the Kansa tribe moved up the Missouri into eastern Kansas. The Omahas and Poncas moved northward into northern Iowa, arriving near the head of Des Moines River before 1673 and joining the Iowas and Otos in that region.

Marquette obtained from Indians on the Mississippi some information concerning the tribes farther toward the west, and he set these tribes down on his crude map. The Panas, evidently the Arikaras, he located either in western Iowa or eastern Nebraska, and a Pawnee group termed Paniassa he placed in southern Kansas. La Salle and his party came into Illinois in the winter of 1679; and they were in the Mississippi valley, exploring and trading until 1700. They had just arrived among the Illini Indians in 1679 when a party of Osages and Quapaws came to see the Frenchmen. They were eager to obtain French knives and hatchets; for they had forgotten their own fate at the hands of eastern Indians, who had metal weapons and had driven them west of the Mississippi, and they were now preparing to raid their new neighbors, probably the Caddoans and Pawnees. Next came

an Oto chief with a horse's hoof tied to his belt, who said that his
people dwelt ten days away toward the west; and five days beyond
their village, in the plains, raids were being made by mounted warriors
equipped with long lances. La Salle was given a Pana boy slave by an
Illini chief. The boy, evidently an Arikara, stated that his people
lived in two villages on a branch of the Mississippi (the Missouri),
more than one hundred leagues toward the west, and to the south of
them were the Gatackas (Apaches or Padoucas) and a tribe called
Manroat. These two tribes traded with the Spaniards and brought
horses to trade to the Panas.[24]

When he returned to Illinois from the mouth of the Mississippi in
1682, La Salle was given a slave boy who may have been a Padouca
from the Nebraska plains; for he had been captured by the Panimahas
(Skidi Pawnees), from whom the Osages had stolen him. The Osages
gave him to their kinsmen, the Missouri tribe, who traded him to the
Illinois Indians. Given to La Salle, the boy presently ran away, taking
a Paniassa (a Southern Pawnee) slave girl with him. Here we have
a picture of what was happening in the lands west of the Missouri in
1673-83. The Southern Pawnees and their Caddoan kinsmen on the
Arkansas in Oklahoma were being raided by Apaches from the west
and by Osages and other enemies from the east; the Skidi Pawnees
in Nebraska were fighting the Padoucas in the west, while at the
same time they were being raided to some extent by Siouan Indians
from the east. The Paniassas (Black or Southern Pawnees) were in
the worst position; and evidently, both in New Mexico and on the
Mississippi, most of the Indian slaves came from their group.

From the French maps of the 18th century it is apparent that these
Paniassas were on the east side of the Arkansas River, in Oklahoma,
extending northward into southern Kansas. They seem to have occupied the district the Spaniards had formerly called Quivira, or lands
immediately to the east and south of that locality. In New Mexico
the Spaniards still used the name Quivira, and they may have included these Paniassas under that designation. The raids on this
group from the east seem to have been mainly the work of the Osages.
As late as 1683 this tribe had only French knives and hatchets and
very few firearms; but they were constantly bringing in Paniassa
slaves; and by 1685 they had extended their raids to include the
Caddoan tribes on Red River, on the northern Texas border.

By 1695 the Caddoans and Pawnees, both in the south and in
Nebraska, were probably better prepared to face the Apache raids
from the west. They now had some horses and metal weapons; they
had drawn their formerly scattered population into more compact

groups some in fortified villages; and the Spaniards of New Mexico reported that these "Quiviras" or "Pananas" (Pawnees) were taking large numbers of Apaches and selling them as slaves to the French. These reports were probably exaggerated; but in 1697 it was reported in New Mexico that the Apaches had been badly defeated by these Caddoan Indians; but in the following year the Apaches struck back hard, destroying three Caddoan villages and a fortified place—the earliest reference in the Spanish records to a fortified place among the Caddoans.[25]

Here we must give some account of these Caddoan groups in eastern Oklahoma, extending up into southern Kansas; for part of them were Pawnees who later moved northward and joined the Skidis in Nebraska; and some of these Indians were certainly the people known to the Spaniards as the Quiviras. As it has been so often stated that the Wichitas were the Quiviras, the situation of the Wichitas at the close of the 17th and opening of the 18th century is of considerable interest.

The first group of Pawnees to move northward into Nebraska, according to the migration traditions obtained by Dunbar and Grinnell, were the Skidis, who came north at a very early period. At a much later date the three other Pawnee tribes came into Nebraska—the Chauis, the Kitkehahkis, and the Pitahauerats; and the tradition was that they and the Wichitas left Red River and moved northward to obtain buffalo; the Wichitas became dissatisfied and returned to the south; the three Pawnee tribes went on northward, remaining in Kansas for a time, and then joining the Skidis in Nebraska. These three Pawnee tribes were clearly the Indians termed by the French the Paniassas, Panis Noirs, or Black Pawnees, and Marquette in 1673 placed them, as nearly as we may judge from his rude map, in southern Kansas or northern Oklahoma, near the Arkansas River. Later French maps located the Panis Blancs or White Pawnees (supposedly the Wichitas) in about the same region: in the lands near the head of the Neosho River, which would have put them to the east of the lands along the Arkansas where Quivira was supposed to lie.

In 1702 D'Iberville stated that the Caddoan group farthest down the Arkansas River was that of the Indians called Mentos, whose settlement was fifty to sixty leagues west of the Mississippi; and to the west of the Mentos were their allies the Panis Noirs, who had 2,000 warriors; which would indicate that at this date these Southern Pawnees had a population of some 10,000 and probably ten villages. Indeed, the French map of Franquelin, 1688, places ten Black Pawnee villages on the east side of Arkansas River, in the country south of the head-waters of Osage River.

The bringing of the Mentos into the picture is a most interesting matter. In 1686 when La Salle's men were attempting to find a route from Texas back to the Mississippi valley, they left the Caddoan villages on Red River and marched twenty-five leagues toward the northeast to two Caddoan villages, those of the Mentos and Cahinnios, on or near Ouachita River in southern Arkansas. By 1700 the Mentos had moved northward to Arkansas River. Later they moved higher up the Arkansas, to a point above the mouth of Canadian River and twenty-five leagues below the Panis Noirs; but in 1719 La Harpe found them west of the Arkansas, on the Canadian River, at a point forty leagues south of the Panis Noirs. Describing the Indians in the two Mento villages, La Harpe named nine tribes or groups that made up the population, including among them some Wichitas and Iscanis. Beaurain also named nine groups in the villages, including Wichitas and Iscanis; and both La Harpe and Beaurain stated that the most prominent group in the villages, smaller in numbers than some of the other groups, but the leaders among these Indians, were the Touacaras, known in later times as the Tawakonis.[26]

Here we have clues that concern the Pawnees and also throw some light on the Quivira problem; for Jaramillo, one of Coronado's captains, stated in 1541 that the people of Quivira called their settlement Teucarea, and this does seem to be the same as the name of the Touacara of La Harpe in 1719. Again, the Wichita Indian agent stated in 1877 that the Touacras (Tawakonis) and Wacos were formerly part of the Wichita tribe; that they separated from the Wichitas when that tribe lived on the Neosho River, and that one of these off-shoot bands built a village near the present city of Wichita, Kansas, while the second band went southward toward Texas. Here we have evidence connecting both the Tawakonis and Wichitas with the old district of Quivira; but the French reports show clearly that the Tawakonis, under the name of Mentos, had gone down near the Texas border before 1685 and had then slowly ventured northward and westward until, in 1719, they were again in close relationship with the Wichitas, actually having some people of that tribe living in their two villages. The composition of the two Mento villages of 1719 is another interesting point; for in these villages, which had a total of 4,000 to 6,000 people, there were gathered remnants of nine tribes, which indicates that these Indians had been severely raided by enemies, and perhaps decimated by epidemic diseases. They had then united to form two strong villages, which in 1719 were holding their own against enemy attacks.

As for the Black Pawnees, these people in 1702-1719 were living in perhaps as many as ten villages on the Arkansas, forty leagues north of the Mentos on the Canadian, and twenty leagues south of the villages of the Wichitas and Iscanis, who were on the Arkansas very close to the present northern boundary of Oklahoma and in what we may term the southern edge of the old Quivira area. The curious thing is that these Black Pawnees, who later moved north to join the Skidis in Nebraska, were removed with the Skidis a century later and resettled by the government on the west bank of the Arkansas, in the exact district in which the Black Pawnees lived in 1702-1719; and neither the white men who moved these Indians, nor the Pawnees themselves, appear to have had the faintest suspicion that these Indians were being brought back and settled on the lands of their ancestors. The French trader Du Tisne who visited the Black Pawnees in 1719, found them on the west side of the Arkansas, evidently in the lands which after 1875 were the new Pawnee reservation.

In Nebraska in the 17th and early 18th centuries the Skidi Pawnees were evidently going through the same ordeal that their southern kinsmen on the Arkansas in Oklahoma were being subjected to. They were losing people because of enemy attacks, and they were combining the population that remained into more compact and defensible settlements. The Closed Man story gave the Skidis seventeen little independent villages (the Franquelin map of 1688 sets down exactly that number of Skidi villages); but by 1715 the Skidis had united their population to form eight strong villages and—like the Caddoans in the south—they were now successfully opposing their old oppressors, the Apaches or Padoucas. This is plainly set forth in a Spanish document of the 1716 period, which states that the Pawnees in Nebraska were close neighbors of the *Apaches*, with whom they constantly warred; and, being better warriors, the Pawnees took great numbers of Apache prisoners and sold them as slaves to the French.[27] Bourgmont, a French trader who was on the Missouri at this period, reported that the Pawnees were a strong tribe, and fine horsemen. They had nine handsome and well-built villages: eight Skidi villages and one Panis village, which was on the Platte south of the Skidis. Rénaudière, who described the Nebraska region in 1723, gave the Skidis eight villages. This Frenchman had not been in Nebraska, but was describing the region from traders' reports. He seems to have confused the Elkhorn (*Rivière Cerf écorne*: River of the Antlered Elk) with the Loup Fork; and he placed the one Panis village on the Platte eight

Top: Restored pot of late Pawnee type from Archer, Nebraska, height 9 inches. *Bottom*: Restored vessel of protohistoric Pawnee type from the Wolfe site near Schuyler, height 4⅝ inches. (Nebraska State Historical Society. From *The Direct-Historical Approach in Pawnee Archaeology*, by Waldo R. Wedel, Smithsonian Misc. Coll., Vol. 97, No. 7)

Historic Pawnee vessels from various sites. (From *An Introduction to Pawnee Archaeology*, by Waldo R. Wedel, BAE *Bulletin 112*)

Pawnee type rim sherds from various historic sites. (From *An Intro-duction to Pawnee Archaeology*, by Waldo R. Wedel, BAE *Bulletin 112*)

Designs on incised tablets ("molds") of stone from the Hill and Linwood sites. (From *An Introduction to Pawnee Archaeology*, by Waldo
R. Wedel, BAE *Bulletin 112*)

leagues below the Elkhorn, with eight Skidi villages on the latter stream, half a league apart. He gave the Panis village 150 lodges, indicating a population of some 3,000 persons. On the same basis the eight Skidi villages would have had about 24,000 people.[28]

Groups of French traders had been established in the Illinois country from the time of La Salle's expeditions of 1679-1682, and in 1699 a new French settlement was made at the mouth of the Mississippi. Unlike the Spaniards in the Southwest, the French were very much interested in trade; and they were soon supplying the tribes along the Mississippi, on lower Red River, on the Arkansas in east Oklahoma, and on the Missouri as high up as the mouth of the Platte. There was no monopoly; and scores of adventurous traders were soon going with two or three companions to the villages of distant tribes, where no Spanish officer would have dared to venture with a force of less than one hundred armed men. Trading knives, hatchets, a few guns, brass kettles, cloth, beads, and cheap ornaments, the French penetrated everywhere that a man in a dugout canoe or with a pack on his back could go; and wherever they went the Indians eagerly traded their furs, slaves, and horses for the French goods, particularly for the metal weapons. Most of all they coveted guns; and the 18th century had not completed its first decade before the effects of this trade in firearms began to be felt in faraway Santa Fé.

The Apaches, the mounted lords of the plains in the 17th century days of the coming of horses, were now getting the worst of it in many of their fights with the Caddoans on the eastern borders of the plains; and bands of Apaches rarely came to the trading-fairs in New Mexico without some report of white men who were bringing guns to their Caddoan enemies, building forts near the Panana and Jumano villages, on the Arkansas in Oklahoma, or even joining the Caddoan war parties and coming into the plains to attack the Apaches in their own camps. Many of these reports were probably much exaggerated, either by Apache imagination or Spanish embroidery; but the officials in Mexico City took it all most seriously, and were alarmed over the alleged building of French forts, the coming of French regulars into the plains, and a general French advance on the Spanish frontiers. The alarm spread to Mexico City and thence to Spain; plans were made to resist the French invasion, and were relayed from one solemn official to another, all the way from Madrid to Santa Fé; but since none of the highly-placed gentlemen who issued orders had the faintest idea as to the true conditions among the tribes east of New Mexico, most of the plans came to nothing.

The Spanish settlements were now suffering from Spain's colonial policy of controls and severe trade restrictions, a policy under which colonists had never been permitted to go out among the distant tribes, seeking for trade; and the French, who not only permitted but encouraged such activities, had not been on the lower Mississippi for five years before they knew more concerning the Indians on the Arkansas River and the Missouri than the Spaniards in New Mexico, who were no farther away, had learned in a century and a half. The French had come to Louisiana in 1699, and by 1702 some French peddlers had been in the villages of the Caddoans in east Oklahoma and had brought back definite reports. The Spaniards of New Mexico had known these Indians since Coronado's day; yet as late as 1719 they did not know where the villages were, and all the little information they had collected concerning these villages had come to them in piecemeal and probably grossly exaggerated Apache reports.

In 1719 Governor Valverde of New Mexico led an expedition to the Apache rancheria known as El Cuartelejo, on the Arkansas River in east Colorado, and there he found an Apache of the Paloma tribe who had a fresh gunshot wound which he stated he had received when his rancheria, far distant from El Cuartelejo, on the most remote borders of the Apaches,[29] had been attacked by Frenchmen, Pawnees, and Jumanos, armed with guns. After this attack part of the Palomas had come to El Cuartelejo, where they now informed Valverde that the French had established themselves among the Pawnees and Jumanos, and that at the villages of these Indians were forts, supposedly French. The absurdity of this is illustrated by the fact that the little French party led by La Harpe and a French trader from the Osage country—Du Tisne—were the only Frenchmen among the Pawnees on the Arkansas River in 1719, and they stayed but a few days. There were no forts. Du Tisne did trade three guns to the Pawnees; and it is quite probable that these Indians promptly went and used their new weapons on the Paloma Apaches, frightening them so badly that they ran away from their rancheria to El Cuartelejo. But the sight of one Paloma Apache with a gunshot wound was enough to throw the Spanish officials into a kind of panic. They pictured French regular troops and fanatical French Huguenots gathering in force in the plains, preparatory to an invasion of Spanish territory; and Valverde was ordered to lead an expedition to the Pawnees, in an effort to wean the tribe away from the French and win it over to the Spanish interest. This seemingly simple enterprise was ruined by official hesitation, delay, and ignorance of the Indians and the country to be visited. Valverde put off the expedition for nearly a year, and then decided for his own reasons to remain at Santa Fé and to send Lieutenant-colonel Pedro de Villasur (an officer of no experience with Indians) in command of the troops.

Villasur left Santa Fé in mid-June, 1720, with all available men: forty Spanish soldiers and seventy Pueblo Indian allies. At La Jicarilla, an Apache rancheria east of Taos, he picked up sixty Carlana Apache warriors as guides. These Carlanas lived in the country south of the Arkansas in east Colorado; and for some reason of their own they misled the expedition. Villasur's orders meant that he was to visit the Pawnees and Jumanos on the Arkansas in east Oklahoma; yet this officer permitted his Apache guides to lead him to the Skidi Pawnees whose villages were on the Loup Fork in Nebraska. The route followed is unknown, for the diary of the expedition was lost and the statements made by the survivors did not touch on this point. In all the Spanish records of the affair the amazing fact stands out that, after being in New Mexico for more than a century, the Spaniards were utterly dependent on Apache guides whenever they attempted an expedition of any distance in the plains. Due to the amiable Spanish custom of naming nearly all streams for saints, then forgetting after a number of years where the streams were, discovering them again and renaming them for new saints, the best-informed military officers were usually at sea and more or less lost as soon as they got beyond the familiar streams and landmarks on the New Mexican borders. Even after the disaster to the Villasur party had startled them into momentary alertness, the Spanish officials on closely questioning the survivors could not learn in which direction the expedition had marched, and the distance traveled was in doubt. The march to the Pawnee country took sixty-three days; but the return journey was made by the survivors in twenty-two days, although they halted for several days at Apache rancherias. The scanty evidence indicates that the Villasur expedition, like all parties led by Indian guides, went by a roundabout way, from one Indian camp to another, with short and cautious advances and frequent halts, to hunt or to permit the guides to renew their courage for a further cautious advance.

On August 10, by pure accident, Villasur came upon a camp of Skidi Pawnees. From the Spanish statements it would appear that the Indians were on the south bank of a river, vaguely supposed to be one known as the Jesus Maria and even more vaguely identified as the Platte. The Villasur party was on the north bank. The colonel sent a Pawnee, who had been captured and brought up among the Apaches, across the river to talk to the Pawnees and to find out if any Frenchmen were in their camp; but when this Pawnee crossed the stream his tribesmen would not permit him to return to the Spanish camp. The Indians were suspicious of the Spanish intentions; but they permitted a few of their warriors to visit Villasur, and by the hands of these men he sent a letter addressed to the Frenchmen he supposed were with the Pawnees. The only reply that came back was a senseless scrawl on a bit of paper, probably the work of some Pawnee worthy who wished to show his friends that he could perform magic with a burnt stick as easily as these white men could.

The Spaniards were becoming alarmed. Villasur held a council of war, the usual Spanish method for deciding anything; and all of the veteran campaigners advised retreat. Abandoning his camp, Villasur made a rapid march back along his own trail. At 4 P.M. on August 13 he encamped on the south bank of another large stream. As night came on guards were set, and they were alert enough to report to the officers when they heard a noise in the darkness, a noise as of many people swimming the river. Some Pueblo Indians were sent to scout; but they found nothing unusual. At dawn the Spanish horse-guards drove the herd into camp, dismounted, and laid down their arms; and at that moment, when most of the men were still asleep and those awake were without weapons, a heavy discharge of musketry was poured into the camp, followed by flights of arrows, and then by a throng of naked warriors charging out of the tall grass with lances in their hands. Villasur's Apache allies made off instantly, taking with them most of his horses; and they were quickly followed by all of the Pueblos and Spaniards who could find mounts. The colonel and all who remained with him in the camp were killed. As nearly as can be made out from the conflicting statements, Villasur with forty-five Spaniards and eleven Pueblos were killed in the camp. Not an Apache lost his life.[30]

Those authors who have placed the scene of the Villasur disaster at the forks of the Platte have put their dependence wholly on the Spanish accounts, on the statements of survivors of the expedition and of Spanish officials, who were confused as to where Villasur had gone, could not tell the direction he took, and gave contradictory estimates of the distance he had marched. Accepting a Spanish opinion that Villasur marched a certain number of leagues in a generally northward direction, and then laying a ruler on the map from Santa Fé northward and marking the site of the battle at the forks of the Platte, is a simple operation; but it fails to take into account that Villasur was in the Skidi Pawnee lands and very close to their permanent earth-lodge villages when he met his fate. The forks of the Platte were in hostile Padouca country, into which the Pawnees could venture only in armed war parties, to strike a blow and hastily retire into their own lands farther to the east; yet A. F. Bandelier and other authorities have measured off the proper distance on the map and located the Villasur fight at the forks of the Platte. They place Skidi Pawnee villages there, in a district where the Skidis never had a permanent village; and they even speak of French forts in the same locality. This last idea is based solely on the Apache statement that the French had forts among the Pawnees and Jumanos *on the Arkansas River,* and even this report was false.[31]

Far from being firmly established at the forks of the Platte, the French had no officers, military or civil, west of Illinois; and it was there that the first reports of the Villasur expedition were brought to official French notice, by Indians and traders. These accounts placed the scene of the Villasur fight *dans environs du Missouri,* and Boisbriant, Commandant at Kaskaskia in Illinois, reported that the Spanish disaster occurred at a point twenty-five leagues west of the Missouri, or fifteen leagues west of the Oto village, which was ten or fifteen leagues from the Missouri on the south bank of the Platte. In effect, the scene of the fight was not farther west than the longitude of the mouth of Loup Fork; and it was on the Loup, near its mouth, that the Skidi villages stood in 1720.[32] Crediting the Indian accounts they received, and the statements of French traders, who seem to have been in the main illiterate men as given to wild exaggeration as the Indians were, the French authorities soon had as handsomely embroidered a version of the Villasur affair as the one the officials at Santa Fé had concocted. A few points of these French versions are of interest. For one thing, they asserted that Villasur had an entire camp of Padoucas, including the women and children, with him, and that on his way to the Pawnees he destroyed five Indian camps, sending back part of his soldiers to Santa Fé with a large consignment of captive women and children, to be sold as slaves. In Santa Fé and Mexico City there were also reports that Villasur, or his superior, Governor Valverde, had turned this expedition into a commercial venture, and everyone concerned had to undergo the most severe questioning; but no solid evidence of wrong-doing could be obtained. Boisbriant reported that no Frenchmen were present when the Indians killed Villasur and his men. The Spanish survivors on the other hand asserted that many Frenchmen, including soldiers in uniform, took part in the fight; and this became the standard Spanish version, which must have comforted the Spanish authorities, who were loathe to admit that the worst military disaster Spain had ever suffered in the plains country had been inflicted by Indians, most of whom were armed only with bows and lances. Starting with a report that the

Skidi Pawnees first contacted Villasur's party and sent runners to call the Otos to their aid, the French built up the story until they had half a dozen tribes involved. The Otos seem to have lied handsomely, taking all the credit for the defeat of the Spaniards for themselves and ignoring the part played by the Pawnees.[33]

In this welter of contradictory reports, the one thing that is historically important about this Villasur affair has been lost sight of; and that is the fact that Villasur set out from New Mexico with a large body of Carlana Apaches as guides, and that these Indians, whose home was in southeastern Colorado, are invariably termed in the French accounts Padouca Indians. Here we have a clear-cut identification of the Apaches as Padoucas, and we also obtain the interesting information that the Indians in eastern Nebraska included the Colorado Apaches under the general designation of Padoucas.

The French officials in Illinois seem to have built up the extent of the Villasur disaster, in the hope that the authorities in Paris would order a French counter-move in the plains west of the Missouri; and that was exactly what occurred. But when the orders came from Paris they were not of a nature to please either Boisbriant in Illinois or the French officials at New Orleans; for the Company of the Indies ignored the men who were on the scene in America and brought the French trader Bourgmont out of his retirement in France and sent him to New Orleans, with full authority to lead an expedition up the Missouri and into the plains. The result was at least two years of delay and the development of much covert opposition among the French officials in America to the Bourgmont enterprise.[34]

To carry out his instructions, Bourgmont had to make a peace between the tribes near the Missouri and the Padoucas in the plains, with the purpose of utilizing the Padoucas in extending French influence and trade among the Indians close to the New Mexican frontier. Coming up the Missouri late in the year 1723, and despite the opposition of the French officials in Illinois, he established Ft. Orleans among the Missouri Indians, near the mouth of Grand River. In the spring of 1724 he went up the Missouri to the village of the Kansa tribe,[35] and with these Indians and his Frenchmen he was presently marching westward up Kansas River, to open negotiations with the Padoucas, whose grand village lay to the westward, evidently in the district where the town of Salina now stands. But Bourgmont fell violently ill of fever and had to turn back. The Kansa tribe continued on westward, to hunt buffalo; and with them Bourgmont sent a French trader named Gaillard, with orders to find the Padoucas and to bring their chiefs to the Kansa village on the Missouri for a peace council. This intrepid French trader left the Kansa camp, accompanied by a party of warriors, and pressed westward into the country of the dreaded Padoucas; and on August 23 he entered the Padouca village, where he was received with every mark of friendship by these loyal allies of Spain. Quickly convincing the chiefs of the good intentions of the French, he conducted them to the Kansa hunting-camp, probably east of the Big Blue River; and there he bribed or cajoled the unwilling Kansa chiefs into making peace and smoking the pipe with the hated Padoucas.

None of the tribes near the Missouri wanted peace. They now had the upperhand over the Padoucas, and their only wish was to press home the advantage that French firearms had given them. The French traders, even the French officials, seem to have opposed peace, which would end the lucrative trade in Padouca slaves.[36] But Bourgmont had his orders from Paris, which he was determined to execute; and he also had a wonderful assortment of peace-gifts, including new French guns, with which to induce the Pawnee, Oto, and other tribal chiefs to make peace with the Padoucas. Gaillard, still with the Kansa Indians and Padoucas, sent word to Bourgmont that all was ready for the peace council; and, coming back up the Missouri to the Kansa village, Bourgmont found that the efficient Gaillard had actually induced several Padouca camps, with their women and children, to venture into enemy territory by coming to the Kansa village. This seems to be the only recorded friendly visit of plains Apaches to the Missouri River. At the Kansa village were gathered the chiefs of the Padoucas, the Nebraska Pawnees and Otos, and some chiefs of the Iowa and Missouri tribes. The peace plan was obviously a white men's arrangement, for the benefit mainly of the French; some of the chiefs were very unwilling to make peace with the Padoucas, who for many years had made mounted attacks on their tribes, destroying their villages and carrying off their women and children into slavery among the Spaniards. Indeed, the chiefs required much persuasion before they would attend this peace council; but Bourgmont, a master of the art of dealing with Indians, did not waste much time in dwelling on the merits of the peace project. Instead he assembled the chiefs for council and ordered his men to open the bales of peace presents. The goods were laid out into three great piles, one for the Iowas, one for the Otos, and one for the Skidi Pawnees, while the chiefs sat and watched with intent eyes. The Kansa tribe had already received their share for making peace in advance with the Padoucas and were not to have a portion of this new largess.

When all the gifts had been laid out and examined by the chiefs,

Bourgmont asked them if this was sufficient payment to induce them to smoke with the Padouca chiefs. For some time no one replied; then one of the chiefs spoke, stating that the women and little girls of his tribe were broken down from carrying heavy loads on their backs when the tribe went on its semi-annual hunts, and that he was willing to make peace with the Padoucas, solely to obtain horses in trade with that tribe, so that his women and girls would not have to walk and carry burdens. The other chiefs seemed to approve of this view of the matter; one by one they gave their assent; the peace-pipe was filled and passed around the circle, and peace with the Padoucas was concluded.

The great assemblage of Padouca camps that the council had brought to the Missouri melted away westward into the plains, and the chiefs from the tribes of Nebraska and Iowa returned home; but Bourgmont had no intention of leaving the Indians to their own devices. He had made peace, which would last just as long as the chiefs found it to their advantage to control their warriors and prevent a fresh attack on the Padoucas; but before that time should come Bourgmont intended to advance the French influence into the Padouca country and to learn something of the Spanish frontier farther westward. Thus on October 8 he set out from the Kansa village with a party of Frenchmen and Indians; and after a rapid march of seventy-five French leagues up Kansas River he entered the grand village of the Padoucas on a salt fork of that stream, probably the Saline Fork of today. He found the village to consist of one hundred *cabins,* whose structure he did not describe; and these Padoucas grew small crops. People from several other Padouca villages had flocked in to see the French, and there were some eight hundred warriors with 1,500 women and 2,000 children present. As to the Padoucas in general, Bourgmont reported that they were not wanderers but dwelt in villages of fifty to one hundred cabins, near which were the little fields for growing crops. Their way of life was exactly like that of the Apaches on the New Mexican frontier—planting their seed in the spring, going on a buffalo hunt, and returning to their villages in time for harvest. Like the other Apaches, the Kansas Padoucas did not grow tobacco, but obtained that article in trade. These Padoucas informed Bourgmont that the Spaniards traded them only knives and bad hatchets. They had obtained no firearms until the recent peace had supplied them with a few such weapons, and they were all very much afraid of guns. These Kansas Padoucas still kept up the old Apache practice of going to war in very large bands of mounted warriors, clad in rawhide armor; but the days in which such war parties in the 17th century had spread terror among neighbor tribes were over; for these other tribes had now obtained horses in considerable numbers and, better still, they were getting French muskets, against which the mounted Apache with his rawhide armor was almost helpless.[37]

As to the events that followed on Bourgmont's success in making peace with the Padoucas in 1724, the French documents are silent; but from the New Mexican records we learn that by 1726 French traders, evidently led by the Kansas Padoucas, had reached the Apache rancheria of El Cuartelejo on the Arkansas in eastern Colorado. The French were now within easy reach of the New Mexican settlements; but their plan for trade with the Spaniards was a dream. Spain had no intention of opening her frontiers to French trade; and the officials in New Mexico (obtaining all their information from garbled Apache reports) regarded the French advance as a hostile movement and became greatly alarmed about an imaginary French plan for an armed invasion.

It was not the little parties of French traders, wandering far out into the plains, that the Spanish should have feared, but the fierce Comanches. The Comanches had made their first appearance in New Mexico when, about the year 1700, their Ute cousins brought a party of them to a trading-fair, probably at the pueblo of Taos. By 1710 the Comanches were aiding the Utes in vigorous raids against the Apaches in eastern Colorado; and at just about the time when Bourgmont made his peace with the Padoucas the Comanches closed the French route into New Mexico by driving the Apaches (Padoucas) out of the district in Colorado to the south of the Arkansas River. About 1726 Bourgmont's post on the Missouri, Fort Orleans, was destroyed, presumably by the Missouri Indians who lived near the establishment. This event appears to have put a stop for the time being to the operations of French traders among the Padoucas in Kansas and Colorado; and the advance of the Comanches and Utes now displaced most of the Padouca and Apache groups and forced them to flee southward through the plains.

In the north the break-up of Padouca power left the Skidi Pawnees the dominant tribe in the Nebraska region; but we are not able to fill in the details as to events in the northern Pawnee country after 1724, as the French who traded with the Pawnees and who were the only white men in the country have left no written records.

NOTES TO CHAPTER II

[13]Wedel, 1940, map on p. 293.

[14]Hill and Metcalf, in *Nebraska History,* v. 22, no. 2.

[15]The Padoucas used to be termed Comanches. The identification of this tribe as Apaches is based partly on a restudy of 18th-century documents and on the evidence disclosed in recent excavations of Padouca village ruins in Western Nebraska, which prove that this tribe had permanent dwellings, made pottery, and grew crops, which agrees with our knowledge of the Apache life in the plains but does not fit in with known facts concerning the Comanches, who did not have permanent dwellings, did not make pottery, and did not grow crops. Then, again, the French traders on Red River, from about 1710 on, used the names Apache and Padouca as synonymous, while in Nebraska and Kansas the French clearly identified the Padoucas as the Indians the Spaniards called Apaches.

[16]This transition from rectangular earth-lodges to circular ones has been also observed by the archeologists in eastern Nebraska and in the Arikara country on the Missouri in South Dakota.

[17]As this tribe was first noted in the plains west of the present city of Wichita, Kansas, and later moved southward to the head of Red River, they must have been Apaches. The name Escansaque may be the origin of the Caddoan Indian name for the Apaches of Red River after the year 1700: Cancey or Kantsi. The *Es* was prefixed by Spanish writers to some other Apache tribal names, as in the case of the Calchufine Apache of southeastern Colorado, who were at times called Escalchufines.

[18]Thomas, 1935, pp. 13-14.

[19]In 1683 a Tejas chief from east Texas visited the Spaniards at El Paso and stated that Quivira was now very close to his country, so close that the Tejas and Quiviras exchanged visits almost daily.

[20]*An Account of Spanish Louisiana in 1785* terms the Apaches of South Dakota (the Gatackas or Prairie-Apaches?) the Pados or Taguibaces (Padoucas or Taguihashes, *hash* being a Caddoan Indian term meaning *people*). This Spanish document calls the southern branch of Loup Fork in Nebraska River the Pados or Padouca River, and it was on this stream that A. T. Hill first discovered broken Padouca pottery and other remains, indicating that this tribe had formerly occupied the district. This account of Louisiana also states that the Padoucas have forts on the Little Missouri (the stream that flows into the Missouri from the west, opposite the present city of Pierre). The forts were probably what the Spaniards of New Mexico termed rancherias. The present writer does not agree with those who state off-hand that it was impossible for Apaches to have villages in South Dakota as late as 1785. The Prairie-Apaches were still in South Dakota as late as 1795-1800, and it remains for the archeologists to demonstrate whether these Apaches had villages east of the Black Hills up to about the year 1785.

[21]Dr. E. B. Renaud's valuable surveys of Indian camp sites in the Colorado plains and adjacent districts were begun in 1930 and continued to be published by the University of Denver until after 1943.

[22]There were villages of Indians, whose culture resembled that of the Pawnees, on the Missouri in South Dakota, as far back as perhaps the year

A large painting on leather, of remarkable detail, thought to show the Villasur-Pawnee battle. Artist unknown. (From *Indian Skin Paintings from the American Southwest*, by Gottfried Hotz, Norman, 1970)

1500; but we do not know that these Indians were called Arikaras. That tribe, according to Omaha Indian tradition and some other evidence, was living in northeastern Nebraska, apparently at least as late as 1673-82.

[23]The Closed Man story was published in Dorsey's *Traditions of the Skidi Pawnees*, 1904, and it also comes into James Murie's *Pawnee Societies* (*Anthropological Papers of the American Museum of Natural History*, v. 2, no. 7).

[24]La Salle, in *Margry*, v. 2, p. 201.

[25]Thomas: *After Coronado*, p. 14.

[26]La Harpe and Beaurain, in *Margry*, v. 6, p. 289; Franquelin map, in Kellog: *Early Narratives of the Northwest*, p. 342.

[27]Spanish document, in Swanton, 1942, p. 269.

[28]Renaudiere, in *Margry*, v. 6, pp. 392-4.

[29]The Palomas were probably Kansas Apaches, termed Padoucas by the French. Dr. A. B. Thomas has suggested that the Paloma country was near the forks of the Platte; but he has no evidence, and that district would have been beyond the reach of the Pawnees and Jumanos of the Arkansas in eastern Oklahoma, who were raiding the Palomas.

[30]In 1949 my friend Mr. Joseph Balmer of Zurich, Switzerland, wrote to me that Mr. Gottfried Hotz of that city was making a study of a painting on deerskin which had been sent in 1757 from northern Mexico by a young priest to his family in Switzerland. Mr. Hotz then wrote to me for information, and sent me a set of photographs showing the scenes in the painting. To my surprise it had every appearance of being a painting of the Villasur fight, as it displayed features of that affair which cannot be fitted into any other Spanish engagement in the plains in the 18th century. There was no other affair in which a Spanish officer was killed and a priest captured by the Indians; and the other details of this painting follow closely the Spanish version of the Villasur story. For one thing, the Spanish witnesses stated that many Frenchmen, including soldiers, aided the Pawnees; and the painting shows French soldiers in uniform mingled among the naked Pawnee warriors.

If this is the Villasur fight, we here have a depiction of Pawnee warriors that is a full century earlier than any other. There are about one hundred warriors shown in the picture. Two have sashes about their waists, but no breech-clouts; the rest are entirely naked except for moccasins and short leggings that do not reach the knee. Every warrior has his face and body painted, usually in plain stripes and spots; and each man has his head completely shaven, with a scarf of cloth or soft leather bound about his brows. A pendant hangs down from the headband on the right side of each warrior's head, coming below his ear. Mr. Hotz states that in the original painting these pendants look very much like those worn by Pawnees and Otos in the McKenny and Hall portraits, made in the 19th century. This painting was probably made by a white man, perhaps by a priest, at one of the missions in northern Mexico or New Mexico; and he apparently obtained details for his picture from men who had taken part in the fight. He makes the Pueblo Indians with the Spaniards stand out most distinctly from the naked Pawnees; and some of the pictures of the Spaniards have the appearance of being intended as portraits of known men. One would at first suppose that the artist had made an error in depicting Pawnees armed with short swords; but some of the Villasur survivors testified that they saw French short swords in the hands of Apaches at El Cuartelejo and that the Apaches stated they had captured these weapons from the Pawnees. Two Pawnees in the painting are carrying ceremonial lances, the shafts ornamented along their entire length with fur. The Pawnees still have similar ceremonial lances, which belonged to the warrior brotherhoods known as Knife-Lance Societies.

[31]It was four years after the Villasur affair that the French built their first post on the Missouri, and they never had one in Nebraska.

[32]The Boisbriant and other French reports are reprinted in *Nebraska History*, v. 6, p. 23 *et seq*.

[33]*Ibid.*, pp. 23-25.

[34]The French officials in Illinois wished to establish a post on the Missouri in 1720; but in 1724 they opposed the building of a post by Bourgmont and did all they could to starve him for supplies and delay him.

[35]This Kansa Indian village was called by the French the Village of '24, because of the Bourgmont councils there in 1724. It stood on the site of the present town of Doniphan, Kansas, and the ruins have been excavated by the archeologists.

[36]This Indian slave trade was extensive, but the French officials kept very quiet about it. On October 5, 1720, Boisbriant reported that the Oto and Kansa warriors had recently brought home 250 Padouca captives; and in the same letter he stated that Frenchmen whom he had permitted to go to the villages of the Paniassas (Black Pawnees on the Arkansas in Oklahoma) to trade for horses had found that these Indians had recently raided a Padouca village, taking one hundred captives, whom they were "burning," a few each day. (*Nebraska History*, v. 6, p. 21.)

[37]The Bourgmont reports are in *Margry*, v. 6, p. 443 *et seq*.

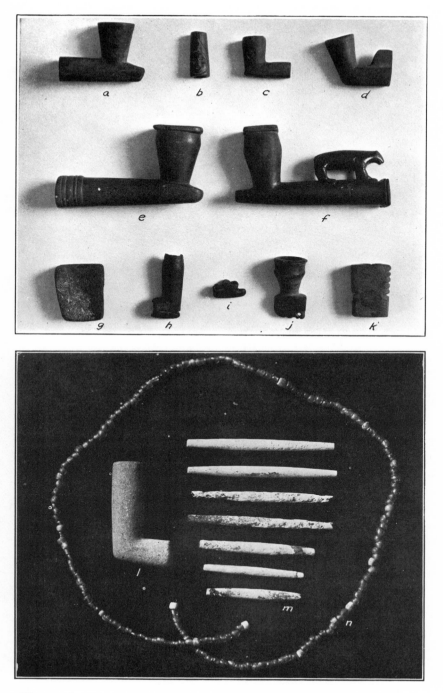

Pipes and mortuary offerings from various historic Pawnee sites. (From *An Introduction to Pawnee Archaeology*, by Waldo R. Wedel, BAE *Bulletin 112*)

Pawnee running buffalo. (Painting by Alfred Jacob Miller, courtesy Walters Art Gallery. From *The West of Alfred Jacob Miller*, by Marvin C. Ross, Norman, 1968)

A Pawnee Indian shooting antelope. (Painting by Alfred Jacob Miller, courtesy Walters Art Gallery. From *The West of Alfred Jacob Miller*, by Marvin C. Ross, Norman, 1968)

Facsimile outlines of paintings on a Pawnee robe representing a medicine man giving freedom to his favorite horse. (From *North American Indians*, by George Catlin)

III

The Pawnees and the French

THE SKIDI PAWNEES TOLD GRINNELL, ABOUT THE YEAR 1880, THAT AT an early period in their history they had four tribes with about five thousand people in each tribe.[38] This would be about the population indicated by the French at the period 1715-25, when they gave the Skidis eight large, handsome, and well-built villages on a northern branch of the Platte, which was undoubtedly Loup Fork, although Rénaudière (1723) stated that the villages were on the Elkhorn. Unfortunately, none of the French traders who frequented these Skidi villages left a detailed description of them; and since the village ruins have not been definitely located by archeological excavation we can only conjecture that they were far up the Loup Fork, in the vicinity of the present town of Cushing. Rénaudière, who was certainly in error when he stated that these Skidi villages were thirty leagues up the Elkhorn, probably meant the Loup; and that distance would place the villages near Cushing, which seems all the more likely because later in the same century the Spanish account of Louisiana (1785) located the Skidi tribe thirty leagues up the Loup.

From this we might suppose that the extensive village ruins along the north bank of the Loup, from the mouth of Beaver Creek eastward to Looking-Glass Creek at Monroe, are the Skidi towns of an earlier period, perhaps of the time when Closed Man first brought the tribe together at the mouth of Beaver Creek. We cannot fix the date of this settlement; but since the Closed Man story places two villages with Arikara names on the Elkhorn, it would seem that the period was late in the 17th century. The French traders' custom of naming streams for tribes that dwelt on their banks is another clue. It was the French who called the Skidi or Wolf Pawnees the Loups and named Loup Fork because the villages of this tribe stood on its banks; and since the French also named the Elkhorn, and the Closed Man story shows that Indians with an Elkhorn or Arikara name dwelt there, we might suppose that part of the Arikaras were still there when the first Frenchmen came to eastern Nebraska, and that the white men named the stream for these Indians.

The French do not appear to have ascended the Missouri as far up as the Nebraska country until after the year 1700; but French wood-runners were on the upper Mississippi and in eastern Iowa long before that year. We have the tale of Radisson and his companions coming to Nebraska in 1658-9 and finding the Arikaras on the Missouri and the Skidis farther west, on or near the Platte. The story is hardly credible in the form in which it has been handed down to us, but there was nothing to prevent a few wandering Frenchmen from accompanying Iowa Indians to the Missouri, to visit among the Arikaras and Skidis, even at that early date; and the probability is that some such journey was made. The Omahas and Poncas (then one tribe) were living in northern Iowa before 1670 and were in touch with tribes to the east on the Mississippi and with the Arikaras to westward. The Arikaras, as the Omaha and Ponca traditions state, were then living on the Missouri, in the region of northeastern Nebraska. The time was late in the 17th century, and these western tribes—the Omahas, Poncas, Arikaras, and Skidi Pawnees—appear to have been still in a very primitive condition. They were being raided by tribes that had obtained metal weapons, and a kind of reign of terror was being created by raiding parties from the east among the tribes in Iowa and farther west on the Missouri. According to Dr. Clark Wissler the Iroquois came west and burnt a Skidi settlement, apparently in eastern Nebraska. The Omahas fled west to the Big Sioux in the Sioux Falls district. Here their enemies found them out, slaughtering many of the tribe, the survivors fleeing to the Missouri, near the mouth of the Big Sioux. Here they joined forces with the Arikaras and part of the Iowa tribe.

By the year 1716 this early period of misty tradition was ended for the tribes on the Missouri and in eastern Nebraska. The Spaniards in east Texas were now obtaining from the Caddoan kinsmen of the Pawnees quite definite information concerning the Skidis and Arikaras; and in 1719 La Harpe visited the Caddoan Indians on the lower Canadian and learned from them that the Arikaras were on the Missouri, 120 leagues south from seven famous villages. They meant the Mandan villages on the Missouri, at the mouth of Heart River; and the distance given would place the Arikara villages of 1719 on the Missouri near the mouth of the Niobrara. A Spanish document of the year 1716, quoted by Swanton, states that the Arikaras have forty-eight villages extending along the Missouri for a distance of ten leagues.[39] Rénaudière completes the picture when he places the Omahas on the north bank of the Missouri, near the mouth of the Big Sioux, with their allies, the Nations of the Ricaras, ten leagues higher up the Missouri.

This very numerous gathering of Indians along the Missouri, from near the mouth of the Big Sioux up to the Niobrara or beyond, seems to have been in the main refugees—people still equipped mainly with flint weapons, who had been attacked, demoralized, and forced to flee from their former homes by tribes armed with metal weapons and even with firearms. The mounted Padoucas in the plains to the westward may also have been responsible for the driving of some of these Indians to the Missouri. The Arikaras had apparently taken into their tribe refugees from several originally separate Caddoan groups, and even people of alien stocks. At the beginning of the 19th century Tabeau, Lewis and Clark, Brackenridge, and some others who sojourned among the Arikaras remarked that these Indians spoke a variety of dialects, some of which were so far apart that Indians living in the same village had difficulty in understanding one another, and sometimes they had to use interpreters when they wished to communicate with their own neighbors. The chiefs stated that there was a purer language, spoken by the upper class; and since both the Arikaras and Skidi Pawnees believed firmly that the former tribe was an off-shoot from the latter, one would suppose that this purer speech among the Arikaras was the dialect of the Skidis. The Arikaras of today speak a dialect very close to the Skidi tongue and differing from the language of the other three Pawnee tribes (the Panis Noirs of the French). Yet, French maps of the 18th century clearly show that some group of Panis Noirs had come northward and joined the Arikaras. The Du Pratz map of the 1750 period sets down these Panis Noirs villages on the Missouri near the mouth of the Niobrara; and as late as 1854 E. E. Hale in his book on Kansas and Nebraska calls the Arikaras *Black Pawnees*. These hints of an invasion of the lands of the Nebraska Pawnees and Arikaras by a Pawnee group from the south may have been the matter referred to by the Mandan Indians of North Dakota when they informed the French explorer Verendrye in 1738 that the Pananas and Pananis (clearly two different Pawnee groups) who had always been at peace had been at war for several years past.

The French, after 1725, reported that the Sioux of the West and their allies, armed with guns, were raiding the Omahas heavily; and Omaha tradition states that their tribe, with the Poncas, part of the Iowas, and the Arikaras, left their old location near the mouth of the

Big Sioux and moved higher up the Missouri, the first three tribes halting at the mouth of White River, the Arikaras going higher up the Missouri, their new villages being apparently from the Great Bend up to the site of the present city of Pierre. Describing the ruins of these Arikara villages in a recent archeological report, Dr. W. D. Strong expressed astonishment at the extent of the remains. The ruins indicate that a mass of Indians had been gathered here on the Missouri which far exceeded the population the Nebraska Pawnees had in historic times. Yet, the building and the history of these great settlements on the Missouri are almost complete mysteries. Some preliminary excavations indicate that small groups of Caddoan Indians may have come to this point on the Missouri to build villages long before the coming of the mass of Arikaras in the 18th century; but of these early settlers we know little. Of the Arikaras themselves, we know hardly more than that they were observed by the French in the district between the Big Sioux and the Niobrara River about 1720 and that the younger Verendrye found them living in the villages above the Great Bend in 1743. Our next information is that the Arikaras contracted smallpox, first apparently about the year 1760, and lost a large portion of their population. Then the Sioux began to raid them. Then smallpox struck again. The Arikara tradition was that, about the middle of the 18th century, they had one thousand lodges, each holding about twenty persons, and they could bring four thousand warriors into the field. Smallpox and enemy action reduced them by 1770-80 to some three hundred lodges; and by 1800 they had only one hundred and fifty lodges left in three weak villages and were practically at the mercy of the vindictive Sioux.

The Skidis in Nebraska must have gone through experiences somewhat similar to those just described, although they were not subjected to the continuous harassment of the Sioux, which was a principal cause of the disaster to the Arikaras. Wars with plains tribes, and smallpox and other diseases introduced by the whites, were probably the causes that reduced the Skidis from eight large villages in 1725 to a single village by the opening of the 19th century. Information concerning this Skidi disaster is even scantier than in the case of the Arikaras; for the Skidis dwelt far from the Missouri, which was the great route of travel for traders, and the few white men who came among the Skidis were illiterate Canadians who could not keep records of events and who as a rule did not trouble to report what they had seen to men who could write it down. Even Bourgmont, on official business in the matter of peace with the Padoucas in 1724, after holding councils with the Skidi Pawnee chiefs in attendance, had nothing

Example of the summer homes of the Pawnees, a tipi of canvas, quite different from the earth lodge. (From *Indian Territory: A Frontier Photographic Record*, by W. S. Prettyman and Robert E. Cunningham, Norman, 1957)

to report concerning that tribe. During these councils the Pawnee chiefs were almost ignored, both by the French and by the other Indians, who treated the Skidis like country cousins. That is evidently what they were. The other tribes at the Bourgmont councils were sophisticates who had known the French so long and were so used to white men's ways that they regarded themselves as far superior to bumpkins like the Pawnees, who rarely saw a white man and still regarded a gun with awe, as if the thing were a piece of magic. These Frenchified chiefs at the Bourgmont councils could hardly be expected to accept as equals the rude Pawnee countrymen from the Loup Fork, who did not even know how to behave in the presence of important Frenchmen and who were so ignorant that they were fair game for any French peddler, who wandered into their villages with a pack of trinkets on his back, and traded them out of their furs and Padouca slaves for knives, beads, red paint, and hawk-bells. The Iowas, Missouris, and Kansa Indians, as men of the world who had known the French for many years, thus looked down on the Skidis and probably made jokes about their bucolic manners; but they were very careful about meddling with these same Skidis on their home grounds or out on the high plains; for a big band of Skidis armed with bows and lances was nothing to laugh at.

After Bourgmont left the Kansa village in 1724, the Skidi Pawnees disappeared behind a misty curtain for another fifteen years. They were then briefly referred to in the account of the Mallet brothers' trading trip from the Missouri River to Santa Fé in 1739. The Mallets, who seem to have been illiterate but highly intelligent men, came into eastern Nebraska with a few French followers and a small stock of trade-goods. They went across from the Missouri to the villages of the Skidis or Panimahas, which they reported were at the mouth of Panimaha River (the Loup Fork) at its junction with the Missouri; but this was an error, probably made by the officials in Louisiana who later wrote an account of the Mallet expedition. The Loup, of course, flows into the Platte, and the Platte into the Missouri. The number of Skidi villages at this period was probably reduced from eight to four or less. The Palairet map (c. 1720) places a group of four Panimaha and Pani villages near the mouth of the Loup, two on each bank of the Platte; while the Bowen and Gibson map of 1763 shows four Panis villages on the north side of the Platte, at the mouth of the Loup and one Panis village on the south bank of the river. The four on the north side must be Skidi Pawnee villages, and their name, Panimaha, is printed in large letters north of the four villages. Father Vivier of the French mission in the Illinois country wrote in

1750 that the Skidis were headed by a grand chief who had recently visited in Illinois. Vivier stated that this chief ruled his people with a strong hand; that he had nine hundred warriors (indicating a population of perhaps 5,000 in 250 lodges), and that the tribe was well provided with horses and hunted in mounted parties with bow and lance. They had a few guns and the French traded regularly with the tribe. In this brief account there is no mention of any other Pawnee groups in Nebraska, and the Skidis are the dominant tribe of the region. To Father Vivier's description of the Skidis at this date we may add that on September 25, 1751, La Jonquiere, a French officer, wrote from the Illinois country that the Panismahas or Skidis were governed by three brothers and that the most important of the three was Stabaco. The eldest of these brothers had recently visited M. de St. Chin, commandant of Fort Chartres, in Illinois; and it was evidently during this visit, in October, 1750, that the so-called alliance between the French and Skidis was concluded. In 1765 the Jesuit, Father Watrin, wrote a description of the tribes on and near the Missouri, and he refers only to the Skidis in the Nebraska region. Thus up to 1765 the French still regarded the Skidis as the dominant tribe in the Nebraska country, and there was no evidence that the Southern or Black Pawnees had yet arrived in force on the Platte.[40]

The little party of Canadians led by the Mallet brothers actually succeeded in crossing the plains in 1739, reaching the Spanish settlements in New Mexico. Tarrying among the Spanish settlers for several months, these Canadians then performed the even more difficult feat of leaving New Mexico. Why they did not suffer the usual imprisonment and often permanent detention which the Spanish officials meted out to French trespassers, is a mystery; but they did get away. In the plains to the east of New Mexico their party divided, some of the men striking northward toward the Skidi Pawnee country, the rest going on eastward, evidently down the Canadian; and this stream may have been given its name from this fact, if the name is of French origin, which it seems to be. These Canadians passed through the country of the southern Pawnees; but in the brief official account of their journey there is no mention of the villages of these Indians.

A hint as to what had transpired among the southern Pawnees after the visits of La Harpe and Du Tisné to their villages in 1719 now appears in the French documents; for the officials were so impressed by the feat of the Mallet brothers in opening a trade route to Santa Fé that they decided to send an official expedition to New Mexico, with some of the Mallet party acting as guides. This expedition, commanded by Fabre de la Bruyère, was sent up the Arkansas in 1741 with the impracticable object of ascending the Canadian River in boats. Fabre found the Tawakoni or Tawehash settlements on the south bank of the Canadian deserted and in ruins. From later records we learn that the Tawakonis and Iscanis had retreated southward into east Texas, while the Tawehash, whose main desire was to be close to the buffalo herds, had gone to upper Red River, west of the Cross Timbers, and there fortified their new village. Fabre reported that these tribes had left their settlements on the lower Canadian about the year 1737.

His boats being stopped in the lower Canadian by low water, Fabre went into camp and dispatched the Mallet brothers in search of the Tawakoni or Tawehash villages, in the hope of obtaining horses from these Indians, so that he might continue his journey toward Santa Fé. The Mallets, unfamiliar with the country and the location of the Indian villages, lost themselves in the welter of rough hills between the Canadian and Red rivers; and after wandering about for some days they returned to camp and proposed that they should go northward, to obtain horses from the Panis Noirs. Fabre rejected the plan, on the grounds that the Panis villages were farther away than those of the Tawakonis and Tawehash, and that the Canadians would probably get lost again. He now left his men encamped near the ruined Indian villages on the Canadian and went down the Arkansas with a few men in boats, seeking for horses among the white settlers. While he was away the Canadians lost patience; and led by the Mallets they shouldered their packs and set off afoot across the plains toward Santa Fé. They were never heard of again. Fabre, returning from Arkansas with some horses, gave up the expedition. He sent part of his men down the Arkansas in the boats, and with the rest mounted on horses started to explore the country south toward Red River. He struck that stream three days' march above the villages of the Tawakonis and Kichais, and thus ended his futile wanderings.[41]

The main historical importance of the Fabre de la Bruyère expedition lies in the reported facts that the Tawakoni and Tawehash villages near the mouth of the Canadian were abandoned about the date 1737 and were in ruins in 1741; the fact that the Tawakonis from this settlement had joined the Kichais on Red River; and the further fact that the Panis Noirs were still near the Arkansas River in northern Oklahoma or southern Kansas in 1741. The French plan, made by La Harpe in 1720, for the establishment of a French post at the mouth of the Canadian and a second one at the Tawakoni-Tawehash villages, had not been carried out, with the result that the Pawnee tribes on the Arkansas and Canadian had not received the full support and encouragement from the French that they had been led to expect. French officialdom had betrayed them to their enemies, for while they were left to be supplied with arms and ammunition by casual traders who did not visit them regularly, their enemies (particularly the Osages) were kept fully armed by a regular French trade. There can be little doubt that it was the Osages who forced the Tawakonis and Tawehash to abandon their old settlements; for the reports of Osage raiding from 1718 until after 1760 indicate it, and the direction of the flight of these Caddoan tribes proves the fact. The Tawakonis from the villages near the mouth of the Canadian, and the Iscanis, who in 1719 were with the Wichitas farther up the Arkansas north of the mouth of the Cimarron, retreated into east Texas; while the Tawehash and some groups from other tribes went to upper Red River. This Tawehash group was made up of those Indians who had a stronger desire to be in the plains, near the buffalo, than the Tawakonis and Iscanis seem to have had. Their old villages on the Lower Canadian were an ideal location for Indians who wished to be near the buffalo range and in touch with tribes in the plains, from whom they could obtain horses. When the Osages made the Canadian villages untenable these Caddoans had three choices: to go up the Arkansas to join the Panis Noirs and Wichitas (but those tribes were also being raided by the Osage), to give up the buffalo and horses of the plains and retire to east Texas, or to flout the waning power of the Apaches in the upper Red River country by going there to live. The Tawehash took the third risk and planted a fortified village on upper Red River, in the heart of the buffalo range; the Tawakonis went to east Texas and submitted to the Spanish authorities, who established a mission among them and attempted to wean them away from paganism and their wild ways; but the Tawakonis soon tired of that and went up Red River, to live with or near the Tawehash.

John Law's colonization of the eastern portion of the present state of Arkansas with European families, about the year 1721, had created a new market for horses and Indian slaves, and this had added to the already heavy troubles of the Caddoan tribes; for most of the slaves were boys and girls taken from their villages in raids made by the Osages, Quapaws, and other tribes. The horses were obtained from the Pawnees on the Arkansas, probably by thieving war parties in the main. The French officials made a public display of frowning on this traffic in stolen children and horses. But it continued to thrive. When the French territory of Louisiana was turned over to Spain at the close of the French and Indian War, the new Spanish commandant of

Pawnee Indians migrating. (Painting by Alfred Jacob Miller, courtesy Walters Art Gallery. From *The West of Alfred Jacob Miller*, by Marvin C. Ross, Norman, 1968)

Arkansas Post, near the mouth of the Arkansas, found that his principal duty was to deal with the Indian slave problem. His heart was filled with grief, not so much over the condition of these Caddoan slaves, but because the creatures persisted in running away; and thus his little garrison of Spanish troops spent most of their time in running after the fugitives. The slaves had a partly secret trail that ran from the Mississippi across Arkansas in a southwesterly direction to the villages of the Grand Caddo on Red River, and over this obscure track through the wilderness the Caddoan slaves were constantly making their way homeward.[42] Most of these Caddoans had been carried off by Osage war parties and sold in the Illinois country; but the Chickasaws from east of the Mississippi were also raiding the Caddoans and carrying off boys and girls into slavery.

The Panis Noirs, who were holding their villages on the Arkansas in north Oklahoma or south Kansas, had with them the Wichitas and, if the Spanish reports are correct, the Jumanos. As far back as 1719 the Apaches had given the Spaniards of New Mexico information concerning the Panana and Jumano villages on the Arkansas, where they claimed the French had established themselves. These Apache reports sometimes stated that the Pananas and Jumanos lived in fortified villages, at other times the story was that the French had forts near the Indian settlements. Armed with French guns, the Indians of these villages took an important part in the raids on the Apache or Padouca rancherias in the southern plains from 1719 on. The Apaches (terrified of guns) were badly shaken; and then, in 1725-35, the fierce Comanches assailed the Apaches from the west and drove them away from their old settlements on and near the upper Arkansas, in southeast Colorado. Thus the Palomas Apaches, who seem to have been Bourgmont's Kansas Padoucas, retreated to El Cuartelejo, on the Arkansas in the Las Animas district of Colorado, only to come under Comanche attack; and presently El Cuartelejo was abandoned by the Apaches, who fled to the New Mexican frontier for protection. By 1754 the governor of New Mexico reported that the Carlanas (the leading group of the southern Colorado Apaches), with their subordinate bands, the Cuartelejos, Palomas, Chilpaines (Apache: *Chilpa inde*), and other bands, were in the plains east of New Mexico, and a large part of them had formed rancherias near Pecos pueblo, where they lived, except when hunting buffalo in the plains.[43]

The Comanches did not follow the fleeing Apaches south of the Arkansas. That is, the victorious tribe occupied the old Apache lands from near the Arkansas northward, in east Colorado; but their war parties were soon penetrating as far south as north Texas. As late as

1751 the Comanche chiefs informed the governor of New Mexico that their camps were not south of the Nepestle (Arkansas River), and their bands still came into northern New Mexico, to trade at Taos. Their most important trade was with the Pananas and Jumanos for French guns and goods; and the Comanche route to these trading villages is clearly indicated in the Spanish report that, just prior to 1750, General Bustamente y Tagle got on the trail of a Comanche band on the upper Arkansas and followed them down the river to the vicinity of the Jumano village. Here is clear evidence that the Jumanos and Pananas were on the Arkansas in east Oklahoma, and that they were not the Tawehash Indians, who at this period were in a fortified village on upper Red River.

The Spanish governor of New Mexico had failed to follow the usual practice and lodge the Mallet brothers and their followers in jail when they crossed the plains from the Skidi Pawnee villages in Nebraska and entered New Mexico in 1739, with the result that other adventurous French traders soon found the way to Santa Fé. As we have seen, Fabre de la Bruyère and his party, guided by the Mallets, had failed in their attempt to cross the Oklahoma plains to New Mexico in 1741; but in 1744 a French trader from the Illinois country, whose name the Spanish documents render as Santiago Velo, reached New Mexico; in 1748 Frenchmen were reported trading at El Cuartelejo—the old Apache rancheria on the Arkansas in east Colorado—the trade evidently being with the Comanches. This tribe now had large numbers of French guns, and one of their first acts was to break with the Utes, the tribe that first brought the Comanches to Taos in New Mexico and aided them in obtaining the two great advantages of horses and metal weapons. In 1749 the Utes asked for Spanish aid against the Comanches; in the following year they allied themselves with their ancient foes, the Apaches, to make common cause against the Comanches.[44]

The concern of the Spanish officials in New Mexico was increased by the report, in 1748, that no less than thirty-three Frenchmen were trading with the Comanches at the old Apache rancheria of La Jicarilla, near the head of the Canadian River. In the following year the enterprising French traders made a peace between the Caddoan tribes and the Comanches, thus opening a route to French trade westward to the gates of New Mexico. In 1750 more French traders entered New Mexico, bringing a report that the Jumanos were trading with the French and then supplying the Comanches with French weapons and goods in exchange for horses. Since most of these horses were stolen by Comanche raiders in New Mexico, the officials at Santa Fé were not exactly pleased with the news of this new trading arrangement. These Frenchmen stated that the Jumanos were at war with the Pawnees; but whether they meant the Pawnees of Nebraska or those on the Arkansas River is not clear.[45]

The peace the French made among the southern plains tribes in 1749 was evidently at the roots of the offensive which the Caddoans of the Oklahoma-Texas region, aided by the powerful Comanches, started, about 1750, against their enemies. The French reported that the Comanches were now joining the Caddoans in attacks on the Osages and on the Kansa tribe of east Kansas; and when the Spaniards in Texas formed a mission for the Lipan Apaches on the San Saba River in 1757 the Comanches came down from the Arkansas River to join the Tawehash and other Caddoans, and with two thousand warriors they attacked San Saba, killing everyone that they could reach and burning the mission. The Lipans fled to the mountains west of the Colorado River; and thus ended the Apache domination of the region at the head of Red River and in northwest Texas, where they had been the great tribe of the plains for over a century. Refusing to recognize defeat, the Spanish officials raised a force of five hundred men and induced the frightened Lipans to join them in an expedition to the Tawehash fortified village on Red River, in the western edge of the Upper Cross Timbers; but here they found six thousand Comanche and Caddoan Indians assembled. Many of the warriors had French guns, and they put up such a fight that the Spanish force retreated, abandoning two cannons. The Lipans were reported to have fought better than the Spaniards; but they were soon forced to retire from the field.

It should be clearly stated that the Tawehash were the Caddoan Indians mainly concerned in this war with the Lipans on Red River and in northwest Texas from 1740 on. To term the Tawehash of this period *Wichitas* is not correct; for the true Wichitas were still on the Arkansas in north Oklahoma or south Kansas, where they remained until about 1770. In 1719 the Tawehash and Tawakonis had two large villages on the lower Canadian, which they abandoned soon after 1735, the Tawakonis going into east Texas, where they were still living in 1748. The Tawehash, who had a stronger desire to be in the buffalo range than the Tawakonis, moved from the lower Canadian to the north bank of Red River, west of the Upper Cross Timbers; and there with the aid of French guns and strong fortifications around their village they held out against the Lipans until other Caddoan tribes and the Comanches came to their aid. They seem to have been joined by at least part of the Tawakonis between 1740 and 1750; after

1772 the Wichitas (and Jumanos?) came to live with them; then other Caddoan groups (including an entire village of Skidi Pawnees from Nebraska) came to live with them; and thus was formed the very mixed tribe which late in the 18th century was termed Tawehash, Taovaya, Pani, Pani Pique, and—after 1850—became known as the Wichitas. In this manner, in the middle 18th century, was created on upper Red River a southern group of Pawnees who recognized the Pawnees of Nebraska and the Arikaras of Dakota as their close kindred. Extended through nine hundred miles of plains, from Texas to South Dakota, these Pawnee tribes always kept a knowledge of the location of each separate group and even exchanged occasional visits, Pawnees from Red River going up to the Platte in Nebraska to visit their kinsmen, and Arikaras from Dakota going into the plains south of the Arkansas, to seek their southern relatives.

Thus by 1750 the old Apache chain of tribes extending down through the western borders of the high plains had been broken to pieces and swept away; but the Caddoan chain along the eastern edge of the plains was still in existence, though weakened by losses in population. With the French actively trading in their villages, the Caddoans were acquiring new strength and confidence, the Tawehash pressing up Red River into lands the Apaches claimed, the Pawnees on the Arkansas not only holding their own but also, with French and Comanche aid, carrying war into the country of their Osage foes, who had persecuted them mercilessly ever since the first Osage warriors had obtained French knives and hatchets in the 17th century and had promptly started to make slave-catching raids against the Pawnees, who had nothing but flint weapons. The position of these Panis Noirs, Wichitas, and (to accept the Spanish reports) Jumanos on the Arkansas now seemed to be secure. With the French trading in their villages they had less fear of Osage guns; and in the matter of horses they were better supplied than the Osages or any of their other eastern enemies. They now had the friendly aid of the powerful Comanches; and through French assistance they had made by 1750 a peace that might well turn into an alliance which included the Comanches, the Tawehash of Red River, and the Skidi Pawnees of Nebraska.

But, as was always the case when any Pawnee tribe placed reliance on white men's help, the Pawnee groups on the Arkansas River soon found themselves in the most serious trouble. Their newfound security rested on a continuation of French trade in their villages, especially a trade in arms and ammunition; but France and England now went to war; the French trade with the Arkansas River Pawnees

Facsimile outlines of paintings on a Pawnee robe belonging to a medicine man and showing him to be a distinguished doctor and warrior. (From *North American Indians,* by George Catlin)

dwindled away to nothingness; and when trade was resumed after the English conquest of Canada the Osages were the first to receive a new supply of guns and ammunition, which they used in wreaking vengeance on the Pawnees of the Arkansas.

Just where these Pawnee villages of the Arkansas were located is a problem. In 1742 Fabre de la Bruyère remarked that it was farther from the lower Canadian River northward to the Panis Noirs than it was southward to Red River, which would seem to place the Panis Noirs villages on the Arkansas in south Kansas; but the Spanish references to the Pawnee and Jumano villages from 1719 until after 1750 locate them on the Arkansas in northern Oklahoma. The earlier Spanish statements (from Apache information) place these villages at or near the mouth of the Colorado—the Spanish name for the Canadian; but the later, and perhaps more accurate, reports from New Mexico indicated a location near the mouth of Rio Rojo (the Cimarron or perhaps Salt Fork). La Harpe and Du Tisné in 1719 seem to locate the Wichitas on the west bank of the Arkansas some twenty-five miles north of the Cimarron, in the immediate vicinity of the present home of the Pawnee tribe, at Pawnee, Oklahoma, with the Panis Noirs villages north of the Wichitas. The only village ruins known at the present time along this stretch of the Arkansas that would fit the Spanish statements concerning the Panana and Jumano villages are the two village ruins near Newkirk, Oklahoma, on the west bank of the Arkansas, within five miles of the Kansas line, sixty miles north of the Cimarron; but here we may note that there is no assurance as to what stream the often rather addled Spanish officials meant when they stated that the villages were near the mouth of Rio Rojo. There are several red-water streams in this northern Oklahoma district. The Newkirk villages are of late date, for they are filled with scrap metal and other indications of a heavy trade with the French. The ruins fit the Spanish description of strong villages or forts; for they are on the bluffs, and there are remains of ditch and wall fortifications. Nearby are the ruins of what may have been a small French trading-post. The Caddoan pottery in these village ruins is of an inferior quality, greatly deteriorated from the fine ware produced by the Red River Caddoans of the 17th-century period; but the pottery found by Dr. Wedel in the so-called Quivira village ruins, a little farther up the Arkansas, is also of a surprisingly low quality, although it has been given a dating as early as 1540. Since the Pani Noir settlements of the 18th century seem to have extended up the Arkansas into or through the Quivira district, it is a fair inference that some of their village ruins are mingled with those termed Quivira; and much additional archeological work will be required to sort out this tangle of Caddoan village ruins and date them properly. As for the village ruins near Newkirk, just described, it seems significant that the lodge type here is an intermediate form, between the grass-lodges of the southern Caddoans and the earth-lodges of the northern Pawnees and Arikaras. One suspects that this Newkirk lodge type is that which De Mezières noted in the Wichita village, immediately after that tribe came into Texas from the north, about the date 1770, and built a village with lodges of a northern type, which De Mezières considered unsuitable to the southern climate.[46]

When Dunbar and Grinnell were collecting material on Pawnee history, after the year 1870, they obtained from both the Pawnees and the Wichitas a tradition that long ago these peoples had left their old home on Red River, near the mouth of the Washita, and migrated northward; that coming into Kansas the Wichitas became discouraged and turned back toward Red River. Dunbar and Grinnell regarded this tradition as a record of an event of ancient times, perhaps going as far back as 1600; but the evidence we now possess suggests that this migration northward began sometime about the year 1685, when there was a movement of Caddoan tribes from Red River, to escape mounted Apache attacks, and that the Wichitas did not return to Red River until after 1770. Moreover, we have the cause for the Wichita decision to turn back in the statement made by French traders to Lewis and Clark in 1804, to the effect that the Wichitas or Panis Blancs were badly defeated by the Osages and then retired to Red River.

Although the Spaniards of New Mexico did not actually visit the Pawnee and Jumano forts on the Arkansas, they obtained frequent information from Indians concerning these forts, and the Spanish records indicate that the forts were still inhabited as late as 1765. The fate of these famous Indian villages we can only surmise. To begin with, it is fairly evident that the strength of the Pawnee and Jumano forts on the Arkansas was in the main due to the fact that the French had made these places their trade headquarters and were supplying the Indians with large quantities of firearms and other weapons. The Tawehash forts on upper Red River owed most of their strength to the same cause. This French trade which was so important to the Indians began to dwindle away when war with England broke out. The taking of Quebec by the English in 1759 stopped the Indian trade in the north; while in Louisiana trade with the more distant tribes became more and more difficult to maintain. About 1768 there was practically a complete stoppage of trade with the tribes in the Oklahoma region, and the taking over of Louisiana by Spanish forces in 1769 merely added to the troubles of the traders by placing them under the stern Spanish system of trade restrictions. Thus the Wichitas and other Caddoan tribes on the Arkansas in Oklahoma were cut off from their vital supplies, particularly of arms; but the Osages were not affected, for the British promptly supplied the French traders in Illinois with quantities of guns, ammunition, and other trade-goods, and these men went regularly to the Osage villages. The Wichitas were now badly defeated by the Osages and fled, appearing in north Texas in 1772. That they were fresh from the north was indicated by the fact that they had built a village of some form of clay-plastered lodges of a northern type, unsuitable for the Texas climate.

Of the Panis Noirs or Black Pawnees, who accompanied the Wichitas on their migration northward, we have little information, after the flight of the latter tribe to Texas. These Pawnees apparently lived to the northward of the Wichitas, and we can only surmise that the Osage assault on the Wichitas cut the Pawnees off from that tribe; and for some reason of their own the Black Pawnees preferred to remain in the north, rather than to attempt a flight southward. From the Dunbar and Grinnell material it would seem that this was the Kansas period of Pawnee tradition, when the three Black Pawnee or South Band tribes built villages on branches of Kansas River, villages whose ruins the archeologists have not yet located. It was at this period, seemingly after 1770, that the Black Pawnees of the Kansas region began to emerge into the light of history as three tribes: the Chauis or Grand Pawnees, the Kitkehahkis or Republican Pawnees (an off-shoot from the Chauis, who gave their name to the Republican Fork of Kansas River, on which stream their villages were often located), and the Pitahauerats or Tapages, sometimes called Smoky Hill Pawnees, because of their early residence on the Smoky Hill Fork of Kansas River, a stream which the Pawnees called *Rahotaka te hehu ru*: Big Black Forest River.

What became of the Jumanos, that favorite tribe of the Spanish chroniclers, when the Wichitas fled southward about the year 1770, is not recorded. In 1768 a Comanche chief informed the Spanish officials in New Mexico that the Jumanos had recently come and traded seventeen horse-loads of guns and ammunition to his tribe. This is the last reference in the Spanish documents to the Comanche-Jumano trade, and since the reports concerning the Pawnee and Jumano forts of the Arkansas also cease, we must suppose that they had been abandoned. Since the Spaniards later termed the Wichita

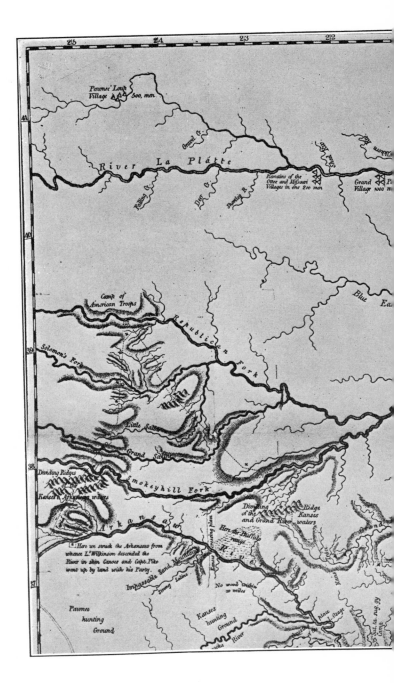

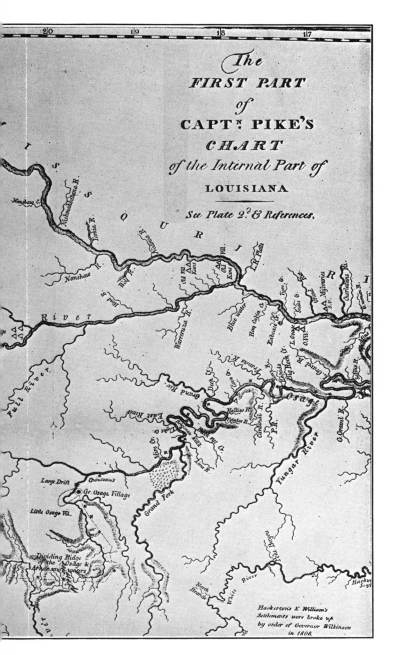

Zebulon M. Pike's Map, 1806. (From *An Introduction to Pawnee Archaeology*, by Waldo R. Wedel, BAE *Bulletin 112*, from *An Account of Expeditions to the Source of the Mississippi*, etc.)

Mountains *Sierra Jumano,* it is apparent that the Spanish officials thought that the Jumanos lived near these mountains late in the 18th century. Indeed, Mendinueta stated in 1778 that the Taovayes (the Tawehash) of Texas were known in New Mexico as Jumanos, and by that year we know that the true Wichitas had joined forces with the Tawehash. Thus down to the end the mystery surrounding the true Wichitas and the Jumanos was left unsolved. In this connection we may note that even after 1870 the Pawnees stated that part of their own Pitahauerat tribe, the band called Kawarakish, were different from the rest of the Pawnees; for they were the only people in the tribe who did not worship Tirawa. They turned toward the west when praying, whereas the other Pawnees always prayed toward the southeast. The name Kawarakish is clearly not Pawnee, but is Wichita, coming from two Wichita words: *kawara,* horse (from Spanish, *caballo*) and *kish,* people; and these Kawarakish folk were perhaps either Wichitas or Jumanos. When the Jumanos were a strong people, in the period 1630-70, part of the tribe at least lived on the head of Red River and had a trade in horses and Spanish articles with the Caddoan tribes to the eastward. We might conjecture that the Apache advance southward drove these Jumanos to seek safety in the east, where they broke up, part of them joining the Tawehash group, which in 1719 lived on the lower Canadian; others going farther north, to join the Wichitas and Panis Noirs. The name Kawarakish may have been a survival from the early times when these Jumanos supplied the first horses to the Caddoans.

The Pawnee tribal names are all curious; and none of them has been explained in a manner that is entirely satisfactory. The popular names for the South Band or Panis Noirs tribes are of French trader origin; but except in the name of the Pawnee Republican band we have no hint as to origin. Knowing the French trader custom of giving the name of a tribe to the stream it dwelt on, we might suppose that the Grand Pawnees formerly dwelt on the Neosho, which was called Grand River by the French; but the same name was given to the present Cottonwood River, north of the Neosho in Kansas, and that stream was still known as Grand River in Pike's day: 1806. The name of the Tapage band or tribe is said to be of French origin and to mean Noisy Pawnees. The native names of these three tribes have not been explained with any degree of plausibility. Major Frank North, who knew the Pawnees better than any other white man in the period 1860-76, and who spoke the language, stated that *Chaui* meant In-the-Middle, *Kitkehahki* On-a-Hill, and *Pitahauerat* Down Stream or Eastward; but these three names do not resemble any Pawnee words known today that bear the meanings Major North indicated. Perhaps the most reasonable explanation of the name *Chaui*, applied to the Grand Pawnees, is that of Dr. Clark Wissler, who believes that the name comes from *itsat*, the name the Grand Caddo gave to their Coon or Racoon clan or tribal division, to which *wi* was added, indicating a part of a tribe. Thus we have *Itsatwi*, shorted to *Tsawi* or *Chaui*.

Kitkehahki does not resemble any Pawnee word meaning On-a-Hill; but Major S. H. Long in 1819 wrote this tribal name as *Kit-ka-Kesh*, which would make this a Wichita name, not Pawnee at all. In Wichita *kesh* meant people; and here we may note that the name of one of the Kitkehahki tribal divisions, the Black Kitkehahkis, is also in the Wichita tongue, the name being *Korash*, which is Wichita for black.

As for the name *Pitahauerat* meaning Down Stream or Eastward, there seem to be no Pawnee words with such meanings that resemble this tribal name. As the Pawnees used to say that the Pitahauerats spoke the Pawnee language badly, one suspects that they were not originally of the same stock as the other Pawnees. In Pawnee the suffix *rat* at times indicated alien people; it also meant *screaming*; and here we may have an explanation as to why the French traders, whose knowledge of the Pawnee language was usually very faulty, called the Pitahauerats the Noisy Pawnees.

With the Wichitas (and Jumanos?) fleeing south to Red River, between the years 1768 and 1772, we have only the three Panis Noirs tribes left in the Kansas region. Just where they were and at what date they went up into Kansas from their older location on the Arkansas south of the mouth of the Cimarron, is another mystery. Still, it is evident that they could not have occupied western Kansas before 1725, as that region was still held by the strong Padouca nation. Bourgmont, when he marched up Kansas River to the Padouca Grand Village in 1724, did not mention the Pawnees at all. The land was held by the Padoucas only. Resorting again to conjecture, we may suppose that the Kansas period of Pawnee history began about 1730 and continued until after 1770; and for all this period we have only one doubtful reference to these Indians, in which a Spanish official states that the Jumanos made peace between the Comanches and Pawnees, about 1750.

When the elder Dunbar accompanied the Pawnees on hunting trips into Kansas in the 1830's, these Indians pointed out the sites of some of their early villages; but unfortunately Dunbar failed to put down the details of the information he obtained. He later recalled two traditional Pawnee village sites on the lower Republican Fork and one (a

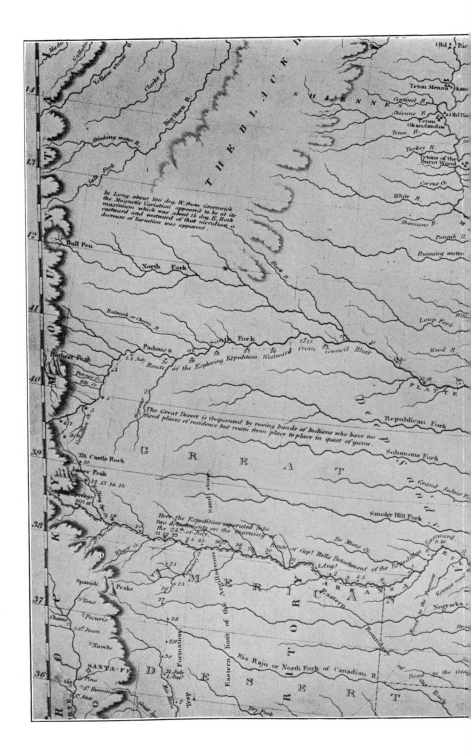

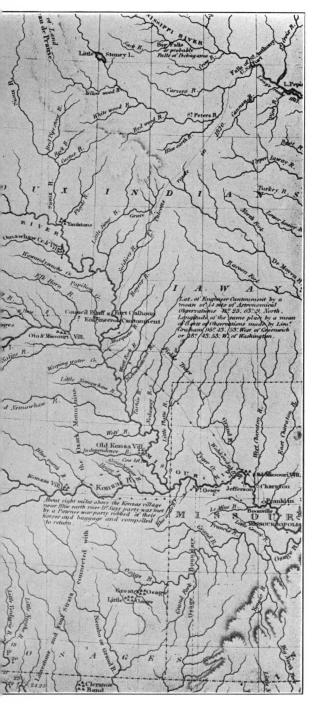

Stephen H. Long's Map, 1819. (From *An Introduction to Pawnee Archaeology*, by Waldo R. Wedel, BAE *Bulletin 112*, from *Account of an Expedition from Pittsburgh to the Rocky Mountains*, atlas)

Pitahauerat village) far up the Smoky Hill Fork. The number of sacred bundles kept by these Panis Noirs might indicate the number of their original villages, as each village had its own sacred bundle. The Grand Pawnees had three bundles; no bundles were recorded among the Kitkehahkis, who were a recent off-shoot from the Grands; while the Pitahauerats had two bands or villages and two sacred bundles. This seems to show that during the Kansas period these Pawnees had from five to six villages; but, due to loss of population, the people may have combined even at that date to form a smaller number of villages.

It is surprising that the archeologists have not thus far found any of the ruined villages in Kansas; but this may be due to the use by the Panis Noirs of a type of clay-plastered grass-lodge which when it fell in ruins would soon lose all surface indications of its former existence.

A piece of evidence that indicates the former occupation of west Kansas by these Indians lies in the location of two of the most famous homes of the *nahurac* or spirit animals, who lived underground in secret homes near every large center of Pawnee population. To these *nahurac* the Pawnees went, seeking spiritual aid and that magic power that all primitive Indians had such faith in. There were two recorded homes of the *nahurac* in the Kansas area: the famous *Pahur* or Hill-that-points-the-Way (the Guide Rock of the whites), on the south side of the Republican Fork, a few miles southeast of the town of Guide Rock; and the still more famous spring on a hill near the present Glen Elder, on Solomon's Fork, for which the Pawnees had two names: *Pahowa* and *Kitzawitzuk*, the latter name meaning Water-on-a-Bank.

In 1870 the Quaker Indian agent who was in control of the Pawnees in Nebraska ordered them to return some stolen horses to the Cheyenne tribe, and Captain L. H. North went with the party of Pawnees who took the horses to Fort Harker, in west Kansas, where the animals were left to be called for by their Cheyenne owners. Going south into Kansas an old Pawnee trail was followed, passing the little town of Belleville; and when the party reached the banks of the Republican River south of that town, Fighting Chief, an elderly Pitahauerat, said to Captain North: "This used to be the Pawnee country. We lived here a long time ago." The next morning the party crossed the Republican and struck across the divide toward a stream the Pawnees called Salt Creek; and presently Fighting Chief pointed at a hill away in the distance. "That is *Pahowa*," he said. "There is a spring on top of that hill, the water ten or twelve feet down in the hole; and the

Pawnees used to go there to offer sacrifices. If there was a great gathering of people and many gifts were cast into the spring, Tirawa was pleased and caused the spring to overflow. In the earth below this spring is a house of the *nahurac*." The Pawnees informed Grinnell, a few years later, that this hill was shaped like a huge Pawnee earthlodge, with the spring deep down in a hole at the top of the hill. When gifts or sacrifices were cast into the spring it at times overflowed, forming a tiny stream that trickled down the hillside to join the waters of Solomon's Fork; and when this occurred the people rejoiced, the women bathing their children in the sacred water and praying to Tirawa to bless them and give them a good life. This holy spring, like so many other precious possessions of the tribe, has been taken away from the Pawnees and has been given the Siouan name of Waconda. It still has a mysterious tide in it that at times causes it to overflow.

NOTES TO CHAPTER III

[38]Grinnell: *Pawnee Hero Stories*, p. 236.

[39]Swanton, 1942, p. 273.

[40]Vivier, in *Jesuit Relations*, ed. Thwaites, v. 69, p. 226; La Jonquire, in *Wisconsin Historical Collections*, v. 18, p. 93; Father Watrin, quoted in *Nebraska Academy of Sciences Reports*, v. 9, no. 1, p. 20.

[41]Fabre's reports, in *Margry*, v. 6.

[42]*Chronicles of Oklahoma*, v. II, p. 226.

[43]Thomas: *Plains Indians and New Mexico*, p. 135.

[44]*Ibid.*, p. 29.

[45]*Ibid.*, p. 107; Bolton and Marshall: *Colonization of America*. p. 282. The Comanche warriors who visited New Mexico at this period nearly all had French guns, two pounds of powder and plenty of ball, a long lance with a steel blade point, and a steel tomahawk.

[46]For a detailed description of these Newkirk Pawnee ruins I am indebted to Mr. Joseph B. Thoburn of the Oklahoma Historical Society, who was in charge of the excavations. The northern village had apparently 80 lodges. the southern 65, which would give the two villages perhaps 2,800 people.

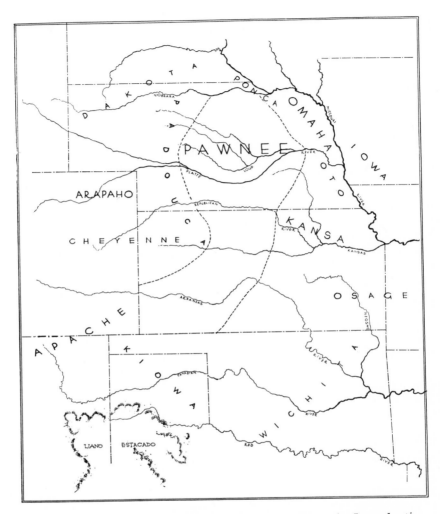

Tribal Map of the Central Plains about 1800. (From *An Introduction to Pawnee Archaeology*, by Waldo R. Wedel, BAE *Bulletin 112*)

IV

The Pawnees in Nebraska

ABOUT THE DATE 1730 THERE APPEAR TO HAVE BEEN FIVE TRIBES IN
eastern Nebraska, and of these the Skidi Pawnees of Loup Fork were
the most important group. To the east of the Skidis, on the south
bank of the Platte, were the Otos, a small Siouan tribe with which
the Skidis had been on generally good terms for at least fifty years.
The Omahas and Poncas, Siouan tribes that had moved up the Missouri with the Arikaras in the first quarter of the 18th century, had
now moved back down the west side of the river into northeastern
Nebraska, the Poncas building a village north of the Niobrara, the
Omahas going a little farther south and building villages about
opposite to the present Sioux City. With the Omahas was a band of
kindred Iowas, who settled on a small stream near the Omahas which
is still known as Iowa Creek. In 1730 western Nebraska was held to
some extent by part of the Padouca Nation. They had settlements
on the Platte, west of the forks, at least one settlement on a head-
branch of the Loup (evidently the present Dismal River), and—according to the *Account of Spanish Louisiana in 1785*—the Padouca
settlements extended up into Dakota, in the district between the
Black Hills and the Missouri. The Kiowas were near the Black Hills
and were apparently allied with the Padoucas; and these two tribes
were being warred upon by the strong Gens du Serpent or Snake
Nation (close kindred of the Comanches of the southern plains), a
mounted tribe that seems to have held the plains of Wyoming, extending northward into Montana.

The French and Indian War (1755-1763) did not directly concern
the Nebraska Indians, but it did affect French trade with the tribes,
on the Missouri and the Arkansas rivers, and in the plains to the
westward. The only Nebraska Indians who were drawn into the
struggle between the French and the British were a few Oto warriors.
In 1806 an old Osage Indian informed Lieutenant Zebulon Pike that

in 1755 a force of Osages and a few Otos from Nebraska took part in
the defeat of General Braddock's army, and that a body of warriors
of the Kansas tribe was also in Ohio, arriving too late to take part in
the battle.[47] The Missouri River tribes were loyal allies of the French;
but the Iowas were hostile. Always inclined to make trouble, the Iowas
in 1755 killed two French traders on the Missouri. By threats, and
probably by stopping all trade with the tribe, the French officers
forced the Iowas to give up the murderers, who were taken to Mon-
treal and handed over to General Montcalm by an Iowa chief. Montcalm pardoned and freed the Iowa warriors, in the evident hope that
such an act of generosity would win the tribe over to the French
interest; but the Iowas remained sullenly aloof in their own villages;
and at the close of the war they bade the French farewell by murdering a French hunter who had ventured into the Iowa lands, west of
the Mississippi.

Fort Cavagnol, a tiny trading-post on the west bank of the Missouri
in northeastern Kansas, was the most northerly French trade center
on the Missouri. This outpost was still in use in 1757, but soon after
that year the war with England killed the French trade with the
Indians. At the close of the war the French officials in Louisiana gave
a trade monopoly on the Missouri River to the New Orleans company: Maxent, Laclede et Cie. The forming of this monopoly had
a very adverse affect on the activities of the little independent French
traders, who for fifty years had been pressing boldly out into
unknown country and opening trade with new tribes on the Missouri
and Arkansas and their branches. The new monopoly did not send
its own traders into the field; but Laclede, the active partner, established himself at St. Louis, from which point he controlled the trade,
retaining that of the Missouri River tribes in his own hands, but
issuing licenses to independent traders permitting them to trade with
the Indians in other parts of the country. The small traders to whom
he gave licenses were forced to buy their Indian trade-goods from
him and to sell to him the furs and other products of their trade.
These small French traders were particularly active after 1763 in the
lands east of the upper Mississippi, which were now by treaty in the
hands of the British.

Laclede's attempt to control the French trade was considerably
weakened soon after 1763, when certain New Orleans merchants began
to smuggle in large stocks of British trade-goods by way of Mobile
and Pensacola; and then every spring large flotillas of batteaux, each
boat rowed by eighteen to twenty men, came up the Mississippi, carrying great loads of fine British goods to various tribes. These traders

went mainly into British lands, in Illinois and to the Wabash country.[48] But, almost immediately, enterprising British traders came into the field in Illinois and on the Ohio and routed out the French traders from New Orleans. Hiring experienced French traders, and some Frenchified Indian mixed-bloods, the British now began an active smuggling of their goods into the lands west of the Mississippi, which were supposed to be controlled by the French trade monopoly. This was about the year 1767, just at the time when the last French traders, going by the Arkansas River route, succeeded in visiting the tribes in the Oklahoma plains. A Comanche chief of the Yamparika tribe who came to the Tawehash Indian village on upper Red River in 1774 and met the French trader Gaignard there, stated that his tribe had not seen a French trader in eight years—not since 1766. The last transaction of the French traders among the Southern Pawnees on the Arkansas seems to be that recorded by Governor Mendinueta of New Mexico, in June, 1768, and from this Spanish report it would seem that the French brought British goods from Illinois to the Pawnees and Jumanos; the Jumanos then went off into the plains to westward with seventeen horse-loads of British guns and ammunition, all of which they traded to the Comanches for horses.[49]

These shifts in the French Indian trade after 1750 are of vital importance in Pawnee history; for there can be little doubt that it was the drying up of the French trade in arms and ammunition with the Pawnees, Wichitas, and Jumanos of the Arkansas that weakened the hold of these tribes on their lands in the old Quivira district in southern Kansas and northern Oklahoma and eventually forced the Wichitas (and Jumanos?) to retire south to Red River, while the Pawnees moved north into Kansas and then to their historic home on the Platte in Nebraska. The course of events may be followed in the few French and Spanish documents we have. Thus we learn that the Pawnees, Wichitas, and Jumanos on the Arkansas obtained a large supply of British guns and ammunition from some unidentified Frenchmen in 1768, but traded most of the arms to the Comanches for horses. They probably kept enough guns and ammunition to supply their own needs for a year, so that they could defend themselves against their most bitter foes, the Osages. From the documents we obtain the additional information that at about this time the Osages were in difficulties and in no position to raid the Caddoan tribes on the Arkansas, because they had been cut off from trade with the whites by the fierce Sacs and Foxes of the upper Mississippi. At this period Prairie du Chien was a great trade center for the Indians; British goods began to reach this point in quantity in 1767, the Sacs and Foxes (in whose territory Prairie du Chien lay) obtaining the first choice of the goods. They equipped themselves with new British guns and ammunition, and immediately sent war parties to the Missouri, to attack the Osages and the Missouri tribe, who were friends of the Osages. The Missouris were overwhelmed, only a handful of their people surviving the Sac and Fox assault; the Osages were hard pressed; and, being cut off from trade, they could not obtain the new supply of arms which they so sorely needed.

It was just at this time that Spain took possession of Louisiana, which had been secretly handed over to her by France at the close of the French and Indian War. The Spanish officials promptly revoked the trading monopoly of Maxent, Laclede et Cie. and clamped the usual Spanish restrictions on trade with the Indians. They established a Spanish garrison at Arkansas Post, near the mouth of the Arkansas, and another at St. Louis, at the mouth of the Missouri; and thus for the time being what little chance the Osages and other tribes west of the Mississippi had had of obtaining some arms and ammunition from the French traders of Louisiana was destroyed. It was the British traders in Illinois who broke up this new effort to strangle trade; for they now began to supply stocks of goods to French traders and Indian mixed-bloods, who smuggled the goods into the new Spanish territory and resumed trade with the Indians, who were starving for goods, and particularly for arms and ammunition. As it happens, we have a record of just how and at what date the Osage tribe began to be resupplied by these smugglers. It was a French trader from Illinois named Ducharme who performed this service for the Osages. He slipped into Spanish territory late in the year 1771, with a large stock of British goods, and spent the winter trading among the Osages. In the spring of 1772 he and his men attempted to smuggle out the furs and other products of their trade; but as they were going down the Missouri in their boats they were captured by a Spanish patrol from St. Louis, who confiscated their furs and other property.[50] At this time an Indian or mixed-blood named Joseph, who had been present at the capture of Quebec by the British in 1759, entered the same business as that followed by Ducharme and began to smuggle British goods to the tribes west of the Mississippi. Joseph was seeking horses, not furs, and he therefore made his way across Iowa to the Skidi Pawnees on the Loup Fork in Nebraska. The Skidis evidently did not have enough surplus horses to fill his requirements; and presently Joseph induced an entire village of Skidis to go with him all the way to the Southern Pawnee villages on Red River, where horses could be obtained in quantities. This seems to have been in the same year 1771 in which Ducharme started to trade among the Osages.

De Mezières, a former French official in Texas, now in the Spanish service, was in control of the Texas tribes, and he and his friends apparently had built up a neat trade monopoly with the tribes on Red River. Just as their plans for reaping great profits were completed they received the blasting news that Joseph and his Skidi Pawnees from Nebraska had arrived from the north with their camp filled with fine British goods, including guns and ammunition, which they were trading to the Pawnees of Red River. Words did not fail De Mezières when he reported this news to his Spanish superiors. He denounced the Skidis from Nebraska as the worst of miscreants, the most dangerous of enemies; but presently he had forgotten his anger and was listing these same Skidis as loyal allies. The truth was that something had happened in Nebraska to prevent the sending of more British goods to Red River; De Mezières' trade monopoly was now safe; and as the Skidis remained on Red River, De Mezières was delighted to enroll their 300 warriors among his Indian allies. These Skidis never returned home to Nebraska. Having joined the Tawehash tribe, they eventually were merged into the modern Wichitas, their group being called *Asidahesh* (*Asida,* Skidi; *hesh,* people). This group is now extinct.[51]

It was evidently during this season when the new stocks of British guns and ammunition were being smuggled to the Osages and to the Skidi Pawnees of Nebraska in 1771 that the Wichitas were forced to abandon their home in the old Quivira district on the Arkansas and retired southward to Red River. The Pawnee tradition states only that the Wichitas became dissatisfied with conditions in the north; but in 1804 Lewis and Clark were informed by French traders that the Wichitas had moved to Red River after being defeated by the Osages. The date of this event is easily fixed; for the Spanish archives of New Mexico show that the Jumanos—the Spanish name for the Wichitas—were still in their village on the Arkansas in 1768, while in 1772 De Mezières found the Wichitas near Red River, freshly arrived from the north. He listed the Wichitas, Tawehash, Tawakonis, and Iscanis as the Panis, one people, speaking one language; and in 1774 the trader Gaignard repeated that these four tribes made up the Panis Nation of Red River.

The Wichitas had now been driven from their old lands on the Arkansas, and apparently at this same time the Panis Noirs or Black Pawnees, who had been neighbors of the Wichitas from as far back at least as the year 1700, also left their old lands on the Arkansas. It was at this time, in the 1770's, that the name Panis Noirs went out of use, and these Pawnees emerged into the clear light of history as three tribes: the Grand Pawnees, the Kitkehahkis, and the Pitahauerats. Why these three Black Pawnee tribes preferred to remain in the north when their ancient Wichita allies removed to Red River in 1771-72, we cannot explain. Perhaps it was because the three Pawnee tribes had already moved northward into Kansas, and learning that British guns were to be obtained from traders on the Platte, they had their attention turned in that direction. The final act came in 1774, when it was reported that part of the Osages had removed to the Arkansas River, to take possession of the hunting grounds which the Wichitas and Panis Noirs had abandoned. From that moment the old Pawnee lands on and near the Arkansas were held by the Osages.

The flight of the Wichitas seems to have left the three Black Pawnee tribes in a precarious position. The advance of the Osages had cut them off from a return to their old lands on the Arkansas; the Kansas tribe, kinsmen and allies of the Osages, occupied eastern Kansas; and thus these Pawnee tribes could not obtain regular trade with the whites who came up the Arkansas or the Missouri. They had either to follow the Wichitas southward or go up to the Platte in Nebraska, and it was the latter decision that their chiefs made. Just when the Grand Pawnees led the advance to the Platte we do not know; but a Spanish report written at St. Louis, November 15, 1777, states that the Panis (Grand Pawnees and Pitahauerats apparently) had a village on the bank of the Platte, fifteen leagues above the Oto village, which was fifteen leagues above the mouth of the Platte. These Panis had 500 to 600 warriors, and their chief was Sokakahige (Long Hair?). The second group of these Panis, the Kitkehahkis, in 1777 were called *Nacion de la Republica* in this Spanish report. They had 350 to 400 warriors, and their chief Escatape bore the same name as their chief who was met by Lieutenant Pike in 1806.[52] This Spanish document clearly locates the Grand Pawnees in 1777 at the village the ruins of which are still to be seen, close to the town of Linwood, on the south bank of the Platte.

Pawnee tradition states that the Grand Pawnees were the first to move up to the Platte from Kansas, that they were followed by the Pitahauerats, but that the Kitkehahkis refused to obey the Grand Pawnee chiefs and remained on the stream now known as the Republican Fork of Kansas River. This revolt of the Kitkehahkis seems to have impressed the French traders and the Spanish officials of Louisiana as an event comparable to the revolt of the American colonies and the forming of the republic of the United States. They called the Kitkehahkis *Republicans*: *Nacion de la Republica;* they gave to the stream on which this tribe had its village the name of Republican Fork; and although we do not have exact information as to the date of these events, it would seem to be a fair inference that the Kitkehahki separation from the Grand Pawnees occurred about 1776. But the coming of the Grand Pawnees to the Platte must have happened a few years prior to 1776. Their village of 1777 was at the present site of Linwood; but Pawnee tradition asserts that on their first arrival on the Platte the Grand Pawnees built a village fifty miles higher up the river, near the place called Lone Tree, the present Central City. The ruins of this Pawnee village seem to be those described by Captain L. H. North, on an island close to the southern end of the Clarks Bridge. That site would seem to fit the situation best; for the older Pawnee villages usually had a home of the *nahurac* or spirit-animals close by; and here near the village ruins was such a home of *nahurac*, which the Pawnees called *Lalawakohtito*: *Dark Island.*

Some fifteen miles to the north of the Grand Pawnee village just referred to, on the north bank of Loup Fork near the present town of Fullerton, were the Skidi Pawnee villages, at least two in number. The Skidi population is said by tradition to have been larger than that of the combined Grand Pawnees and Pitahauerats; but the contemporary reports of traders gave that group 500 to 600 warriors and the Skidis about the same—600 warriors. In 1771 the Skidis had 900 warriors; but, as we have seen, 300 of these went south to Red River with the Indian trader Joseph and never returned to Nebraska.

The Skidis resented the intrusion of these Black Pawnees from the south on lands which they regarded as their own; still the Skidi chiefs decided to take no action, as long as the Grand Pawnees and Pitahauerats kept to the south side of the Platte. The Skidi chiefs then paid a ceremonial visit to the Grand Pawnee village and smoked with the chiefs of the Grands. For the moment there was a friendly feeling; but presently the Grand Pawnee chiefs haughtily demanded that they should be recognized as the heads of the nation, superior to any of the Skidi chiefs. To this the Skidis would not consent, and they returned to their own villages in no pleasant state of mind. Ignoring the Skidi request that they should keep out of the lands north of the Platte, the Grand Pawnees now sent a large hunting party north of the river, to hunt buffalo on Prairie Creek, within sight of the Skidi villages. The enraged Skidis mounted and swarmed across the Loup, attacking the hunters, killing a number of them, and driving the rest south of the Platte.[53]

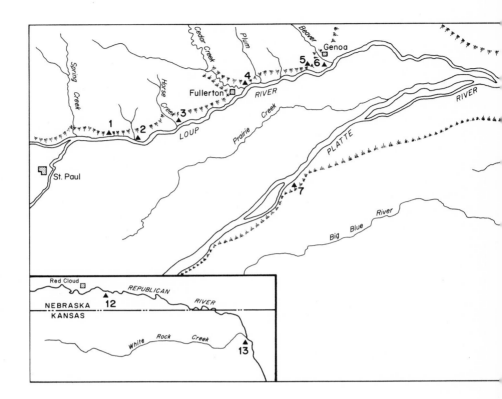

Spring Creek

Cedar Creek

Plum

Beaver

Genoa

5 6

4

Fullerton

LOUP RIVER

Horse Creek

3

1 2

Prairie Creek

PLATTE RIVER

St. Paul

7

Big Blue River

Red Cloud

REPUBLICAN RIVER

12

NEBRASKA

KANSAS

White Rock Creek

13

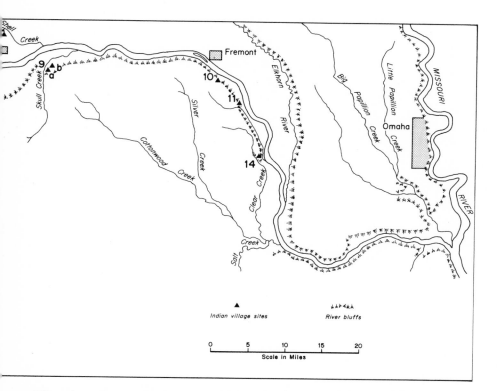

Historic and Late Prehistoric Pawnee Sites. 1 Palmer site, 2 Cotton-
wood Creek site, 3 Horse Creek site, 4 Fullerton site, 5 Burkett site (?),
6 Genoa site, 7 Clarks site, 8 Schuyler site (?), 9 Linwood site, 10 Mc-
Claine site, 11 Leshara site, 12 Hill site, 13 Kansas site, 14 Yutan site
(Oto). (Redrawn from *An Introduction to Pawnee Archaeology*, by
Waldo R. Wedel, BAE *Bulletin 112*)

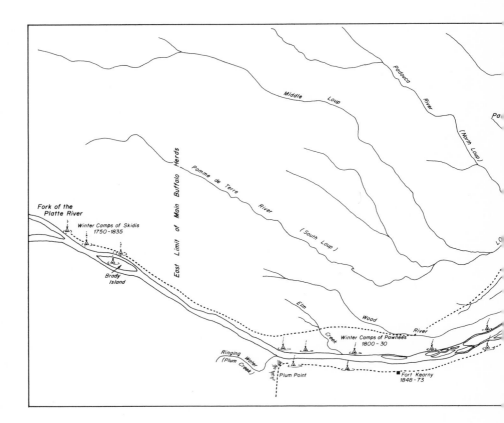

Middle Loup

Paducca River

(North Loup)

Pa

Pomme de Terre River

(South Loup)

Fork of the
Platte River

Winter Camps of Skidis
1750-1835

East Limit of Main Buffalo Herds

Brady
Island

Elm

Wood River

Creek

Winter Camps of Pawnees
1800-30

Ringing Water
(Plum Creek)

Plum Point

Fort Kearny
1848-73

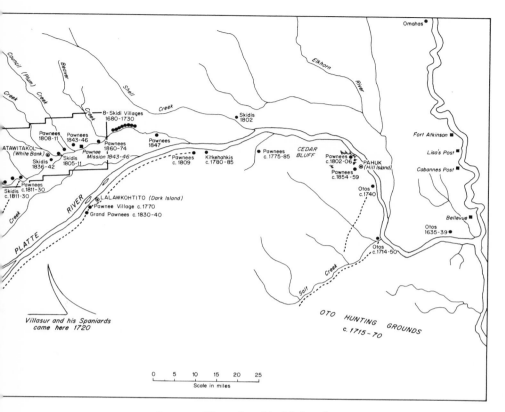

Omahas

Elkhorn River

Council (Plum) Creek

Beaver Creek

Shell Creek

8-Skidi Villages
1680–1730

Skidis
1802

Pawnees
1847

Fort Atkinson

Lisa's Post

Cabannes Post

Pawnees
1808–11

Pawnees
1843–46

Pawnees
1860–74

Pawnees
1843–46

Pawnee
Mission 1843–46

ATAWITAKOL
(White Bank)

Skidis
1836–42

Skidis
1805–11

Pawnees
1847

Pawnees
c.1809

Kitkehahkis
c.1780–85

Pawnees
c.1775–85

CEDAR
BLUFF

Pawnees
c.1802–06

PAHUK
(Hill Island)

Pawnees
c.1854–59

Skidis
c.1811–30

Pawnees
c.1811–30

PLATTE RIVER

LALAWKOHTITO (Dark Island)

Pawnee Village c.1770

Grand Pawnees c.1830–40

Otos
c.1740

Otos
1635–39

Bellevue

Otos
c.1714–50

Salt Creek

Villasur and his Spaniards
came here 1720

OTO HUNTING GROUNDS
c. 1715–70

0   5   10   15   20   25
Scale in miles

Pawnee Homeland in Nebraska

The Grand Pawnee and Pitahauerat chiefs now held a council and decided on war, but they are said to have been afraid to attack the Skidis at once, who were supposed to outnumber them. They therefore sent messengers to their third tribe, the Kitkehahkis, whose village was on the Republican Fork of Kansas River, summoning all the warriors of that group to their aid. The Kitkehahkis (not caring to leave their women, children, and old people unprotected) now abandoned their village and moved up to the Platte with all their people and possessions. When they arrived at the Grand Pawnee village preparations were made for an advance against the Skidis.

The Skidi villages, on the north bank of the Loup, were just to the east of Cedar River, a northern tributary of that stream. Here, on the south side of the Loup, there is a long sandy ridge, six or eight miles east of the town of Fullerton. The ridge runs parallel to the river, and between the river and ridge is a narrow valley, four to five miles long and about one-half mile wide. Hiding their main force behind this ridge, the Pawnees sent forward a decoy party to draw the Skidis into a trap. The warriors of the decoy party lay down on their horses' backs, covering themselves with hairy buffalo robes; and as day dawned they rode over the ridge slowly in single file and moved down toward the river, having the appearance from a distance of a band of buffalo coming down to the stream to drink. These warriors started from the east end of the ridge, crossed the open valley, and vanished among the thickets along the river bank; but the watchers in the Skidi villages had seen them; and the cry *Taraha! Taraha!—Buffalo! Buffalo!*—rang out in the dawn. Mounting in haste, a large body of Skidi hunters came pouring from the villages, splashed across the river, and rode swiftly eastward down the narrow valley. Approaching the point where the buffalo had been seen, to their amazement they were suddenly charged by a large force of Pawnees, who burst out of the brush along the river bank and slammed into them; and at the same moment a still larger body of Pawnees appeared on the ridge, cutting off their line of retreat up the valley. Here many of the Skidis died, bravely fighting against overwhelming numbers. Some of them broke through the Pawnees, swam their horses across the river, and rushed back to the villages, to protect the women and children.

According to the Grand Pawnee version of this story, obtained by Grinnell after 1870, while the fight in the valley was raging part of the Pawnees rode up the river, crossed, and captured the villages, holding all the women and children. Captain L. H. North's version was obtained from the Kitkehahkis as early as 1864, and it differs from the Grinnell story in stating that when the Grand Pawnees reached the ford across Loup Fork near the villages the Skidi warriors were on the north bank and opposed the crossing. After some fighting, the Skidi chiefs went down to the river bank and made signs of peace. A quarrel ensued among the Pawnees, the Grands and the Pitahauerats being very vindictive and demanding that the attack should continue and that the Skidi villages should be burnt. The Kitkehahkis maintained that the Skidis had been punished enough and should be given peace. There was a long and angry argument among the chiefs; but in the end the signal was made for the Skidi chiefs to cross at the ford. When they arrived they were told that they could have peace if they would abandon their villages, move down to the Platte, and live near the Pawnees, accepting the leadership of the Grand Pawnee chiefs. After another long argument the Skidi chiefs are said to have accepted these terms, and the pipe was smoked.

This war between the Skidis and the other Pawnees made a profound impression on the minds of the Indians, and a century later they remembered many details of the fight. Old men, who had been born around the year 1800, stated that the battle took place when their grandfathers were young, and this agrees with what little additional evidence we have in fixing the date between 1770 and 1775. The Pawnees termed this battle and the peace that concluded it their conquest of the Skidis and stated that from that time on the Skidis were compelled to live close to the other Pawnees, the Skidi village always being a little to the west of the others; but this does not appear to be correct, for we have proof that at some periods after 1775 the Skidi village was quite distant from those of the other Pawnees. The continued independence of the Skidis was also demonstrated by their hunting and wintering in their own lands near the forks of the Platte, while the other three Pawnee tribes hunted toward the south, on the Republican and other branches of Kansas River. The claim that the Skidis were conquered seems to be a gross exaggeration of the truth. Pawnees who were alive in 1875 had taken part in fights between the Skidis and the other Pawnees, and we have much evidence of the independent spirit of the Skidis, who refused to be controlled by the Grand Pawnee chiefs during the first half of the 19th century. The Skidis called the other Pawnees Big Shields, implying that they lacked courage and hid behind shields of unusual size. Some of the early French traders, and Americans of the later days, were of the opinion that the Skidis were superior to the other Pawnees: more intelligent, more reliable, and better warriors; but after 1850

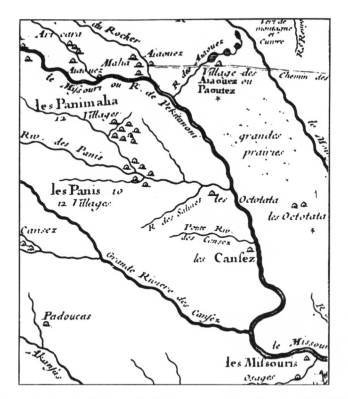

Portion of the Guillaume Delisle map, 1718, showing the Pawnee
Towns on the Loup and Platte Rivers in East-Central Nebraska.
(From *The Direct-Historical Approach in Pawnee Archaeology*,
Smithsonian Misc. Collections, Vol. 97, No. 7)

there was little difference to be noted in the quality of the fightingmen of the Skidis and the other Pawnees. Perhaps the Skidis on the whole were steadier and more amenable to discipline, the warriors of the other Pawnee groups being wilder and more inclined to act independently. Every man for himself is a poor rule in war; the headlong charges of the Pawnees often ended in sudden flight. By 1850 they had learned this lesson and obeyed their leaders.

Although after 1870 the Pawnees could give details of the battle with the Skidis a century before, their minds retained almost no memory of the less striking events in the period 1770-1825. We are therefore compelled to seek in the scanty historical records and in the gropings of the archeologists in village ruins for information with which to fill in the history of the Pawnees during this rather obscure period. From the records kept by Spanish officials at St. Louis it would appear that, if the Pawnee story is true and the Skidis were compelled to abandon their villages on Loup Fork after their defeat by the other Pawnees, they did not keep the agreement to live near the Grand Pawnees for any length of time, but were soon back on the Loup, living independently in their own country. They were there on the Loup by 1777, and (perhaps because of this new movement of the Skidis), the Grand Pawnees and Pitahauerats left their village near Lone Tree and moved fifty miles down the Platte, building a village near the present town of Linwood. From their new location, it will be noted, the Grand Pawnees were in a position to stop French traders coming up the Platte, and thus to cut off trade with the Skidis. The Kitkehahkis seem to have gone to this Linwood location with the other Pawnees; but presently they quarreled again with the Grand Pawnee chiefs and returned to their old home on the Republican Fork. They were there before 1777, as is shown by a Spanish document of that date, and Cruzat's letter of 1780 confirms this.[54]

The smuggling of British goods to the tribes on the Platte was resumed in 1777; and in 1780 Cruzat, the Spanish governor of Louisiana, reported that British traders were very active west of the Mississippi, with the Iowa tribe aiding the traders. The Iowas, he stated, had gone to the Otos on the Platte and won them over to the British interest; but despite these efforts of the British in Illinois the chiefs of the Otos and Pawnees were going pretty regularly to St. Louis, to pay their respects to the representatives of the King of Spain, and to receive the customary gifts, including Spanish medals for the leading chiefs.

The report of 1777 placed the Pawnee village on the south bank of

the Platte, fifteen leagues west of the Otos, but the Spanish account
of Louisiana in 1785 located this village twelve leagues west of the
Otos and three leagues east of the mouth of Loup Fork. This document terms Loup Fork *Rio de Papas*, which may be an error to Lobos,
the Skidis being known to the French traders as the Loups or Wolves.
Papas or Popes might be a reference to the famous brotherhoods of
priests among the Skidis. In this document of 1785 the Kitkehahkis
are given the quaint names of *aldea de la Republica* (*little village of
the Republic*) and *Maniguacci* or *Ojos de Perdiz* (*Eyes of the Part-
ridge*). This latter name for the Kitkehahkis does not occur again
after 1800. It does not seem to make sense, but we must remember
that the Pawnees called the Wichita people *Kiri-kuruks*: Bears' Eyes.
The Omahas called the Kitkehahkis *Zitka-akithisin*, *zitka* meaning
turkey. As there were no partridges in Kansas or Nebraska, the Spanish
writer must have meant some other bird, possibly the wild turkey,
which abounded in the Kitkehahki country. Solomon's Fork of Kansas
River, near their village, was called Turkey River by some of the
Indians. As the Spanish word *ojos* means either eyes or a spring of
water, and as the Pawnee sacred spring was close to Solomon's Fork,
we might guess that this name was given to the Kitkehahkis because
they lived near the sacred spring on Turkey River.

The distances given in these Spanish reports are not correct, but
it is perfectly clear that the Grand Pawnee village they refer to in the
period 1777-85 is the ruin which Dr. Walter Wedel describes in his
Introduction to Pawnee Archeology, page 29. This ruin is on the east
bank of Skull Creek, three miles south of the Platte and about one
mile south of the town of Linwood. The Indian village stood on the
bottomlands, covering about forty acres, and it was defended by an
earth wall and ditch. The ruins are featured by a huge enclosure,
about ninety feet in diameter, near the center of the village, which
the archeologists conjecture may have been an open-air council
ground. It might more probably be the remains of a huge grass-
thatched sacred lodge or temple, such as Dr. Wedel found in the
Caddoan village ruins on the Arkansas in southern Kansas.

Not far from this Grand Pawnee village ruin there was a second
village of apparently the same period, on the south bank of the Platte
and the east bank of Bone Creek, where Shinn's Ferry crossed the river
in pioneer days, the Indian village being on the site of the old town
of Savannah, which has now disappeared. In that rare little volume,
The Centennial History of Butler County by George L. Brown, there
is a map made in 1876 which shows both the Linwood and the Savan-

nah Pawnee village ruins. The author gives us some hints as to the dates of these villages; for he questioned some of the oldest Pawnees living in 1875 on this subject, and he quotes Mr. D. R. Gardiner, who also sought information among the oldest of the Pawnee men. Mr. Brown states that the Linwood village was that of the Grand Pawnees (and Pitahauerats) while the Kitkehahkis occupied the Savannah village. A very old Kitkehahki told Mr. Gardiner that his tribe left this village when he was about seven years of age, removing to Republican Fork, and Mr. Gardiner gave the date of this event as about the year 1785.[55]

It would be impossible today to follow all the movements of these Pawnees. The Kitkehahkis were originally part of the Grand Pawnee tribe, and even after 1800 part of their group wished to live with the Grands, while the other faction opposed that idea and wished to live on the Republican Fork as an independent group. The result of this situation was continual quarreling in the Kitkehahki village and periodic movements north to the Platte or from the Platte back to Republican Fork. This was kept up from a time apparently near the date 1770 until about 1825. Of the Pitahauerats both Pawnee tradition and the historical records are silent for the period of the 18th century. This tribe appears to have lived with the Grand Pawnees from the first arrival on the Platte until after the close of the century.

The main interests of these Black Pawnees lay in the southern plains, and even after they had established themselves on the Platte they spent the greater part of every year in the south, returning to their villages on the Platte only to plant their little crops in the spring and to harvest them in early autumn. Their war parties nearly always headed southward, and it was from that direction that they obtained the great numbers of horses and mules that constituted their principal wealth. Their one important interest on the Platte was trade; for it was only by having permanent villages there that they could be assured of a steady flow of trade-goods, particularly guns and ammunition. In trading with the whites, every tribe was jealous of its neighbors and strove by every possible method to prevent traders passing by their villages, to go to some other tribe and trade freely with it. Thus the Pawnees from the moment they arrived on the Platte seem to have striven to cut the Skidis off from direct trade with the whites who were bringing goods up the river. Every time the Skidis shifted the location of their village the Pawnees also moved, building new villages so situated that they could easily stop traders

going to the Skidis. It might be argued that the traders could have
avoided this Pawnee blockade by going on up the Missouri above the
Platte, to a point near the present city of Omaha, and carrying their
goods overland to the Skidi village on the Loup; but the fact is that
these early French traders were wedded to water transportation, they
did not usually have the means of obtaining horses on the Missouri
above the Platte for carrying their goods overland, and we have evidence in the written records that they did not try to do this. From
the time when the Pawnees moved up to the Platte, around the year
1772, until the end of the second decade of the 19th century, the white
traders made the village of the Grand Pawnees their headquarters,
and in 1804 Lewis and Clark stated definitely that the Skidis had to
come to the Grand Pawnee village and trade there, clearly under
restrictions set by the Grand Pawnee chiefs. The little Oto tribe, close
friends of the Skidis, is said to have had a village on the south bank
of the Platte, about opposite to the present town of Fremont, at the
time when the Black Pawnees moved up to the Platte. At first these
Pawnees settled far to the west, near Lone Tree; but about 1775
they moved down the Platte to the Linwood location, which was quite
close to the Oto village—too close, apparently, for the comfort of that
small tribe. The Otos now moved down the Platte and built a fortified village near the present Yutan, where they held their ground; for,
although they were few in numbers, they had a much better supply
of firearms than the Pawnees and knew how to use such weapons.
Moreover, they had known the French traders much longer and, their
village being farthest down the Platte, they obtained the first choice
from any stocks of goods the traders brought up the river. The Skidis,
far away on Loup Fork, were the worst off. In trade with the whites
they obtained the leavings from stocks of goods which the Otos and
Grand Pawnees had already picked over; and when the Pawnees were
in a particularly vindictive humor, they cut the Skidis off from all
trade.

After 1870 some of the Pawnees gave the younger Dunbar an account of their successful wars against the Siouan tribes, after their
arrival on the Platte, and Dunbar accepted these tales at face value,
terming this the heroic age among the Pawnees. Every author who
has written of the Pawnees since Dunbar's time has repeated these
statements; but if any of them had attempted to do a little independent research he might have found reason for suspicion that these
Pawnee claims of conquest were without any solid foundation of truth.
Their absurdity is evidenced from the fact that, among other claims,

the Pawnees asserted that they had conquered the Osages, a statement so droll that it does not require further notice. The Siouan tribes who Dunbar supposed were the principal victims of Pawnee conquest were those in eastern Nebraska: the Otos, the Omahas, and the Poncas. As for the little Oto group, it was on the Platte when these Black Pawnees came up from the south; it remained on the Platte, and—far from being conquered or cowed—the Otos regarded themselves as better warriors, man for man, than the Pawnees, and even after 1840 they did not hesitate to fight back if the Pawnees injured them.

The Omahas and Poncas, as Dunbar wrote, were not only defeated by the Pawnees, they were driven out of Nebraska. At a later date they were permitted to return as subject tribes; but when the Pawnees and Omahas hunted together the Omahas were under Pawnee control. This last statement is true to the extent that when, late in the 19th century, the Omahas occasionally hunted with the Pawnees *south of the Platte* on lands that were unquestionably Pawnee, they were guests of that tribe and naturally accepted the leadership of the Pawnee chiefs. In their own lands, north of the Platte, the Omahas did not permit any interference with their control of their own hunting grounds.

One point we must note here, and that is the fact that from early in the 18th century down to about 1740 or 1750 French maps and some statements by French traders placed one village of Black Pawnees on the Platte and a group of Black Pawnee villages on the Missouri, in northeastern Nebraska. Here there is a suggestion of a Black Pawnee incursion into Nebraska and an advance northward to a point at which contact between these Pawnee invaders and the Omaha and Ponca tribes may have occurred, on the Missouri, near the mouth of the Big Sioux, at a date prior to 1725. It is therefore possible that at this early period the Black Pawnees from the south may have attacked and defeated the Omahas and Poncas; but those tribes were not in Nebraska. They were east of the Missouri; and moving up the river into Dakota, they crossed the stream and then came down into northern Nebraska, at about the date 1740-1750— long before the main body of Black Pawnees left their home in the south and moved up to the Platte (c.1772). Was it to events of the period 1720 that the Pawnees were referring when they informed Dunbar that they had conquered the Omahas and Poncas? They did not give details from which we might form a real judgment; and it must be remembered that at the time when they spoke to Dunbar

Spanish medal of Carlos III from a Pawnee grave in Nebraska.
(Courtesy Mr. A. T. Hill)

none of the Pawnees had a detailed memory of any event farther back than their defeat of the Skidis, around the year 1775. Still, even in 1870, some of the oldest Pawnees may have had a vague memory of the coming north of a group of their people, as far back as 1720 or 1725. We might conjecture that what happened was that part of the Black Pawnees of the Arkansas, having a good supply of horses and a temporary stock of goods obtained from the French, including possibly a few guns, moved up to the Platte; finding themselves among tribes that had few horses and no guns, they raided them. At this period the Omahas and Poncas were on foot and without metal weapons—the easy victims of mounted warriors, particularly if those warriors had some firearms. Thus the Pawnees may have driven the Omahas and Poncas (also the Arikaras) up into Dakota. But, why did not the Pawnees speak of this to Grinnell, who came among them after Dunbar and collected every scrap of information he could obtain; and why did they not speak of these early conquests to the North brothers, who were with them for years before Dunbar came out to seek information?

After 1775 the Omahas and Poncas were certainly free of any Pawnee claim to overlordship. The Omahas, in particular, under the leadership of their great chief Blackbird, ranked as high in power as the Grand Pawnees, and these two tribes apparently had some kind of friendly agreement and were generally on the best of terms, their friendship probably having its roots in the fact that the Grand Pawnees had large numbers of horses for barter, while the Omahas had excellent British guns and goods to exchange for horses. Chief Blackbird of the Omahas had made a trade arrangement with the Sacs and Foxes of the upper Mississippi, to whom he traded furs and horses for British arms and goods, which the Sacs and Foxes brought across northern Iowa to the Omaha village on the west bank of the Missouri, south of the present Sioux City. This trade made the Omahas independent of the Frenchmen who brought goods up the Missouri from St. Louis, and the Omahas robbed and mistreated the French traders habitually. From the high bluffs near their village, the Omahas could overlook the river for many miles, and they usually discovered the traders' boats toiling slowly upstream long before they reached the vicinity of the village. Blackbird would make his arrangements to block the passage of the boats by stationing his warriors at strategic points; then he would compel the Frenchmen to unload all their goods and carry the bales to the village, where he would arbitrarily fix very low prices on the goods and force the traders to barter on his own terms. If they resisted he stripped them of everything and had his warriors toss all the Frenchmen over the bluff edge toward the river. The traders hated and feared him, but the Spanish officials at St. Louis were anxious to keep his friendship. He seems to have paid several visits to St. Louis, returning home loaded with gifts, including Spanish flags; but when he was given the usual chief's medal he refused haughtily to take it, asserting that it was too small a medal for such a great chief. The bedeviled Spaniards then took several chief's medals and had them soldered together, to form a large flat plaque—the finest and largest medal any chief on the Missouri had ever seen, and this Blackbird condescended to accept.

In the opinion of contemporary traders and Spanish officials at St. Louis, Blackbird was the dominant figure in Nebraska from about the year 1770 to the time of his death thirty years later. During his time the Omahas were feared by all their neighbors, and any claim of the Pawnees that they conquered the Omahas at this period is simply not true. Edwin James was with Major S. H. Long's expedition, which wintered on the Missouri in eastern Nebraska in 1819-20, and during the stay in this district James collected from traders and Indians a fairly complete history of the Indians in Nebraska from about 1770 to 1819. In the James narrative there is no hint of any trouble between the Grand Pawnees and Omahas; nor is there one word on that subject in the Omaha tribal traditions, collected since 1850. The traditions tell only of several victories of the Omahas over the Skidi Pawnees, in the district north of the Skidi villages on Loup Fork.[56] In this war between the Omahas and Skidis the Grand Pawnees apparently maintained an attitude of benevolent neutrality: benevolent toward the Omahas, but not toward the Skidis, whom the Grand Pawnees heartily detested. It may have been these Omaha attacks on their people that forced the Skidis to abandon their villages far up Loup Fork and move eastward, a movement which seems to have been made toward the close of the 18th century. They established themselves on Shell Creek, north of the Platte and east of the mouth of Loup Fork; and the Grand Pawnees promptly moved to a position on the south side of the Platte, at Cedar Bluff and built a village from which they could again prevent traders from going to the Skidi village.

Having defeated the Skidis in several fights and put down an attempt of the Ponca tribe to flout his authority, by 1795 Chief Blackbird was at the height of his power. About this time, in 1798, apparently, a famous Omaha warrior, Little Grizzly Bear, went with a group of comrades to the Kitkehahki Pawnee village on the Republican Fork with the object of performing the calumet ceremony in honor of the Pawnee chiefs. This ancient peace ceremony had now degenerated into a form of begging which the Omahas termed *smoking for horses.* That described it accurately, the purpose of the Omahas being to parade about in fine costumes and obligate their hosts to give them feasts and present them with large numbers of horses; but the Kitkehahkis were by this time highly annoyed at the frequency with which parties of Omaha warriors came to honor them in this manner; and now when Little Grizzly Bear and his friends arrived in their village it was just too much, and they lost their tempers. They stripped the Omaha worthies bare, beat them, and turned them over to the older Pawnee women, who heaped every possible insult on them and then drove them from the village with sticks.

Two days later the Omaha warriors reached home, entering the village naked, bruised all over, and covered with the filth the Pawnee women had thrown at them. Chief Blackbird listened to their story; then he ordered the entire tribe, including the women and children, to march against the Kitkehahkis. They moved their camp to the Platte. The Grand Pawnees did not oppose this movement—they had probably quarreled with the Kitkehahkis again and did not care what happened to that tribe. The Omahas crossed the Platte and went on southward to a small stream near the Kitkehahki village; there they set up their camp and left their women, children, and old people. Amazing as it may seem, after this long and perfectly open march the Omaha warriors took the Kitkehahkis completely by surprise, charging into their village on horseback and driving the Pawnees from lodge to lodge. They plundered and set fire to all the earth-lodges they drove the Pawnees out of, until presently the Kitkehahki fightingmen were crowded into four very large lodges near the center of the village. Here a fierce fight took place; but, finding that they could not get at the Pawnees without sacrificing many of their own men, the Omahas drew off. They plundered the village at their leisure, set all the remaining lodges in a blaze, and withdrew to their own camp. They had killed about one hundred Pawnees with a loss of some fifteen of their own warriors.[57]

It was the Skidi Pawnees who finally conquered the Omahas, but not by fighting. About the year 1801 a Skidi horse-stealing party went to the New Mexican border and brought home a large quantity of plunder. They also brought the smallpox. A great many Pawnees died; then the epidemic spread to the Omahas, and within a few weeks Blackbird and half his tribe lay dead. The stunned survivors abandoned their village, which had become a charnelhouse, and took to wandering. Almost overnight they had lost their great position and become a broken remnant, the easy victims of any tribe that chose to attack them.[58]

As has been stated, about the end of the 18th century the Skidis, harassed by the Omahas, abandoned their village on Loup Fork, seemingly the ruins near the present town of Fullerton, and moved eastward, building a new village on Shell Creek near the present Schuyler. With the probable purpose of controlling the Skidis and cutting them off from direct trade with the whites, the Grand Pawnees and Pitahauerats left their village near the present Linwood and built a new one near Cedar Bluff, on the south bank of the Platte, opposite to the present Fremont. The Skidis were still in the Shell Creek village when the smallpox destroyed the Omaha tribe, and now a band of Omahas under a chief named Voleur (the Thief) came to live in a camp just west of the Skidi village. The Ponca tribe, close kindred of the Omahas, wished to attack the Skidis, but were afraid of offending the Grand Pawnees. They therefore sent men to the Pawnee village to ask permission to assault the Skidi village, and the Grand Pawnee chiefs gave their consent. The Ponca war party now approached the Skidi village openly, making signs of peace and pretending to be on a friendly visit; but the Skidi chiefs were suspicious, and they put all their warriors under arms and concealed them in the earth-lodges before going out of the village to greet the visitors. Advancing toward the Poncas, the Skidi chiefs were suddenly attacked, and the Poncas, raising the war cry, rushed after them into the village. The Skidi warriors poured out of the lodges to meet them, and after a hard fight drove them in rout and pursued them across the prairie. In this affair the Omahas of Voleur's band fought side by side with the Skidis, but the Pawnees stayed in their village on the south side of the Platte and did not lift a hand to aid the Skidis. We here have another demonstration of the fact that the Grand Pawnees did not consider the Skidis to be a part of their nation.

The Skidi village on Shell Creek and the Grand Pawnee village at Cedar Bluff were apparently occupied for only a few years, being abandoned before 1806. According to Edwin James the Grand Pawnee village was burned down by the Oto chief. This chief had warned his young men not to do anything to offend their powerful Pawnee neighbors; but some of the young Otos disregarded his words and went to the Pawnee village, just as that tribe was setting off on its semi-annual buffalo hunt, and stole a number of Pawnee horses. When they brought the animals to the Oto village the chief became infuriated. He told the men that, since they seemed to wish to have war with the Pawnees, he would see that they had their desire. He then mounted his horse, rode up the Platte to the Pawnee village, and set it ablaze. The Pawnees were away on their hunt for two or three months. When they returned and found the village burned down they knew that the Otos had done this, and they prepared for war; but in the meantime the Otos had prepared to purchase peace, accumulating large supplies of guns and other gifts, with which to placate the Grand Pawnee chiefs, and inducing the white traders to speak to the Pawnees for them. The trouble was therefore settled, but the Pawnees did not rebuild the burned village.

As we have seen, the Skidis apparently had been forced to remove from Loup Fork because of the attacks the Omaha tribe had made on them, but the Omaha power had been destroyed by smallpox, about the year 1802, and the Skidis soon after that date returned to their old country on the Loup. This they did at about the time when the Grand Pawnee village at Cedar Bluff was burned by the Otos; and the Grand Pawnees now followed the Skidi movement westward, building a village on the south side of the Platte, about six miles east of the mouth of the Loup. The new village was very close to the one near Linwood, which the Grand Pawnees and Pitahauerats had built about the year 1776, but the village of 1806 was on high ground. Here the Grand Pawnees and Pitahauerats lived until 1809.

It must be admitted that, for such a powerful tribe, the Pawnee activities in Nebraska, from about 1772 to 1806, are not very impressive. They did not assert themselves; they were not united, and the Grand Pawnees looked on without taking any action while the Omahas and Poncas attacked the Skidis and Kitkehahkis. The fact seems to be that the Grand Pawnees were not much interested in the course of events in Nebraska, all their important activities centering in the plains to the southward, where their war parties went as far as New Mexico and northern Texas. Unfortunately we have no details of these activities in the southern plains, as the Pawnees are rarely referred to in the scanty Spanish records; but we do know that the tribe was warring on the Comanches and their allies, and that every year they brought surprising numbers of horses and mules back to their village on the Platte, many of these animals having Spanish brands. Occasionally they brought home large quantities of Spanish goods, including silver coin and gaudy Mexican blankets—the spoil taken from some captured Spanish caravan. The extent of these southern operations was illustrated by the fact that the Pawnees, more than any other northern tribe, were strongly inclined to imitate the Spaniards of the Southwest. Many of the warriors had Spanish saddles, bits, bridles, and huge Spanish spurs, and the Pawnee chiefs had picked up that Spanish practice of preferring fine mules (not for war or hunting, but for riding on a journey).

NOTES TO CHAPTER IV

[47]Pike, Coues edition, v. II, p. 223, p. 300.

[48]*Illinois Historical Collections*, v. XI, p. 146, p. 228, p. 300.

[49]Bolton: *A. de Mezières*, v. II, p. 88; Thomas: *Plains Indians & New Mexico*, p. 38.

[50]*Missouri Historical Review*, April, 1930.

[51]Bolton: *A. de Mezières*.

[52]Spanish document of 1777 in *Wisconsin Historical Collections*, v. XVIII, p. 260.

[53]Captain L. H. North informed me that the oldest Pawnees at the date 1860-65 could still name the principal actors in this fight between the Pawnees and Skidis. They said that twenty to thirty Grand Pawnees were killed in the Prairie Creek fray; but a few years later, when the old men were dead, the Pawnees said one hundred were killed. Thus the story shifted from history to tradition.

[54]Houck: *Spanish Regime in Missouri*, v. I, p. 143; Cruzat, quoted in *Wisconsin Historical Collections*, v. XVIII, p. 412.

[55]The archeologists have not found the Pawnee village ruins at Savannah; but when John Dunbar came up the Platte with the Pawnees in 1834 he observed the village ruins clearly indicated at the Savannah and Linwood locations, and also at a third spot, on the south bank of the Platte about opposite the mouth of Loup Fork. Robert Stuart's party of Astorians, on their way down the Platte, in 1813, noted a Grand Pawnee village ruin in this district, on high ground, about six miles below the mouth of the Loup, and stated that this village was occupied until 1809. This last ruin does not seem to have been noted by archeologists.

[56]In Fletcher and LaFlesche's history of the Omaha tribe there is a map which shows the locations of these battles between the Omahas and Skidis, all in the country north of Loup Fork. The true character of this fighting is indicated by the statement of Edwin James that in 1799 the Omahas surprised the Skidis while hunting buffalo north of the Loup and killed sixty of them. This was always the method of the enemies of the Pawnees: to conceal a big party of mounted warriors, to wait until the Pawnee men were scattered over the prairie, pursuing the buffalo, and then to charge and drive the Pawnees in confusion back to their hunting camp, killing large numbers of them.

[57]This is the Edwin James version, written in 1819. The Omaha traditional account, set down some fifty years later, agrees in substance, but has been softened down by the missionary unwillingness to call a spade a spade.

[58]Lewis and Clark seem to have the wrong date for this epidemic. It broke out among the Tawehash Pawnees on Red River in 1801 and it spread from tribe to tribe, clear up into North Dakota.

V

Sharitarish the Angry Chief

BOTH DUNBAR AND GRINNELL STATE THAT THE PAWNEES SPENT MUCH
of their time at a very early period in making raids into New Mexico;
but the barrenness of the Spanish records of any references to such
raids, down to the last decades of the 18th century, cast doubt on these
assertions. The very early period should mean 1550 to 1700, and during that time the Pawnees are hardly mentioned in New Mexico,
except as slaves brought in and offered for sale by the Apaches and
Navahos. Until after 1750 the Pawnees were to the officials and
people in New Mexico a very distant tribe, beyond the great plains
toward the east, of whom the Apaches occasionally brought in some
vague report. Even after 1750 the great numbers of horses and mules,
many with Spanish brands, which the Pawnees brought to their villages in Nebraska, and the quantities of Spanish articles which they
also obtained, were not taken during raids into New Mexico, but
were the fruit of trading or raiding expeditions in the Indian country
east of New Mexico.

It must be admitted that we know very little of a definite nature
concerning the activities of the Pawnees in the southwest plains until
after 1830; yet the tribe spent more than half its time in those plains.
Their permanent earth-lodge villages on the Platte were deserted most
of the time. In the spring the women cleared, dug, and planted their
little gardens, and the people remained at home long enough to give
their corn one hoeing; then the entire tribe set out for the buffalo
plains, in June or July. They hunted buffalo, moving their camp
every day or two, always farther and farther toward the west and
south. In August or early September they came home to their villages
with great quantities of dried buffalo meat, tallow, dressed hides, and
other product of the chase; and generally they also brought many
new horses and mules and quantities of Spanish articles. They then
harvested and dried their crops, and after depositing a large part of

Indian corn braided for storage (courtesy of George F. Will) and gardening tools, digging stick, willow rake, iron hoe, antler rake (courtesy Montana Experiment Station)

the corn, dried pumpkin, and beans in carefully-built pits called
caches, they deserted their villages and again vanished into the mysterious silence of the plains, to spend the autumn and most of the winter
hunting and raiding. Until after 1830 they never took with them into
the plains a white man who kept a record of their doings; and except
for a few brief Pawnee statements and a rare reference in the Spanish
documents, we have nothing to indicate the exact nature of the tribe's
operations in the plains.

Until late in the 19th century the Skidi Pawnees—treated by the
other three Pawnee tribes almost like aliens—hunted by themselves,
to the west or north of their village; yet the Skidis sent war parties as
far south as Red River. The other three tribes always operated as a
separate group, a group that evidently claimed the hunting grounds
south of the Platte as their own country, from which they did their
best to exclude all other tribes. Their advance north to the Platte had
been brought about mainly by their desire for a regular trade with
the whites and with the tribes in east Nebraska; but they were still
southern Indians whose real interests were on the Arkansas River and
in the plains farther toward the south.

When they left their earth-lodge villages on the Platte in June or
July they struck south toward the Republican and then turned westward up that stream, hastening forward in anxious quest of the
buffalo herds; for at the beginning of the summer hunt they generally
had no food except a small supply of last year's corn. There were
good seasons and bad ones. Some years they set out from their villages
with no food and in a condition of semi-starvation, keeping themselves
alive by digging and devouring wild roots and hunting small game
until they came into the eastern edge of the buffalo herds.

This great throng of Indians, with their thousands of horses and
mules and their packs of wolfish dogs, moved across country in parallel
columns, leaving a wide trail of trodden grass and dropped articles in
their rear. Miles ahead, or out on the flanks of the marching columns,
groups of scouts were scanning the country for signs of game or indications of the presence of enemies. The grand chief of the Grand
Pawnees was in control, marching at the head of the central column,
surrounded by his priests and subordinate chiefs. The make-up of
the columns seems to have varied from year to year; for these Pawnees often quarreled, and old alliances were broken up that new ones
might be formed. In 1835 the center column was made up of part of
the Grand Pawnees headed by the grand chief, the left column
was a second division of Grand Pawnees and all of the Pitahauerats,

while the right column was formed of Kitkehahkis alone. When they camped at night the Kitkehahki camp was always to the west, the Grand Pawnees headed by the grand chief camped in the center, while the second division of Grand Pawnees and the Pitahauerats camped farthest toward the east. In 1835 they had some 4,000 people in these camps, in about 600 buffalo-skin lodges, with thousands of horses and mules, and some 7,000 half-wild dogs. By day, and more particularly by night, the noise that this congregation of Pawnees, horses, mules, and wild dogs made was prodigious. All day long and on into the small hours of the night the men were talking, shouting, singing war-songs, while the women's shrill voices never ceased. Babies and small children that were ill wailed and screamed; babies and small children that were just spoiled and cranky yelled for anything they wanted, and kept on yelling until their mothers came and filled their needs; horses neighed, mules brayed; and at night the thousands of dogs, half wolf and half cur, assembled in packs and howled at the moon. It was claimed in the 19th century that the Pitahauerats were called Tappage or Noisy Pawnees by the early French traders; but why should they have been singled out, when all the Pawnees habitually produced all the noise that human lungs could develop? On a still night you could hear the roar of the Pawnee camp miles away across the lonesome plains; and it is little wonder that enemy war parties frequently found the camp at night, slipped into its very center, cut loose the best of the horses, and made their escape. The only guard consisted of little groups of young men, who at night went out from the camp in every direction and lay down on the grass, to talk, to sing war-songs, and to sleep. They were not ordered to do this; it was simply an age-old custom for young men to sleep away from the camp; and as guards they were not particularly useful. If an enemy party approached and was discovered, it was more of an accident than an expected result.

While in the plains the Pawnees usually broke camp about four in the morning. They ate no breakfast, fasting until the noon halt. The march was directed by the grand chief who rode at the head of the column; and it was he who selected the camping places. They usually marched twelve miles before the noon halt, sometimes as much as fifteen miles. Camp was not set up at noon; the people simply halted to rest and eat; then in the afternoon they made a shorter march, usually about eight miles. The marches were irregular in length, as it was necessary to bring the people at the end of the day's journey to a camp where good water and wood were available. The great chief was constantly consulting the priests, and if those worthies decided that the omens were adverse, the entire tribe might be kept in camp for two or three days at a time. It was the same in hunting buffalo. With herds of these animals in sight of the camp, the Pawnees often had to sit idle, because the priests insisted that the gods or spirits were not in a good humor.

The buffalo-skin lodges of these three southern Pawnee tribes were utterly different from the tipis used by the other plains Indians. The Honorable Charles A. Murray, who accompanied the Pawnees on their summer hunt in 1835, lived in one of these skin lodges for weeks and has left a detailed description of this type of dwelling. On reaching the camp-ground, the women unpacked and unsaddled the horses and a young boy took the animals away, to water them and let them graze. The women then arranged all the baggage, rawhide cases, saddles, and the rest, in the form of a semicircle, the open side facing due east. This wall of baggage was two to three feet high, and on its open side four straight poles were driven into the ground in a row. A number of curved willow poles were next inserted in the ground behind the wall of baggage, the poles spaced about three feet apart and all bent forward and bound with leather thongs to willow rods which were tied along the tops of the poles at the front of the lodge. A lodge-cover made of dressed buffalo-skins sewed together was now fitted over the frame of poles, forming a lodge in the shape of a quartered sphere, the flat side, facing east, having a doorway in its center; but in fine weather the whole east or flat side of the dwelling was left open. Some of these curious lodges had additional straight poles driven into the ground on the east side, over which skin covers were spread, to form a flat awning under which the people could sit or work in the shade on hot summer days. The place of honor at the center of the west wall of the lodge, facing the door, was where the buffalo robe of the head of the family was spread; there he sat, ate, and slept, his gun, bow, quiver, and other weapons hanging from the tent pole above his head, his saddle, bridle, and other belongings piled against the wall of baggage at his back. The other members of the family sat or slept on buffalo robes ranged around the back wall of the lodge, their positions carefully arranged in order of their rank. At the front of the lodge of every chief or important man stood a tripod of poles on which the lodge-owner's shield was hung; as each shield had its own device painted on it, even a stranger among the Pawnees soon learned to find his way about the camp by looking at the shields. Samuel Allis, the missionary, who lived among the Pawnees for many years after 1830, stated that they were divided into clans, and that you could tell to what clan a man belonged either by his name or "paintings." One family painted a bear on its tipi, another an eagle; and Allis mentioned particularly as Pawnee clans the Buffalo, Elk, Deer, Bear, Wolf, Beaver, Otter, Eagle, Owl, and Hawk. Mr. Dunbar, the other Pawnee missionary, bore out these assertions, stating that each Pawnee band and family had its mark, such as Bear, Beaver, Sun, and not only the tipis but other articles of property were painted with the family mark. The French explorer La Harpe found in 1719 that in the Caddoan villages in Oklahoma the head of each family had his "coat-of-arms" painted on a sheet of leather and hung up over the door of his big grass-lodge.

The buffalo hunt was to the Pawnees a means of life, and also a passionate pleasure. As the very life of the tribe depended on success-ful hunts, there were innumerable rules which were enforced by warriors who were selected by the chief to police the camp and the moving columns of Indians. Herds of buffalo were at times encoun-tered while the camp was on the march, and an immediate hunt was organized; but the strictly-controlled communal hunts took place when the people were in camp, when the scouts reported the location of large herds of buffalo, and when the priests decided that the gods were propitious. On such a hunt the men moved from the camp in a column with warriors serving as police keeping every man in his place. The chiefs and priests led the march, making occasional halts to confer. At the conclusion of such a halt, a crier came back along the column, shouting out the decision that had been made. Every hunter who could afford one had a special hunting pony, which was usually led by a youth of the class Grinnell termed the servants. Only when the signal to attack the herd was about to be given did the hunter mount his buffalo pony, handing over to his servant the horse he had ridden. When the signal was given the hunters charged the herd, usually from several directions at once, to prevent the huge animals from getting away. Like all the other plains Indians, the Pawnees preferred the bow for hunting buffalo. This was not sur-prising, considering that the guns the early traders supplied them with were in general little more than a very poor grade of light fowlingpiece. When the hunt was over the men and the youths who acted as servants skinned the buffalos and cut up the meat, which they loaded on the backs of the horses and took to camp. The women then set to work cutting part of the meat into thin sheets, which were hung up to dry. After a good kill the camp remained where it was for two or more days, waiting for the meat to dry sufficiently so that it could be packed in the rawhide cases in which it was to be carried.

On these buffalo hunts the Pawnees followed a regular beat: west up the Republican Fork, going on until they came to the district in the high plains where there was no wood and little water. They then struck southward to the head of the Saline Fork of Kansas River and on across the Smoky Hill Fork to the divide between that stream and the Arkansas River. Here they often waited in camp for the return of their war parties or trading parties that had gone south of the Arkansas to obtain fresh supplies of horses and mules. In early times, as they informed Dunbar, the Pawnees frequented the district at the great bend of the Arkansas, where they have left their name at Pawnee Fork and Pawnee Rock. At times entire bands of Pawnees went south of the Arkansas, with their camps, women, and children, to obtain rock salt at the Grand Saline and Rock Saline. These places they had known from ancient days, when their villages had been on or near the Arkansas, in Oklahoma. The Grand Saline lay between the Nescatunga (the present Salt Fork of the Arkansas) and the Cimarron, in the present Alfalfa County, Oklahoma. It was later known as the great Salt Plain. The Rock Saline was about seventy-five miles northwest of the Grand Saline, and was a place of wonder, where the Pawnees went to worship. In early times this famous place was a level flat of hard red earth about five hundred acres in extent, surrounded by awesome cliffs of naked red clay and gypsum. The flat enclosure was divided into two unequal parts by a salt stream flowing from a spring that issued from the base of a towering hill. Other salt springs oozed their water over the flat to form layers of rock salt which in places were twenty inches thick. There was here an ancient red cedar tree, to which the Pawnees prayed and made sacrifices. Caddoan Indians from Red River, Pawnees from Nebraska, and occasionally even an Arikara from faraway Dakota, came to this place to pray and to gather lumps of rock salt to take home.

After 1820 the Pawnees rarely ventured to take their camps, with their women and children, south of the Arkansas. Instead—having finished their hunting—they often hovered for some days or weeks on the high divide between the Arkansas and Smoky Hill Fork, waiting for parties of their warriors to come in from the country father south; then the village marched east and north, crossing Kansas River above the mouth of the Republican Fork, and so on northward to their permanent villages in Nebraska.

The return from the summer hunt inaugurated what was usually the happiest season of the year for the Pawnee: harvest-time. If they came early from the hunting grounds there would be green corn waiting in the gardens; and even if they missed the green corn season, there would be, with luck, a plentiful supply of corn, vegetables, and even melons. To this supply of vegetable food they added the dried meat they had brought home in their rawhide packing-cases; feasting went on day and night in the villages. There was, too, that great festival, the Big-Sleight-of-Hand, lasting for twenty thrilling evenings, with all the great doctors and magicians performing the best of their new feats, to the accompaniment of singing and instrumental music.

This happy harvest season ended, the tribe put away in the village caches part of what remained of their food supply and set off into the plains for the autumn and winter hunt. It was during this hunt that they obtained the robes for which the traders were ready to give them European goods. The summer buffalo skins were of no value in trade, the fleece being of poor quality. The women shaved the hair off the skins, using part of them for making rawhide packing-cases and similar articles, while the rest were made into lodge-covers or cut into long strips, for the making of braided lariats. Winter robes had hair fine as fur, and the Pawnees kept part of them for personal wear, part for bedding; the surplus went to the white traders.

The tribe came home from the winter in the plains in early spring (in late February if the hunt had not been very successful, more often in March), bringing with them all the robes they had made and a new supply of meat. In good years they generally had enough food laid up to see them through the spring season, until their gardens were planted and they were ready to go off on another summer hunt. But there were bad years when hunts failed and crops were damaged or destroyed, leaving the people to endure long bouts of hunger and, at times, actual starvation. Despite the fact that these Pawnees spent at least eight months in every year wandering in the plains, they undoubtedly regarded their villages on the Platte as home and loved them. These villages, standing deserted the greater part of the time, were fixed points toward which the wanderers turned their thoughts. It was at the villages that all or nearly all of their most sacred rituals were performed and their great festivals were held; and there in the great earth-lodges rest, food, and comfort were waiting for everyone, particularly for the aged and the small children. Yet the business of wandering in the plains was the most important part of tribal life; for it was in the plains that the people obtained the great supplies of dried meat and skins which made life possible for them; and from these plains they brought back the fresh stocks of horses every year, to add to the tribal wealth and to its strength in war.

By 1750 there had been a notable shifting of tribes in the high plains, and by the time the three Pawnee tribes from the south had moved up into Nebraska, changing conditions had broken the old chain of Apache and Padouca tribes and replaced them by a new arrangement of Shoshonean tribes, extending from the plains of eastern Wyoming down through east Colorado and into west Oklahoma. First there were the Comanche bands or tribes. In the last decades of the 18th century the plains east of New Mexico were held by the Comanche division known as Kotsoteka (Buffalo Eaters); farther north, extending from the Arkansas River to or beyond the Platte, were the Kwahari (Antelope Eaters), the Yamparika (Yampa-root Eaters), and a group known to the Spaniards as the Yupini or People of the Pole; while in the Wyoming plains were the Gens du Serpent or Snakes, close relatives of the Comanches.

Few white men who kept records visited these Comanche and Snake tribes during the 18th century, and there is considerable doubt as to their exact location and identity. Thus the oldest people among the Cheyennes in 1910 believed that the Kwahari Comanches were the northern group, still lingering in the Black Hills region of Dakota about the date 1770; but the Comanche traditions place the Yamparikas in the north, in close contact with the Snakes. Here there must be an error; for a Yamparika chief visited at the Tawehash village on Red River in 1774. He said that his band had not seen a French trader in eight years; from this statement it would seem that the Yamparikas were one of those Comanche bands who lived in southeast Colorado, near the Arkansas River, and had trading relations with the French in the period up to 1766. Again, we cannot state surely whether the great Gens du Serpent tribe of the period 1740-70 were really Snakes or a northern division of the Comanches. The Serpents were mounted and armed in 1740 and were following the old Apache practice of sending out great parties of mounted warriors to destroy the camps of tribes in the Black Hills region, carrying their raids as far as the Arikara villages on the Missouri, and taking numerous captives, some of which they sold as slaves to the tribes on the New Mexican frontier.

From tradition it would seem that the Gens du Serpent had established themselves as far east as Old Woman's Fork, immediately south of the Black Hills; but they were then attacked by the Kiowas, Arikaras, Crows, and evidently by the Prairie-Apaches; by 1775 their power was gone and they had disappeared from their old haunts near the Black Hills. The tribe known in the plains as Snakes continued to rove north and south along the western border of the plains until as late as 1825. They had a large trade in horses and Spanish goods with the northern tribes. Larocque in 1805 found some of them with the Crows near the Yellowstone. British goods and guns were reaching the Mandans and other tribes on the Upper Missouri, and as these tribes greatly desired horses and Spanish goods, while the Snakes in the plains were anxious to obtain British guns, the intertribal trade was quite extensive. The Ietans were also engaged in trade. This mysterious group has been identified variously as a band of Utes, a division of the Comanches, or Snake Indians; but it now seems more probable that they were originally Apaches: perhaps that group of Padoucas who, as far back as 1680, were engaged in a trade with the Arikaras on the Missouri River. In the Spanish documents of New Mexico for the years after 1740 there are a number of references to the *A* or *Ae* tribe in the plains to the northeast. These Indians could not have been Comanches; for in the spring of 1749 a party of French traders left the Jumano village on the Arkansas and crossed the plains to a Comanche camp on the New Mexican frontier, where they found the Comanches preparing to attack the Ae tribe.[59] The true identity of the Aes is apparently disclosed by the passage in *An Account of Spanish Louisiana in 1785,* which reads: "One must note in passing that all the wealth of the Indians on the Missouri consists in having many horses which they get from the Laytanes or Apaches and from frequent raids that one nation makes on another." Here the Ietans are Apaches; and from this it would seem that a band of that tribe (Padoucas of the northern region) who had always been engaged in trade between the Missouri and the New Mexican frontier had continued that trade, despite the intrusion of the Comanches and Snakes into the plains after 1730. The Mallet brothers in 1739 found these Laytanes encamped on the Arkansas in east Colorado and saw an Arikara slave from Dakota among them. In 1752 a French trader reported in New Mexico that the Comanches had recently allied themselves with the Pawnees and also with the Ae tribe.[60] If the Aes were really Apaches, this is the only recorded instance of the Comanches being on friendly terms with any members of that tribe; but the Ietans are known to have lived with a band of Comanches (the *Têtes Pelés* or Baldheads) over a long period of years in the late 18th and early 19th century. Tabeau (c.1802) speaks of these trading Indians visiting the Arikaras, bringing horses and Spanish goods, which they obtained at San Antonio, evidently the Spanish town of that name in Texas. Curiously, he states that the article these Indians valued most and were most eager to trade for was the Arikara native tobacco. Here we may have a clue as to why part of the Padoucas were trading horses to the Arikaras as far back as 1680. It was the tobacco raised by the Arikaras that they were anxious to obtain and which they probably traded to Padouca tribes farther south for fresh supplies of horses and Spanish goods. The Apaches were driven from east Colorado and the plains east of New Mexico by the Comanches after 1730; but we have no proof that the Apache or Padouca groups farther north, in northeast Colorado and west Nebraska, made a general withdrawal southward. Indeed, some of these Padoucas seem to have lingered in the north as late as the close of the 18th century. In *An Account of Spanish Louisiana in 1785,* we are informed that a branch of Loup Fork was still known in 1785 as the River of the Padoucas, and it was here, on the Dismal Fork of the Loup, that in recent years Mr. A. T. Hill and other archeologists discovered quite extensive remains of Indian villages which they have termed Padouca. The same account of Louisiana in 1785 refers to Padouca forts (probably only camps) on Bad River, the stream that flows from near the Black Hills east and empties into the Missouri opposite the city of Pierre, South Dakota. When the Omahas and Poncas moved down the Missouri into northeast Nebraska after 1750 they were at once raided by the Padoucas, coming from what the Omahas termed a fort in the sand hills region of west Nebraska. The Poncas had a war with these Padoucas, and when James Mackay, the trader, came up the Missouri in 1795 he went on a hunt into west Nebraska with the Omahas and marked on his map a Padouca fort on a branch of Loup Fork. The fine Collot map of 1796 sets down Padouca settlements on both banks of the South Platte, in northeast Colorado, and even after 1800 this branch of the Platte was called by the fur traders Padouca Fork. One suspects that the Comanche and Snake occupation of the plains was mainly along their western border, near the mountains, and that the Padoucas in scattered locations continued to camp and rove from the South Platte up through the sand hills of west Nebraska, to near the Missouri in South Dakota, where (under the name of Gatackas or Prairie-Apaches) they were allied with the Arikaras and Kiowas against the Snakes.

The part the Pawnees played in plains activities in the 18th century is obscured by our almost total lack of information. In 1752 they were reported to be in alliance with the Comanches; but after that year they vanished from the Spanish records of New Mexico until 1786, when Anza made peace between the Comanches and Utes, and it was suggested that the Spanish officials in Louisiana (at St. Louis) should be urged to make a similar peace between the Comanches and Pawnees. This indicates that the alliance between the two tribes, made in 1752, had been the usual Indian peace, lasting for a season or two, and that in 1786 a war between these tribes was well enough known for the officials in New Mexico to be concerned and to desire an end to hostilities. At this time (1786) the Comanche chief Toro Blanco (White Bull) bitterly opposed peace with the Spaniards; but he was murdered by the faction that favored peace. His band then split to pieces, his immediate family going off alone in a small camp of their own; presently it was reported that they had all been killed in an attack on their camp "by the Pawnees and other pagans."[61]

The Pawnees who lived nearest to New Mexico were the Kitkehahkis, whose village from about 1775 until after 1800 was usually on the Republican Fork. In 1792 the officials in New Mexico sent a Frenchman named Vial to explore a route from Santa Fé to the Spanish town of St. Louis at the mouth of the Missouri. After being in New Mexico for over two centuries, the best instructions the Spaniards could give Vial were that he should proceed to the *Magages* Indians and then turn northeast and head toward *Los Ylinneses*; or, in simple English, he was to find the Kitkehahki Pawnees (called Maniguacci in *An Account of Spanish Louisiana in 1785*) and then head for the Illinois country. Employing his Frenchman's sense of direction, Vial seems to have followed the route later known as the Santa Fé Trail as far as the great bend of the Arkansas; but there he and his two companions fell into the hands of the Guachaches (clearly a band of Pawnees or *Ouaches,* the old name for the northern Pawnees). They held Vial and his companions until the middle of August, then set them adrift in the trackless plains, naked and without arms. By great good fortune the white men found their way to a Kansa hunting camp, where French traders provided them with all they needed and put them on the right trail for St. Louis.[62]

Even before the Louisiana purchase the Spanish officials at St. Louis and Baton Rouge were becoming uneasy at the activities of American agents in the West. An attempt to penetrate to New Mexico was feared, for the Americans were at work questioning Indian traders, hunters, and anyone else who knew the plains country and its tribes. They seemed to be particularly eager to get in touch with men who knew the Pawnees and had some influence with the chiefs of that tribe. The Spaniards were reminded of conditions in 1700-1720, when the French had attempted to penetrate to New Mexico by making use of the Pawnees and Padoucas, and of their own counter action of sending the Villasur expedition to make an alliance with the Pawnees against the French: a venture that had led to disaster. Some similar action now seemed necessary, and about the year 1802 (evidently through their agents at St. Louis) the Spaniards got in touch with Joseph Gervais, a trader among the Pawnees on the Platte, who was reputed to know the plains and the plains Indians better than any other man.

In 1803 Gervais turned up at Santa Fé with a party of Pawnees, and some arrangement for these Indians to come regularly to trade in New Mexico seems to have been made, for in the following spring, 1804, Gervais and his Pawnees paid a second visit to the Spanish settlements. But Gervais now seems to have gone over to the American interest, for on August 10, 1804, Colonel Charles de Lassus, former Lieutenant-Governor of Spanish Upper Louisiana, wrote to warn Casa-Calvo that two French traders, Jeannot Metoyer and Baptiste Labarde (the LaLande of Lieutenant Zebulon Pike's journals?) had gone up the Missouri with merchandise in boats, intending to meet Gervais and accompany him and his Indians to New Mexico. De Lassus stated that the Americans were filling the towns along the Mississippi with great stocks of fine merchandise, that they were intent on driving a trade through to New Mexico, and that if the Spanish officials at Santa Fé were not awakened, boatloads of Spanish silver dollars, instead of loads of furs, would be coming down the Missouri to St. Louis.

The officials at Santa Fé had already been aroused, however; for all unheralded two French traders, LaLande and Durocher, had appeared with a band of plains Indians, possibly Pawnees; and soon afterward James Pursley and two Frenchmen from the upper Missouri arrived in New Mexico, having come down from the Platte with the trading Ietans. These men were arrested, and the alarmed officials ordered a military force to proceed to the Pawnee villages in the fall of 1804, to make an alliance with that tribe. With their usual bad luck, the Spanish troops became embroiled with a large force of Indians on the Arkansas River, were defeated, and had to return home without visiting the Pawnees.[63]

Louisiana was now in the hands of the Americans, and that archplotter, General James Wilkinson, was at St. Louis, laying secret plans for an invasion of New Mexico. Within a few months he had gathered more accurate information on the plains and plains tribes than the Spaniards had obtained in two centuries. Informed by veteran French traders that he could accomplish little against New Mexico without first winning over the Comanches, and that the best method for reaching that tribe was through the Pawnees, Wilkinson prepared to send Lieutenant Zebulon M. Pike to visit both of these tribes; at the same time he dispatched a party to build a post at the mouth of the Platte and get in touch with the Pawnees; but after proceeding up the Missouri for three hundred miles this expedition had a fight with Indians and had to turn back.[64]

Thus the Pawnees, without knowing anything about it, had become suddenly very important in the view of many white men at St. Louis and Santa Fé, who were busily at work hatching plots and counterplots. In 1805 the Spaniards sent another expedition to find the tribe, the results not being known, unless Pike recorded them in his confused account of the expedition of 1806. He seems to be speaking of two expeditions, one that went to the Skidi Pawnees, and the expedition of 1806 to the Kitkehahkis. Referring to the Spanish visit to the Skidis, he states that this tribe was met while on its semi-annual buffalo hunt; the Spaniards camped near the Indians, a peace was made, and then in the night the Skidis took down their camp and slipped away, their young men at the same time stealing most of the Spanish horse herd. Since in other reports Pike indicates that in 1806 the Spaniards visited only the Kitkehahkis, it would seem that the affair with the Skidis was in 1805.

In the summer of 1806, according to Pike, Lieutenant Don Fecundo Malgares set out from Santa Fé with one hundred regular troops, five hundred mounted militia, 2,075 animals, and ammunition and supplies for a six months' expedition. His orders were to visit all of the Pawnee tribes, and also the Otos, Kansa, and Omahas; to make peace with them, distribute gifts, Spanish medals and flags, and to attempt to form an alliance with these Indians. Malgares marched 233 leagues to Rio Rojo (the Cimarron?) where he met the "grand bands of the Ietans." Here Pike meant the Comanches. After councils with the chiefs, Malgares marched up to the great bend of the Arkansas, where he left part of his men and animals in a strong camp on the south bank. He later informed Lieutenant Pike that he left half his force at this camp because the horses were tired and some of them lame; but Pike was of the opinion that the Spanish officer had a plan to attack the Skidi Pawnees and avenge the death of *Villineuve*. Taking into account Lieutenant Pike's inability to get any Spanish name correctly, we here must have a memory of the Villasur defeat at the hands of the Skidis in 1720. Pike states that the Pawnees remembered the killing of Villineuve and were filled with guilty suspicion that the Spaniards were now seeking vengeance.

From the Arkansas Malgares marched north to the Kitkehahki village on the south bank of the Republican, between the present towns of Red Cloud and Guide Rock, Nebraska.[65] The chiefs of the

Grand Pawnees had come from the Platte to meet the Spaniards. In a great council Malgares presented Spanish medals, flags, and commissions to the chiefs; he then proposed a joint expedition against the Skidi Pawnees; but although the Kitkehahkis were at war with that tribe and the Grand Pawnees felt none too friendly toward them, the chiefs refused to join forces with Malgares. Their attitude hastened his departure; for, instead of going on, as his instructions required, to visit the Kansa, Otos, and other tribes, he now hastily withdrew to his camp south of the Arkansas.

Shortly after Malgares had left the Pawnee village, Lieutenant Z. M. Pike arrived with a score of soldiers of the First Infantry, coming from the Osage villages. Having succeeded in frightening the Spaniards, the Pawnees now attempted to do the same for the Americans, but they failed. The display of three hundred mounted warriors made no impression on Pike; and he and his handful of infantry promptly resisted every attempt the Pawnees made to rob or intimidate them.

Sharitarish or White Wolf, also called Angry Chief, was the head-chief of the Kitkehahkis in 1806. He was a Grand Pawnee, but had come to the Republican village some years back and thrust aside the Kitkehahki chief. Sharitarish had a small General Washington medal and a much larger Spanish one. The second chief, Iskatappe or Rich Man, was apparently also a Grand Pawnee. He refused to accept a small American medal from Pike on the grounds that two young Pawnees who had been to Washington and had returned with Pike's party had been given large American medals. This chief was very angry that he should be offered a small medal when these boys, who were of no importance in the tribe, had received large ones. Since a Spanish report from St. Louis in 1777 stated that *Escatape* was chief of the Kitkehahkis, Lieutenant Pike's Iskatappe would seem to be the chief he referred to when he stated that, some years prior to 1806, this chief and the chief of the Grand Pawnees had a violent quarrel at the Pawnee villages on the Platte, and that the Kitkehahki chief then led part of the Indians to the Republican Fork, to build the village they still occupied in 1806. After this separation of the bands, Sharitarish and his family of Grand Pawnees had come to the Kitkehahki village and had pushed Iskatappe out of power.

In the autumn of 1806 this Kitkehahki chief was sullenly awaiting the opportunity to regain his independence. The fourth chief in the village was American Chief (*Lachikuts Lasharo*).

Whether Sharitarish belonged to the family of hereditary Grand

Pawnee chiefs or not we do not know. He is the first recorded chief
of the name, said to have been father and grandfather of later chiefs
of the same name. It seems extraordinary that the Pawnees should
retain no memory of these once famous chiefs; but today the best
information one can obtain from the tribe is to the effect that this
name was claimed by a family descended from a chief who bore it.
They explain the name as an abbreviation of *lesharo* (*chief*) and
charish (*angry* or *cross*) which would make the name *'Sharo-Charish*.
Murray (1835) translated the name as meaning Wicked Chief.

In McKenney and Hall, *History of the Indian Tribes of North
America,* it is stated that this first Sharitarish had three sons who one
after the other succeeded him as head-chief of the Grand Pawnees;
an assertion that disregards the fact that the Pawnees counted descent
in the female line and that, theoretically at least, a chief's son could
not succeed him as chief. This statement in McKenney and Hall
(added by an editor of a reprint edition) names Sharitarish's sons
as Long Hair, Sharitarish, and Iskatappe, and records that the first
Sharitarish died prior to 1819, Long Hair in 1822, and the younger
Sharitarish in the autumn of the same year. These statements have
been accepted and repeated by the few men who have dealt with
Pawnee history; yet the facts alleged have never been verified, and
there is reason for doubting the truth of at least part of them. Long
Hair was the bitter enemy of both Sharitarish I and Sharitarish II,
the latter chief once challenging Long Hair to a duel and treating
him with the greatest contempt when he refused to fight. It is true,
however, that Sharitarish II and Iskatappe were brothers, who in
turn succeeded Long Hair as head-chief of the Grand Pawnees.[66]

The first Sharitarish and Long Hair seem to have been engaged
in a struggle that involved the leadership of the Grand Pawnees
from before 1805 until the older chief's death before 1819; and from
that year onward the son of Sharitarish, who bore his father's name,
continued this struggle. We cannot judge just what the situation
was; but the removal of the Kitkehahkis from the Platte to the
Republican Fork had something to do with it, and Sharitarish in
1806 was living in the Republican village because his family interests
could best be served there. He needed the support of the Kitkehahki
tribe to enable him to control the Grand Pawnees, and he probably
was working to induce this tribe to move back to the Platte, to
reinforce his faction in the Grand Pawnee village, which was not
strong enough to oppose Long Hair. Which of these men, Sharitarish
or Long Hair, was hereditary chief of the Grand Pawnees, we will
probably never know. One suspects that this almost-sacred position

belonged to Long Hair. He seems to have been a weak, vacillating man. Sharitarish, on the other hand, had the strong, decisive characteristics of a self-made man. In 1806 Lieutenant Pike called him White Wolf or Angry Man. Now, White Wolf was not so much a chief's name as a rank of military honor among the Pawnees. The name refers to the mythical white wolf that was the symbol of war, and this name was conferred, like knighthood, on the field after a victory. Some leader had distinguished himself; a council was held after the battle, and the name White Wolf was given to the distinguished warrior. Major Frank North was given this name of honor by the Pawnee Scouts after a victory over the Cheyennes in 1865.

In 1806 the Kitkehahkis had made peace with the Kansa tribe to the east of their village and were trading with them. The other Pawnees on the Platte traded with Frenchmen from St. Louis, but about once in three years made a trip to the southwest to trade with the Spaniards. The Pawnees had one gun to each two warriors and, as Pike noted, they generally went to war on foot, intending to ride home on stolen horses.

Pike's instructions from General Wilkinson were to employ the Kitkehahki Pawnees in opening friendly relations with the Comanches; but on reaching the Pawnee village the lieutenant was informed that the Comanches had recently killed some Pawnees, and the two tribes were at war. Later, on his way up the Arkansas, Pike encountered a war party of sixty Grand Pawnees returning northward from an unsuccessful attempt to steal horses from the Comanches. The Indians, all on foot, made a bold attempt to rob Pike's party; but the grim faces and prompt action of Pike and his men deterred them. Pike observed that the Comanches had very few firearms, which placed them at a marked disadvantage in their frequent fights with the Pawnees.

In 1807 the Spanish authorities continued their efforts to win over Sharitarish, sending messages to him both from Santa Fé and from the Spanish post at Baton Rouge on the Mississippi.[67] These efforts of the Spanish and American agents to gain his goodwill, must have impressed the Pawnee chief strongly; but he was probably much less interested in the maneuvering of these white men than in his own efforts to gain control in the Grand Pawnee village. The ignoring of Long Hair, then head-chief of the Grand Pawnees, by the white officials seems to have encouraged Sharitarish to act with increasing boldness and to pose as the big man among the Pawnees; but his attempts to impress his tribesmen led him into the error of quarreling with the Kansa tribe. In 1809 they defeated him, and he was compelled to abandon the village on the Republican Fork and retire to the Platte with his mixed following of Kitkehahkis and Grand Pawnees.[68]

As we have seen, at about the date 1802 the Skidis had a village on Shell Creek and the Grand Pawnees were at Cedar Hills, south of the Platte and a little east of the Skidis. About 1804 the Skidis returned to their old home on Loup Fork, and the Grand Pawnees followed suit by removing farther up the Platte and building a village on the south bank, east of Bellwood and about seven miles west of the present town of Edholm—a good point from which to watch the Skidis and cut off white trade with that tribe. The bad feeling between these Pawnee tribes had now increased, for the Skidis were openly at war with the Kitkehahkis on the Republican and were raiding the Spanish settlements, at the very moment when the Grand Pawnee and Kitkehahki chiefs wished to be on good terms with the Spaniards. At this time the Poncas, smarting from the defeat they had suffered when they had attempted to attack the Skidi village on Shell Creek by treachery, came down from the north and again asked Long Hair's permission to attack the Skidi village. The Grand Pawnee chief not only gave his consent, he also mustered all his warriors and marched against the Skidi village. Young Pitalesharo, the son of the Skidi chief, came out with his men to meet the enemy, but found that he was hopelessly outnumbered. He boldly advanced alone and defied Long Hair to single combat, which the older man curtly refused. Knife Chief, the Skidi head-chief, then came forward and by diplomatic negotiations settled the trouble amicably.[69]

The appearance of Sharitarish and his followers at the Grand Pawnee village on the Platte in 1809 apparently precipitated the quarrel between this chief and Long Hair. In the *Missouri Gazette* for April 25, 1811, there is an article describing the Pawnee villages which appears to refer to conditions in 1809. In this article the Grand Pawnees and Otos (seemingly an error for Grand Pawnees and Kitkehahkis) are placed in a village on the south bank of the Platte, east of Bellwood, while the Skidis *and Pawnees* are located in a village far up Loup Fork. This is a curious situation; and one suspects that it represents the result of the return of Sharitarish: that when he brought the Kitkehahkis to the Grand Pawnee village there was a quarrel, and that Long Hair and his faction moved to Loup Fork and joined the Skidis. Such a view is supported by the journal of Robert Stuart, which states that in the spring of 1813 Long Hair was chief of the Grand Pawnee village, which was on Loup Fork at the mouth of Cornfield Creek, a small stream about twelve miles west of the modern Cedar River. One league or about two and one-half miles farther up the Loup was the Skidi village, in which Knife Chief was still the principal man. Stuart passed the village on the south bank of the Platte, east of Bellwood, and found it deserted.[70]

In the spring of 1811 Major G. C. Sibley, the son of Dr. John Sibley of Natchitoches in Louisiana, left Fort Osage on the Missouri for an official visit to the tribes in Kansas and Nebraska. He reached the Grand Pawnee village May 28, finding that these Indians had recently removed from their old location on the Platte to a point on the north bank of the Loup, ten miles east of the Skidis. The Indians had built 170 earth-lodges, but part of the families had recently come from the Platte, crowding the lodges, and the chief stated that the number of lodges would have to be doubled to accommodate all of the people. Long Hair, the Grand Pawnee chief of 1809, had gone, and Sharitarish was chief in this village, which contained people of three Pawnee tribes: Chauis, Kitkehahkis, and Pitahauerats. Long Hair was clearly with the Skidis, who were not visited by Sibley, for this chief later returned to the Grand Pawnee village and became again head-chief, after Sharitarish had died.

The location of the Sibley Pawnee villages of 1811 is still an unsolved problem. The archeologists have suggested that the Sharitarish village, occupied by three tribes, is the ruined village on Horse Creek; and if this is correct the Skidi village of Sibley's day may be the ruin east of the town of Cushing which was discovered by Captain L. H. North about 1870. Captain North stated that this ruin contained more lodges than were occupied by the entire Pawnee tribe of 1870. The Omaha tribe used to call Cottonwood Creek, near Captain North's Skidi ruin, *Skidi Village* (*Stream*), and they called Horse Creek, where the archeologists wish to locate the 1811 village, *Little Pawnee Village* (*Stream*); but this does not describe the situation found by Sibley; for the village here was a large one, 170 lodges, and the chief stated that when completed the village would be much larger. The most significant point is that Sibley found three Pawnee tribes crowded into this new village and stated that two of these tribes (clearly the Kitkehahkis and Sharitarish's band of Grand Pawnees) had recently moved up here from the Republican Fork.

Thus by 1811 Sharitarish had made himself the head of three Pawnee tribes. He had won the power he had toiled and schemed for years to gain, and he evidently believed that he was now in a position to begin paying off old scores. The first of these scores was not an old one, for he and his followers were still hot with wrath over the Kansa tribe's attack on them, about 1809, which had forced them to abandon their village on Republican Fork and move north to the

Platte. Sharitarish now called all the warriors of the three Pawnee tribes to arms and set forth with a great mounted array to teach the Kansa a lesson. Early in the morning the Pawnees appeared at the Kansa village, near the mouth of the Big Blue, and began charging up and down, shooting and yelling. The Kansa warriors, though greatly outnumbered, wished to mount and charge the Pawnees; but their chief, Burning Heart, shouted for them to stay inside their earth-lodges and let the Pawnees use up their ammunition and tire their horses out. The Pawnees were at their worst on horseback in early days, for their chiefs had little comprehension of the proper way in which to make a mounted charge effective. The warriors simply rode furiously about, shooting at random and doing very little damage to the enemy. After this performance had gone on for a long time, the Kansa chief sent out two parties from either end of the village, the warriors crawling through ravines to positions in rear of the Pawnees. Suddenly assailed with deadly volleys from the rear, the Pawnees fled in panic, the Kansa warriors mounting and pressing them so hard that they had to take refuge in ravines, into which they jumped their tired horses. They soon found that they could neither defend the ravines nor get their horses out, and they had to abandon the animals and escape on foot. In this sorry affair the Pawnees had eighty warriors killed and lost nearly all of their horses. They evidently lost Sharitarish as well; for he does not appear again. This fight was evidently in 1812. In the spring of 1813 Robert Stuart's party came down the Platte, and Stuart noted in his journal that Long Hair was the head-chief of the Pawnee village on Loup Fork. This village he located about twelve miles west of the modern Cedar River, and he placed the Skidi village, with old Knife Chief still the principal man, one league or two to three miles west of Long Hair's village. Going on down the Platte, Stuart noted the deserted village in which the Grand Pawnees had lived in 1809, on the high southern bank of the river.

In the period 1806-1812 the Pawnees were constantly sending war parties south of the Arkansas, to steal horses from the Comanches. Sibley in 1811 reported that the Pawnees had incredible numbers of horses and mules, all stolen from the Ietans. Here the name Ietan is applied to all of the Comanches. The camp of trading Indians, to whom this name was at times specially applied, had been on the upper Platte in 1800-1804. It had then gone south to trade in New Mexico, but was ordered away by the Spanish officials and went on south, to trade on Red River. These Indians started for the upper Platte again in 1813, having in their camp a band of Ietans and a

band of Penateka Comanches called Baldheads from the name of
their chief. On reaching the North Platte they announced to the
northern tribes that they were going to hold a horse-fair at their camp
on a stream near the east line of Wyoming which is still called Horse
Creek. Here the northern Indians came to trade: Kiowas, Arapahoes,
Prairie-Apaches, Cheyennes, Crows, and a band of Teton Sioux.
Trade had hardly started when a Brulé Sioux quarreled with a Kiowa
and split his head open with a tomahawk. The Sioux then attacked
the Kiowas and their friends, broke up the fair, and drove all the
Indians into the mountains near the head of the Platte.

The trading Indians did not move south of the Arkansas again until about 1817, and when they went they took camps of Kiowas, Prairie-
Apaches, Arapahoes, and Cheyennes with them, thus familiarizing
these northern Indians with the country as far south as Texas.

During the period 1800-1835 the Skidi Pawnees hunted buffalo near
the forks of the Platte and often wintered in that district; yet in the
contemporary records and in traditions we find no references to contacts between the Skidis and the tribes in the plains whose movements
have just been described. It was during this period that the Sioux
began to penetrate the country south of White River and the Black
Hills, and the Sioux winter-counts contain some entries which seem
to refer to contacts with the Skidis. Thus in 1802-1803 the counts
record that horses with iron shoes were first stolen by the Sioux, and
it is difficult to see where they could have obtained shod animals unless it was from the Pawnees, who were stealing horses and mules in
New Mexico. In 1804-1805 the Brulé winter-count records that a war
party of Sioux set out, and somewhere while on their expedition
danced the Calumet, a Pawnee ceremony employed in making peace;
and here again there is a hint of contact with the latter tribe. Indeed,
the same Brulé count records that in the preceding year the Sioux
stole many horses from the Pawnees. In 1807-1808 Broken Leg, a
Sioux chief, was killed in a fight with Pawnees, and in 1811-1812 six
Sioux winter-counts record that the people first went to catch wild
horses with lassoes, some state in the sand hills north of the Platte,
others in the plains south of that river. As we have already noted,
the Brulés came to the trading-fair on the North Platte in 1813 and
broke it up. These meager reports in the winter-counts are all that
we have concerning the Sioux advance, which a generation later was
to prove such a terrible scourge to the Pawnee tribes.

In 1816 the Skidis captured an Ietan girl and decided to sacrifice
her to Morning Star. This dreadful rite was to be performed at

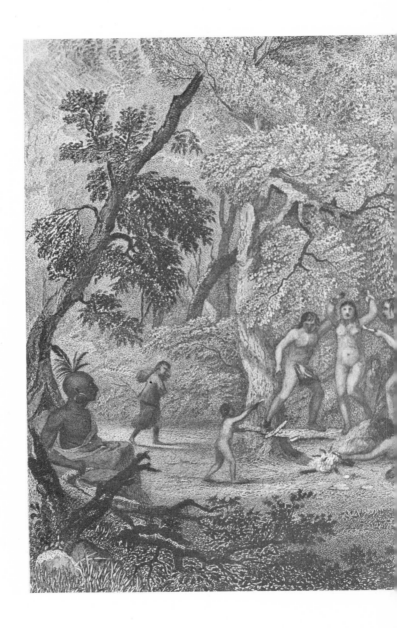

Pawnees torturing a female captive (the Morning Star Sacrifice cere-
mony), from an engraving after Seth Eastman, from *The Indian
Tribes of North America*, by Henry R. Schoolcraft. (From *Indian
Sketches*, by John Treat Irving, Jr., Norman, 1955)

planting-time in the spring of 1817. Knife Chief (Lachelesharo) was opposed to the holding of the sacrifice, which he knew the whites regarded with abhorrence; but the people listened to his talks coldly, for they believed that if Morning Star were not propitiated by sacrifices their crops would fail and the men would have no success in the hunt or in war. This chief, a tall, fine-looking elderly man with hair graying at the sides of his head, had been to St. Louis to visit the Indian superintendent, William Clark, and had come home with his views concerning some of the ancient customs of his tribe greatly altered. He had a son, Pitalesharo (Man Chief) born in 1795 or 1797, a tall, handsome youth, who was regarded by all as the bravest warrior in the tribe.

On the day of the sacrifice the Ietan girl was taken to the place of torture and was there bound with thongs to the scaffold of poles. All was ready for the final bloody act, when suddenly young Pitalesharo appeared. Facing the throng of Skidis, he told them that his father disapproved of what they were about to do, and that he had come either to rescue the girl or to leave his body on the ground. He then stepped to the scaffold, cut the girl free, and swiftly led her away, no man daring to lift a hand to prevent his act. He put the girl on a horse, mounted his own, and took the girl several days' journey toward the Arkansas; then gave her a supply of food, with instructions as to the route she should take to reach her own people, and bade her farewell. She soon met a war party of her own tribe and reached home in safety.

That winter, or in the early spring of 1818, a Skidi party came upon a group of New Mexicans who were hunting buffalo, evidently in the plains of Oklahoma. The Skidis killed seven men in this party and captured a Spanish boy about ten years old, who was at once dedicated to Morning Star. When the boy reached the Skidi village, Knife Chief intervened to save him; but the warrior who had taken the boy refused to give up his plans for the sacrifice. At last the chief called a council, at which the other Skidi chiefs and the French trader, Pappan, were present, and asked all these men to contribute articles for the ransom of the Spanish boy. Most of the chiefs gave liberally; Pappan added a large quantity of new trade-goods, and the warrior was summoned and offered the great pile of articles on the floor of the lodge if he would surrender his captive. He refused, and Knife Chief in a blazing fury sprang at him with a war club, his son Pitalesharo shouting for him to strike hard. By a great effort of will the old chief withheld the blow. He turned and added to the pile of goods several articles from his own property; he then asked the warrior again to give up the boy for the goods, and the man consented, giving the goods to the priests to be sacrificed to Morning Star in the boy's stead. Guarded by Knife Chief and his warriors, Pappan took the boy to Manuel Lisa's trading-post on the Missouri, north of the present Omaha, and Lisa induced the old chief to come with him and the boy to St. Louis, where they arrived in the middle of June, 1818. The boy was so terrified by the fear of sacrifice that he could not sleep soundly for months after his release.

The *Missouri Gazette* of St. Louis (June 19, 1818) recorded the arrival of Manuel Lisa with Knife Chief and the Spanish boy. This paper gave all the credit for saving the boy to Lisa; and it was not until 1820-22 that the story was told in full by Edwin James and Jedidiah Morse, who recounted the splendid conduct of Knife Chief and his son Petalesharo, and the generosity of A. L. Pappan, who had contributed most of his trade-goods toward the ransom of the boy.

This same issue of the *Missouri Gazette* refers to another case of attempted human sacrifice that does not appear to be mentioned elsewhere. It states that some years prior to 1818 a Skidi warrior captured a Padouca woman and dedicated her to Morning Star; but the priests found that the woman was with child and refused to make the sacrifice. The Indians kept her until her child was born, intending to sacrifice her later, but she anticipated their purpose by stealing a horse and making her escape. The priests then sacrificed her infant to Morning Star.

There can be no doubt at all that the Skidis had practiced these horrible rites on Nebraska soil from very early times, and that the few instances of human sacrifices that have been recorded are but a small fraction of the total of such acts of blood. The fact that the French traders, who frequented the Skidi villages from about the year 1717 on, never referred to these sacrifices is merely proof of the callous indifference of these men to any matter that did not directly concern their trade and its profits. It has been stated that the Skidi Pawnees were alone in making such human sacrifices; but Prince Maximilian, who visited the upper Missouri River tribes in 1833, records that the Arikaras, close kindred of the Skidis, formerly had this custom but had abandoned it. The coming of the Americans spelled the doom of such practices. By 1816 the Skidi chiefs were fully aware of the horror in which the American officials held these ancient rites, and the chiefs were doing all that they could to discourage the practice; Pappan, and probably most of the other traders, supported the chiefs.

But the mass of the Skidi tribe, led by the fanatical priests, were still convinced that if the sacrifices were given up crops would fail and the tribe would be overwhelmed by every form of misfortune.

In the autumn of 1821 young Pitalesharo went East with a delegation of Pawnee chiefs. By this time the detailed story of his rescue of the Ietan girl had been published, and when he reached Washington the girls at Miss White's select female seminary contributed the necessary money to have a large silver medal made, which they presented to the Pawnee hero at a public ceremony. Dr. King painted the chief's portrait, and later a colored reproduction of the painting was included in the McKenney and Hall volumes on the Indian tribes. When this picture was painted Pitalesharo was about twenty-three, a handsome boy with pink cheeks and fine eyes; but even at this age he had greatly distinguished himself in war and was the war-chief of the Skidi tribe. Through a strange misapprehension, J. B. Dunbar in his authoritative work on the Pawnees depicted Pitalesharo as living to old age, becoming head-chief of all the Pawnees, and signing the treaties of 1833 and 1857. These Dunbar statements have been copied unquestioningly by every author who has written about the tribe; but it is obvious after a little investigation that Pitalesharo, the Skidi hero, died before 1833; that the chief of the same name who signed the treaty of 1833 was a Grand Pawnee; and that it was a third chief of this name, another Grand Pawnee, who signed the treaty of 1857. These three chiefs named Pitalesharo have been combined by J. B. Dunbar to form a single person. Being a Skidi, Pitalesharo could not possibly become head-chief of the Grand Pawnees. In 1883 Alonzo Thompson found this Skidi hero's *Bravest of the Brave* silver medal, presented to him by the young ladies of Miss White's seminary in 1821, in an Indian grave near Fullerton, on the Loup Fork, at the location of the Skidi village, which was built about the year 1830; and here the hero must have died. He signed the treaty of 1825, but did not sign that of 1833.

Dunbar gave most of the credit for the rescue of the Ietan girl and the Spanish boy to Sharitarish, the chief in whose lodge the elder Dunbar lived in 1834-5. He makes Sharitarish play the combined roles of Knife Chief and his son Pitalesharo in a manner that cannot be reconciled with contemporary accounts. These human sacrifices were practiced by the Skidis alone, the other three Pawnee tribes having no part in the matter; and it is difficult to see how a Grand Pawnee chief could have intervened to save the victims. When the Spanish boy was taken to St. Louis, it was Knife Chief of the Skidis, and not

Silver medal given to Pitalesharo for saving the Ietan girl in 1817. (Courtesy Bert Ellsworth, North Platte, Nebraska)

Sharitarish, who accompanied him; and when young Pitalesharo was given the silver medal and publicly praised in Washington, Sharitarish was present and made no effort to claim that these honors were by right his own.

Dunbar found an undated French pamphlet giving an account of a Skidi attempt to sacrifice a boy to Morning Star, and he thought this a very early account of this Skidi custom, perhaps belonging to the 18th century. But an examination of the French narrative discloses that it is a garbled account of the rescue of the Spanish boy in 1818. It states that when the boy reached St. Louis he was befriended by Bishop Dubourge. This is not 18th century material; for Dubourge became a bishop as late as 1812. He was in St. Louis in 1818, when the Spanish boy was brought there.

NOTES TO CHAPTER V

[59]Thomas: *Plains Indians and New Mexico*, p. 20.

[60]*Ibid.*, p. 119.

[61]Thomas: *Forgotten Frontiers*, p. 310, p. 322.

[62]*Chronicles of Oklahoma*, v. VI, p. 212.

[63]Casa-Calvo, in Tabeau: *Loisel's Expedition*, p. 240; Cox: *Opening the Santa Fé Trail*, in *Missouri Historical Review*, October, 1930.

[64]Cox: *Opening the Santa Fé Trail.*

[65]Consult *Nebraska History Magazine*, v. X, No. 3; Wedel, 1936, p. 35. Mr. A. T. Hill, now in charge of the Nebraska Historical Society Museum, bought the land on which this Pawnee village ruin is located, and over a period of years he excavated the village and cemetery. He has found military buttons belonging to the First Infantry (Pike's regiment) and many Spanish, British, and American Indian medals, bearing dates between 1762 and 1801.

[66]J. B. Dunbar appears to be mainly responsible for the Pawnee notes in the McKenney and Hall later editions. His father, John Dunbar, lived in the lodge of Sharitarish for some years from 1834 on, but does not seem to have kept notes concerning this chief and his family.

[67]Report in the *Missouri Gazette*, May 16, 1811, reprinted in *Nebraska History Magazine*, July-September, 1927, p. 203.

[68]*Nebraska History Magazine*, July-September, 1927, p. 202.

[69]Edwin James: *Expedition from Pittsburgh to the Rocky Mountains*, Thwaites edition, v. II, p. 161.

[70]*Ibid.*, v. II, p. 91. Robert Stuart journal (in *The Discovery of the Oregon Trail*) p. 221.

VI

Civilization Demands Attention

OLD SHARITARISH DIED IN 1812, HIS DEATH PASSING UNRECORDED BY THE whites. His rival, Long Hair, now resumed his position as grand chief of the Grand Pawnees, but he had to face the persistent and bitter opposition of the old chief's family, led by another Sharitarish. Long Hair's first important action after recovering his position at the head of the tribe was to answer a summons from Red Head (General William Clark, Indian superintendent at St. Louis) to bring the head-chiefs of all four Pawnee tribes to his town for a council. The chiefs who went down to St. Louis were Long Hair (Chaui), Knife Chief (Skidi), Fool Robe's son (Kitkehahki, whose personal name seems to be unknown), and an old Pitahauerat chief whose name is also uncertain. In Red Head's Town, as they called St. Louis, these chiefs signed a simple treaty of peace and friendship with the United States, which ended for all time the efforts of the Spanish authorities in New Mexico to win this tribe over to the side of Spain. On this treaty Long Hair's name is written down as Big Hair. In 1819 Edwin James set down the chief's name as Tararicawaho. *Waho* would mean *great circle, great bend,* the *sky,* the circle of the horizon. Just what the name meant is obscure. Most of these old-time Pawnee names had a story attached to them; but as the stories are usually lost, we are left to conjecture the true meaning of the names. Four of the chiefs who went to St. Louis on this occasion received United States medals.

The chiefs came home with their minds filled with bewilderment, but with a strong impression that this new tribe of white men, the *La-chi-kuts,* the Americans, were not like the easy-going Spaniards and French, who were content to let people alone, to live their own way. This Red Head chief and his white men seemed determined to take hold of the Pawnees and force them to obey the behests of a mysterious being they called the Great Father who was said to dwell in a village far toward the east. Red Head's talk had impressed the chiefs, and they had been even more impressed by the swarm of whites they had seen at St. Louis; but they had the greatest difficulty in attempting to pass on these impressions to their people. The Pawnees saw only an occasional American—a tribe with a handful of men and, apparently, no women or children at all. How could such a people be compared in strength with the Pawnees? They regarded most of the tales their chiefs had brought back from Red Head's Town as false; they did not like to be lied to by their chiefs; they did not like all this talk of peace the chiefs had brought home, and many of them said the chiefs had returned from Red Head's Town half white man and half squaw. That very winter the wild Kitkehahkis, on a hunt in Kansas, showed what they thought of the new peace by killing two American trappers whom they found hunting beaver on the Arkansas River; in the same locality they captured another white hunter and his son, and after robbing them carried them to their village and mistreated them so dreadfully that the captives begged to be put out of their misery.

By 1815 the Kitkehahkis had established a fine reputation for hostility toward the new tribe of *La-chi-kuts* or Americans. In 1819 the government sent an exploring expedition, headed by Major Stephen H. Long, up the Missouri into Nebraska, a detachment of the main party going up Kansas River to visit the Kansa tribe and then starting across country toward the Pawnee villages. They were hardly out of sight of the Kansa village when they were set upon by a large mounted war party of Kitkehahkis, who plundered their baggage and then made off with the white men's horses. A neat piece of work, as the Pawnees thought; but they were soon to realize that Americans were not inclined to put up with such treatment.

The main body of the expedition, proceeding up the Missouri, established winter-quarters at Engineer Cantonment, on the west bank of the river about ten miles north of the center of the present city of Omaha. Major Long here learned of the attack on his detachment near the Kansa village, and men were promptly sent down to the mouth of the Platte, to stop all traders going up to winter among the Pawnees; at the same time the Indian agent, who was with the troops, sent John Dougherty to the Pawnee villages with the curt demand for the return of the horses and other property taken by the Kitkehahki warriors, and for the surrender of the principal culprits. The American trapper and his son, who had been taken by the Kitkehahkis in 1818, had now been released on the solicitation of the French traders and were at Manuel Lisa's trading-post, close to the new camp of Major Long's troops. The story this trapper told greatly increased the anger of the military officers against the Kitkehahkis.

It now began to dawn on the Pawnee mind that *La-chi-kuts,* the Americans, were dangerous people to trifle with. Here it was September, time to get ready for the journey to the Kansas plains, for the winter hunts and the war expeditions south of the Arkansas; but they must have trade first, to outfit themselves for the coming season's activities; and at a word from this new American soldier-chief all the traders had stopped where they were, and seemed to be afraid to visit the Pawnees. The demand for the surrender of the Kitkehahki warriors still further opened the eyes of the Pawnees as to what they had to expect from the Americans. What would be the fate of these warriors, if they were given up? The Pawnees had never given up one of their men at the demand of another tribe since the world began; the very proposal outraged them, and they could not comprehend the object of the Americans. Were they going to kill the warriors as soon as they were handed over to them, or was that old Frenchman right in his claim that the American soldiers would tie the Pawnee warriors to posts and beat them with whips that had many tails? Pawnee public opinion rejected the very thought of giving up the Kitkehahki warriors, to be killed or (worse) to be publicly whipped by white men; but the chiefs now knew that they must go warily. The entire Sixth Infantry was on its way up the Missouri to establish a permanent post, and the traders had warned the chiefs that these officers at the camp near Lisa's place had the power to loose this force and send the soldiers to burn the Pawnee villages.

Early in October seventy Pawnee chiefs, all mounted on fine mules[71] and all looking worried, came to Engineer Cantonment. They approached the camp warily, dismounting in the midst of a thicket and standing there, holding their mules and shooting sharp glances here and there for signs of a possible ambush. At this moment a body of the Sixth Infantry which was coming up the river fired a salute of artillery as a greeting to their comrades at Engineer Cantonment, at the same time letting off a brassy blare of trumpets; some of the Pawnees in the thicket, shocked by the roar of thunder such as they had never heard before, gave themselves up for lost. The head-chiefs, however, had heard big guns roar at Red Head's Town; they now harangued their alarmed companions and after a time coaxed them out of the thicket and into Major Long's encampment.

On the following day a grand council was held, and the chiefs were soundly scolded. They returned nearly all of the articles the Kitkehahkis had stolen; but give up the Pawnee warriors they would not. Pitalesharo, a Kitkehahki chief (not to be confused with Pitalesharo, the heroic son of Knife Chief of the Skidis), gave his word that on returning to his village he would soundly whip the chief offenders, a promise which he never kept. In this council the Chauis spoke first, the Skidis second, the Kitkehahkis third, and the Pitahauerat chief last, a fact that indicates the importance of the several tribes at that period. The chiefs vied with each other in pledging obedience to Major Benjamin O'Fallon, the Indian agent, and they spoke with open abhorrence of the very thought that any Pawnee could ever injure an American. As for Mexicans, they could hardly believe that the agent really wished them to be at peace with that black people in the Southwest.

The tribe went on their winter hunt, and the Chauis promptly sent out a strong war party to invade Mexican territory. What these warriors did is not clearly known. They returned in the spring with many Mexican horses and mules, many gaudy blankets, quantities of Spanish merchandise, and silver coins. The chiefs informed Major O'Fallon that the warriors had met a Mexican caravan, from which all the men had run away as soon as they sighted the Indians. Major O'Fallon suspected that there had been a fight and that the chiefs concealed the truth, fearing that the tribe would be accused of a breach of the peace. The Mexican records speak of a victory of their troops over the Pawnees in this year, but the Grand Pawnee war party here referred to certainly was not defeated. The Mexican victory was on paper; the Grand Pawnees had their village full of plunder to demonstrate the success of their warriors.

The Skidis in 1819 were assuming an air of superior virtue. No matter what the other Pawnees did, the Skidi chiefs claimed that their tribe had never killed a white man. One must suppose that the chiefs counted Mexicans as blacks; but even if we acquiesce in this Skidi attempt to draw a color line, we still have to face the report of John Jamison, Indian agent in Louisiana, who states, August 17, 1817, that a few weeks earlier a large party of Americans who had been trading with the northern Comanche bands in the plains of west Oklahoma had been attacked at the Grand Saline by a body of Tawehash and Omaha or Maha Indians (here meaning Panimahas: Skidi Pawnees), and that in the ensuing fight twenty Mahas had been killed and seven wounded. After this affair, as Major William Bradford reported, March 28, 1818, the Indians issued a call for a general council to meet at the Grand Saline in June, 1818, with the purpose, as was supposed, of taking common action against the Americans. The Spanish officials in New Mexico were suspected of engineering this council, and this may have been the fact; for the Osages had been invited to attend, and no Pawnee or Comanche chief would have dreamed of inviting these enemies to a council. In April, 1818. forty-eight Osage warriors were journeying through the plains, fifty or sixty miles west of the Arkansas River, and coming on a small party of Pawnees, they started to chase them. The next thing they knew they had been led into an ambush in which some four hundred Pawnees were concealed. The Osages started back, but in a running fight the Pawnees killed forty-seven of them. They captured forty-seven rifles, only one Osage warrior escaping. Nothing further was heard of the great Indian council to be held at the Saline in June. [72]

These activities of the Pawnees in the plains toward the south (or, as they put it themselves, *Kirikurukstu*: toward the Wichitas) are very interesting; there can be no doubt that all four of the Pawnee tribes in Nebraska had special friendships and special enmities in that quarter. The Skidis, who had now dwelt in Nebraska for perhaps three centuries, were still keeping in touch with their Tawehash cousins on Red River; indeed, there was an entire village of Skidis who had gone south about 1770 and had remained with the Tawehash. This band, which still had a village of its own after the year 1800, hunted in the plains near the Canadian, the Skidis of Nebraska going down at times, either for a visit and hunt, or to engage in some war expedition.

In the winter of 1819-1820 a party of ninety-three Skidi warriors went south to steal horses from the Ietans. The camp of trading Indians to whom this name was often specially applied had moved south of the Arkansas in 1818 and wintered on Red River. The following winter they were again in camp on Red River, and with them was a party of American traders. The Indians were making raids into Mexican territory and trading stolen horses and mules to the Americans. Unaware of this situation, the Skidi warriors made their way southward, all on foot, expecting to ride home on stolen horses. Led by a brother of the Skidi second-chief (the Mestizo chief) the party proceeded with the usual Pawnee caution, scouts out ahead and on the flanks, often many miles away. One day a group of scouts came back to the main party and reported that they had seen mounted men but had not been seen themselves. Presently another group of scouts brought a similar report, adding that they had not been seen by the strange horsemen. The Skidis halted and began to put in order the braided rawhide lariats with which they intended to lead stolen horses from the enemy camp that night; but while they were thus engaged they were surprised to observe in the distance groups of mounted warriors coming over the prairie hills from several different directions.

There was a creek nearby with timber along it, a good place to make a stand, but the Skidis had been surrounded so quickly that it was already too late to make for the shelter of the timber. They had to fight in the open plain, men afoot against mounted warriors; and to make it worse these enemies had been trading for guns and ammunition with the Americans who were in their camp, while Major Long had cut off all the Pawnee trade because of the robbery of the party of his men by the Kitkehahkis, and the Skidis were badly off for both guns and ammunition. The enemy were in great force, circling furiously around the embattled Skidis under a rolling cloud of dust, yelling and shooting as they raced by, and contracting the circle until they were close enough to attack the Skidis in hand-to-hand combats in which war clubs and even knives were used.

The Skidis were very brave men, but their situation was a hopeless one. Their leader was mortally wounded, but as he lay on the ground dying he continued to direct the fight. He said with almost his last breath that his men should try to fight their way to the timber, and when he was dead the men who were still on their feet did break through the enemy forces toward the creek bed. Instead of following them, the great mass of mounted warriors made a rush for the spot where half the Skidis lay dead or dying, for they were more intent on gaining the great honor of counting coups by striking dead Pawnees than pursuing and killing living warriors. When the rush toward the timber was made only one prominent Skidi warrior was still on his feet; when he reached the comparative safety of the trees along the stream he was smitten with shame and, although his stiffening wounds made it difficult to walk, he turned back into the plain to die among his old comrades.

Forty of the Skidis reached the timber, all but seven of them wounded. Not being closely pressed, they started a slow retreat.

They had thrown off all their clothes on going into the fight and had left them on the prairie. It was winter and very cold; they were hundreds of miles from home, all afoot and encumbered by a large number of desparately wounded men. They made pole-drags on which to transport the men who could not walk. Some of the warriors died of their wounds, the others made their way slowly northward. A few buffalo were killed and the raw hides employed to cover the wounded men. These warriors got home to Loup Fork in March, 1820. They had made the big news for that year in the plains, but they had paid a dreadful price.[73]

The government had given up the plan of sending Major Long's expedition up the Missouri to the Yellowstone. Instead the troops were to remain near Old Council Bluffs while the major with a small party explored westward up the Platte and then southward toward upper Red River. In April Long sent Major O'Fallon, the Indian agent, to the Pawnee villages to purchase horses and mules. Long Hair, the head-chief, had invited O'Fallon to the villages and should have come out with all his warriors to greet the whites, but he failed to perform this act of courtesy. The Indians were quarreling among themselves; the warriors, still under the impression that the tribe was much stronger than the Americans, were all for treating the Indian agent insolently. Long Hair sided with the warriors, Sharitarish quarreled fiercely with him and took the opposite stand. The Kitke-hahkis had forgotten all of their promises and, instead of awaiting at their village for O'Fallon's arrival, they had made up a big war party and set out on a plundering expedition. The Skidis were in mourning for their dead. O'Fallon assumed a threatening attitude, which at any rate impressed the chiefs. In council Long Hair made a speech to the warriors, telling them bluntly that they could not fight the whites, and asking them how they would like it if the Americans should cut them off from a supply of arms and ammunition.

It was in this manner that the Pawnees lost most of their opportunities to impress American officials and citizens with their friendliness and worth. Their petty tribal feuds were more important to them than anything else in the world; so they quarreled, ignoring or treating badly any Americans who came to visit their villages and the whites went away spreading the report that the Pawnees were a bad lot who would bear watching.

When they entered the Pawnee villages in the spring of 1820 Major Long's party did not set down in writing as detailed an account of these Indians and their homes as we might wish to have; but by piecing together Edwin James' account we might have what is perhaps the best picture of the towns as they were when the Pawnees were still a numerous and important tribe.

Major Long with his twenty men (including a tiny detachment of seven members of the Rifle Regiment), left the camp of the large body of troops on the Missouri River on June 6, following an Indian trail westward, crossing the Elkhorn near its mouth and ascending the valleys of the Platte and Loup Fork. As they approached the Pawnee towns the travelers observed that the one path they were following was being added to, until the grass on the north side of the Loup Fork was scored by fully twenty well-beaten paths, all leading to the Indian villages. When within a few miles of the first village, that of the Grand Pawnees and Pitahauerats, Long's party met a group of Indian women with hoes and other gardening implements, who were on their way to the corn patches. They were accompanied by one young Pawnee man. Near the villages such groups were always to be seen, going to the distant gardens early in the morning, or returning to the villages at close of day. Some of the parties had a man or two with them, but usually the women took only their small children and dogs. With no effective tools for breaking the tough sod, the Pawnee women usually selected for a garden the ground in the edge of some ravine, where the grass had been removed by erosion and the ground was easily worked with a digging-stick and hoe. Many of these corn patches were miles from the villages and hardly a week went by without some of the women and children being killed by lurking war parties of Sioux or other enemies.

When within two or three miles of the Grand Pawnee village the wide grassy river-plain ahead was seen to be thickly sprinkled with groups of people, and throngs of grazing horses and mules were observed everywhere watched by small boys and a few men; groups of women and girls were plodding across the flatland toward the village, carrying loads of corn and vegetables from the gardens or fuel from distant patches of timber; while other groups of women were at work on the sunny stretches of grass, tanning hides. Children and dogs ran about, shouting and barking.

In 1820 the village of the Grand Pawnees and Pitahauerats had 180 earth-lodges, with an estimated population of 900 families, 3,500 people. The big dome-shaped earth-lodges, with their earth-covered vestibules extending out from the doorways, were set quite close together, most of the lodges having in front or to one side of the dwelling, a log corral in which the horses and mules were kept at night. Despite such precaution, it was a common occurrence for small groups of enemies to slip into the village at night, open the corrals, and make off with the best of the horses. The lodges were set irregularly in the village; and strangers usually lost their way until they learned to recognize the painted designs on the shields of the leading chiefs and warriors, which on clear days were always displayed in front of each man's dwelling. The shields, and also the large cylindrical rawhide cases in which the men's war finery was carefully packed, were hung on tripods of poles. Many lodges had war trophies displayed: captured weapons and war-bonnets; a common sight in the village was the display of red-painted wands about two feet in length, usually stuck upright on the earth roofs of the lodges, each wand with a piece of enemy scalp attached to its tip, the long hair streaming in the wind.

When Major Long entered this first village in June, 1820, the chiefs did not come to greet him. They had sent word that they were engaged in a medicine ceremony which could not be interrupted even if the village were attacked or on fire. Major Long and his companions went to the big earth-lodge belonging to head-chief Long Hair, where they were soon seated on mats spread on the hard clay floor at the back of the lodge, the place of honor, facing the doorway. A big wooden bowl of boiled sweetcorn was placed before them, with one large buffalo-horn spoon for the party to eat with. The interior of the lodge was dimly illuminated, the only light coming in through the smokehole in the center of the roof. Through this hole a bar of sunlight entered aslant to light a circular spot on the earth floor. A large saucer-like depression in the center of the floor was the hearth where fires were kindled and cooking was done. The air in the lodge was smoky, which added to the dimness of the interior. In the place of honor at the back of the lodge, facing the doorway, was a clay altar on which a buffalo skull lay.

The Pawnee earth-lodges ranged from about twenty-five to above fifty feet in diameter. They were circular in form, with a hard earth floor a little lower than the level of the ground outside. A series of large center posts with small posts around the outer wall supported the roof poles, over which were laid layers of long grass and a final thick covering of packed earth. In each lodge dwelt a group of families, the usual number in early days being five families or twenty persons to a lodge. The beds were against the wall of the lodge and were made by driving short poles into the floor to form a frame across which were stretched small springy wooden rods laced together with elm bark. A mat woven from rushes was spread over this spring to complete the bed. Each apartment was separated from the next and also curtained off from the open space in the center of the lodge by a partition made of intertwined willow rods or a curtain of woven rushes. Each family kept most of their personal belongings in their own compartment behind this curtain; but there were also large storage pits or caches, some under the floor inside the lodge and others outside, which were used mainly for storing corn, beans, dried pumpkin, and other food supplies. A typical Pawnee cache measured six feet or so across the mouth, seven feet across the bottom, and was five feet deep.

The Pawnee earth-lodge was an easily and quickly constructed dwelling, reputedly cool in summer and warm in winter, but with the drawback (from the viewpoint of some white visitors) of being dark inside, smoky, and gloomy. The Indians, however, did not spend much of their time indoors, and the lodges were certainly comfortable shelter, especially in bad weather. Moreover, the earth roofs were fine places for the older people to sit and sun themselves; when anything unusual was happening either in the village or out on the open valley lands that surrounded it, the roofs were usually thronged with sightseers.

Four miles up the Loup Fork from the Grand Pawnees Major Long's party found the village of the Kitkehahkis, which contained only fifty lodges, 250 families, 1,000 people; three miles farther up the river was the Skidi village of one hundred lodges, 500 families, 2,000 people. In all the Pawnees had 330 earth-lodges, with an estimated 1,650 families, 6,500 people. The tribe had between six and eight thousand horses and mules, a large part of the animals bearing Spanish brands, and many of the warriors had Spanish saddles, bits, bridles, and spurs.

Major Long's party went on its way westward to explore the upper Platte, the Colorado mountains, and the country southward toward New Mexico. They found the land empty of Indians until they came to the upper Arkansas River in southeast Colorado, where they met camps of the trading Indians, who were on their way north toward the Platte. Pitalesharo, the son of the Skidi head-chief, had requested Major Long to inform these trading Indians that the Skidis desired peace; but Long found that a band of Cheyennes who were with the trading Indians had already sent out a war party to raid the Skidis. Thus the long Cheyenne war with the Pawnees was begun in 1820. To one group of these trading Indians Long gave the name of "Ietans or Camanch, a band of Snake Indians." Thus if the name Ietan originally was applied to the Apaches, its application had been altered by 1820.

When the Pawnees returned to their villages from the summer hunt, in October, 1821, Major O'Fallon induced a number of the chiefs to accompany him East. The government was still attempting to impress the Pawnees with the power of the whites, but the warriors would not believe the stories brought back by the chiefs when they returned from the white men's towns. Long Hair refused to go with this party, Sharitarish, the Grand Pawnee second chief, taking his place as head of the delegation. The Kitkehahkis were represented by Pitalesharo, the young chief who had made many promises to O'Fallon in 1819 and promptly forgotten them. For the Skidis there was another Pitalesharo with the delegation, the youthful hero who had rescued the Ietan girl in 1817. These Indians went to Washington, Baltimore, Philadelphia, and New York, everywhere being greeted by large crowds and showered with gifts. The church people had their eyes on the Pawnees, but when approached on the subject of a mission, one of the older chiefs replied: "It is too soon to send missionaries among us. We are not starving yet. We wish to enjoy hunting until the wild animals are extinct. Let us use up the wild animals before you make us work and spoil our happiness." This chief hoped that the time of happiness would last out his day, but he was sufficiently worried over the matter to complain of the custom of trading for buffalo robes, the traders inducing the Indians to kill buffalo when they did not need meat, remove the skins, and leave the carcasses on the prairie for the wolves. The Pawnee hunting expeditions in earlier years had been made on foot, at no great distance from their home villages. They were now traveling hundreds of miles each summer and winter to obtain buffalo. But it must be noted that these long journeys were necessary for another reason. They could not feed their great herds of horses and mules at their permanent villages for more than a few weeks at a time. In summer they had to shift the herds frequently, and in winter they moved from one timbered stream to another to obtain shelter and fuel. In the coldest weather they fed their horses on the sweet bark of cottonwood trees destroying great numbers of these trees each year. On Loup Fork there was very little timber for building purposes and fuel, and few cottonwood trees to provide horse-fodder.

While the Pawnees were in Washington the portraits of the two Pitalesharos and of Sharitarish were painted. The portraits curiously confirm the opinions of these chiefs which were expressed by government agents and other white men who knew them. Pitalesharo, the Skidi hero, is a handsome youth, with a resolute almost stern facial expression, which verifies his reputation for courage and steadfastness. The other Pitalesharo, the Kitkehahki, is depicted as a man of

Pitalesharo, last grand chief of the Pawnees in Nebraska. (From *Ab-Sa-Ra-Ka, Land of Massacre,* by Henry B. Carrington)

about thirty with a bold hawk-like expression. He was bold enough, but shifty and unreliable, with a bad reputation among the whites who knew him well. McKenney and Hall labelled his portrait, *Peskelechaco or Republican Pawnee*. He was killed in 1826 when some Delawares were discovered while attempting to steal horses at the Kitkehahki village. This chief rushed out of his lodge to meet the raiders and was shot dead during the ensuing fight. Sharitarish, as shown in his portrait painted during this visit in Washington, was an older man: a fine-looking chief with a stern and reserved expression. When Long Hair died in 1822, Sharitarish succeeded him as grand chief of the Grand Pawnees, but he lived only a few months after gaining this greatly coveted rank.[74]

The attempt of the American government to control the Pawnees was not very effective even while Major Long and Major O'Fallon were in Nebraska, holding frequent talks with the chiefs; and no sooner had the white men gone away than the Indians returned with eagerness to their own interests, which lay mainly south of the Arkansas River. The Grand and Little Osages now claimed most of the old Pawnee lands in northern Oklahoma, making two extended buffalo hunts each year in the plains west of the Arkansas. usually wintering on the Red Fork (Cimarron) or on the Salt Fork, farther north. The Pawnee country, so termed by the Osages and the white traders of the region, lay south of the Cimarron, and the Pawnees referred to, after 1800, were the southern Tawehash and Wichitas; but there was a surprising lack of accurate information concerning these plains tribes as late as 1820, and when a band of supposed Pawnees was closely inspected the Indians at times turned out to be Kiowas or Comanches. The hunting grounds of the Nebraska Pawnees lay north of the Arkansas River, three of the tribes hunting from the Republican Fork southward, the Skidis hunting westward from their village, up the Platte, and often wintering at Brady Island below the forks of that river. There is no record of the Pawnees having a village on the Republican after Sharitarish brought them up to the Platte in 1809, although Dunbar obtained from some old Pawnees statements that the Kitkehahkis lived on the Republican when they were boys, presumably about the year 1812.

In June, 1822, two parties of American traders, the Glenn and James party returning from New Mexico and the Cooper party on their way from Missouri to Santa Fé, met and camped together at the great bend of the Arkansas; here on June 18 they were visited by "an army of 2,000 Pawnees" who stated that they had recently made peace with the Comanches and Arapahos, and were on their way south to the salt plains to visit these tribes.[75] These were Grand Pawnees and Kitkehahkis, for the Skidis are known to have been still at war with the southern tribes in 1822. In this year the Grand Pawnees had also made peace with the Osages, and thus a general revival of Pawnee interests in the southern plains had been brought about.

In 1824 a deputation of Spaniards from New Mexico ventured across the plains and arrived at Fort Atkinson, on the Missouri in Nebraska, where they begged the military officers to use their influence to stop Pawnee raids into Mexican territory.[76] It was late in this year that the large trapping party led by W. H. Ashley and Jedidiah Smith made its way through the Pawnee lands to the mountains. In early winter these Americans found the three Pawnee villages on Loup Fork deserted; but on December 3 they came up with the Grand Pawnees, Kitkehahkis, and Pitahauerats, encamped at Plum Point, on their way to their usual winter grounds between the Republican Fork and the Arkansas. Plum Point was said to be the most southerly point on the Platte. It seems to have taken its name for the high point of bluffs on the south side of the river, close to the mouth of Plum Creek, where there was an Overland Stage station in 1864, which was said to be most exposed to Sioux and Cheyenne raids, as this station was the nearest point on the Overland to the hostile camps on the Republican Fork. The three Pawnee tribes met here by Ashley in 1824 usually camped at this place in early winter, before starting for the Republican. The Skidis used a ford higher up the Platte, below the forks and near the present town of Gothenberg.

A few miles above the Pawnee camp, Ashley found the Skidis, who were on their way to their usual wintering ground on Brady Island, below the forks of the Platte. The Skidi chiefs sent five of their warriors up the South Platte with the American party, with orders to go to the Arapaho and Kiowa camps on the upper Arkansas River and to attempt to make peace with those tribes.[77]

In September, 1825, the Pawnee chiefs were summoned to Fort Atkinson, on the west bank of the Missouri a few miles north of the present Omaha, where on the 30th they signed a new treaty, under whose terms they agreed not to molest American citizens on their way to and from Santa Fé. The United States on their part agreed to give the Pawnees "from time to time such benefits and acts of kindness as may be convenient or seem just and proper to the President." Sharitarish II was now dead, and his younger brother,

Iskatappe or Wicked Chief, signed as head-chief of the Grand Pawnees. Sun Chief signed second. For the Skidis, Knife Chief and his son Pitalesharo signed (their last appearance in history), while another Iskatappe, or Bad Chief, signed for the Kitkehahkis, and Singing Crow as head-chief of the Pitahauerats.

Here we may note that the name Sun Chief, that of the second chief of the Grand Pawnees in 1825, was the name of the nephew of Pitalesharo, head-chief of the Grand Pawnees in 1864-74, and that this Sun Chief was head-chief after Pitalesharo's death.

This treaty meant little to the Pawnees. They continued their war expeditions toward the south, and in November, 1828, we find the Indian agent, John Dougherty, sending a messenger to Fort Leavenworth in eastern Kansas with the warning that 1,500 Pawnee warriors had recently gone southward with the probable intent of plundering white parties along the Santa Fé trail. That this was their intention seems improbable; here we seem to have another example of the injury that Indians and white men in the Osage country were doing the Nebraska Pawnees by applying the name *Pawnee* to the Comanches, Kiowas, or any other strange band they met in the plains.

Late in the year 1829 or early in 1830 the Pawnees met with one of those recurring disasters, each of which cost them the lives of from fifty to one hundred people. In that winter the Osages sent out a war party of three hundred men to seek the Pawnees near the upper Arkansas. They found a Pawnee camp near a large lake and apparently attacked it by surprise, for they drove the Pawnees into the lake, the Osage warriors jumping in after them and tomahawking men, women, and children as they stood helpless in the water. The Osages came home in February, 1830, boasting that they had shed more Pawnee blood than in any fight since they had first known that tribe. They had killed eighty to ninety people, without the loss of a single warrior, and they had brought home eighty-four Pawnee horses and five women captives. At this period (the 1830's) H. L. Ellsworth, who had been present at treaty-makings with the Pawnees of the Platte and with several southern plains tribes, remarked that these northern Pawnees were at war indiscriminately with all tribes south of Kansas River. He also stated that all the tribes knew that the Pawnees of the Platte and the Pawnee Picts were the same people, connected by language and blood, but that of 10,000 Pawnees on the Platte only one could be found who could understand the language of the Picts. The Skidis were raiding the Picts and the Wichitas, and the other three Pawnee tribes in Nebraska, who regarded the Picts and Wichitas as their relatives, were very angry with the Skidis.[78]

It was about this time that the Skidi Pawnees enraged the Cheyennes by killing an entire war party of that tribe, caught while
attempting to steal horses in the Skidi camp. Part of the Cheyenne
tribe had moved south from the Black Hills of Dakota and were
now living on the North Platte west of the Skidi hunting grounds.
These Cheyennes, with their Arapaho allies, hunted on the Platte and
in the lands between that river and the upper Arkansas. Here they
often met the Skidis and fought with them, and in idle seasons the
Cheyennes made up war parties and went to the Pawnee villages or
hunting camps to steal horses. In the summer of 1829 (as nearly as
the old Cheyennes could fix the date in 1912) a party of Cheyennes
was discovered near the Skidi camp, and after a hard fight the Skidis
killed all of the enemy, cut their bodies up, and threw them into a
creek. Here another Cheyenne party later found and identified their
missing warriors. This disaster threw the Cheyennes into mourning,
and the relatives of the dead warriors besought the chiefs to "move
the arrows" against the Skidis. That winter war-pipes were taken
around from camp to camp, and all the Cheyenne chiefs, as well as
some Arapaho and Sioux chiefs, accepted the pipes. In August, 1830,
all of the Cheyennes, taking their women and children with them
and being accompanied by a large force of Arapahos and Sioux,
moved down the Platte with the intention of striking a terrible
blow against the Skidis. They found the Skidis on the South Loup
and sent out a great mounted force to attack them. Some Skidi
buffalo hunters were charged and driven to their camp, where they
spread the alarm. A great fight seemed on the point of beginning, but
now a very strange incident occurred. A Pawnee who had been ill for
a long time and was feeling very despondent asked his friends to carry
him out and leave him on the prairie where he could die an honorable
death. They took him out and left him sitting alone on the grass,
directly in the path of the advancing Cheyennes. That tribe was
taking into battle their great tribal medicines, the Buffalo Cap and
the Medicine Arrows. One of their medicine-men named Bull had
tied the arrows to the shaft of his lance and was leading the advance
in perfect assurance of victory. Seeing the sick Pawnee sitting on the
ground, Bull rode swiftly out before the line of Cheyenne warriors
and struck at the man; but the Pawnee leaned sharply to one side,
avoided the stroke, and jerked the lance out of his assailant's hand.
The medicine-man, thunderstruck by this great misfortune, turned
his horse and rode slowly back, crying and mourning. The Cheyennes
rushed forward; but the sick man had already signaled to his

friends that he had captured something very important, and the Skidi warriors rushed toward him and after a hard fight succeeded in carrying off the lance with the sacred arrows still tied to its shaft. The Cheyennes on seeing their great medicine borne off by the enemy completely lost heart and withdrew from the field in the deepest dejection.[79]

Many of the Cheyennes firmly believed that the misfortunes their tribe suffered after 1830 were due to the loss of the Medicine Arrows. But the sacred arrows certainly brought no good fortune to their captors. In 1832 a big war party of Skidis was badly whipped by the Comanches on the Arkansas. In this same year a Pawnee chief who approached a Santa Fé train to shake hands was shot dead, and another Pawnee party that was permitted to visit the camp of some Santa Fé traders contracted smallpox, the contemporary reports stating that the whites hated the Pawnees so much that they had brought a bottle of smallpox virus with them which they spread on tobacco and some articles of clothing and gave to their Pawnee visitors. The disease, brought home by the war party in early spring, swiftly spread to all four of the Pawnee villages causing terrible loss of life. The agent reported that nearly all the Pawnees over thirty years of age died, while the missionary Isaac McCoy asserted that half the tribe—over 3,000 persons—perished within a few days. It was probably during this dreadful epidemic that old Knife Chief and his son Pitalesharo of the Skidis died: Iskatappe of the Grand Pawnees also disappeared at this time, and when the tribe signed a new treaty in 1833 almost none of the chiefs who had signed in 1825 were present.

To add to the tale of disasters for this year 1832, the Pawnees now for the first time were attacked by large mounted war parties of Sioux. Lone Horn's father (not the father of that Lone Horn who was killed by a buffalo bull in 1832, but the father of Lone Horn who was chief of the Miniconjou Sioux from 1859 to 1876) led a war party against the Pawnees in 1832 and was killed, his famous warbonnet falling into the hands of the Pawnees. In revenge the Sioux got up a great war party and attacked the Pawnees at their villages, killing one hundred people. In later years Lieutenant G. K. Warren stated that in this fight the Sioux drove the Pawnees from their villages on Loup Fork and forced them to flee south of the Platte, but contemporary records seem to refute this assertion. Indeed, the fight may not have been at the Pawnee permanent villages but at a Skidi hunting camp. Joseph LaBarge was trading in the Skidi permanent village in 1832 and 1833 and does not mention the fight. Maximilian heard of it in 1833, recording that a famous Sioux chief was killed by the Pawnees; and in a later fight the Sioux saw a Pawnee wearing this chief's warbonnet, which they attempted to recover by making a combined charge, but the man was mounted on a swift pony and got away from them. The Sioux winter-counts record the death of Stiff-Leg-With-Warbonnet in 1832-33, and he seems to be the famous chief the Pawnees killed.

About 1833, according to the Cheyennes, a large war party of Pawnees was surrounded by Cheyennes and Arapahos on a hill north of the present Fort Lyon, on the Arkansas in southeast Colorado, and here all of the Pawnees were killed. The place was later called the Pawnee Hills. It was near Old Bent's Fort. Every year the Pawnees were suffering heavy losses because of their custom of sending out war parties on foot. When surprised by large forces of enemies, the Pawnee warriors took to the timber along a creek or to some nearby hill, and fought until they were all killed.

On the South Platte, a few miles northeast of Fort Morgan, Colorado, are the Pawnee Buttes and Pawnee Creek. Here in the early Thirties another Pawnee war party was surrounded on the buttes by Cheyennes and Arapahos. No Pawnees escaped. Another party, which took shelter on the top of the huge Court House Rock on the North Platte, escaped by tying lariats together and climbing down the cliffside in the night, slipping away between the tipis of their enemies, who had camped all around the base of the rock to prevent their escape.

In the early 1830's it was the government's policy to remove the remnants of eastern tribes to new homes in the Indian territory, west of the Missouri. The Delawares and Shawnees had thus come into eastern Kansas; and these Indians were sending hunting and trapping parties into the plains, where they sometimes encountered the Pawnees. In 1832 the Grand Pawnees killed a hunting party of Delawares, and no sooner had the news reached the Delawares than the chief, Souwanock, organized a war party and set out for the Grand Pawnee village on the Platte. He found the tribe had left for the hunting grounds; but that did not prevent his taking vengeance, for he had his warriors set the village on fire and grimly stood watching until every lodge had been destroyed.

The Grand Pawnees, coming home from their buffalo hunt, found the village in ruins and set to work to rebuild it. This was the village on the south bank of the Platte near the southern end of the present Clarks Bridge.[80] The village was rebuilt on the same ground, and the Pawnees, with half their warriors dead from smallpox, formed an alliance against the immigrant tribes with their neighbors the

Otos, whose village was near the mouth of the Platte. The Osages—those ancient foes of the Pawnees—promptly joined forces with the Delawares and other immigrant tribes, and it seemed probable that a war was about to start that would involve the Pawnees, Otos, Osages, Delawares, Shawnees, Kansa, Iowas, Kickapoos, Sauks and Foxes. To prevent this disaster the government sent a commission to the Pawnees, and at the Grand Pawnee village on October 9, 1833, a treaty was signed. The chiefs of all the tribes were then summoned to Fort Leavenworth, where peace councils were held. The Pawnees and Otos were talked into giving up their exclusive claims to lands in western Kansas, so that the immigrant tribes might hunt in peace on those lands; and the Pawnee chiefs were coaxed into going from Fort Leavenworth to Fort Gibson in Indian Territory, where peace talks were held with the Osages, Creeks, Cherokees, and Choctaws. It was reported at the time that these Pawnee chiefs walked all the way from their villages in Nebraska to Fort Leavenworth, went on afoot to Fort Gibson, and then returned in the same manner to their villages on the Platte and Loup—a journey afoot estimated at 1,000 miles.

The year 1832 which had already witnessed the defeat of the Skidis by the Comanches, the smallpox epidemic, the battle with the Sioux, and the burning of the Grand Pawnee village had yet other surprises in store for the tribe. It was in this year that the Arikaras, who had deserted their own lands on the Missouri in South Dakota, came down to live with the Skidis. When the Arikaras had migrated up into Dakota a century or more earlier they had been a numerous people, tradition stating that they had ten tribes and at least that number of strong villages. By 1790 smallpox epidemics and Sioux attacks reduced them to three weak villages, and after being driven from one location to another for some ten years, they fortified themselves on the Missouri at the mouth of Grand River. Here they made the fatal mistake of assuming a hostile attitude toward the American traders, from whom alone they could hope to obtain a regular supply of arms and ammunition. As the culmination of a series of assaults on Americans, they made a treacherous attack on W. H. Ashley's large brigade of trappers in 1823, while the whites were trading in the Indian villages in supposed security. Ashley extricated his men with the greatest difficulty and fell back down the Missouri to await the arrival of United States regulars from Fort Atkinson. On the arrival of Colonel Henry Leavenworth with these troops, Ashley and the other trapping and trading leaders with all their men and with a large force of Sioux joined in an attack on the Arikara towns; but the

Indians put up a stout fight, and in the end managed to slip out of
their villages at night and get away with all their women and children.
They later reoccupied the villages; but drought destroyed their crops,
the Sioux harried them, and the whites, who regarded them as the
worst of miscreants, missed no opportunity to do them an ill turn.
They held out until the summer of 1832; then, led by their head-
chief Starapat,[81] they abandoned their towns and set out with all
their possessions on an amazing journey through hundreds of miles
of hostile country to the land of their Skidi cousins in Nebraska.
Their first stop was in the Black Hills, which they evidently reached
by going up Grand River. In the hills they hid themselves and began
to send out raiders against the hated whites. Their war parties were
reported as far south as the Santa Fé trail and westward to the
Rockies. In the spring of 1833 they established themselves on the
North Platte near its mouth and contacted the Skidis, who hunted
buffalo each winter and summer in that locality. They now sent out
war parties, one of which stole all the horses belonging to Captain
Bonneville's trapping party. They also got all of Harris' horses and
all of those belonging to Henry Fraeb's trappers, and again their
warriors were reported as far south as the Santa Fé trail. The traders
and trappers were frightened and furious. They were afraid to use the
trail up the Platte to the mountains; and unable to injure the
Arikaras in any other way, they lynched poor Garreau, an Arikara
half-breed, near Bellevue, Nebraska, and threatened to kill La
Chapelle, who was an Arikara interpreter with an Arikara wife.

When the missionary Samuel Allis came to the Skidi village on
the Loup in October, 1834, he found 2,200 Arikaras there. These
people went on a winter hunt with the Skidis and returned with
them to their village in the spring of 1835, but by that time the
Skidis were tired of their visitors and were trying to get rid of them.
The other half of the Arikara tribe did not join the Skidis, but
stayed in their own camp near the forks of the Platte in 1834-1835.

In May, 1833, a Pawnee half-breed rode to Bellevue on the
Missouri and informed John Dougherty, agent for the Pawnees,
Otos, and Iowas, that the Skidis had captured a Cheyenne woman
during the winter and were about to sacrifice her to Morning Star.
Dougherty took five men from Bellevue and set off at once for
the villages on Loup Fork. At the Skidi village he was greeted in
grim silence by a throng of scowling Indians; but the head-chief,
Big Axe, gave him a friendly welcome, took him into his lodge and
agreed at once to aid him in ransoming the captive. The Cheyenne
woman was brought to the chief's lodge that night. She knew the

fate that awaited her and seemed stunned with terror. The chiefs and headmen assembled, and Big Axe made a speech imploring the men present not to anger their father, the agent, by carrying out their plans but to accept his good advice and let him have the captive. One hundred Skidis yelled a fierce refusal. Big Axe grew angry and defied anyone to touch the Cheyenne woman. He brought in two warriors to guard her. The chiefs and headmen withdrew from the lodge. They were nearly all opposed to Big Axe's interference in what they regarded as a sacred act of devotion to the gods. Black Chief, a very swarthy man with a great reputation for bravery, sided with the chief.

With all the white men and a few friendly Pawnees on guard, a night of tense anxiety was passed in the big earth-lodge where the Cheyenne woman sat staring before her, as if watching an implacable fate creeping toward her. At dawn some of Big Axe's men brought news to him and the chief informed Agent Dougherty that if he wished to get the woman out of the village he must start at once. Dougherty (a veteran Indian trader) was fully aware of the danger of the situation. He got his men and horses ready at once, mounting the Cheyenne woman on a horse between two of his staunchest men, the rest of the whites and a few friendly Pawnees mounting and forming around the three in the center.

The village was a death-trap. The great looming earth-lodges stood close together, often with only the narrowest passage between them; and all the open spaces and the earth roofs of the lodges were crowded with groups of angry Skidis, all armed and ready for instant action. Only their knowledge as to what would happen to their village and their tribe if they killed these interfering white men kept them quiet; but among the groups of scowling warriors the Skidi priests were at work—blind fanatics, who talked of the anger of the gods, which could ruin the tribe more surely than the anger of a few white men.

Through these packed masses of scowling Skidis John Dougherty rode with an air of unconcern, pushing his horse through the crowd, to make way for his men and Pawnee allies, who pressed close behind him. It was slow work, and ticklish. The people stood stubbornly in the way and could hardly be pushed aside. Some of the warriors had chips prominently displayed on their shoulders and were waiting for anyone to dare to jostle them; but John Dougherty managed to keep moving.

They got as far as Soldier Chief's big earth-lodge, a dangerous corner. The lodge had a vestibule or earth-covered passageway stuck straight out from its rounded wall, and as he pushed his horse slowly through the packed crowd of Indians Dougherty saw one of the most fanatical of the Skidi priests standing just inside the vestibule. As the little group of white men, formed up closely around the captive woman, came in front of the chief's lodge, a bow twanged sharply and an arrow buried itself to its feathers in the woman's breast. She gave a choking scream, threw up her arms in despair, and fell forward on the neck of her horse. Instantly two warriors seized the bridle, the close-packed crowd opened like magic, the warriors rushed the horse with the dying woman on its back through, and the crowd closed its ranks, fronting the white men with a solid mass of angry opposition. Dougherty struggled fiercely to get through, but in vain. Savage shouts rang out behind him; and looking over his shoulder he saw Black Chief gripping Soldier Chief by the throat with both hands, while a pack of infuriated Skidi warriors fought their way through the yelling crowd, some to join Black Chief, others to help Soldier Chief. Dougherty jerked his horse around and literally fought his way up to the two chiefs, for he knew that if blood were shed now a general fight would be precipitated and that every white man in the village would be killed. With the aid of some of the chiefs he managed to stop the fight between Black Chief and Soldier Chief but by the time this was accomplished the Cheyenne woman had vanished. The priests had had their way. A mob of Skidi warriors had taken the dying woman out in the prairie, where she was sacrificed and her body torn to pieces. When Dougherty had a moment free to look about him, he saw that the whole prairie was covered with Skidis, galloping their horses in madly swirling groups, each party led by a warrior who held aloft a bleeding portion of the Cheyenne woman's body. As they rushed their frantic horses here and there, some of these men whirled pieces of bloody flesh above their heads on leather thongs, whooping with triumph. John Dougherty realized now that he could accomplish no good by remaining among these maddened Skidis. He got his tiny party of white men together and rode for Bellevue.

John T. Irving, Jr., who visited the Skidi village in October, 1833, less than six months after the enactment of this horrible affair, is the principle authority as to the events leading up to the killing of the Cheyenne woman. Joseph La Barge was trading in the village in 1833, but his brief account of the affair was set down many years later, when he was an old man. Big Axe (*Kuttaratit Kuchu*), the Skidi head-chief, certainly did all that was humanly possible to save the

Cheyenne woman. This chief has been forgotten by the Pawnees. James Murie, the Pawnee historian, must have meant Big Axe when, in 1910, he wrote that Big Eagle was head-chief of the Skidis at about the date 1833. There is no contemporary record of a Skidi chief named Big Eagle. The Reverend Samuel Parker met Big Axe in 1835 and described him as a fine-looking, dignified, and benevolent old man. His later history is unknown, but Captain L. H. North stated that a very old Skidi chief named Big Axe was killed by the Sioux near Fort Kearney on the Platte in 1859.[82]

La Barge asserted that Spotted Horse was the man who shot the Cheyenne woman with the arrow. If this is correct, we must suppose that there were two prominent men of this name among the Skidis in 1833 for John Dougherty was not the man to forget easily; and it is incredible that he should have spoken for the murderer when, a few years later, he urged the government to push aside the hereditary Skidi head-chief and give the position to Spotted Horse, whom he described as the best chief the Skidis had.

NOTES TO CHAPTER VI

[71]Unlike all other northern plains tribes, the Pawnees had an inordinate love for fine mules, not for use in war or hunting, but for riding on ceremonial occasions. They must have picked up this custom from the Spaniards of New Mexico, among whom the priests and prominent men often rode fine mules when they went on journeys.

[72]Foreman: *Indians and Pioneers*, p. 46. *Advancing the Frontier*, p. 138.

[73]This story comes from Edwin James, who had it from men who were present when this Skidi war party came home.

[74]In a catalogue of autographs published about 1935 the following curious item was listed: "Signature of Sharitarouish, a great chief of the Pawnee Nation of N. American Indians. It represents himself spearing an enemy. He gave it to me at Washington in 1822. J. Halkett."

[75]Thomas James: *Three Years Among the Indians and Mexicans*, p. 171.

[76]A. E. Sheldon: *Nebraska, the Land and the People*, v. I, p. 195.

[77]H. C. Dale: *The Ashley-Smith Exploration*, pp. 120-24.

[78]Foreman: *Indians and Pioneers*, pp. 246-7.

[79]Grinnell: *The Fighting Cheyennes*, p. 69; Dorsey: *How the Pawnees Captured the Cheyenne Medicine Arrows* (*American Anthropologist*, n. s. v. V, No. 4). Grinnell was informed that the Skidis were preparing to sacrifice a captive to Morning Star when the Cheyennes attacked them. This seems highly improbable, as the fight was apparently at a Skidi hunting-camp, far from their village, and the Cheyennes agreed in stating that the time was August. Sacrifices to Morning Star were always made at the permanent village, in spring.

[80]S. W. quarter of section 17, T. 14, N, R. 4, W, in Polk County. The date given to this village ruin by the archeologists seems a bit arbitrary. They

date it 1820-45; but the Grand Pawnees lived in a village on Loup Fork from 1811 until after 1824, and the village here referred to is known to have been occupied as late as 1849.

[81]Bloody Hand. The name really refers to a small hawk with bloody talons. The whites called this chief Old Star.

[82]Information supplied to the author by Captain L. H. North. Agent Dougherty was urging that Spotted Horse should be made head-chief of the Skidis soon after 1833. Whether Big Axe was dead or superannuated by that time is not clear. He may have lived on, to be killed, as Captain North stated, in 1849.

VII

Civilization Advances and Retreats

THE DELAWARES, REMOVED FROM THEIR OLD HOME EAST OF THE
Mississippi to new lands on lower Kansas River in 1831, were
given by the government an outlet corridor straight westward to
Solomon's Fork, into the heart of the Pawnee hunting grounds. The
Delaware chief sent his wampum with a friendly message to the
Pawnees on the Platte and received a friendly response from the
Pawnee chiefs; but when the Pawnees met parties of Delawares
in their hunting grounds they attacked them, and in reprisal the
Delawares went up to the Platte and burnt the village of the Grand
Pawnees while that tribe was away in the hunting field.

At this time (1832) the Reverend Isaac McCoy was employed by
the government to survey the new Deleware lands; he reported
that recently three thousand Pawnees, about half of the tribe, had
died of smallpox within a few days' time, the bodies being left to
decay in the open fields near the Pawnee villages. He recommended
that an effort should be made at once to extinguish the Pawnee rights
to lands in southern Nebraska and Kansas; a treaty commission was
sent to the Grand Pawnee village on the Platte, where the chiefs
were quickly talked into signing away all the vast Pawnee territory
south of the Platte.

The Pawnee chiefs seem to have believed that in signing this
treaty, October 9, 1833, they were merely giving the Delawares and
other immigrant tribes permission to hunt on their lands. They do
not appear to have comprehended the government's true purpose,
which was to obtain the Pawnee lands and then to attempt to end
the ancient practice of wandering in the plains and to induce the
Pawnees to settle down on Loup Fork, to give up hunting and roving,
and to learn to live by agriculture alone. The treaty therefore
provided that whenever the tribe exhibited an honest purpose to

abandon hunting and war and settle on the Loup Fork the government was to send farmers to teach the Indians the white man's
methods of agriculture. Blacksmiths and school teachers were also
to be provided, as well as a grist mill and agricultural implements.
As the Pawnees had not the slightest intention of giving up hunting,
all that they received for the vast tract of land ceded was $1,600 in
goods handed to them by Mr. Ellsworth when they signed, and the
promise of an annuity of $4,600 in goods each year for twelve years.

For the Grand Pawnees this treaty was signed by Sharitarish,
seemingly the third chief of that name since 1806, with Big Horse
(*Asahkuchu*) signing below him; but everyone seems to be agreed
that Big Horse was the head-chief and Sharitarish the second chief, or
principal war-chief. For the Kitkehahkis *Capot Bleu* or Blue Coat
signed as first chief; the Pitahauerat who signed was Little Chief,
whose Pawnee name *Tarawicadia*[83] does not mean Little Chief; while
for the Skidis four chiefs signed: Big Axe, Middle Chief, Spotted
Horse, and Soldier Chief.

We know very little about these chiefs. Big Horse of the Chauis
signed the treaty of 1818, his name immediately following that of
Long Hair, the head-chief. He may have been a son of that chief.
There was always a Sharitarish among the Grand Pawnee chiefs; and
the man who signed in 1833 as head-chief seems to be the one who was
killed by the Sioux in 1843; yet another Sharitarish signed as head-
chief of the Chauis in 1848. Ellsworth in 1833 described Big Horse
as an elderly and dignified man whose son, named Sharitarish, was
second chief of the Chauis. This may be an error as the missionaries
who lived among the Pawnees after 1834 said that the Chaui head-
chief's son died while a little boy, but they may not have meant
Big Horse's son. Big Horse said in 1844 that his father, his son, and
his son-in-law had all died at the Chaui village on Loup Fork, which
means the village of 1819-24, abandoned when the Chauis moved
to the south bank of the Platte, after 1824.

The split among the Grand Pawnees adds to the confusion as to the
identity of the chiefs. In 1835 the Honorable Charles A. Murray lived
with the Pawnees for several weeks; he found that the Grand Pawnees
were split, as they had been at the beginning of the 19th century,
part of the tribe led by Sharitarish living with the Pitahauerats,
while the rest of the Grands headed by the grand chief had a camp
of their own. Murray did not name the grand chief, but named his
son, Pitalesharo. The Sharitarish who lived with the Pitahauerats also
had a son named Pitalesharo. Was either of these Pitalesharos the
chief of that name who became grand chief after 1850? We do not

know certainly. Some authorities state that the last grand chief, Pitalesharo, was the son of Iskatappe, either the head-chief of that name who died about 1826, or the chief of the same name who was alive in 1833.

Before starting on their winter hunt in October, 1834, a large party of Pawnee warriors rode to Bellevue, the Indian agency on the Missouri immediately south of the present city of Omaha, to receive their first annuity goods under the treaty of 1833. There they learned that two good white men had come to teach the Pawnees the ways of the white people. These young men, the Reverend John Dunbar and Mr. Samuel Allis, had been sent out by the Presbyterians of Ithaca, New York, to start a Pawnee mission. The chiefs, doubtless regarding these two humble Christians as great magicians who could give them power in war and the hunt, were eager to obtain their services, Sharitarish of the Grand Pawnees demanding and getting the Reverend Dunbar and the leading Skidi chief taking control of Brother Allis. They then returned to their villages and set out at once on a six-months buffalo hunt, taking the missionaries with them. These unfortunate men, separated from each other, living alone among thousands of Indians whose language they did not understand, suffered very severe hardships. The monotonous diet of unseasoned meat, badly cooked by the women, was in itself enough to kill any but a strong man, but Dunbar and Allis survived the winter and came back to Bellevue in the spring of 1835 with a working knowledge of the Pawnee language and their zeal for saving souls not much dimmed.

The autumn of 1834 that witnessed the arrival of the missionaries among the Pawnees brought the first regular trading-post to the upper Platte; Fort William was built on the site of the later Fort Laramie, and the traders induced Chief Bull Bear to bring his Oglala Sioux camp down from the Black Hills to hunt and trade on the North Platte. This event brought several thousand hostile Sioux within reach of the Pawnee hunting grounds. With the thousands of Arikaras already intruding on the lands near the forks of the Platte, the Skidis had a poor hunt and returned home in spring with meager supplies of dried meat and skins. An event that occurred in March, 1835, illustrates how far-reaching Pawnee interests were at this period. Two Panis Piques from Red River had come all the way up to the Platte to visit the Grand Pawnees, and in 1834 they lived in the lodge of the head-chief of that tribe. In March, 1835, these men went home, accompanied by a large party of Pawnees, all afoot and loaded with packages of European goods and guns and ammunition.

which they intended to trade to the Panis Piques, Ietans, and Kiowas on Red River for horses. They told Dunbar before they set out that this journey on foot to Red River would take sixty sleeps.

When Colonel Henry Dodge brought his dragoons up the Platte in June, 1835, he visited only the Grand Pawnee village, and the chiefs openly attempted to set the dragoons on the Skidis, whom they accused of bad conduct toward the whites. Something was evidently said concerning the Skidi practice of human sacrifice, for when the Skidi chiefs came to visit Colonel Dodge he asked for and obtained their promise to end such sacrifices. The old bitter feeling between the Pawnees and Skidis had been much increased at this time, and the Grand Pawnee chiefs were very angry because of recent Skidi attacks on the Panis Piques, whom the Grand Pawnees regarded as their close kinsmen. What appears to have been back of this trouble was the persistent and vindictive effort of the Grand Pawnee chiefs to treat the Skidis as an alien and even hostile tribe. Now in 1836-1837, with the new treaty annuity goods, including arms and ammunition, at their disposal, the Grand Pawnees, Kitkehahkis, and Pitahauerats had the opportunity to increase their friendly relations with the Panis Piques and other southern tribes by starting a new trade with them; but from these operations they jealously excluded the Skidis. That tribe then increased its raiding operations in the lands south of the Arkansas River, and by 1837 there were continuous reports in Indian Territory of Panimaha or Skidi depredations. A. P. Chouteau, who had a trading post on the lower Canadian River, reported that the Wichitas and Wacos of Red River suffered particularly from Skidi raids; the Osages were also victims of Skidi horse-lifting incursions and in the winter of 1837-38 Chouteau reported that war parties of Skidis were roving in the country near the lower Canadian, stealing horses from immigrant Indians and white traders. As to who the Pawnee Piques were, Chouteau (who had investigated these Indians for the government) reported that they were the Wichitas, Tawakaros (Tawakonis), Wacos, and Kichais, who had a total of about one thousand warriors. Captain Bonneville, who was serving in Indian Territory at this time, reported in 1837 that the Tawakonis and Wacos lived together on Red River at a point fifty miles west of the Cross Timbers; they had two hundred warriors; and west of them, 120 miles west of the Cross Timbers, the Wichitas and Tawehash lived together and had one thousand warriors. These Panis Piques or Southern Pawnees were raiding into Texas, carrying off horses and some captives, but presently the Texans began to strike back. The Wichitas and Tawehash then abandoned their villages on Red River and moved up near the Wichita Mountains, the Wacos and Kichais moving farther north and establishing themselves on the south bank of the Canadian, north of the Wichita Mountains.

Colonel Dodge marched his troops up the Platte, and near the forks induced the Arikaras to meet him in council. This tribe, informed in advance by Indian messengers that the dragoons were coming to attack them, had been greatly alarmed; but the colonel reassured the chiefs, stating that if their people refrained from any fresh attacks on the whites the government would treat them kindly. Both the Skidis and Arikaras were eager to make peace with the Cheyennes; and when they found that the dragoons were to march southward, striking the Arkansas River near Bent's Fort (the Cheyenne trading-post), they formed a peace party of one hundred men to visit the place and attempt to make peace while the dragoons were present. The plan succeeded, peace being made while Colonel Dodge and his officers looked on, the Skidis and Arikaras giving the Cheyennes fifty guns as peace gifts. The brother of Big Axe, the Skidi head-chief, told the officers that this was the third or fourth time that the Skidis had come to the Cheyenne camps to make peace, but that the Cheyennes had never visited the Skidi village in friendship. The Cheyennes now demanded that their Medicine Arrows should be given back by the Skidis as a peace offering; but to this the Skidi chiefs demurred. They said that in the winter of 1833-34 they had been tricked into giving one of these arrows to a peace-making party of Cheyennes, and the peace had hardly lasted until spring.

This was the Skidi presentation of the story. On the Cheyenne side one must record the Skidi attempt to sacrifice a Cheyenne woman in May, 1833, ending in her brutal murder, and the fact that the Cheyennes had visited the Skidi village to ask for peace. It was White Thunder, the Keeper of the Arrows and the highest ranking man among the Southern Cheyennes, who had made that effort. Accompanied by his devoted wife, by two Cheyenne men and one woman, White Thunder had made a dangerous trip across the plains in the winter of 1833-34 and had faced death to approach the Skidi village. He had made peace pledges and had been given one of the sacred arrows: and the fact that the peace had not lasted was not to his discredit. With all the warriors thirsting to distinguish themselves, no Indian peace could be more than a brief truce. Walking Whirlwind, a famous Cheyenne warrior, took part in the peace-making which Colonel Dodge witnessed; and a

short time later he led a war party against the Pawnees. Leaving camp
on a branch of the Republican Fork on a very foggy morning these
Cheyennes blundered straight into a big Pawnee camp. Chased out,
they were surrounded and all slain. [84]

When Colonel Dodge left the Grand Pawnee village these Indians
immediately set out on their summer hunt, accompanied by the
Kitkehahkis, the Pitahauerats, and a few Skidis. The Skidi tribe was
making its usual hunt along the north bank of the Platte, but this
summer they turned south toward the Republican Fork and hunted
westward up that stream. The Chauis led the rest of the tribe from
their own village on the Platte directly southward to the Republican,
thus avoiding the Skidis, with whom they were still on very bad
terms.

Before this hunt started a delegation of Pawnees had gone to
Fort Leavenworth in eastern Kansas for a council, and there they
were seen by the English traveler, the Honorable Charles A. Murray.
Murray and his German traveling companion wished to accompany
the Pawnees on the buffalo hunt; the chiefs at the fort consented to
the proposal and took the two white men with them across the
prairies to the Pawnee hunting camp on the Republican. Murray
later devoted over one hundred pages of his volume of travels to
his experiences among the Pawnees, giving a rather full but probably
much biased account of the leading chiefs. Sharitarish, the Chaui
head-chief, had been described in June by Colonel Dodge's officers
as a friendly and very talkative man, but Murray depicted him as a
morose and vindictive savage. Murray and his German friend were
living in the lodge of another Sharitarish, who was a chief in the
mixed camp of Chauis and Kitkehahkis; and the true cause of the
trouble between Murray and the grand chief Sharitarish probably
lay in the fact that the two white men refused to come and live in
his lodge. By living with the other Sharitarish, who was his rival,
they were increasing the importance of that chief and lowering his
own prestige in the view of the watching tribe.

Murray certainly saw the Pawnees that summer with their company
manners laid aside, and in his ignorance of the rivalries between the
chiefs he probably caused many heart-burnings. He was really
fond of old Sharitarish, in whose lodge he lived, but his attitude
toward the other chiefs was critical. As a British gentleman he could
not forgive some of these Indians for failing to behave always as
British gentlemen should. The Dunbar account is to the effect that,
having annoyed the Pawnees and their chiefs very much, Murray
and his German friend were ordered to leave the camp. There seems

to be no truth in this assertion. The Dunbars were evening the score because Murray had described young John Dunbar as a lumpish, silent, and empty-minded youth: the worst material in the world from which to make a good missionary.

During this summer hunt the Pawnees sent a large party of their men south of the Arkansas to trade their government annuity goods (guns, ammunition, blankets, cloth, and trinkets) to the Ietans, Panis Piques, and Kiowas, mainly for horses. Considering the great need the tribe had for guns and ammunition with which to protect its own people, one can only regard the Pawnee action as very foolish.

The Skidis, still keeping apart from the rest of the tribe, had a good summer hunt in 1835. Their crops of corn and vegetables were also excellent, and they might have been happy for a season if it had not been for the Sioux and *Pahukatawa*. For us moderns, Pahukatawa is a character in a quaint Pawnee myth, but in 1835 he was a very real person and a most serious problem for the Skidis. He was a Skidi youth. About 1830, early in the spring, Pahukatawa was killed by the Sioux on the South Loup while he was trapping beaver, but the *nahurac* or spirit animals took pity on him and breathed new life into him. He was no longer a human being, but a spirit; still he could speak and he had magic power. He went to the Skidi village and talked in the dark to his mother, his brother, and to the chief Big Ax (called the Big Eagle by James Murie). He gave the chief advance information when the Sioux were coming and instructed him where to have earthworks thrown up to protect the village; in several battles with the Sioux he appeared in the form of a white wolf, the Skidi symbol of war, aiding his people against the enemy; and with his help the Skidis defeated the Sioux in a number of engagements. Then Pahukatawa's brother and the chiefs began to neglect and slight him, and he went away. In 1835 all the Skidis believed Pahukatawa was aiding the Sioux, and they were terribly depressed. That winter the Skidis were encamped for a time near the upper end of Grand Island on the Platte, and the Sioux came and defeated them. The Skidis told the missionary, Samuel Allis, who was in their camp at the time, that they could not win, that Pahukatawa caused their guns to flash in the pan and the bullets to roll harmlessly from the muzzles. This angry spirit also broke their bowstrings.

Grinnell put the tale of Pahukatawa in that part of his *Pawnee Hero Stories* that was devoted to myths. He had no idea as to the supposed date of the events he set down, but Samuel Allis heard the Skidis talking almost daily in 1835 of Pahukatawa's latest doings. In 1868 the pioneer photographer, W. H. Jackson, took a photograph

of Pah-hoo-kah-tah-wah, a man with the same name as this Pahukatawa of 1835. This later Pahukatawa was a leader of the Skidi clan
called Skidirari (Wolves-Standing-in-Water). The picture shows him
wearing a fine buffalo robe with the skin side painted with the Skidi
star deities.

The Arikaras were also troublesome to the Skidis in 1835. This
tribe in December was hunting west of the Skidis, only thirty miles
from their camp, preventing the buffalo herds from moving eastward
within reach of Skidi hunting parties. The Skidi chiefs sent their
Buffalo Soldiers to ask the Arikaras to come and camp with them, so
that the two tribes might hunt together and obtain all the buffalo
they needed. The land belonged to the Skidis, and only through their
kindness were the Arikaras permitted to hunt on it; yet the Arikaras,
angry over some injury or slight they imagined the Skidis had put
upon them and giving way to that perverse spirit which so often
brought disaster on their heads, insulted the Skidi Buffalo Soldiers
and remained camped where they were, continuing to do all they could
to spoil the Skidi hunting. The Skidis said that Pahukatawa had put
the Arikaras up to this; and many Skidis firmly believed in later years
that Pahukatawa went back to Dakota with the Arikaras about
1836. At any rate, he was never seen again near the Skidi camps.
Meantime the Arikaras seem to have paid the price that was generally
exacted from them for bad conduct; for it appears that later this
winter the Sioux came down on them in force, defeated them, and
drove them away from the Platte.[85] If they had accepted the fair
offer of the Skidi Buffalo Soldiers, the whole Skidi tribe would have
been with them to aid them against the Sioux. The Skidis, cut off
from good hunting on the upper Platte, had moved eastward, at
last finding buffalo herds on the Cedar River, a northern branch of
Loup Fork; there the tribe camped for the remainder of the winter.

By 1835 the missionaries, Dunbar and Allis, had learned the
Pawnee language and were ready to begin the work of teaching
their religion to any of the Indians who were willing to listen, but
there were great difficulties in the way of founding a permanent
establishment among the Pawnees. It was with the children that
the best work could be accomplished, but how was anything to be
done while the tribe continued its custom of spending over half of
every year wandering about the buffalo plains? It seemed impossible
to establish a mission at the villages on Loup Fork, for here the
little group of whites would be at the mercy of the Sioux, who
constantly lurked about the Pawnee villages while that tribe was away
on its semi-annual buffalo hunts. In the hunting field there was no
scope for missionary work, the Pawnees, young and old, being very

busy and in a constant state of excitement over the locating and surrounding of herds of buffalo and the frequent raids on their camp by enemies. Dunbar and Allis had now married and brought their wives to the Indian agency and trading-post at Bellevue on the Missouri.[86] Allis settled down here, but in 1836 Dunbar went on another hunt with the Pawnees. He found the Pitahauerat, Kitkehah-ki, and Skidi villages on the north bank of the Loup, apparently about in the same locations as in 1830; but the new villages were all on high ground, the Sioux having compelled the Pawnees to abandon the valley and take up strong defensive positions on the bluffs. It was this year that Dr. Benedict Satterlee went with Dunbar on the winter hunt. In the spring of 1837 Satterlee was returning to the Pawnee villages with some of the young men when, near the forks of the Platte, he became separated from his guides and either starved to death on the prairie or, as some said, was murdered by an insane fur trader near Brady Island on the Platte.

This winter of 1836-37 the Skidis hunted in their lands near the forks of the Platte. The troublesome Arikaras had decided to return to their own country on the Missouri and were encamped in the Powder River country or the Black Hills; but the Sioux were in force near the forks of the Platte, and the Skidis had some fights with them.

In the winter of 1837-38 the Skidis were again hunting near the forks of the Platte, and again they had fights with the Sioux. At this period there was a well-known Oglala Sioux named Paints-His-Chin-Red. In the winter of 1837-38 this man was encamped with a few lodges of Oglalas, away from the main camp of that tribe, when a war party of Skidis swooped down on the camp, killing Paints-His-Chin-Red and several others and carrying off about twenty women and children. When this war party returned to the Skidi camp, the chiefs were alarmed; they believed that all the Sioux would combine and come against them with a great force. A council was held, and it was determined to abandon the winter hunt and to retire at once to the per-manent Skidi village on Loup Fork. The tribe went home and spent a miserable winter. They had lost the meat and robes which were the fruits of a winter hunt, and their horses were dying because there was little grass and less cottonwood bark near the village for them to live on. As if these misfortunes were not sufficient, some of the captive Sioux women and children now went down with smallpox of the most virulent type, which spread swiftly through all four of the Pawnee villages killing about two thousand people.

That devoted man, Samuel Allis, left his family at Bellevue and hurried to the pest-hole villages with vaccine obtained from the

Indian agent, who was afraid to go near the Pawnees. Allis persuaded a great many of these ignorant and prejudiced Indians to submit to vaccination. In all he treated about two thousand persons, saving nearly all of them. In this outbreak nearly all the Pawnee children under fourteen perished. Those over fourteen had had the disease in 1832 and were immune.

These outbreaks of smallpox among the Indians in early days were catastrophic. In this case the disease was brought up the Missouri River in the summer of 1837 on the American Fur Company's steamboat. When some of the crew went down with smallpox the captain of the boat sent an express, a messenger, up river ahead of the steamer, to warn the chiefs not to permit their people to crowd onto the boat in their usual fashion. When the boat reached the first permanent village, that of the Mandans in North Dakota, the Indians disregarded the captain's warning. Nothing short of firing on them with rifles could have kept the Indians off the boat. The frightful result was that of 1,600 Mandans all but thirty-one died. The Arikaras had recently returned to Dakota from Nebraska and were hunting in the plains west of the Missouri. Their hunt ended, they went to the infected villages on the Missouri and promptly came down with smallpox, losing about half of their four thousand people. The Sioux became infected that fall, and all winter the disease raged in their camps. The fur-traders called it smallpox, but if it was really that it was of amazing virulence. The stricken Indians complained of pain in the head and loins, and within a few hours they fell helpless, their bodies swollen to three times the natural size and turned black. It was termed smallpox because those who had had that disease or had been vaccinated were spared, and a few Indians who contracted the disease and lived had their faces badly pitted.

In spite of this terrible visitation, or perhaps because of it, the Skidi priests insisted that the gods must be placated with a sacrifice; and in April, 1838, these Indians sacrificed an Oglala girl named Haxti to Morning Star to insure a more prosperous year with good crops, good hunting, and success in war. De Smet states that this was in 1837; but Schoolcraft, giving full details, says that Haxti, about fourteen years old, was captured in February, 1837, and (after a council in which eighty Skidi worthies participated and decided on her fate) she was sacrificed on April 22, 1838.[87]

This is the last record of a human sacrifice at the Skidi village. Either the pleading of Samuel Allis and other white men, or the waning faith of the Skidis themselves in the value of these bloody rites, brought the ancient practice to an end with the killing of the

Oglala Sioux girl. The Skidi priests kept a star chart, painted on a large piece of hide, which from astronomical evidence seems to date back to the 15th century; and since the human sacrifices were an integral part of the Skidi star worship, this practice must be of very early origin. Since the French traders did not mention these sacrifices in the 18th century, all of the recorded instances, except, perhaps, the sacrifice in 1838, seem to have taken place at the old Skidi village on the north bank of Loup Fork, about five miles east of the present town of Cushing.

When the Grand Pawnees came home from their winter hunt in March, 1838, they found that enemies had again burned part of their village on the south bank of the Platte thirty miles above the mouth of Loup Fork. Then they got the smallpox from the Skidis and lost very heavily. The Pawnee chiefs were growing anxious about the fate of their tribe. Recurrent epidemics and the constant attacks of enemies were steadily reducing the population; the four tribes were no longer strong enough to maintain themselves in separate villages, and the agent and the missionaries were urging the chiefs to settle all of the people in one or two compact villages on Loup Fork, to give up going on buffalo hunts, and to take to farming for a living. The thought of giving up their old wild life was very repugnant to all of the Pawnees, but something had to be done to save the remnant of the tribe. Year by year the Sioux menace increased. The Sioux in Dakota had been raiding the Pawnees for a long time, but after the Oglalas and part of the Brulés had established themselves on the North Platte in 1834 the raids had increased in frequency and deadliness. When the Pawnees were at their permanent villages in early spring and late summer, the Sioux came down on them, at times with parties of hundreds of mounted warriors who charged into the midst of the villages, driving the Pawnees from lodge to lodge, taking horses from the log corrals, and setting fire to the big earth-lodges. At other times small war parties of Sioux harassed the Pawnees, lurking near the villages to cut off little parties. Some of the corn patches were five miles or more from the villages, and although the Pawnee women at times had a few young men with them to act as guards, they usually went to work in the gardens alone; every season scores of them were killed and scalped while at their work. At night little groups of Sioux slipped into the villages, opened the horse pens and led out fifty or one hundred animals, making their escape before their presence was discovered. When the Pawnees went on hunts they buried part of their corn, beans, and dried pumpkins in caches, in which they also concealed articles of clothing and other property which they could not care for on the hunt. When the tribe had left, the Sioux came into the deserted village, robbed the caches, set fire to some of the lodges, and then in their hate went to the corn patches and rode their horses up and down, destroying as much of the growing crops as possible.

The Pawnees had no allies, unless their kinsmen on the faraway Texas border could be regarded in that light. All the tribes that were their neighbors were either at war with them or ready to plunder them whenever the opportunity came. The little Oto tribe came nearer to being allies of the Pawnees than any other northern people, but the Pawnees could not trust them. The Otos, living farther down the Platte than the Pawnees, close to the Missouri and the trading-posts, looked down on the stronger tribe as barbarians and bumpkins. In the early thirties the Otos were busily engaged in drinking themselves to death. Officially there was no liquor trade in eastern Nebraska; but the traders generally had a plentiful supply of raw alcohol, and this source of liquor was added to by the Iowa tribe, groups of Iowas slipping across the Missouri every summer with kegs of liquor just at the time when the Otos and Pawnees returned from their buffalo hunt with great supplies of dried meat, skins, and many new horses that their war parties had brought home from the southern plains. The Otos traded all that they had to the Iowas for liquor, and when the grand spree was over found themselves without food, weapons, or horses, and in a condition of complete destitution. They then generally tracked off to visit the Pawnees, remaining at their villages until all supplies were eaten. Many of the Otos were too sodden with drink to go on buffalo hunts. They remained at home; and when the Pawnees started on a hunt, leaving their villages unprotected, the Otos slipped in and robbed the caches of food and of any articles that could be traded for liquor. In mid-August, 1836, an Oto party went to the deserted Grand Pawnee village on the Platte, broke into the cache pits, and carried off four horse-loads of fine buffalo robes and chiefs' coats.[88]

Many of the Pawnee chiefs were now greatly perturbed over the situation of their tribe. A century back the Pawnees had possessed a vast tract of plains, through which they could hunt and rove in relative safety, while their permanent villages could be left deserted during the hunting seasons with every expectation that they would be safe from enemy molestation. But now, in 1838, the plains were swarming with hostile tribes; and when the Pawnees went on a hunt they never knew whether on their return home they would find everything safe or discover that their caches had been robbed, their crops destroyed by malicious enemies, and perhaps the entire village burned to the ground.

The Sioux were the worst. Powerful in Dakota, holding strongly the lands as far down as the Niobrara in Nebraska, part of the Sioux had now moved down to the upper Platte; and both at their home villages and in their hunting grounds the Pawnees were under almost constant pressure of Sioux hostility. A map showing the numerous removals of the Pawnee villages on Loup Fork from 1820 and on will have SIOUX printed all over it. The Sioux were raiding the Pawnees before 1820; soon after that year the Grand Pawnees left the Loup and built a village south of the Platte. The Skidis, Kitkehahkis, and Pitahauerats remained on the Loup, but seem to have moved to stronger positions, as Dunbar reported in 1836 that their villages were on high ground in good defensive locations. After the smallpox of 1838 the situation of the greatly weakened tribe grew unbearable, and a shift to new locations was started. The Kitkehahkis had been divided for many years, the main body living with the Pitahauerats on Loup Fork, the rest in a small village of their own west of the Pitahauerats. Now, in 1839, the Kitkehahkis broke up into four groups, the main body leaving Loup Fork and building a new village a little west of the Grand Pawnees on the south bank of the Platte.

In May, 1839, the Pawnees went to Bellevue for their annuities, and while there the chiefs earnestly begged the Indian agent to give them the aid promised in the treaty of 1833. They stated that they were ready to settle down and attempt to farm. They wished to have a mission and government agency near the Grand Pawnee village on the Platte, to which neighborhood the Kitkehahkis had now removed; the head-chief of the Skidis stated that his people also wished to remove south of the Platte. At this council it was arranged that in the autumn the missionaries should visit the Pawnees and aid them in selecting the site for a mission. In the meantime the agent was to take up the matter with the Indian superintendent at St. Louis.

The Pawnees had a poor hunt, and when they returned to their villages in the fall they found that enemies had again robbed their caches. The missionaries, Dunbar and Allis, now appeared with the government interpreter, Louis LaChapelle, who visited the different villages and held councils. As Dunbar stated in a letter written at the time, the chiefs had changed their minds and now wished to settle on Loup Fork. The Indians went with the three white men and selected the site for a combined Pawnee village on Council (now

Plum) Creek and the site for the mission on Plum (now Council) Creek, a little farther east.[89]

The die was now cast. Superintendent Thomas Harvey at St. Louis had given his consent to the proposal for a mission and government farm on the Loup and was preparing to send to the Pawnees the farmers, blacksmiths, teachers, and other assistance promised in the treaty of 1833. In the spring of 1840 missionary Dunbar and Indian agent J. V. Hamilton visited all the Pawnee villages to make the necessary preliminary arrangements, only to find that the chiefs had changed their minds for the third time and now wanted the agency established near the Grand Pawnee village on the Platte. What lay back of this strange vacillation of the chiefs we do not know. Perhaps the Sioux had demonstrated again that Loup Fork was no safe place for the Pawnee villages. But the government agent refused to alter his plans, pointing out that the treaty provided that aid would be given to the tribe only if all the Pawnees moved north of the Platte, away from the Oregon Trail. Big Axe, the great Skidi head-chief, had died this spring, and the Pawnees and whites no longer had his wise counsel and strong support.

During this inspection trip Dunbar and Agent Hamilton visited all of the Pawnee villages which, due to faction feuds, now numbered six (there had been seven a year before) ; they took a census, finding 6,244 Pawnees, as against the current government report of about 12,000. The smallpox and the Sioux accounted for most of this dreadful shrinkage. Two of the missionaries, Samuel Allis and a younger man who had recently come out, G. B. Gaston, now entered the government employ and plowed some patches of land on Council Creek with the evident object of enticing the Pawnees to this locality by exhibiting the honest purpose of the whites to help the people. The Indians, however, did not remove to the new location. Instead they went off on their summer buffalo hunt.

By this time it was growing apparent that leading the Pawnees up the trail toward civilization was to prove a difficult task. On returning to Bellevue Dunbar learned that the Commissioner of Indian Affairs had interpreted the treaty of 1833 as meaning that the government was not called upon to aid the Pawnees until that tribe gave up hunting entirely and settled down to live the year round in permanent villages, supporting themselves by farming. The usually meek missionary wrote a very angry letter to the mission board, in which he stated that the official at Washington might just as well have interpreted the treaty as meaning that if the Pawnees settled down and farmed for one year, at the end of the year the United States government would expend the necessary funds to dig a big grave in which to bury the entire tribe, for if these Indians were induced to move to Loup Fork without government aid and protection being given to them in advance, they would all be massacred by the Sioux. Dunbar had talked the chiefs around by employing this bait of government aid and protection. He knew better than any other white man that the tribe would not suddenly abandon hunting, and that the only hope was to make the government settlement and the mission on the Loup in advance and then coax the Indians into gradually settling down there. On October 12, 1840, Dunbar, Allis, and Gaston wrote a letter to the mission board stating that, whether the government aided them or not, they intended in the spring of 1841 to move their families to the Pawnees and start the mission. They were still not decided as to whether they would make their settlement on the Loup or the Platte. The absence of wood on the Platte was a great objection, but opposed to the Loup location was the opposition of the Pawnees and the fear of the Sioux.[90]

In April, 1841, the missionaries left Bellevue and moved their families to the Loup, where on the Council Creek they plowed land and began a settlement. This location was to be that of the new Pawnee village, but Dunbar had been right in judging that to induce the Indians to remove would be a slow business. The Pawnees went about their usual occupations. In early spring a big war party of Skidis went to steal horses from the Cheyennes, but they were discovered, and in the ensuing battle lost fifty warriors. A large number of Cheyennes had fallen, but the Skidis were in mourning for their own dead. Another band of Pawnees, their identity not given, was on a hunt this spring (Niles Register reported the affair on April 3), and while the Pawnee men were away from their camp hunting, a war party of sixty-three Kansa or Kaw Indians attacked the camp, slaughtering the women, children, and old men. Of this Pawnee camp only eleven persons escaped.

The head-chief of the Grand Pawnees, Big Horse, met the missionaries when they came to Loup Fork and did all in his power to induce them to build the mission on an island in the Platte, near his village. They refused to do this, and the Indians went off on their usual summer hunt, some families promising that in the fall they would move to the vicinity of the mission. There were fifteen whites in the mission party, and most of the Pawnees were very much astonished to see white women and children coming among them. The Indian women were even more surprised to see white men plowing, planting, and doing other tasks which among the Pawnees were regarded as purely women's work.

The missionaries had intended to settle on Council Creek, and they did come to this location first and built two small log houses; but they now found that the Indians had marked all of the bottom-lands along the creek for corn patches, which they insisted that the whites should not use. The missionaries therefore plowed some land below, on Plum Creek, and put in a crop of corn. In the winter of 1841-1842 they took down their houses and set them up again on Plum Creek, which now became the permanent site of the mission. As finally established, this Pawnee Mission stood on the west bank of old Plum (now Council) Creek, a half mile north of the bank of Loup Fork, in the northwest quarter of section thirty-six, Council Creek Township, Nance County. The new village the Pawnees were building was about one mile west of the mission with the Indian cornfields along old Council (now Plum) Creek. The government blacksmith shop was midway between the mission and the Indian village; in 1846 the government added a school and agency stockade near this blacksmith shop.

In September, 1841, the Pawnees came home from their hunt, harvested their little crops and, instead of keeping their promise to remove to the Council Creek site, set off again on a winter hunt. The missionaries were much discouraged, but held on through the winter; at last, in May, 1842, when the Indians were home again, some of the families of Grand Pawnees, Kitkehahkis and Pitahauerats moved to the Loup and began a new village on Council Creek. Part of the Skidis also removed from their old village and established a new one on the east side of Willow Creek (now Cedar River). To assist the Skidis, Samuel Allis and a government blacksmith went to live near the new village. With the consent of Dunbar, Allis had en-tered the government employ as a teacher for the Skidi children. Allis was a man of little education whose letters were badly written and worse spelled, but he was full of eagerness to help the Skidis. His method of teaching was to send some of his warrior friends through the Indian village to smoke out the little boys and girls. The warriors drove a flock of these youngsters to the school, which at first was in an earth-lodge. Allis then took off his coat and, pointing at the letters of the alphabet on a board, shouted the name of each letter in turn, the children yelling the names in chorus. When this task had been completed the teacher led his school in song, good old Presbyterian hymns turned by Allis himself into rough-and-ready Pawnee. The children loved the singing, and their parents and relatives came and listened with pleasure and pride. The children were going to learn a great deal from this wise and good white man.

The Pawnees still showed no signs of settling down to farming. The women planted their corn patches, and then the tribe set off on the summer hunt, taking the school children with them. By this time young G. B. Gaston was growing very impatient. The son of a Baptist deacon, he had been educated at Oberlin College in Ohio, and had come to join the mission burning with ardor to help the Pawnees and firmly believing that if offered a helping-hand these Indians would give up hunting, turn to farming, and accept conversion. Gaston was the first crusader who had ever come among the Pawnees, Dunbar and Allis both being simple-minded, plodding Christians, more addicted to the slow processes of commonsense conduct than to fervid zeal to press forward. They understood the Pawnees, and were too wise to attempt to force sudden and great changes on these Indians. Young Gaston had no experience and no patience. Fretting over the disappointments he had met with, he began writing letters to his father, complaining that the Reverend Dunbar did not preach, either to the Indians or to the whites at the mission, and that instead of attempting to spread Christianity among the Indians he was devoting all of his time to farm work and to the care of his herd of stock. The deacon passed these messages on to the mission board, and presently Dunbar grew aware of the fact that he was being severely criticized back home. His defense was that having lived for eight years among the Pawnees his first faith in a sudden conversion of the tribe had gradually been replaced by a conviction that the adult Pawnees were so set in their heathenism and ancient customs that very little could be done with them. It was in the education of the children that the true hope for improvement lay; but as long as the children were taken from school to go on two buffalo hunts each year, this work would be retarded. Patience was necessary if the tribe was to be led into the way of a better life. Dunbar was pinning much hope on the cooperation of the chiefs, whose word was law among the Pawnees. When some families had moved to the new site about one mile west of the mission this spring, the head-chiefs of the Grand, Kitkehahki, and Pitahauerat Pawnees had been among the first to come, and these men had all displayed a great willingness to help the whites.

Young Gaston was not willing to wait for the Pawnees to advance at their own pace, but was determined to force them along toward Christianity and civilization. In the fall of 1842 he received a strong reinforcement, James Mathers coming out with his family, which included two grown sons, to labor among the Skidis on Willow Creek. Mathers was one of those Ohio farmers of ante-bellum days who could combine practical farming with a college education and a mighty zeal for the improvement of all humanity. He seems to have been an Oberlin College man; he brought a good library with him to Loup Fork, and he immediately joined young Gaston in opposing Dunbar and Allis in their policy of coaxing the Pawnees along. Gaston and Mathers were for driving the Indians.

The breach between the whites on Loup Fork had grown into a feeling of hostility, almost of hatred, and Dunbar was referring to Gaston and Mathers in his letters as the advocates of *Oberlinism*, by which he clearly meant the doctrine that humanity if it lagged along the upward path of progress should be assisted by being vigorously kicked behind. Mathers, setting to work as government farmer to teach the Skidis the first steps in civilization, was soon knocking the Indians down with his fists. He then took a whip to them, and in this his sons and young Gaston enthusiastically aided him. Dunbar and Allis were appalled. Could this slave-driving be the fruit of all their years of kindly effort to aid the Pawnees? They protested, and warned the enthusiasts that the Pawnees were wild people who sooner or later would reply to mistreatment by killing all the whites. The new Indian agent, Daniel Miller, came from a slave state; he supported Mathers and Gaston, his view being that colored people, Negroes or Indians, must be handled firmly and forced to do what was for their own good. Here on Loup Fork in 1842 we find the strange phenomenon of anti-slavery humanitarians from Ohio joining forces with a slave-owner from Missouri in an effort to whip the Pawnees forward. To indicate clearly on which side he stood, the Indian agent made James Mathers superintendent of the government establishment at the Skidi village on Willow Creek, putting Allis and the other men there under Mathers' orders.

These developments on Loup Fork seem all the more astonishing when we learn that the Pawnees, whom Gaston, Mathers, and the Indian agent imagined that they could whip like slaves, were at this very time perhaps the most feared Indians in the southern plains. While Mathers and his sons were knocking the Skidis down, the Creek tribe in Indian Territory was calling a general council in the hope of putting a stop to raids, and it was Skidi Pawnee raids that they had particularly in mind. So alarmed were the Creeks and some of the other immigrant Indians that they held a second general council in 1843 and, after solemn consultations among the tribes, a peace was made; but the council was hardly ended when the Osages broke the peace. At this time, in the summer of 1843, a party of Skidis came south to trade part of their annuity goods, including guns and ammunition, to the Comanches. They then went on southward to Red River to visit at the Wichita village. Here an Osage visitor saw them. He hastened home, assembled a party of Osages and set an ambush at the crossing of Canadian River. When the Skidis on their way home came to this spot and went into camp the Osages attacked them by surprise, killing nine men and capturing a Skidi woman. Foreman (*Advancing the Frontier,* pp. 214-16) states that the wily Osages, hoping to place the blame for this deed on another tribe, gave some of the Pawnee scalps to the Kickapoos, who started scalp-dances; but the chiefs of the Creeks heard of this and stopped the Kickapoo dancing. In some manner the Osages seem to have avoided war with the Skidis, for in 1844 a band of Osages was camped at the Rock Saline on the upper Cimarron, with a Skidi camp not far from theirs, and the Skidis and Osages were evidently on good terms. But this was an additional worry to the Creeks and other immigrant Indians, who feared that the Skidis were planning a general attack on them in which the Osages might become allies of these Pawnees.

Dunbar had induced his old friend Sharitarish of the Grand Pawnees to use his influence in starting the people along the new trail. In the spring of 1843 this chief persuaded sixty picked warriors to give up the summer buffalo hunt and remain with him in the new Pawnee village near the mission as a guard, thus making it possible for part of the Pawnee children to remain in school and for some of the old people to stay in the Indian village and care for the crops while the tribe was off hunting. This was a real start, and Dunbar had not beaten any Indians to produce the change. The Pawnees were hard at work building new earth-lodges in the village within sight of the mission, and four miles farther up the Loup the Skidis were at work on their new village, which they were protecting with a high sod wall with a deep ditch outside it. Samuel Allis stated that the Skidi head-chief and many warriors worked with their hands in building these defenses. Part of the Pitahauerats had joined the Skidis at this new site on Willow Creek; the rest of the Pitahauerats, part of the Chauis, and part of the Kitkehahkis were building the lower village, close to Dunbar's mission.

From the time the missionary party had reached the Loup in the spring of 1841 little had been seen of the Sioux, and some of the whites were inclined to belittle the danger of attack. Indeed, none of these men had ever seen a Sioux attack in force on a Pawnee village; they had no realization of what such an affair was like, and Allis went so far as to represent the fortifications at the new Skidi villages as a sod fence to keep horses out of the corn patches. In mid-June a large Sioux war party came to the old Skidi village, the one on the bluff above Willow Creek, and stole 100 horses, killing four Skidis; but no white man was present, and this affair did not impress them. About June 25 the Pawnees reported Sioux lurking in the vicinity of the new villages, the Indians seemed much alarmed, but again the whites were not particularly interested.

At dawn on June 27 a Pawnee chief drove his horses out of the new village near the mission and, having turned the animals loose on good grass, he lay down on the ground and went to sleep again. Some Sioux, lurking in the thickets near the river, rushed upon this man, killed him, and started to drive his horses toward the bluffs north of the river. The Pawnees in the village now took the alarm, and a party of warriors mounted and started after the Sioux, chasing them toward the bluffs. But here the Pawnees suddenly found themselves faced by a mounted war party of from 300 to 500 Sioux, who drove them pellmell back into the village. Here the Sioux killed a number of people before the Pawnees could take shelter in the earth-lodges; then part of the Sioux got on top of the lodges and began firing bullets and arrows down through the smokeholes. The Pawnees fired back at these assailants; they also cut loopholes in the walls of the lodges and fired at other parties of Sioux, who were opening the horse pens that stood between the lodges and driving out the Pawnee horses. The Sioux set fire to several lodges and then withdrew with the horses and other plunder to a hill north of the village, but this was only the opening scene of the battle.

The whites at the mission, within a mile of the Indian village, had fled to their log houses at the first alarm, and with their wives and children they watched in dismay the scene of carnage. From the green hill where they had assembled the Sioux leaders sent party after party to attack the village. A band of mounted Sioux would come roaring down the green slope, blowing their war-whistles and singing as they charged in among the Pawnee lodges. Here they would kill some Pawnees, open the horse pens and get out a number of horses, set fire to a lodge or two, and then ride slowly back to their companions on the hill. Then another party would collect into a group and charge down into the village.

This fight went on furiously for hours. During all this time part of the Sioux were in the village, fighting and collecting horses and other plunder; when one party went back to the hill another charged down the slope and into the village. The Pawnees were driven from lodge to lodge, fighting desperately, but they were out-numbered and had few good guns. As soon as the Pawnees had been driven from a lodge, the Sioux plundered the dwelling and then set it on fire. It was the horses that they were most interested in, but many of the horse pens were right up between the lodges from which the Pawnees fired at point-blank range on the Sioux who attempted to get at the animals. Nothing would keep the Sioux off for long. They lost man after man, but always came back, and in the end got the horses out of the pens.

The Skidis in their village some three miles up the river had fortified themselves, and they made no attempt to aid the Pawnees in the village under attack; but other Pawnees from the villages on the Platte rode fifteen miles to join in the fight. About noon, soon after this reinforcement came up from the Platte villages, the Sioux withdrew, taking with them about 200 horses (all there were in the village) and a great quantity of plunder. They left the Pawnee village a shambles in which dead men, women, and children lay among dead horses. Twenty of the forty-one new earth-lodges had been burnt, and many others were almost wrecked. Capot Bleu, the Kitkehahki head-chief, had been killed, and the head-chief of the Pitahauerats, who was old and sick, had fallen dead of shock. The Pitahauerats had had thirty-five killed, the Kitkehahkis twenty-six, the Chauis six, a total of sixty-seven killed and twenty-six wounded. The Pawnees were so frightened that they threw their dead into corn caches and ravines, gathered up a few of their belongings and fled south of the Platte.[91]

Sharitarish, John Dunbar's friend (apparently the chief Murray liked so much in 1835), may have been killed by the Sioux in this battle. His death is not referred to in contemporary letters, but years later the younger Dunbar stated that the old chief was killed by the Sioux at the village on the Loup in this year 1843. At dawn the chief started out to water his horses, riding a favorite animal, the other horses following in single file down the narrow path through the thickets to the river. A Sioux suddenly sprang out of the bushes and slashed Sharitarish across the stomach, inflicting a mortal injury. The horse whirled and rushed back into the village, the old man shouting warnings to the people until he fell dead.

This havoc, falling out of a clear June sky, left the missionaries and government employees aghast. They now knew the meaning of a Sioux attack. The Pawnees they had worked so long to aid had been swept away; the chiefs who had shown the only true desire for progress lay dead, and the children for whom the new schoolhouse had been erected were fugitives on the prairie.

This disaster was only one in a series that had befallen the Pawnees this spring. Three large war parties had set out in March to steal horses and had met disaster, coming home to report the loss of a total of eighty to ninety men. Samuel Allis reported on July 1, 1843, that between March 1 and that date the tribe had lost 200 to 250 people killed by enemies, and about 400 horses and mules stolen by enemies.

After the battle on the Loup the Pawnees took their sorrows into the plains, but they could not hunt buffalo properly for want of horses. They came home in August with little meat, and found a poor corn crop awaiting them. By an irony of fate, the only good corn was in the fields close to the village the Sioux had attacked, and the Pawnees were afraid to reoccupy the place. They camped some distance off in a strong position and sent parties of women under guard to gather part of the crop. Then they moved up the Loup to join forces with the Skidis at the mouth of Willow Creek. Thus the new village near the mission was deserted just when more government employees and teachers arrived to aid the tribe.

In November the Skidis and part of the Pitahauerats were hunting near the forks of the Platte when a great force of Sioux, Cheyennes, and Arapahos suddenly appeared, surprising the camp. Some brave Pawnee boys saved the horse herd by driving the animals into camp, but the people had only time to mount and get away. They lost the camp and all their equipment, with all the fresh dried meat and robes. On returning to their village late in February, 1844, they found the corn, beans, and dried pumpkins in their caches too mouldy to be eaten. This winter the Sioux attacked one of the villages, killing about eighty Pawnees and burning 100 lodges.[92]

In the spring of 1844 some of the Pawnees returned to the village near the mission which the Sioux had attacked on June 27, 1843. Here they had the missionaries to help them, and a farmer and blacksmith employed by the government. The Skidis and Pitahauerats were three or four miles above on Willow Creek with a school, farmer, and blacksmith. The Indian agent had promised 200 guns and ammunition, and this promise of aid had drawn the Pawnees back to the Loup; but at the moment they were starving. All they had to eat was the wild *pomme de terre* which grew in abundance along the Loup. The whites had a surplus of corn left from 1843; Dunbar was trading corn to the Indians. James Mathers, G. B. Gaston, and Lester Platt were mission-workers, although they were taking government pay for their labors among the Pawnees. Some of these men now wrote letters to Christian friends back East stating that the Reverend Dunbar was trading corn to hungry Indians, corn that had been grown on mission land worked at mission expense. In eastern Christian circles Dunbar was severely blamed; his justification of his conduct made no impression on men and women who knew nothing about Indians and who judged all conduct by the narrow standards in vogue in small town church circles. Dunbar stated that in the Indian country it was not considered right to make free gifts to common Indians, which encouraged begging and angered the chiefs whose authority rested mainly on their people looking to them for occasional distributions of gifts. Dunbar traded his corn to the Indians for hoes, axes, and similar articles; he then gave these articles to the friendly chiefs, who passed them back to the Indians as gifts from themselves. Both Dunbar and Allis were anxious to support the power of the chiefs who were the protectors and helpers of the missionaries and teachers, but the Ohio men were true crusaders who refused to compromise with the heathen but were determined to make a clean sweep of all Indian ways. They abhorred Indian customs, and they intended to make their own rules and enforce them. While accusing Dunbar of trading corn to hungry Indians, some of these men were hoarding their own corn; and when they caught Pawnee women and children in their cornfields they beat them with their fists and with whips. Samuel Allis warned them that they must not touch an Indian. If they would complain to the chiefs the culprits would be punished and Indian guards would be set to prevent further pilfering. But the Ohio faction refused to listen to advice. They said that the Pawnees must be taught that stealing food, even when you were starving, was wicked.

These self-appointed teachers of the Pawnees soon had to take a lesson themselves, and a bitter one. Soldier Chief, the new Skidi head-chief, was very angry over the whipping of Pawnee women and children by these newcomers; one day he told James Mathers that since he (Mathers) and his friends had seen fit to flout the authority of the chiefs and take matters into their own hands, the chiefs would no longer protect them. The next day a party of Skidis armed with bows and arrows marched a large number of Indian women into Mathers' potato field and set them to work, digging and carrying away the potatoes. While the women worked, the warriors challenged Mathers and his friends to get their weapons and try to interfere. No one took up the challenge, the Ohio men looking on helplessly while two friendly chiefs pleaded with the warriors and finally induced them to leave the potato field.

In the summer of 1844 the Reverend Timothy E. Ranney and his wife came to join the Dunbar mission. At Bellevue on the Missouri River Mr. Ranney was buttonholed by Indian agent Daniel Miller, who filled his ears with bitter complaints against John Dunbar, whom he charged with being at the roots of all the feuds among the whites on Loup Fork. On his arrival at the mission, Mr. Ranney took no side but watched and listened; he was convinced very soon that the agent's charges against Dunbar were not justified in fact. When the Indians came home from their summer hunt Ranney noted at once how fond they seemed to be of Dunbar and Allis. On the other hand, the Indians were very angry with Mathers, Gaston, and Platt at the Willow Creek village. These advocates of muscular Christianity at Willow Creek told Ranney that Dunbar and Allis were incompetent and were doing nothing to improve the Pawnees. Allis had now been dismissed as government teacher and had come back to Dunbar's place on Plum Creek, his school having been turned over to Lester Platt and his wife Elvira.

The Indians had been home from their hunt only a short time when James Mathers' eldest son, Carolan Mathers, caught a Pawnee taking some roasting ears from a field and shot him in the back, the duck shot penetrating the boy's intestines and inflicting an apparently mortal wound. Young Mathers had recently whipped a Pawnee girl so severely that she almost died. This young man was sent away to prevent the Pawnees killing him.[93]

These affairs brought matters to a head. The Indian agent came out from Bellevue early in October and held a council, all the chiefs and whites being present. He told the chiefs to speak their minds, and one after another they arose and stated that Dunbar and Allis were good men but that Mathers and his friends were hard men who whipped and even shot Indians. A Skidi chief brought in the young Pawnee who had been so badly wounded by young Mathers, but Agent Miller exhibited no sympathy for the injured Indian. He demanded angrily what this youth was doing when he was shot, and the Pawnee replied that he was hungry and was taking some ears of corn. The agent began to storm up and down and roar. He shouted that the whites were right to whip or even to shoot Indians they caught stealing, and that the chiefs should then have the men whipped a second time. White men were whipped for stealing, and the Pawnees should also be whipped. At this most of the chiefs got up and started to leave the council. Miller yelled at them to come back, and a few returned.

The agent then called the names of the few government employees the chiefs had spoken well of and dismissed these men on the spot.[94]

The agent continued to harangue the gathering in the manner of a southern slave-holder. He was for a color line to be drawn between whites and Indians. If a white man whipped or shot an Indian without just cause, all honorable white men must side with the man of their color. Dunbar and Ranney indignantly refused to conform to any such standard of conduct.

This visit of Agent Miller practically destroyed the Pawnee mission. Every man at all friendly with the missionaries was removed from the government payroll and ordered to leave. Mathers was left in charge, to continue his policy of beating and driving the Indians. In the spring of 1845 Thomas Harvey, the Indian superintendent from St. Louis, visited Loup Fork and, after listening to the statements of the chiefs and the white men, he warned the government employees that they must cease their harsh treatment of the Indians. But he left in charge men who believed in harsh treatment, and there was little change in the conduct of Mathers and his friends.

This spring the Pawnees who still lived south of the Platte and had refused to have anything to do with the experiments in civilization being tried out on Loup Fork were informed by the government agents that they would not be permitted to live near the emigrant road on the Platte any longer and that if they did not move to Loup Fork troops would be sent to drive them there. Some of the wilder young men of this Pawnee group now expressed their opinion of the government's threat by going to the Loup and killing five head of stock belonging to the whites there. The Pawnees from the Platte villages then started on their summer buffalo hunt, but on the way west they met a camp of Otos and promptly became embroiled with them. A fight ensued, the Pawnees having five men killed and four wounded, the Otos losing five men and a woman. The Pawnees moved into the buffalo range, but the Otos returned to the Platte and robbed the caches in the deserted Pawnee villages. They then killed four Pawnees at Bellvue Indian agency and, when Mathers came there with six wagons to haul supplies to Loup Fork, sixty armed Otos forced him to unload all ammunition and leave it at Bellevue.

The double life the Pawnees were living at this time was something really surprising. At home in Nebraska they had been repeatedly beaten by the Sioux in battle; the Sioux had stolen nearly all their horses; and on Loup Fork a little group of white men—part of them missionaries at that—were flouting the authority of the chiefs and whipping the Pawnees. At this same time, in the lands south of the

Arkansas, the Pawnees were spreading alarm among both Indians and whites by their raiding, and there were even reports that the Pawnees were trying to form an alliance of plains tribes with the object of driving all the immigrant Indians and whites out of Indian Territory. In the winter of 1844-45 a camp of Skidis near the Rock Saline on the upper Cimarron was systematically stealing horses from Indians and whites, and there were rumors that this band was planning to start war in Indian Territory in the spring. In February a party of Creek Indians caught up with a group of Skidi horse-stealers and killed six of them; but this success only increased the alarm in Indian Territory, where it was now reported that the Skidis, seeking revenge, had come down in force on the Creek settlements near the lower Canadian and were besieging the immigrant Indian families there. Before the falseness of this report could be established, the immigrant Indians were almost in a panic. They now decided to call a peace council in the Creek country, inviting the plains tribes to attend; but it was soon learned that the plains Indians were going to hold a council of their own at Great Salt Plain: not a peace gathering but, as was reported, a council to discuss plans for a general attack on the immigrant tribes. A peace message was now sent by the immigrant Indians, through the Kickapoos settled in eastern Kansas, to the Pawnees of the Platte, but apparently no reply was received. In June, 1845, a war party of Skidis penetrated almost as far south as Red River, where they had a fight with the Wichitas; at about the same time the Piankashaws in eastern Indian Territory caught some Skidis trying to steal their horses, and killed one of the raiders and ate part of his body. The Piankashaws then became alarmed as to the possible consequences of their act and hastily sent off a message of great friendliness to the Pawnees. The Creek chiefs also sent white wampum and tobacco with a peace message to the Pawnees by the hand of Black Dog, an Osage chief.

Not a whisper of these Pawnee performances in the southern plains reached the whites in Nebraska; yet there can be no doubt at all that the tribe was very active in Indian Territory during the ten years between 1836 and 1846. Grinnell's story of Comanche Chief, the Skidi who went south and made peace with the Comanches and other tribes, refers to this period; although the evidence is not clear, there is good reason for thinking that at this time a peace and some form of alliance existed between the Skidis, Comanches, and Osages. The other three Pawnee tribes of Nebraska were trading with the Comanches for horses at this period; but in the case of the Skidis most of the horses obtained in the south were stolen during raiding operations of a bold character, and it was always the Skidis and never the other Pawnees who caused such alarm among the Creeks and other immigrant Indians.

On the Loup Fork in Nebraska progress in civilization was not notable during this summer of 1845. Ten or twelve Pawnee children had been left by their parents at Lester Platt's government school when the tribe had set off on the summer buffalo hunt, and a few Pawnee men and women, most of them old or infirm, had remained to care for the deserted Indian village and the crops. Soon after the tribe left on the hunt a Pawnee boy was ambushed and killed by the Sioux within sight of the school and the Indian village. When the cry was raised *Teradeda! Teradeda! Chahrarat wata! (Enemies! Enemies! The Sioux are coming!)* Mrs. Platt hurriedly concealed the Pawnee children, but the Sioux did not approach the school. A short time after this a large Sioux war party appeared and started a brisk fight with the handful of Pawnees at the village. These Sioux were riding furiously about, blowing war-whistles and yelling. Lester Platt and some other white men rushed in from the hayfield to protect the women and children. They had a cart and horse, and as they drew up near the school some Sioux rode up, cut the horse out of the harness and made off with him. The white men, who were so bold at whipping Pawnee boys and women for stealing roasting ears, did not dare lift a hand against the Sioux.

When the Pawnees came home from their buffalo hunting they inquired anxiously for the ammunition the government agent had promised them, only to learn that the Oto warriors had forced James Mathers to unload all of the ammunition and leave it at Bellevue. Not knowing whether to believe Mathers' story, the Indians were suspicious and angry. Soldier Chief, the Skidi head-chief, went to Mathers' farmhouse and demanded ammunition; but Mathers stated that only a small quantity was on hand, and he refused to give any to the chief. There was a violent quarrel. Many horns of powder were hanging on the walls of the room in which the two men were arguing, and Soldier Chief rushed to the wall and began taking down the powderhorns. Mathers shouted at him to stop, then seized an axe and hewed at the chief's arm, cutting through the bone and leaving the hand dangling by a few shreds of flesh. The chief ran in on his assailant as he raised the axe again and grappled with him, holding him with his wounded arm while with his sound hand he tried to wrench the axe out of his hand. Mathers' son Marcellus now rushed in to aid his father, but the wounded Pawnee hurled Mathers across the room and turned to face the younger man. Marcellus turned to run, and Soldier Chief pursued him; but he was now weak from loss of blood and, finding that he could not overtake the white man, he threw the axe and the blade sank into the flesh of young Mathers' back between his shoulders. Soldier Chief staggered out into the Pawnee village, shouting for the people to avenge him until he fell unconscious.

The village was in an uproar. The fallen chief was surrounded by a throng of furious Skidis. Indians were running for weapons; but from the roofs of some of the big earth-lodges the chiefs were haranguing the people, urging them not to kill the whites. Mathers and the other white men had barricaded themselves and their families inside their log houses and were preparing to fight for their lives. Among the Indians there was no leadership. The chiefs were calling for peace while some of the warriors were shouting for vengeance. If they could not kill the white men, there was the property of these white men to be avenged on. A number of warriors rushed to the farm buildings and began to shoot the cattle and destroy wagons, harness, and other articles; but before they could begin an actual attack on the whites some friendly chiefs placed a picked body of warriors inside the log houses. Faced with this opposition, the mob of angry Skidis sullenly withdrew to their village.

This affair occurred just as the Indians were ready to set out on their winter hunt, and the chiefs, who were strongly opposed to killing the whites, hastened the departure of the tribe, hoping that before the people came home in the spring their anger would subside. Soldier Chief had died of his wound; young Mathers was dying. James Mathers had had enough of trying to civilize the Pawnees by violent methods. Gaston and Platt had had enough also; as soon as the Indians had gone on their hunt the whites abandoned the government farm, school, and blacksmith shop at Willow Creek and moved to the vicinity of the mission, where they built new log houses which they fortified with a high log stockade. This was a confession of defeat. Civilization on Loup Fork was on the defensive, and there was a general feeling that the end was not far off.

Young Mathers died at Dunbar's mission house; Mathers was dismissed from the government service and took his family to Bellevue, the whites fearing a general massacre if the Pawnees found this man at the settlement when they returned in the spring. Mathers and his wife bitterly accused the missionaries of causing all the trouble by supporting the chiefs in their opposition to what the Mathers family regarded as progress. In December the

Otos came and burned the Pawnee village near the mission, its second destruction by enemies in two years. In January, 1846, the Sioux attacked the Skidi and Pitahauerat hunting camp near the forks of the Platte, killing thirty-two persons; when the Pawnees came back to the Loup in the spring the Sioux followed them and resumed raiding. It was becoming clearer every day that neither the Pawnees nor the whites could maintain their position on the Loup.

Curiously, it was at this time when the Pawnees were suffering defeat in Nebraska that the tribe was most feared in the plains south of the Arkansas. It was in the early months of 1846 that the Skidis in alliance with the Osages made an expedition down to Red River and attacked the Wichitas and Tawehash, burning their villages and sweeping off all the horses these tribes possessed. It was by such raids in the south that the Pawnees replaced the horses which the Sioux were stealing from them in such numbers.

When the Pawnees started on their summer hunt, June 12, 1846, they left twenty children with the whites on Loup Fork, the parents having been persuaded that the little boys and girls would be safer and better cared for in school than in a hunting camp. On June 14, two days after the tribe had departed, smoke was seen curling from the Pawnee village on Willow Creek, where the bloody feud between the Skidis and the Mathers family had been fought out; then a war party of Sioux appeared, riding very fast. The Pawnee children were hurried to places of concealment. Only a few Sioux came inside the stockade. They looked everywhere, but did not find the children. Some of the warriors went to the mission, where they fired on Samuel Allis and another man and then rode off. On the 17th a larger war party appeared, and the whites deserted the mission and fled to the stockade. The Sioux pretended friendship, but the Reverend Dunbar, armed with a gun, held the gate and refused to let them enter the stockade. While he was talking in signs with the chief, the warriors got the stable door open, ran out every horse the whites owned and made off with them. This war party set fire to the Pawnee village at Willow Creek, but the whites were afraid to go up the valley and did not know whether the village was entirely destroyed or not.

The open hostility displayed by the Sioux toward the whites in these two raids was alarming. The government employees took a vote and decided to leave at once, before the Indians should kill their ox teams and make removal impossible. The mission families sadly acquiesced in this decision, and the men set to work at once preparing for departure.

Thus in sadness and bitterness the first attempt to civilize the Pawnees came to an end. Dunbar took his family to Missouri, his heart filled with anger against Mathers, Gaston, and Platt. Those three advocates of stern measures went their separate ways, hating the missionaries for spoiling their plans for forcing the Pawnees into progressing. This was the sole fruit of the great experiment on Loup Fork—the fruit of bitterness and hate left in the hearts of both the whites and Indians.

NOTES TO CHAPTER VII

[83]The name in Pawnee does not bear the meaning Little Chief. Captain L. H. North knew a Pawnee in the 1860's named Little Chief, called in Pawnee Leshero-kitbuts.

[84]This story was told by Porcupine Bull, a Southern Cheyenne who was about seventy-six years old in 1912, to George Bent, who passed it on to the present writer. Porcupine Bull also told of White Thunder's visit to the Skidi village.

[85]This event is recorded only in the Sioux winter-counts, whose dates are sometimes a year too early or too late. The same pictograph is used in these counts to represent the Pawnees and Arikaras, and there is at times some doubt as to which of these tribes is meant.

[86]When John Dunbar went East in 1836 to get married he had the first book in the Pawnee language printed: a simple elementary reader in cheap booklet form, seventy-four pages, edition of five hundred copies. Two copies are said to be still in existence.

[87]Schoolcraft: *Indian Tribes*, v. V, p. 77, footnote; also v. IV, p. 50.

[88]Merrill diary, in *Nebraska Historical Society Collections*, series I, v. IV, p. 185.

[89]Dunbar letters, in *Kansas Historical Society Collections*, v. XIV, p. 630.

[90]*Ibid.*, p. 644.

[91]There are several accounts of this fight. The present narrative is prepared mainly from the letters of Dunbar and Allis, written immediately after the event.

[92]Samuel Allis is the authority for the attack of the Sioux on the Skidis and Pitahauerats. The *Daily Missouri Republican* reported the burning of the 100 earth-lodges in the Grand Pawnee village.

[93]These events are fully detailed in the Dunbar, Allis, and Ranney letters, in *Kansas Historical Society Collections*, v. XIV.

[94]Ranney's letter, in *Kansas Historical Collections*, v. XIV, p. 762.

Middle Chief, Terrarecawa, chief of Pitahauerat Pawnees, about 1865–74. (Photograph by William H. Jackson, from BAE, Smithsonian Institution)

White Horse, Asataka, a Pawnee scout. (From BAE, Smithsonian Institution)

The Conqueror, Tizawatkadahuk, Grand Pawnee chief, taken about 1860. (Pitt Rivers Museum, Oxford University)

Medicine Pipe Chief, Larktahure Sharu, Grand Pawnee, taken about 1858. (Pitt Rivers Museum, Oxford University)

VIII

The Homeless People

HAVING BEEN DRIVEN FROM THEIR VILLAGES ON LOUP FORK BY THE
great Sioux attacks of 1842-1846, the Pawnees wandered about for
a time, confused and more than a little worried as to their fate,
then settled down in new villages south of the Platte, where they
hoped the Sioux would not trouble them.

The tribe was now in much worse condition than it had been in
1841, when the chiefs had listened to the government officials and
missionaries and, against their better judgment, had given in to the
white men's view that the Pawnees would be happy and prosperous
on the Loup. The government might have saved the situation in
1846 by aiding the tribe and sending a few dragoons to teach the
Sioux a lesson when they next came to attack the Pawnee villages,
but the officials' way of regarding the matter was that the Pawnees
were the tribe that should be punished. It was claimed that the
Pawnees had broken the treaty of 1833 by returning south of the
Platte, where they were directly on the Oregon Trail in a position
to cause annoyance to emigrant parties. The fact that the Pawnees
had gone to the Loup only at the government's urgent solicitation
and had left only when Sioux raids had made life there unbearable,
was ignored by the whites. The Pawnee chiefs insisted that the
white men who had talked them into signing away the tribal lands
in 1833 had promised government aid against the Sioux, if the
tribe would settle on Loup Fork. Such accusations were usually
made by Indian chiefs who had been induced to relinquish tribal
lands, and it is not difficult to believe that the men who negotiated
many of these treaties made verbal promises that were never heard
of again. There was no promise of aid against the Sioux written
into the treaty of 1833; but the government in 1844 had made a
trifling start at providing such assistance when it had sent two
hundred muskets to the U.S. farmer on Loup Fork, the guns to be

kept in his hands for arming the Pawnees when the Sioux actually appeared, but to be returned to the farmer when the Sioux had gone. The value of this contribution had been destroyed by the Oto tribe, which had stopped the shipment of ammunition for these muskets from Bellevue to the Pawnee villages in 1845 and 1846. Moreover, the benefits to the Pawnees under the treaty of 1833 were to end after twelve years—just at the moment when the Pawnee need for help became really urgent. It was useless to talk to the Pawnee chiefs of government policy, its shifts and changes, or to try to explain to them friendship that was to last twelve years and then end. From their untutored way of looking at it, such a friendship, measured with a stick and cut off at a certain point, was a sham.

The emigration to Oregon, started in a very small way in the 1830's, had become nationally important by 1843; and by 1845, when 600 wagons traveled the new road, the Platte Valley had become a white man's thoroughfare to the west. The emigrant parties had destroyed all of the wood within easy reach along the lower Platte; they had driven away the game, and their great herds of oxen were destroying the wild pastures. In 1847 thousands of Mormons, migrating to Salt Lake valley, were added to the Oregon emigration, most of the Mormon parties taking a new road of their own up the north bank of the Platte, thereby placing the white man's mark on that side of the river, the south bank having been already spoiled for Indians by the groups on their way to Oregon.

Trouble between the emigrants and the Indians was certain to come. Most of the emigrants were much afraid of Indians and strongly inclined to shoot first and talk it over afterward. In every train there were fools who went out alone to hunt buffalo or antelope, improperly equipped and careless of the danger they were courting. There was also among the emigrants a liberal supply of the type of frontiersmen who mistreated any Indians and shot them if they resisted.

Although the Pawnees were not guiltless in their dealings with the emigrants along the Platte after 1840, in justice it must be said that on the whole their conduct was surprisingly good. Usually the emigrant parties had nothing to complain of except the visits of small groups of Pawnees to the camps, begging for food, clothing, and other small donations. Every year there were cases of little groups of emigrant men being robbed or even attacked by Indians while away from the main trains. The Pawnees were nearly always blamed for these outrages, although usually no one knew which tribe had made the attack. Most of the men who were waylaid were hunting game or traveling in parties of three or four in a country where no experienced man would take such a risk; but the Oregon emigrants seemed to think that the Platte valley should be as safe as a road back home in York state, and when they discovered that it was not, they wrote angry letters to the newspapers and protests to the government officials. Even before 1840 the Pawnees had been given a bad reputation, and it stuck.

In the spring of 1845 the emigrants filled the air with plaints that the Pawnees were preying on them along the lower Platte; yet when Colonel S. W. Kearny marched up the river in June with three companies of the First Dragoons, he did not come to seek the Pawnees but to go to Laramie Fork and warn the Sioux to stop molesting the emigrants. The military knew the truth, and Colonel Kearny was not concerned over the petty annoyance caused by the Pawnees, but about the very real danger that hundreds of Sioux and Cheyenne warriors would make a combined attack on the wagon-trains west of Laramie Fork and overwhelm them. Even the most timid of the emigrants had little fear that the Pawnees would attack their trains in force.

As has been recorded, the Pawnees were in the plains on their summer hunt when the government employees and missionaries abandoned the establishment on Loup Fork and fled to Bellevue taking a score of Pawnee school children with them. Daniel Miller, the Indian agent, had been removed and J. L. Bean appointed in his place; but Bean had not even troubled to come to Bellevue, and the missionaries found no one there to whom they might turn over the Pawnee children. The dilapidated log warehouse in which Pawnee annuities were stored was standing empty; and as there was no other possible shelter, this was now broken into and the second Pawnee school established in its damp and gloomy interior. In August when the tribe returned from the buffalo hunt, some of the Pawnees made the journey of over one hundred miles to Bellevue and took their children home. Eight were taken, the other twelve being left to their fate.

The Mormons, fleeing from Illinois, were crossing Iowa in great numbers, gathering on the east bank of the Missouri at the site of the present Council Bluffs, crossing the river here and establishing winter quarters in the northern edge of the present city of Omaha. To the latter place went the Pawnee missionaries to appeal to Brigham Young to aid the destitute Pawnee children, and it was not in vain. Mr. Young ordered that warm clothing, food, and other supplies should be provided for them. The Pawnee missionaries and government employees wintered at Bellevue, still in doubt as to whether their mission and their government jobs were ended or were to be given a new lease of life by the Washington officials. In May, 1847, they had the answer from a new Indian agent, John Miller, who came to Bellevue and dismissed all of the Pawnee employees and teachers. The feud between the mission people and the Oberlinists flared up for the last time in a struggle for control of the twelve Pawnee children, and Agent Miller enraged the Oberlin group by appointing Samuel Allis as the sole teacher. Allis who was so nearly illiterate that he could not teach his own son, but had to send him to Lester Platt for instruction! This was the view of the Oberlin party, headed by Mrs. Platt; the Pawnee view was that Allis was a kind man, who understood and liked the Pawnees and would not beat their children with a whip.

In the autumn of 1846 an advance guard of Mormons, on their way to Salt Lake, had moved out to Loup Fork and established themselves for the winter in the deserted buildings of the Pawnee Mission. When they left in 1847 they took plows and other farm implements, the property of the government, claiming them as their due in return for aid supplied to the destitute Pawnees. The rest of the government equipment on Loup Fork was later loaded into wagons on the orders of Agent John Miller, who had the government wagons, harness, farm implements, and blacksmith tools taken to the Mormon settlement north of Bellevue, and there sold them at public auction. This enterprising gentleman forgot to report the transaction to his superiors.[95]

The Pawnees returning from their summer hunt in 1846 found the mission abandoned and their children gone. Having harvested what little crop the Sioux had failed to destroy, they started out on their winter hunt in October. The Skidis, hunting by themselves near the forks of the Platte, were set upon by the Sioux in January, 1847, losing thirty-two killed in a big fight in which the Sioux had only one warrior killed.

In the spring of 1847 the Pawnees were nearly destitute and in deep trouble. The government by supplying the tribe with annuity goods had cut into the business of the traders; annuities had now been stopped, trade had not been resumed, and the Pawnees were starved for supplies of very necessary goods. The Iowas and the wily Sacs and Foxes knew of this and in May they attacked a Pawnee hunting camp, taking seventeen scalps. The Sioux attacks continued, threatening the very existence of the Pawnees as a tribe.

In May, 1847, a great war party of from 700 to 800 Sioux set out to attack the Pawnees. They went to the Skidi village at the mouth of Cedar River—the only Pawnee village remaining on Loup Fork— and finding the tribe away from home, they set fire to the village and destroyed it. Later they came upon a camp of some 200 Pawnees and in a fierce attack killed eighty-three persons.[96]

The Sioux were now carrying their attacks as far east as the Missouri River near the mouth of the Platte, where they were raiding the Omahas and Otos. In September, 1847, 300 men of the Oregon Battalion of Missouri Mounted Volunteers were sent north of the Platte to hunt down the raiders; but after marching several hundred miles and wearing out most of their horses the troops returned without having seen an Indian. In the meantime another detachment of this regiment was sent up the Platte to select the site for a new military post near the upper end of Grand Island. This island, some sixty miles in length but very narrow, was to be included in the military reserve, as was also more Pawnee land on the north side of the Platte. In the spring of 1848 the new post, Fort Childs (later Fort Kearney) was established and the land was bought from the Pawnees, who were so destitute that they eagerly accepted $2,000 in goods for the large tract of fine land and timber involved. A new Sharitarish, the fourth of this name since 1806, signed as first chief of the Chauis, but the officers speak of him as the principal war chief of the tribe. All of the old head-chiefs had died in the smallpox of 1838 or had been killed during the great Sioux attacks on the Loup Fork villages since that year. The Skidis were now led by Iskatappe or Wicked Chief and by French Chief (Chahikstakalesharo: chahiks, man, taka, white, being the Pawnee name for a Frenchman, as distinguished from Lachikuts, Big Knife, an American). The Kitkehahkis and Pitahauerats were led by chiefs whose names have been forgotten.[97]

For ten years Pawnee anger had been growing over the trade in arms and ammunition with their Sioux enemies at Fort Laramie. In 1846 some traders from that district were coming down the Platte with their packs of furs loaded in skin boats, and because of shallow water they became stranded just opposite to the Grand Pawnee village. The Indians, led by some of the minor chiefs, robbed the traders of everything they had, tied some of the men up, and soundly whipped them. The commanding-officer at the new fort nearby now informed Sharitarish and the other chiefs that such outrages against the whites must cease, if the Pawnees did not wish to see the troops marching against them. Four or five days later two officers left the post and rode down the Platte, on their way to the Missouri River. When they reached the Grand Pawnee village an old chief, known to them as a very friendly man, rushed up to them and began talking excitedly in signs, repeating as he did so, *Sharitarish! Sharitarish!* and all the while making vigorous signs of throat-cutting. Much alarmed by the thought that this friendly old Pawnee was warning them that Sharitarish was about to set out with his warriors to cut the throats of all the emigrants strung out along the Platte road, these officers sent a rider in haste back to the fort. At midnight the bugles blew and the garrison flew to arms. At dawn 250 mounted men rode down the Platte and on reaching the Pawnee village drew up in battle array, their shining brass howitzers trained on the Indian town. A French interpreter came out with some frightened chiefs, and on being questioned he explained that what the old Indian had said to the two officers was this: Sharitarish's daughter was temperamental. In a recent quarrel with her husband she had gone too far and he had beaten her; she had then beaten him even worse; he had then shot her with an arrow; whereupon Sharitarish, regarding the arrow incident as a little too much, had cut his son-in-law's throat. Colonel Powell took the chief back to the fort and placed him in the guardhouse, not for killing his son-in-law but on the general grounds that he was a man of bad reputation.[98]

In the spring and summer of 1848 over two thousand five hundred wagons traveled up the Platte on their way to Salt Lake and Oregon. Most of the wagon-trains passed within sight of the Pawnee villages. The Sioux were continuing their attacks on the Pawnees, who were very much disturbed; and many of the people instead of planting and caring for their crops hung about the emigrant camps, begging or stealing from the whites. Early in October the entire tribe with 1,200 warriors turned up at Fort Childs, and having gained the release of their chief Sharitarish they went on their winter buffalo hunt, taking with them (as was reported) nearly everything at the fort that was not too heavy to lift or too bulky to be concealed under a blanket.[99]

The Skidis had lost their village on the Loup—burned by the Sioux; and their last attempt to hunt in their old lands near the forks of the Platte in the winter of 1846-47 had ended in their being driven away by the Sioux. The Skidi chiefs now swallowed their pride and asked the Grand Pawnees for permission to hunt with them in their lands, and the Grand Pawnee chiefs, also swallowing their pride, assented. Thus the ancient feud between the Skidis and the other Pawnees was ended, because both parties had to end it or starve. The Skidis could no longer hunt near the forks of the Platte; and the other three Pawnee tribes were being so bedeviled by the Sioux, Cheyennes, and other enemies in their own hunting grounds on the Republican Fork that they were glad to have the Skidis join forces with them.

In October, 1848, the whole Pawnee tribe, including the Skidis, set out to hunt on Republican Fork. They had a troubled winter with poor hunting and in the spring of 1849 they came back to the Platte near Grand Island discouraged and alarmed, for the whites reported that the Sioux were coming down the river in great force. The Grand Pawnees now decided to desert their old village on the south bank of the river, south of the present Clarks, and in May they moved east to the vicinity of the present Ashland and built a new village on Salt Creek. At this date the Skidis were on the south bank of the Platte, at Pahuk, south of the present Fremont.[100]

In the spring of this year, 1849, some 20,000 whites with 60,000 animals left the Missouri frontier and took the Oregon Trail through the Pawnee country. To the usual hordes of Mormons and Oregon emigrants had now been added the thousands going to the new gold fields in California. Asiatic cholera had broken out in the emigrant camps, hundreds dying along the trail east of Fort Kearney. Many Pawnees were loitering near the trail, visiting the camps of the whites, and presently the cholera broke out among these Indians, who promptly introduced the disease among the people at the Pawnee villages. As the tribe was about to set out on the summer hunt, it was hoped that the people would shake off this sickness; but the hopes were vain, and by the end of the year the cholera had taken a toll of 1,234 Pawnees: about 900 women and children and 250 men, one-fourth of the tribal population.

On July 6 a war party of 500 Sioux and Cheyennes came down on the Grand Pawnee village on the south bank of the Platte below Grand Island. Finding the village deserted, these warriors had to vent their rage by setting the place on fire and destroying it. A wagon-train owned by an army contractor named Hughes was on its way east from Fort Kearney, and on July 7 the Sioux and Cheyennes surrounded the train and robbed the whites of everything they had. Two days later this wagon-train met a party of 700 Pawnee, Oto, and Omaha warriors, who were looking for their enemies. On being informed as to the direction the Sioux and Cheyennes had taken, the warriors set off in pursuit. The contemporary reports are silent as to the results of the chase.[101]

Some of the Pawnees had not gone on the summer hunt. Instead, they were infesting the Oregon Trail east of Fort Kearney, living on the emigrants, obtaining food by begging, and when denied often taking what they required by force. In the middle of June troops had to be sent from the post to drive these parties of Pawnees away from the emigrant trial. These Indians, who had been persistently represented by the emigrants and western newspapers as fierce banditti, made no effort to resist but left the trail at once when ordered to do so. They were in the main destitute families whose horses had been stolen by the Sioux or other enemies, making it impossible for them to accompany the tribe on its buffalo hunt. Occasionally real outrages were committed against the whites by small parties of young Pawnees who refused to listen to the counsel of the chiefs.

Late that fall a party of Pawnees was accused of murdering two mail riders near Ash Hollow, but the tribe to which the murderers belonged was not clearly established. The government was right in doing all that it could to protect the emigrants, but it was in fault for making no effort whatever to aid the Pawnee tribe in its time of desperate need. At this very moment the Indian Office was greatly concerned over the well-being of the Sioux, Cheyennes, and other strong tribes of the Upper Platte region, and Congress had been induced to vote a sum of $100,000 for the purpose of holding a great council with these Indians and giving them handsome presents as a kind of bribe to keep them quiet. Much has been written about this great Indian peace council near Fort Laramie and the government's kindly intentions; the truth is that the government treated liberally the Sioux and some other tribes that it feared, while the Pawnees, whose need was so desperate but who were not strong enough to be a serious menace to the emigrant movement westward, were ignored. To the officials the Pawnees were a tribe who had broken their treaty obligations by permitting the Sioux to drive them south of the Platte, where they were now annoying the emigrant trains. To the emigrants and certain western newspaper editors the tribe were "pestiferous banditti," "Indians who have covered themselves with white blood," "those grand rascals, the Pawnees."

In the spring of 1850 some 10,000 wagons with more than 40,000 whites gathered at different points on the frontier, preparatory to taking the Oregon Trail to the west. It was predicted in the newspapers that few Indians would be seen, as all of the tribes had suffered so terribly from cholera in 1849 that they were afraid to approach parties of whites; but the Pawnees were so destitute that even the fear of death could not keep them away from the emigrant trail; and with the appearance of the first wagon-trains little parties of hungry Indians began visiting the camps of the whites, begging, pilfering small articles, and even running off oxen, which were almost as good

food as buffalo in the opinion of many Pawnees. The tribe was summoned to Fort Kearney, where the commanding-officer soundly be-
rated the chiefs. Finding that part of the tribe (the Skidis) had disregarded his summons, a small force of mounted troops was sent in
pursuit. The Skidis, who had had nearly all of their horses stolen
from them by the Sioux the year before, could not make much speed;
moreover, they were being chased up the Platte, straight into the arms
of the Sioux. They therefore halted to await whatever fate the white
chief had allotted to them, but the major was just and did not attack
these unresisting people. He told them, however, that if they annoyed
the emigrants again he would "wipe them off the face of the earth."

There were amazing numbers of buffalo south of the Platte in 1850,
and the Pawnees had a good hunt. At their permanent villages they
were still being greatly harassed, both by Indian enemies and by emigrant parties, who often let their stock feed in the Pawnee corn
patches. It was apparently in the fall of 1850 or spring of 1851 that
the tribe deserted their village at the mouth of Salt Creek and built a
new one at the old Linwood site on the south bank of the Platte,
about twenty-five miles above the Skidi village at Pahuk. In the winter, 1850-1851, the Skidis had a piece of luck, running off a large herd
of horses from the Sioux and their white traders, who were encamped
on the North Platte near Scott's Bluffs. In spite of all their losses and
troubles the Pawnees were still sending out many war parties, most of
them going south of the Arkansas to steal horses from the Comanches
and Kiowas.

In early August, 1851, Superintendent D. D. Mitchell of the Indian
service came up the Platte with a wagon-train loaded with nearly
$100,000 worth of food and gifts which he was taking to the Sioux and
other tribes who had been summoned to a great intertribal peace council near Fort Laramie. The Pawnees do not appear to have been invited to this meeting, although they were anxious to make peace. Just
before the Mitchell train reached Fort Kearney a party of eighty Cheyenne warriors rode into the post and informed Major Clifton Whar-
ton that they had come to make peace with the Pawnees. The major
gave the Cheyennes a quantity of army rations to reward them for
their good intentions, only to learn a few days later that the Cheyennes
had attacked a party of Pawnee buffalo hunters, of whom they killed
four. These Indians then attached themselves to Superintendent Mitchell's peace caravan, with which they traveled all the way to Fort
Laramie, being fed on government supplies while on the road.[102]

Mr. Mitchell and his peace party returned down the Platte early
in October, bringing delegations of Sioux, Cheyennes, and Arapahos,

who were to be taken east. At Fort Kearney the Pawnee chiefs met this party in council, and the Skidis offered the pipe to a Cheyenne named Alights-on-the-Clouds. He refused to smoke, saying that he did not wish to deceive the Pawnees by pretending to make peace with them, for he thought it likely that at the very moment war parties of his tribe were on their way to attack the Pawnees. In the following summer this Cheyenne was killed by the Skidis under remarkable circumstances.

In the spring of 1852 the Pitahauerats were camped north of the Platte, near the present Fremont, when a wagon-train of emigrants crossed the Elkhorn and camped on a small western branch of this river. Among the emigrants was a hero who had been boasting of his courage ever since the party left the settlements. He vowed repeatedly that he would kill the first Indian he saw; and now when a young Pitahauerat woman was seen near the camp this man went out with his rifle and shot her dead. The train moved on; but the Pitahauerats heard of the murder, stopped the train, and took the white man back to the scene of the crime, where they skinned him from neck to heel while his companions looked on. "Skinned him," wrote Samuel Allis, the Pawnee missionary, "I do not know whether dead or alive, and it matters not in my estimation." Some missionaries could express themselves rather neatly on occasion. The creek on which this occurred is still known as the Rawhide.

The summer hunt of 1852 is a good example of the way the Pawnees lived when they were not haunting the emigrant road. In the spring the women planted the corn patches near the villages, with some hope that when the tribe returned from the hunt a part of the crop might have been spared by Sioux and emigrants. Three of the tribes then set out for the Republican Fork. The Skidis, still trying to maintain some part of their old freedom from the other Pawnees, started off by themselves up the Platte toward their old hunting lands, hoping to obtain buffalo before the Sioux came. Some distance west of Fort Kearney they grew alarmed about the Sioux and turned south toward the Republican. On that stream they encamped and were about to begin hunting buffalo when enemies, probably Brulé Sioux, attacked them. A Skidi chief, his wife, and child were caught away from the camp and killed. The enemy then attacked in force and there was a big fight. The Skidis were now afraid to hunt, but they had to have meat, so the chiefs decided to move south and join the other three Pawnee tribes. They found these people camped on the Beaver, a southern tributary of the Republican. The next day the Pawnees hunted buffalo. Two days later the enemy came down in force and fought the Pawnees from noon until mid-afternoon. By this time everyone in the Pawnee camp was showing the strain of this ceaseless harassment, and the cry was constantly heard: *Chah-ra-rat wata!* —*The Sioux are coming down!*[103] On the fifth day after reaching this camp the chiefs decided that the Sioux annoyance was too bad; it made hunting impossible; and they ordered a move toward the southeast, one day's march. But the day after this move the Sioux came down and fought the Pawnees, preventing their hunting. The next day they came again, and there was a fight lasting several hours. Dusty Chief, a Skidi, was killed this day. The next day camp was moved toward the southeast; the following morning enemies came down and made a bold attempt to run off the entire Pawnee herd. They came very near succeeding in putting the Pawnees on foot, but the heroism of small boys who were guarding the herd prevented this. This new attack was made by Comanches and a few Kansa or Osages from the Arkansas; but the Pawnees thought that they were Sioux, and the next day they broke camp in alarm and made a long march toward the southeast to get away from the enemy. Their new camp was on the Solomon Fork, some fifty miles west of the Pawnee sacred spring, which is near the present Cawker City. By making this march to the Solomon the Pawnees had put themselves directly in the path of a great war party of Cheyennes, Brulé Sioux, Arapahos, Kiowas, and Prairie-Apaches who had recently set out from the Arkansas to attack them. The morning that this war party appeared a misty rain was falling. Small parties of Pawnees were scattered over the prairie hunting buffalo when the enemy came down and opened the attack. The Pawnees ran for camp; there they made a stand, then came out in force and drove the enemy back. Presently the Cheyennes and others made a stand. Alights-on-the-Clouds, the Cheyenne who the autumn before had refused to smoke with the Skidis at Fort Kearney, was riding up and down the Pawnee line. The Pawnees were frankly afraid of him. They had shot him many times without wounding him, and they believed that he was protected by the spirits and could not be killed. Wherever he rode the Pawnees turned their horses and gave ground. At last he rode toward a young Kitkehahki named Big Spotted Horse, a mere boy some fifteen or sixteen years old. Big Spotted Horse turned his pony and started away, but to his terror found that the dreaded Cheyenne was keeping after him.

It was considered much braver to strike and count coup on an armed enemy than to kill him, and Alights-on-the-Clouds evidently intended to count coup on this Pawnee boy before shooting him. He had a sheathed sword in his hand which he was using to count coup with. Big Spotted Horse had only a bow. Now, a man with a bow, when mounted and trying to hit a following foe, can only shoot toward the left. The Cheyenne warrior took full advantage of this fact, maneuvering to get up on the righthand side of his intended victim. He came up close and reached out to strike, and at that moment the boy, who was lefthanded, turned and let fly an arrow. He said afterward that he was so frightened he did not even look where he was shooting, and having shot he started away as fast as he could go. Then he heard a great shout from the Pawnees, and looking around beheld the terrible Cheyenne stretched on the grass with an arrow sticking in his eye. The Pawnees made a hard push and got to where the Cheyenne lay. They then discovered that he was wearing under a red cloak or blanket a coat of Spanish armor that protected him from neck to knee from arrows or even from the fire of the old-fashioned smoothbore guns with which most Indians were then equipped.[104]

The Pawnees were greatly pleased over the killing of Alights-on-the-Clouds. This Cheyenne had worried them very much; to find that he was after all only a man in an iron shirt was a relief. They cut his coat-of-mail into several pieces and carried these off as trophies.

The enemy having withdrawn, the Pawnees completed their hunt and returned to their villages on the Platte to harvest their crops. In October they set out again to hunt on the Republican; and now the Kitkehahkis sent out a war party to steal horses. These warriors found the Arapahos encamped near the crossing of the Arkansas. Here there was a camp of United States dragoons, and near it two big Arapaho camps about three miles apart, with all of the Arapaho horses grazing on the prairie between the two camps. With the consummate skill for which they were famous in such operations, the Kitkehahkis got in between the two Arapaho camps unobserved and, in broad daylight, mounted the best horses and drove the entire herd off toward the north, leaving the astonished Arapahos without mounts on which to pursue them.[105]

With part of this treasure trove the Kitkehahkis made peace with the Prairie Potawatomies, with whom they had been unwise enough to go to war about two years before. They put the Potawatomies into a good humor by giving them many fine Arapaho horses. And it was well they did, for the Arapahos were filling the air with threats, and the Cheyennes, still mourning Alights-on-the-Clouds and the other warriors they had lost in the recent battle, were preparing to send around war pipes to get up a crusade against the Pawnees.

In June, 1853, this great war party of prairie Indians set out to hunt the Pawnees. All the Cheyennes were present with their women and children. At the head of the tribe were being carried the two great medicines, the Medicine Arrows and the Buffalo Cap, which were taken into battle only when the tribe had suffered some particularly heavy loss. With them were the angry Arapahos, a band of Brulé Sioux, some Kiowas, Prairie-Apaches, and even a few Crows from the far north.

Meantime the Kitkehahkis had met their new brothers, the Prairie Potawatomies, with whom were a few Sacs and Foxes. These Indians hunted together and camped together on the Republican, then separated. On the day after they had left the Potawatomies, Sky Chief of the Kitkehahkis decided to ride back to the other camp to complete a horse trade he had begun with a Potawatomi. He had just left the Pawnee camp when he saw the advance parties of the prairie warriors coming over the hills. Hesitating whether to turn back, he decided that the best thing to do was to ride to the Potawatomi camp for aid.

The Pawnees had taken position, with their women and children and horses, in the bed of a creek, the warriors fighting from behind the protecting banks. The prairie warriors charged up and down, losing men and doing little execution. The Pawnees simply would not leave the protection of the creek banks. This went on for a long time; then a body of horsemen appeared on a hill: the Potawatomies led by their chief and Sky Chief. These Indians were armed with splendid rifles and fought like troops. A platoon rode forward and fired a volley into the mass of prairie Indians, then fell back to reload, the second platoon at once advancing and firing a volley. They came on and on, being driven back a little at times by a hard charge, but always coming on. This mode of fighting proved too much for the Cheyennes and their friends; after fighting back as best they could for a time, they fled from the field.[106]

During the early 1850's the Pawnee buffalo hunts in summer were gambles with death. At times the tribe saw few enemies and had a good hunt. At other times, as in 1852 and 1853, they had to fight hard, but succeeded in driving off their foes and returned home with plenty of meat and skins. Every few years, no matter how great the precautions they took, they were caught in one of those sudden catastrophes that featured Indian life in the old days.

The prairie Indians had been defeated in 1853 by the Potawatomies and Kitkehahkis; but they were determined to get back at these tribes, and in June, 1854, they assembled a great camp on the

Arkansas at the mouth of Pawnee Fork. Early in July a war party of 1,500 warriors set out toward the north, telling the white men on the Arkansas that they were going to wipe out all of the "eastern Indians" they found in the buffalo range. The Pawnees were included under the title of eastern Indians. In the contemporary reports no attack on the Pawnees is recorded; but J. B. Dunbar states from Pawnee authority that a great body of Cheyenne and Kiowa warriors cut off 113 Pawnees from the main camp and killed them "almost to a man." It would seem that the war party of prairie Indians divided after leaving the Arkansas, most of the Cheyennes and Kiowas going in search of the Pawnees. The rest of the party, a very large force of Comanches, Osages, and Prairie-Apaches, with some Arapahos and Cheyennes among them, on July 10 came on a hunting party of 200 Sacs and Foxes on the Smoky Hill Fork. The Sacs and Foxes, all armed with good rifles, got into a ravine, and firing by sections so that half the rifles were always loaded, they beat off charge after charge and won the fight handsomely. In this affair the prairie Indians had twenty-six killed and about one hundred wounded. The Sac and Fox loss was trifling.

Such was the life of the Pawnees when they went into the plains for buffalo in the early 1850's. These Indians were making an heroic effort to support their families by hunting in the face of almost ceaseless attacks by enemies and the steady loss of Pawnee men, women, and children killed in these bloody affairs. From their association at this period with the Prairie Potawatomies, Sacs, Foxes, and other immigrant tribes now settled in east Kansas, the Pawnee chiefs learned the value of good rifles and discipline; but their tribe gained nothing from this knowledge. The Pawnees were now too poor to purchase good rifles and the government still exhibited no inclination to assist the unfortunate tribe. To the travelers on the Oregon Trail (now beginning to be termed the Overland Road) and to the western editors, who knew nothing of the courageous efforts of this tribe to support itself by hunting in the plains, the Pawnees were nothing more than troublesome beggars and thieves who infested the roads, preying on the emigrants, and did not deserve any assistance.

NOTES TO CHAPTER VIII

[95]His successor, Agent James W. Gatewood, reported these facts in 1853.
[96]*Daily Missouri Republican*, May 28, 1847. This newspaper reports the burning of the Pawnee village in May, 1847. The Sioux had set the village

afire the year before; in May, 1847, they finished the work. Dunbar reported the killing of the eighty-three Pawnees.

[97]This treaty is dated August 6; but the *Daily Missouri Republican* states that the lands were bought and the Pawnees were paid in the spring of this year.

[98]*Daily Missouri Republican,* various dates in September, 1848. We have a Pawnee version of this affair in "Sharitarish's Lament for His Grandson" (in Dinsmore: *Pawnee Music*). In this song the chief's name is given as Sharitarish or Mad Chief.

[99]*Ibid.,* correspondence dated Fort Childs, October 6, 1848.

[100]The *Daily Missouri Republican* reports that the Grand Pawnee village (seemingly the one near the present Clarks, Nebraska) was in use up to the spring of 1849, and that the Pawnees from here started building a new village at the mouth of Salt Creek in May, the old deserted village being burned by Sioux and Cheyennes on July 6, 1849. The paper refers to the new village again in September, 1849.

[101]*Daily Missouri Republican,* July 27, 1849.

[102]*Ibid.,* August 26, 1851.

[103]*Chah-ra-rat* (Sioux) *wata* (coming). Like the Assyrians, the Sioux always *came down*. Chah was a very old name for the Sioux, first recorded by La Salle. Pawnee, *Chah-ra-rat* (Chah enemies); Arikara, *Chaone;* Prairie-Apache, *Shanana;* Oto and Osage, *Shahan.*

[104]George Bent of the Cheyennes described this armor to the present writer as a long leather coat with small metal discs sewn all over it, overlapping like shingles on a roof. Dr. George Bird Grinnell states (*The Fighting Cheyennes,* pp. 78-9) that a Pitahauerat Pawnee on foot shot Alights-on-the-Clouds with a magic arrow, and he gives old Eagle Chief of the Skidis as his authority. Many old Cheyennes in 1912 (and some of them were in this fight) agreed that Alights-on-the-Clouds was killed by a left-handed Pawnee who was riding a horse when he shot the arrow. Captain L. H. North heard this story over and over, and the Pawnees (around 1863-73) always said that it was Big Spotted Horse, mounted, who killed the Cheyenne. Captain North knew Eagle Chief very well and found it difficult to believe that he had given a different version to Grinnell; indeed North suggested that the interpreter (Tom Morgan) had twisted old Eagle Chief's words and given Grinnell a false interpretation. It may be noted that Tom Morgan was the man who produced this story of the magic arrow, and that he said it was his own father who killed the Cheyenne.

[105]*Nebraska Historical Society Publications,* series 1, v. III, p. 294.

[106]Grinnell: *The Fighting Cheyennes,* pp. 88-91; D. C. Bean, in *Nebraska Historical Society Publications,* ser. 1, v. III, p. 294. The *Daily Missouri Republican,* December 4, 1853, states that the Cheyennes lost seventeen, Arapahos five, Kiowas two; a great many were wounded; 170 ponies were killed, and the Cheyennes were still "all in tears." The Pawnee loss was five or six men killed. The paper dates the fight August 16, 1853. These losses were heavy from the prairie Indians' viewpoint, and the men killed were their best warriors.

Pahukatawa, chief of the Skidirari clan of Skidi Pawnees. (Photograph by William H. Jackson, from BAE, Smithsonian Institution)

Blue Hawk and Coming-Around-with-the-Herd, Pitahauerat Pawnees.
(Photograph by William H. Jackson, BAE, Smithsonian Institution)

Pawnee Indians watching the caravan. "Of all the Indian tribes," said Alfred Jacob Miller, "I think the Pawnees gave us the most trouble." (From painting by Alfred Jacob Miller, courtesy Walters Art Gallery. From *The West of Alfred Jacob Miller,* by Marvin C. Ross, Norman, 1968)

IX

Back to the Loup

In 1834 THE POLICY OF THE GOVERNMENT HAD BEEN TO TURN the country west of the Missouri River into an Indian Territory where the native tribes and the immigrant Indians from the East could be settled permanently, all whites except traders and government representatives to be scrupulously excluded from the Indian country. The white men, however, had already gained a foothold in the new Indian district, and by opening trails to Santa Fé and Oregon they had rapidly developed their claims on the country. By 1850 public clamor in the West was demanding the opening of all these Indian lands to settlement, and by the signing of the Kansas-Nebraska act, May 30, 1854, by President Pierce, this public demand was met.

New treaties were immediately made with the Omahas and Otos in Nebraska, these tribes being given small reservations, the remainder of their lands being opened to settlement. Nebraska Territory was organized and divided into counties; lands were surveyed, towns laid out, and a swarm of whites came to settle on the best lands near the Missouri and along the Platte, Elkhorn, and other streams. Although the Indian Office officials had been considering a new treaty with the Pawnees for a number of years, the government still took no action to aid this tribe. Part of the lands the Omahas had sold by the treaty of 1854 were Pawnee lands, and the Pawnees were very angry over this. Their lands north of the Platte were being settled by the whites without the tribe receiving any payment whatever; at the same time they were being treated by the whites as intruders on the lands south of the Platte. White men of the roughest frontier type took up land immediately adjacent to the Pawnee villages, where some of them by cunning and others by acts of open violence attempted to crowd the Indians off. They let their stock run in the Pawnee corn patches, cut off most of the timber on the Indian lands, stole the Pawnee horses, and committed acts of violence against any small parties of the tribe that came within their reach. These men were making life unbearable for the Pawnees south of the Platte, and the tribe did not dare to remove north of the river for fear of the Sioux.[107]

The Brulé Sioux had had a fight with the troops at Fort Laramie in 1854, and now in the summer of 1855 the government was sending an expedition up the Platte to punish them. The Sioux took being warred upon by the United States very coolly, going about their usual business of hunting buffalo and raiding the Pawnees and Omahas, as if the Americans were a very small tribe of no importance. In July the entire Omaha tribe was hunting on Beaver Creek north of the Loup, when 500 Laramie Sioux with many Cheyennes and a few Arapahos came down on them and drove them from their hunting grounds. In this affair Logan Fontenelle, the head-chief of the Omahas, was killed. The tribe did not dare to return to their own reservation near Blackbird's Hills, but fled for protection to the Indian agency at Bellevue. This attack on the Omahas had been made immediately north of the old Pawnee villages on the Loup; when the Indian Office officials urged the Pawnees to return to the Loup, stating that there was now no danger from the Sioux, the Pawnee chiefs refused point blank. The Indian agent at Bellevue, George Hepner, reported that the Pawnees were anxious for a treaty, but that they wished to have a reservation south of the Platte, so that the river would form a protecting barrier between their villages and the Sioux. This Indian agent reported that in 1855 the Pawnees were in three villages south of the Platte. The Skidis were still where they had been since 1850, on the high bluffs near Pahuk or Hill Island, a home of the spirit animals or *nahurac*, on the south bank of the Platte, opposite the present Fremont. They had by 1855 a strong village here, protected from attack by a high sod wall. They had been joined by the Pitahauerats. The Grand Pawnees were about four miles southeast of the Skidis, on the site of the later town of Leshara. The third village of 1855 was probably that of the Kitkehahkis, on the south bank of the Platte, west of the Skidi village.[108]

Caught between *Chah-ra-rat* (the Sioux) and *La-chi-kuts* (the Big Knives or Americans), the Pawnees did not know what to do. The new territorial government of Nebraska immediately took sides with its own citizens; when in the spring of 1855 settlers on the Elkhorn complained that Pawnees were stealing their stock, Governor Izard appointed John M. Thayer brigadier-general of militia and sent him to the Pawnee villages to investigate. Both at the Skidi village and that of the Grand Pawnees Thayer was informed by the chiefs that the settlers' stock had been stolen by a war party of Poncas, who had also attempted to steal the Pawnee horses. General Thayer was strongly inclined to believe the chiefs; but when he discovered that some Pawnees had robbed his wagon of a large stock of fine groceries while he was attending the council, he began to have doubts as to the probity of all Pawnees.

The truth of the situation was that nearly all of the chiefs and a majority of the warriors were very anxious to be on good terms with the whites; but the tribe had suffered so terribly that the authority of the chiefs was now little regarded, and many of the destitute people were ready to take what they required either from Indian enemies or the white settlers. The worst sign was that the Pawnee women were losing heart and giving up. They had always been noted for their industry; but they were growing tired of building villages, to be burned by the Sioux, and of planting crops, to see them destroyed by the Sioux and the whites. When surveyors arrived at the Pawnee villages in May, 1856, and began throwing up mounds in the corn patches to mark corners, the Pawnee women could hardly be prevented from mobbing the white men, and they angrily tore down the mounds as soon as the surveyors had left. The Indian Office officials were discussing placing the Pawnees with the Otos on a reservation on the Big Blue, near the Kansas line. The Pawnee chiefs evidently approved of this scheme, but nothing came of it.

In the summer of 1856 a war party of Cheyennes came up to the Platte to raid the Pawnees, but became involved with the whites and were attacked by troops from Fort Kearney. The Cheyennes at once broke out into a series of bloody raids along the Platte, which for the moment quieted the outcry of the whites concerning the petty misdeeds of the Pawnees. By autumn, however, the whites were again making threats; Samuel Allis, the Pawnee missionary of earlier years, made a report to the superintendent of Indian affairs in which he stated that if a treaty were not made and the Pawnee villages removed from their present location there would be serious trouble. He added that the tribe was ready to set out on its winter hunt and that a treaty council could not be held until the following spring.[109]

The winter of 1856 was a hard one, with great cold and deep snow. The Pawnees came home in the spring, destitute and worried, to find that the white settlers had wrought great havoc about their villages during their absence in the plains. A new agent,

William W. Dennison, had been sent out, to care for both the Otos and the Pawnees. He arrived in March and devoted all of his time for two months to keeping peace between the Pawnees and the whites. The tribe then, having planted their crops, set out on the summer hunt; but, with the Cheyennes gathered in force on the Republican Fork and the United States troops preparing to attack that tribe, the Pawnees had poor hunting. The whites were now also encroaching on the Pawnee hunting grounds on the Republican and Solomon forks, many families having established themselves on both of these streams, living mainly by going on buffalo hunts twice a year: white Indians, who went into the plains with wagons and came home with loads of dried meat and hides.

Returning from their hunt, the Pawnees found the Oregon Trail, now transformed into the great Overland Road, crowded with emigrants and troops. The army was not only campaigning against the Cheyennes but was sending a large force to deal with the Mormons in Utah, and after the troops had passed, the road was still crowded with army supply trains and herds of beef cattle. The Pawnees had pickings this summer; some of their warriors also enlisted as scouts to go with Colonel E. V. Sumner against the Cheyennes. These Pawnees did not add much to the tribe's renown, the officers stating that when the fight with the Cheyennes started the Pawnees lurked in the rear, following the troops, picking up Cheyenne ponies and other plunder. Hearing that the soldiers had captured a Cheyenne, the Pawnees went in a body to Colonel Sumner and offered him all the Cheyenne ponies they had gathered in, and also all their pay as scouts, if he would turn over the Cheyenne captive to them, to be tortured to death. On their way home with their new ponies and a large quantity of supplies and presents Colonel Sumner had given them, these Pawnees were set upon by a band of white frontiersmen, who took everything that they had and attempted to murder them.[110]

At last, in the middle of September, 1857, the Pawnee chiefs were summoned to a treaty council to be held on Table Creek, near the present Nebraska City. Here they met Commissioner J. W. Denver (for whom the city of Denver is named), and on September 24 the chiefs signed away the last of the Pawnee lands, accepting a small reservation and government aid in compensation. At this council Samuel Allis advised the chiefs, and J. Sterling Morton looked after the interests of Nebraska Territory. For some reason the idea of placing the Pawnees with the Otos on the Big Blue

was given up, and with Allis' aid the chiefs were talked into accepting a small reservation on Loup Fork; but they agreed to this only
when promised that the government would actively protect them
from Sioux attacks.

This treaty gave the Pawnees the option of choosing another
reservation, if they did not like the one on Loup Fork; but they
were expected to be prompt in their decision, and the tribe was so
split up into factions that prompt decision was impossible. They
took what the whites pressed them to take, the Loup Fork lands,
a tract thirty miles from east to west and fifteen from south to
north, including lands on both banks of the river. The tribe was
to receive for five years an annuity of $40,000 a year; $30,000 there-
after each year in perpetuity; the government was to build an
agency, with a sawmill, gristmill, blacksmith and other shops, and
a school; the tribe was to have an agent, a farmer, blacksmith,
teachers, and other employees at public expense; and the promise
of protection from the Sioux was written into the treaty.

To the Pawnees, who had been cut off from all government aid
for twelve years and practically outlawed, this treaty seemed a proffer
of new life. Pitalesharo or Man Chief signed the document as head
of the Grand Pawnees—the last Pawnee head-chief to rule in
Nebraska. By a strange misapprehension this chief has been identified as the Skidi of the same name (born 1784 or ten years later),
who saved the Ietan girl from being sacrificed in the spring of 1817;
but that chief had died (1841?), and the Pitalesharo who signed
the treaty of 1857 was a Grand Pawnee, born about 1823, and
reputedly the son of the Grand Pawnee head-chief of the period
1833-43. Mrs. Elvira Platt, who knew this last Pitalesharo intimately,
stated that he was the nephew of Sharitarish, the chief who signed
this same treaty of 1857.[111] The other chiefs who signed were, for
the Skidis, Comanche Chief; for the Kitkehahkis, Nasharosedetarako;
for the Pitahauerats, Kewekonasharo (Buffalo Bull Chief).

For the second time in the tribe's history some Pawnee chiefs
were now taken to Washington. Samuel Allis went with them as
interpreter and adviser. They were kept idling about the capital
city all winter, waiting for the Senate to approve the treaty. When
this was accomplished, the chiefs were taken on a tour of the great
eastern cities, where they received much attention and were presented with many fine gifts. They came home in the spring of 1858.

The year 1858 among the Pawnees was a repetition of 1857. They
could not hunt on the Republican Fork because of the hostile
Cheyennes, and at their villages on the Platte they were almost

besieged by hostile whites. The Indian agent, William W. Dennison, reported that a majority of the whites who had settled near the Pawnee villages were less civilized than the Indians. The moment these men learned that a treaty had been signed they swamped the Indian Office with claims for depredations, hoping to obtain most of the $40,000 Pawnee annuity money. Late in September the tribe received their first annuities under the new treaty, mainly in the form of needed goods, and set out on their winter hunt.

The treaty had provided that the Pawnees should remove to their new reservation on Loup Fork within one year of the date of ratification. That meant by April, 1859; but at that date the Pawnees were still at their villages on the Platte and exhibited no intention of moving to the Loup. In this they were justified. They had been promised aid and protection, and the officials now expected these destitute Indians to move to the Loup unaided and to remain there at the risk of their lives, waiting for the promised protection. The assurances of white men, who had never seen a Sioux raid, that they would be safe on the Loup only angered the Pawnees.

The Sioux and Cheyennes were unusually active in the spring of 1859, carrying their raids to the reservations of the tribes with whom they were at war. The Pawnees again were afraid to go to the Republican Fork to hunt, but had made an arrangement with the Omahas to meet that tribe on the Elkhorn and hunt with them for mutual protection. In mid-June the Pawnees crossed north of the Platte and headed for the Elkhorn. The next morning they saw smoke rising in heavy clouds south of the Platte, and realized that their village had been set on fire. Indians who recrossed the Platte reported later that the entire village had been destroyed. The *Nebraska City News* of July 2, 1859, stated that a small party of Sioux had recently set fire to the Pawnee village, after killing a number of old people and children whom the Pawnees had left behind when they started on their hunt; but this newspaper was so habitually hostile in its attitude toward the Pawnees that the truthfulness of its report may well be questioned. Many Pawnees certainly believed that white men had burned their village.

The next day when the Pawnees started up the Elkhorn, little parties of Indians began plundering the whites. They were furious at the destruction of their village, and they were destitute, many of them with no food at all. The chiefs attempted to keep order; but they could not be everywhere at once, and small parties of roving warriors continued to take cattle and other property from isolated settlers. The whites drew together in armed groups. One party of twenty-five armed white men came on a few Pawnees at a house near the little town of Fontanelle; and although the main Pawnee camp was in plain sight and the chiefs might have been applied to for aid, the whites took matters into their own hands, with the result that one white man and three Pawnees were shot. It was then observed that the Indians in the main camp were mounting their horses, and the whites hastily withdrew.

Messengers were sent to Omaha and to Fort Kearney for help, and a force of militia supported by a few United States dragoons from the fort was gathered on the Elkhorn. The Pawnee tribe had gone on up the river to meet the Omaha Indians and hunt buffalo. On July 12 the whites found a small camp of Omahas, who said that the Pawnee camp was ten or twelve miles ahead. At two in the morning the "army" set out, intending to surprise the Pawnees in their camp: wagons rattling, men talking and shouting, all the noise of a picnic party on the move. The Pawnees packed up and went elsewhere, and the amateur soldiers were astonished to find the Indian camp deserted. Pressing ahead, they soon sighted the Pawnee tribe in rapid retreat; the village (the women, children, old men and impedimenta) was hastening toward a high plateau near the bank of the Elkhorn, but the warriors, 500 to 600 in number, had taken a position in the deep bed of a dry creek, where they stood grimly watching the approach of the whites. They had thrown off every stitch of clothing, as they always did when going into a fight.

As the whites came up and jostled themselves into a rude line of battle, Sharitarish, called the head-chief, advanced toward them, making signs of peace. Lieutenant B. H. Robertson, Second Dragoons, promptly whipped out his pistol and fired, but missed the chief and wounded his horse. The chief threw away his bow and arrows and came boldly on, shouting in English that he would not fight the whites, that he had been to Washington the winter before, and that after the good talk of the Great Father he was ready to die, but would not shoot at white men.

He was now joined by Pitalesharo, who had an American flag wrapped about his naked body. The experienced Indian-fighters among the dragoons were all for an instant charge; but Governor Samuel W. Black, who had joined the army on the march, demurred. The sight of these Pawnee chiefs earnestly begging that no blood should be shed was too much for the governor, and he ordered that no more shots should be fired.

The Pawnee women had taken fright and were fleeing with their children and old people. Some were swimming the Elkhorn, others running for the high bluffs. The dragoons and some of the settlers were cursing loudly on seeing their prey escape. The governor was parleying with the chiefs through an interpreter. The chiefs were extremely anxious that there should be no fight. They said that some of the people, who were starving, had taken food from the settlers. They would pay for all the damage from their annuities, and they would give up the worst offenders. To this Governor Black willingly assented; and thus was ended what was known in Nebraska pioneer circles as the Pawnee war of '59. One shot had been fired at an utterly friendly chief by a brainless and bad-tempered dragoon officer. Some frontier humorist dubbed the little stream on which the meeting took place *Battle Creek*, a name which has stuck; and the members of the volunteer force were made the butts of many robust jests that had to do with their coming home without a single dead Pawnee in their game-bags; but the more sensible volunteers were content with the bloodless outcome of their campaign. They had seen the array of grim Pawnee warriors and knew that but for the brave stand of the chiefs for peace not a white man would have left the field alive.[112]

The Pawnees and Omahas had a poor hunt. The dragoons and Nebraska militia while still in sight of the Indian camps saw many mounted Sioux on the bluffs, evidently waiting for the whites to withdraw. No sooner had the whites gone than the Sioux began attacking the Pawnee and Omaha hunting parties; this they kept up during the entire hunt. A large party of Omaha women, with old people and children, who did not have many horses and could not keep up with the moving camps, started to return to their reservation on the Missouri; on the way they were attacked by Sioux, who killed a large number of them.

Although the Pawnee treaty of 1857 had been ratified in April, 1858, Congress had not made an appropriation for a Pawnee agency, agent, and employees. The Indian Office officials, however, were so impressed with the need for immediate removal of the tribe that in the spring of 1859 men were sent to Beaver Creek on Loup Fork, where they began building a mill and agency. The Pawnee troubles with the whites in June and July still further alarmed the officials; and in August Judge J. L. Gillis of Pennsylvania was appointed special agent for the Pawnees and came up the Missouri with Superintendent A. M. Robinson to council with the chiefs and induce them to remove at once from their villages south of the

Platte. The officials were aided by Samuel Allis, former missionary and government teacher for the Pawnees, and by William G. Hollins, an old American Fur Company trader. These men met the chiefs as soon as they returned from their hunt in August. The tribe had been forced to leave the buffalo range north of Loup Fork by Sioux and had come home with little meat. The annuities under the treaty were now used as a bait to induce the Indians to move to the Loup, for they were told that they would be fed and clothed by the government if they agreed to move. The agent also stressed the government's promise of protection from Sioux raids. About twenty of the chiefs now went with the Indian officials to Loup Fork to select the new location for the tribe. Several Mormon families had settled on the Loup a few years before this, founding the little village of Genoa, and now the Pawnees decided to have their new home at this town; but the agent wanted the Genoa location for the agency, and he induced the Pawnees to select a beautiful plain on the west side of Beaver Creek, immediately southwest of Genoa, as the site of their villages.[113] He then ordered the white settlers off the Indian reservation, but paid them for some of their buildings and part of their crops. The main body of the Pawnees remained in the old villages south of the Platte until they had harvested their crops. Late in October the agent induced them to come to Loup Fork; but they moved with deep forebodings, for they remembered very well the great Sioux raids which had broken up their former villages on the Loup in 1843-1846.

In 1859 the Loup was no longer a primitive Indian country. The old fur-trader trail up the river was now a road over which thousands of emigrant teams and freight wagons passed each season. There was a regular ferry on the Loup within a mile of where the Pawnee agency had just been established; here also was the little settlement of Genoa, and although Agent Gillis had ordered the whites to leave, many of the families refused to go, and they were still here two years later. The town of Columbus, some five miles above the mouth of the Loup and eighteen miles east of the Pawnee agency, had 200 people and was rapidly growing. A stage line had been established from Omaha to Columbus and thence westward between the Loup and Platte to Fort Kearney, with stations all along the line. On the south bank of the Platte was the great Overland Road with mail coaches, swarms of emigrant teams, and long trains of freight wagons. Stage stations, trading-stores, and ranches were clustered along this highway; Indians were not welcome; the country had become a white man's land, and this was also true of the Elkhorn district east of the Pawnees. To the west and north of the Pawnee reservation lay untouched Indian country, given over to the buffalo and other wild game. But here the Pawnees were no more welcome than in the white men's lands south of the Platte and east of the Elkhorn, for it was through these lands to the west and north that the Sioux and their allies came prowling, hunting for Pawnee and Omaha camps to attack.

The Pawnees left their reservation to hunt buffalo in the late fall of 1859, and again in the spring and late fall of 1860; but Agent Gillis made no mention of this fact. *Progress in civilization* was the slogan at the new Pawnee agency, and taking the women and children on extended buffalo hunts was not progress. The hunts were therefore left out of the agent's discreet reports, which stressed more pleasing subjects: farming and crops, building improvements, and the bright prospects for advancement that lay in education. In 1860 the agency farmer and his white employees planted 160 acres, and in spite of the drought had a good crop. The Pawnee women had their own little patches, some 800 acres in all; but their crop was very light, because of the drought and the ancient custom of going off on a buffalo hunt after hoeing the corn for the second time in early June, leaving it to take care of itself until the tribe returned home at harvest-time. The saw and grist mill had been finished. It ran by steam, and the whistle was the wonder and delight of the tribe. The agency buildings were log houses bought from the Genoa settlers. The agent's report hinted at extensive building he had accomplished, but in fact he had built only one large granary. There was no school, but on the urging of the Washington officials Judge Gillis was planning to put up a brick schoolhouse. He had already built a bridge across Beaver Creek, connecting the agency with the Pawnee villages.

These villages were in the level plain west of the creek. At first there seem to have been three—two Skidi villages to the west, and one large village farther east in which the Chauis, Pitahauerats, and Kitkehahkis lived together. The villages were protected after a fashion on the north by the high bluffs; but as the Sioux had a trick of slipping across Loup Fork and attacking suddenly from the thickets south of the villages, the Pawnees presently built a high sod wall to defend their settlement on the west, south, and east. That some such protection was needed became apparent at once. In 1860 the Sioux, Cheyennes, and Arapahos made attacks on the Pawnee villages on April 10, May 19 and 21, June 22, July

5 and 11, September 1 and 14. The agent's report does not cover events after September 14, but the raids probably continued all fall and winter. The chiefs had demanded the protection promised in the treaty of 1857, and in August Captain Alfred Sully arrived with a few soldiers and a brass howitzer. While he was at the agency the Sioux made two attacks. He recommended that a blockhouse be built on the bluffs north of the Pawnee villages and that a small detachment of soldiers be stationed there with a howitzer to keep the Sioux off. The Pawnee chiefs urgently desired peace with the Sioux, Cheyennes, and Arapahos; Captain Sully sent an officer to Fort Laramie to attempt to arrange a peace council, but nothing came of this. The Sioux, who were very strong and well armed, simply were not interested in a Pawnee peace.

The Sioux raid on September 14 made it evident that this tribe was as heartily bent on driving the Pawnees away from the Loup as it had been in the great days of 1843-1846. It was on this day that the Sioux burned sixty earth-lodges. They came down with 250 warriors and charged into one of the villages. The Pawnees quickly rallied in force, and with some aid from the whites drove the Sioux out, killing thirteen of them and taking several scalps. Captain Sully had gone back to Fort Kearney to report that he had made the Pawnee agency safe, when the news of this raid took him by surprise.

It was during this year 1860 that the Pawnees learned to love *Atiputa* (Grandfather—their term of honor for the agent). Judge Gillis was a man after their own hearts. He was seventy and white-haired; but when the warning rang out: *Chah-ra-rat wata!* (The Sioux are coming down!) the old man ran for his pistols, mounted a fast horse and rode out, banging away at the Sioux and lustily cheering his Pawnees on. He had discovered almost at once that his Indians were keeping up the ancient custom of stealing horses from other tribes; he was working to stop this, not as some of the later agents did, by threats and by calling in the sheriff, the U.S. marshal, or the military to arrest the culprits, but by talking the chiefs around and gaining the support of many leading warriors. He had organized a police force of six prominent warriors from each of the four Pawnee tribes and put them into brilliant uniforms made from the Indian cloth which was a part of the tribal annuity goods. These men were so pleased with their uniforms and authority that they willingly took away from their best friends the horses which these young men had stolen at the risk of their lives from the Potawatomies, Delawares, and other tribes.

In the spring of 1861 Abraham Lincoln removed Judge Gillis. Indeed, he made the cleanest sweep of agents and superintendents thus far seen in the Indian service, his appointees being men unknown to fame except in certain local political circles. Most of these men were of a low type, interested mainly in making money by shady methods for themselves and their relatives whom they put on the agency payrolls. Their principal contribution to the service was to add greatly to the popular legend that all Indian agents were rascals of the worst type.

In the Lincoln changes the Pawnees were given an agent named H. W. DuPuy, a western politician who at once set up a patronage mill of his own at the agency, promising places to a large number of persons and inducing them to leave their homes and come to Nebraska, where he kept them waiting for months while he busied himself in attempting to find out which of these prospective employees would prove most profitable to himself if he placed their names on the payroll. He neglected his Indians completely. The Sioux came down and raided the reservation; the Civil War began, the regular troops left Fort Kearney, volunteers were called for and mustered in; but Agent DuPuy continued to spin his little webs. Spring came; no plowing was done, the Pawnee women being left to dig up the ground with their hoes as they had always done, while the government teams stood idle in the stables. No school had been started; after three years of reported progress there was no schoolhouse, and the new agent had not even got to the point of planning one.

At last the crowd of appointees this man had enticed from their homes lost all patience, formed an association and sent a representative to Washington to accuse him of corrupt practices. Deserting his Indians, DuPuy hastened to the capital to fight his accusers. The Indian Office did not care for the publicity this vulgar quarrel was bringing it, and presently Mr. DuPuy was quietly dismissed, and all the other men engaged in the squabble were debarred from holding any position under the government.

Lester Platt and his wife, who had taken a leading part in the quarrels that had disrupted the Pawnee Mission and the first government agency on Loup Fork in 1843-46, had obtained a DuPuy promise of positions as teachers at the new agency. Failing to gain their appointments, the Platts took part in the denunciations of DuPuy and were ordered to leave the agency. Platt moved just outside the eastern boundary of the reservation and set up in the store business, running a trading place for the Pawnees. The ruling of

the Indian Office had debarred all the men engaged in the DuPuy
affair from entering government employment, but it did not mention
their wives; in 1862 Mrs. Elvira Platt was appointed as a teacher
for the Pawnee children. Thus the Platts, who had now known the
Pawnees for twenty years, remained closely associated with these
Indians. The Pawnees had noted that the name Platt was the same
as that applied by the whites to the Platte River. Platte was the
French for shallow or flat, and the Pawnee name for this stream,
Kizkatus, had the same meaning of shallow. For this reason the
Pawnees always called Lester Platt Kizkatus.

The new Pawnee agent, Benjamin F. Lushbaugh, reached the
agency June 20, 1862; two days later a force of Brulés and Yanktons
made a raid, killing sixteen Pawnees, nearly all women who were
working in corn patches far from the villages. L. H. North, then
a youth in his teens, was hauling wood. He had camped near the
hills east of the agency for the night, and in the morning he found
that his team had strayed. Without a gun and mounted bareback
on a mule, he set out to hunt his runaways, looking into the ravines
that cut through the hills. Suddenly the Sioux rode out of the hills
between him and the agency buildings, but he whipped his mule
into a run and headed south toward the trading store of H. J.
Hudson. One of the Sioux who carried a long lance was mounted
on a very fast horse, and it was soon so obvious that this warrior
was going to catch North that the other Sioux turned off and began
to pursue some Pawnee women who were running from the corn
patches toward the Indian villages. Just as the warrior came up
with North and was preparing to lance him, his horse stepped in a
prairie-dog hole and threw him. North rode on and reached the
trading store. The Sioux jumped on his horse and started after a
Pawnee woman who was also running toward the trading store.
With the white men at the store shooting at him, this Sioux rode
up, caught the woman by the hair with his left hand and with his
knife in his right hand scalped her alive without getting off his
horse. He then made off. By this time the Pawnee warriors and a
company of the Second Nebraska Cavalry that was stationed at the
agency had armed and mounted; but the Sioux split up into small
groups and made off in different directions with little loss.

The Pawnees went on the usual summer hunt, leaving in the
villages some women and children and a few men, most of the latter
being sick or crippled. On August 27 six hundred Sioux, said to
have been Brulés and Yanktons, appeared suddenly on the hill to

the northwest of the Pawnee villages (the hill on which the Skidi burial ground was located), and came riding down toward the villages. This was in the morning, and the Sioux, who seemed to know that the villages were almost deserted, did not make a charge but advanced slowly in perfect order, the sun gleaming on their lances and guns, the fringes of their white war-shirts and the feathers of their warbonnets streaming in the breeze; as they came on at a slow steady pace, holding their excited ponies in, they were singing war songs.

In the Skidi village there was a man named Crooked Hand (*Skadiks*) who had a great reputation as a warrior although, as some informants stated, he was born with a deformed or palsied hand. According to other Pawnee informants Crooked Hand had had a leg broken in a fight with the Cheyennes in 1852, and he was lame in that leg. He was lying sick in his lodge when news was brought of the appearance of the great war party of Sioux; he instantly sprang up, threw off his buffalo robe, and seized his weapons, issuing orders for everyone to prepare to fight. Mustering sick men, old men, boys of twelve, and even a number of women, Crooked Hand got a force of about two hundred together and mounted, some of the women armed only with iron hoes and similar weapons. Some of the Pawnees wanted to stand behind the high earth wall that had been thrown up around three sides of the villages, as a protection from Sioux raiders, but Crooked Hand refused angrily to listen to their advice and led his motley force boldly out on the open plain to face the Sioux.

The Pawnees always recounted that when the Sioux caught sight of Crooked Hand's little force, including women, soft-cheeked boys and men almost too old to sit their horses, they burst into laughter and began to jeer at the Pawnees; but a fierce charge led by Crooked Hand soon ended that. The fight was the old-fashioned prairie Indian kind of affair: ride up and down and yell, shoot and charge in, kill a man or two, and then draw off for a rest before resuming the performance. As a spectacle it was prodigious: six hundred Indians careering up and down through clouds of powder smoke and dust. Sick as he was, Crooked Hand killed six Sioux during the day and had three horses shot under him. The fight started in the middle of the morning; the Sioux, who had expected to kill all the Pawnees in a few minutes and then plunder the villages and set them ablaze, were astonished to find that they could not break the Pawnee resistance. As the afternoon wore on the Sioux began to be

worried about themselves and started drawing off, and as the day
ended this slow withdrawal suddenly turned into a panic flight with
Crooked Hand and his old men and boys (now mounted on fresh
ponies brought from the villages) riding them down and killing
them. The Pawnees claimed that a great many Sioux were killed
in this final retreat. The Pawnees had about sixteen killed. Crooked
Hand, wounded in several places, rode into the villages at dusk
covered from head to heel with blood and with a Sioux arrow
through his throat, the iron arrowhead sticking out at the back of
his neck. Somehow the Skidi medicine-men got the arrow out and
patched him up, but the throat wound bothered him for the rest
of his life. It did not reduce his pugnacity in the slightest degree,
and up until the time of his death in 1873 Crooked Hand continued
to be a leading warrior among the Skidis.[114]

When the Pawnees returned from their summer hunt and heard
of this fight at the villages, the chiefs angrily told the new government agent that the white men's promise to protect the villages
from enemy raids was not being carried out. Their women were
afraid to work in the corn patches, and even in the villages there
was no safety for the old people and children who were left at home
when the tribe went on a hunt. Agent Lushbaugh was an intelligent and energetic man—a businessman who had many irons in the
fire—but it is difficult to avoid the impression that he was not
interested in the welfare of the Pawnees. The exposures he made
in his reports of the shortcomings of agents Gillis and DuPuy had
the ring of righteous indignation; yet when he in his turn was
removed from office his successor had to make a similar righteous
report on Lushbaugh's misdeeds. Ever since the agency had been
formed in 1859 the government had been paying out money to aid
the Indians; in particular, a farmer and several laborers had been
employed to teach the Pawnees improved agricultural methods. But
Lushbaugh found that in four years no land had been plowed. The
old Mormon settlers had plowed some land in 1859; part of this
land had been turned over to the Indian women, and for four years
they had hoed up the ground and planted their little patches with
no aid whatever from the government farmer. What this man and
his several teams and laborers did to occupy their time is a mystery.
Mr. Lushbaugh at once inaugurated a new farming policy that
would aid the Indians, as he claimed; but his plans appear to have
been paper ones in the main, intended to impress the officials at
Washington and, perhaps, to obtain more government funds for his

agency. This agent's repeated assertions that the Pawnee men were eager to take up farming was not the truth. Even the eight little boys who had been herded into the new agency school rebelled when the teachers ordered them to pull weeds. Weed-pulling was for girls and women; even ten years later the Pawnee men and boys were stubbornly refusing to do any work with their hands. Curiously, the women, who did all the farm work, built lodges, chopped and carried wood, and performed all the other manual labor, were even more outraged than the men at this government attempt to turn their warriors into drudges.

When Lushbaugh arrived, June 20, 1862, it was too late in the season to do more than talk about planting crops, but there was another matter demanding attention—education. Since the agency had been established four years before there had been no school, the agents contenting themselves by making elaborate plans for a large and costly brick school building, the funds for the construction of which would pass through the agent's hands. But it was war-time, and public money for such schemes was unobtainable. Agent Lushbaugh realized this, and he now decided to start a school first and talk about an expensive schoolhouse at a more auspicious time. He engaged Mrs. Elvira Platt as teacher, a position which she had held at the old agency and mission in 1843-46. At that time the Platts had belonged to the Oberlin College faction on Loup Fork, to the group that had attempted to force the Pawnees to progress; now in 1862 Mrs. Platt intended to take up this forcing process. Her plan was to separate the school children completely from their parents and rapidly train her charges into imitation whites. The trouble lay in the fact that the Pawnee parents understood enough of the proposed program to realize that they were to be lumped together as an objectionable class and the children taught to despise them, so when the call came for children for the school there were few volunteers. It took time and the making of many promises to obtain eight boys and eight girls for the school, and part of the sixteen—probably most of them—were mixed-bloods, whom the Pawnees did not regard as real members of the tribe. These children were lodged in a delapidated log cabin which the Mormons had abandoned several years before, and there they were held prisoners, for this was a boarding-school. Once committed to it a child might as well have been in prison; there was no release. The school was started in July, 1862, just when the tribe was leaving for the summer buffalo hunt, and the children of the new school wailed with fright and grief as they saw their parents and playmates move over the hills, leaving them to an unknown fate. Mrs. Platt was strict with them. One of her first acts was to snip off the scalplocks of the eight boys, who, deprived of these badges of manhood, were stricken with renewed outbursts of grief. Education seemed to mean being insulted in every possible manner. All Pawnees of the period detested hats, so the eight boys had to wear them. Some families had remained in the Indian village when the tribe had gone hunting, and the boys of these families spent a happy summer, parading their manly scalplocks and their unlimited supply of perfect leisure before the aggrieved eyes of Mrs. Platt's victims. They shouted taunts at the shorn warriors of the school and jeered when they beheld them being driven to do squaw work, such as weeding, hoeing, and woodcutting. But the little outlaws kept carefully out of Elvira Platt's way. She was not like other white women, but could express herself very forcefully in Pawnee. She knew them all by sight and was ready to report them to the Indian soldiers of their village and get them soundly whacked.

Year after year the Pawnee buffalo hunts were becoming a greater gamble with death, yet the people would not hear of giving up this ancient custom of going on two hunts each year. At the moment when the tribe set out on the summer hunt of 1862 the military reported that over 1,000 lodges of Sioux and Cheyennes were in camp on Beaver Creek, in the heart of the Pawnee hunting grounds on the Republican Fork. These enemies outnumbered the Pawnees two to one, yet the latter tribe managed in some way to obtain a good supply of buffalo. They also sent out a war party, caught the Sioux off guard, and stole sixty of their horses.

The Pawnees returned from this hunt just as the news of the great Sioux massacres in Minnesota was spreading alarm along the whole frontier. It was rumored that the Minnesota Sioux were moving southward and would soon attack the Nebraska settlements. The whites were in terror of the Sioux, and great alarm was caused when 600 Sioux warriors made the attack at the Pawnee villages on August 27. After the raid Agent Lushbaugh reported that his white employees behaved like heroes, the truth being that he and his white men were at the agency, across Beaver Creek, more than two miles north of the scene of action; as for their heroic conduct, contemporary reports state that they fled in panic down the Loup to the little town of Columbus, where they spread a report that the Minnesota Sioux had come down on the Nebraska frontier. In the wild excitement that ensued many farmers abandoned their places and fled to the nearest towns. Meantime the Sioux—who were not Minnesota Sioux—had gotten the worst of it in their fight with Crooked Hand and his heroic band of Pawnee old men, little boys, and women and had fled from Loup Fork. All was peace again; but the panic among the whites continued to spread, and the government became alarmed for the safety of the vital Overland Stage line, the one means for communication with the country west of the Missouri. A regiment of cavalry was ordered to Nebraska; but rumors of impending Indian attacks were still being spread abroad, and at each fresh alarm the western governors sent frantic appeals to Washington for more troops.

With the panic among the whites continuing, the Pawnees stayed close to their agency until October, but they had to hunt buffalo or starve. Late in the fall they set off, armed with many new papers signed by their agent and other white men, attesting that the bearers were Pawnee Indians of the best repute. They also had with them a Pawnee half-breed who could speak some English, the chiefs imagining that he might prove useful if some enterprising officer of volunteer cavalry mistook the Pawnee camp for a hostile Sioux outfit and ordered an attack.

NOTES TO CHAPTER IX

[107]Samuel Allis, in *Annual Report of the Secretary of the Interior* for 1856, pp. 656-7. The recognized line between the Pawnees and Omahas touched the Platte at the mouth of Shell Creek, but in their treaty of 1854 the Omahas had sold all lands as far out as the mouth of Beaver Creek, forty miles west of their western boundary, the whites immediately moving in and starting to settle on these Pawnee lands.

[108]Thayer saw only two villages in May, 1855: the Skidi-Pitahauerat village at Pahuk and the Grand Pawnee village at Lashara. The same two villages are referred to in the reports on election frauds in 1859 (*Nebraska Historical Society Publications*, series II, v. XIX, p. 213, p. 255) ; in these reports witnesses state that the Pawnee agent removed the Indians from these villages to the reservation in October, 1859.

[109]Allis to Superintendent Alfred Cumming, October 28, 1856 (*Annual Report of the Secretary of the Interior* for 1856, p. 656).

[110]These statements concerning the Pawnee scouts were made by one of Sumner's officers (*Kansas Historical Society Collections*, v. VIII, p. 498). The scouts were Pitahauerats, a band that had a poor reputation for courage and reliability in the 1850's.

[11] Mrs. Platt called Sharitarish *Malan*, perhaps an abbreviation of the French Maligne. His Pawnee name was interpreted as meaning Angry Chief, but the Skidis called him the Malignant Chief.

[112]In the main this account of the Pawnee troubles of June-July, 1859, is made up from the reminiscences of R. W. Hazen, a pioneer settler at Fremont, who lived within four or five miles of the Pawnee village, knew the Indians well and, unlike some other pioneers, was quite fair-minded in his attitude toward them. In these accounts "the headchief Carrow-na-Sharrow" is Sharitarish, and Pitalesharo, later the head-chief, is spoken of as "the former chief and orator of the Pawnees."

[113]The Pawnee agency was in the eastern edge of the present town of Genoa, in the southwest quarter of section 13, township 17, range 4, Nance County, Nebraska. The Pawnee villages were built some three miles south of the agency, a mile west of Beaver Creek, the combined Grand Pawnee, Pitahauerat, and Kitkehahki village being in the present section 23, the Skidi village, a mile farther west, in section 24. On February 21, 1861, the *Huntsman's Echo*, a little pioneer paper whose editor had just visited the Pawnees, stated that the Indians then had three villages, with three tribes or bands in the eastern village, the two western villages being occupied either by Skidis or one village by that tribe and the second smaller one by some of the Pitahauerats, who had been living with the Skidis on the Platte in the 1850's.

[114]Grinnell: *Pawnee Hero Stories,* London edition, pp. 319-21, gives an account of Crooked Hand and this famous fight. Captain L. H. North knew Crooked Hand well, and stated that he was born about 1828. He belonged to the *Tuhitpiyet* (Village-on-a-point or Peninsula Village) clan of Skidis. He had a son whom Elvira Platt tried to make over into a little Christian at the Pawnee school. The boy was renamed Simon Adams, Pawnee names being frowned on as a survival of heathenism, and his scalplock was snipped off. He later horrified his Christian teachers by enlisting in the Pawnee Scouts and reverting, as they believed, to heathenish ways.

Man Chief, Pitalesharo, last head chief of the Pawnees in Nebraska, taken about 1858. (Pitt Rivers Museum, Oxford University)

Eagle Chief, last head chief of the Skidis in Nebraska. (Photograph by William H. Jackson, from BAE, Smithsonian Institution)

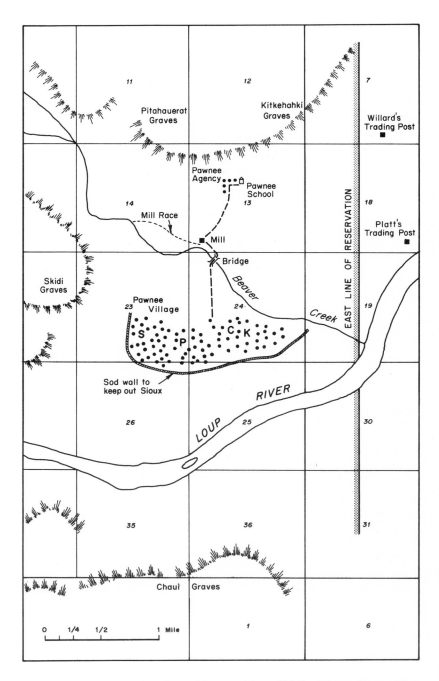

Pawnee Agency, Nebraska, 1860–75. S = Skidi village, P = Pitahauerat village, C–K = Chaui and Kitkehahki village

X

"Progress in Civilization"

WHEN AGENT LUSHBAUGH HAD BEEN AMONG THE PAWNEES FOR A FULL year, he began to make bright forecasts of rapid improvement for the tribe. His Indians desired peace with other tribes; they were industrious, and with proper government aid would soon be progressing nicely. He had reorganized the police force of Pawnee warriors and, as he claimed, was successfully dealing with the Pawnee custom of stealing horses, a practice which he said was "completely hereditary" and would require careful work to break up.

This agent, in his reports at least, was a consistent optimist. His Indians did desire peace with the Sioux, but they were still a very primitive people; war was the breath of their nostrils, and they had no intention of giving it up. It was true that the Pawnee women were noted for their industry, but the men and boys were utterly opposed to working with their hands. Despite the agent's little successes in recovering a few stolen horses from returning war parties, the ancient custom of taking horses from enemies was so ingrained that nothing short of breaking up the tribe could end the practice.

The white settlers in Kansas knew the Pawnees much better than Agent Lushbaugh did, and had a great deal less hope of reforming them. As soon as the whites came into the country west of Fort Riley they became aware of the fact that there was a Pawnee war trail coming down from the Platte in Nebraska, passing east of the Pawnee sacred spring, near the present Cawker City on the Solomon Fork, and going on southward through Mitchell and Lincoln counties to Pawnee Fork and the Cheyenne Bottoms at the great bend of the Arkansas. War parties of Pawnees were constantly traveling this trail, coming south on foot or returning northward with stolen horses and mules. Some of these parties went to lift stock from the Potawatomies, Delawares, Kansa and other reservation Indians in Kansas (and from whites settled near the reservations); others were going farther, to raid the Comanches and other tribes on and south of the Arkansas. Occasionally parties of Pawnees went down to Red River on the Texas frontier, to visit the Wichitas or to steal horses; there are several recorded instances of Pawnee parties going clear down into Mexico and coming home months later with horses, mules, and other booty.

These Pawnee war parties numbered from two to thirty-five warriors, generally young men, the larger groups being led by older men, who carried the war-pipe or some other sacred object and conducted the ceremonies whose scrupulous observance was supposed to aid powerfully in bringing an expedition to a successful issue. Each warrior had a bow and quiver of arrows, a knife in a leather sheath, four or five extra pairs of moccasins attached to his belt, and on his back a small pack of about twenty pounds, containing dried buffalo meat both lean and fat, pieces of leather, thongs, and awls for repairing equipment. They also carried coiled rawhide ropes, to be used in stealing horses; occasionally one of the warriors had a light gun, a pistol or a small squaw axe. When met on their way south, these parties of Pawnees were always afoot; on their way back they were (if successful) mounted on stolen animals. Sometimes they were driving an entire herd. White men did not trust these Indians, for there were many stories in circulation concerning small parties of whites who had encountered Pawnees and had been robbed by them of everything they possessed, including their clothing. The Pawnees, however, were generally friendly; the occasional outrages against whites appear to have been the work of the wilder young warriors who had been unsuccessful in their attempts to steal horses from their Indian enemies. The wounding or killing of whites by Pawnee war parties in Kansas was practically unknown, for if white men resisted an attempt to rob them the Indians almost invariably desisted and made off at top speed.

In the winter of 1862-1863 the Pawnees had a poor hunt. Their enemies, the Sioux, Cheyennes, and Arapahos were encamped in great force on the Republican Fork and its branches, and the Pawnees did not dare venture far into the plains in quest of buffalo. In March, 1863, part of the tribe on its homeward march came among the settlers on the Solomon; being destitute and hungry, some of the Indians took food from the whites. Once started in this work, they began to take horses and cattle. The alarm spread swiftly, and Company "I" Ninth Kansas Cavalry was dispatched from Fort Riley in pursuit of the Indians. Coming up with a large camp of Pawnees, the officer in command decided that he was hopelessly in the minority and ordered a retreat. The Pawnees went home to their reservation, where their agent at the moment was penning a report to the effect that his Indians had given up their old practice of wandering about the country and that complaints of Pawnee depredations on settlers were never heard now. Evidently the uproar over the recent Pawnee activities on Solomon Fork in Kansas had failed to reach his ears.[115]

When the tribe came home in April, 1863, the women went to work in their corn patches. The agent's reports showed that he was spending about $10,000 a year to aid the Indians in their farming, but what he spent the sum on is a mystery. The Indian women had about 1,400 acres in widely scattered little patches, and this spring the agent reported that his white employees plowed 700 acres for the Indians. Apparently the women dug the other 700 acres by hand, and they did the planting, hoeing, and harvesting unaided. Agent Lushbaugh had established a model farm of one hundred acres, which was supposed to give the Pawnees an object lesson in good farming practices; but this tract was left untended by the white employees and by the boys of Mrs. Platt's school, who would only work when driven to it, and in 1863 the model farm had a total crop failure. Lushbaugh reported in June that the Pawnee women had the finest crops of corn and vegetables on record, and this he seemed to believe was to his credit. In late June grasshoppers settled on the Indian fields and in a single day devoured most of the crops. This the agent did not report.[116]

The Sioux were very troublesome this summer. They started with a big raid on June 22, when they charged straight into the Pawnee villages, killing and scalping some Indian women, with Agent Lushbaugh and the officers of the cavalry company which was supposed to be on guard looking on. Later in the summer 300 Brulés made an attack on the Pawnee villages, wounding the captain of the cavalry company with an arrow and killing one soldier and a number of Pawnees before the Indians and cavalry could mount and drive them off. The cavalry company seemed useless, small parties of Sioux getting in almost daily to kill Pawnee women in the corn patches and to enter the Indian villages at night to steal horses. The agency white men were so frightened that they neglected all work, remaining close to the agency buildings where the troops were stationed.

Agent Lushbaugh had a new scheme: a Pawnee-Sioux peace conference to be financed by a large appropriation of public money. Every man on the Nebraska frontier knew that the Sioux would not make a real peace with the Pawnees; but Lushbaugh had talked Superintendent E. B. Branch into giving his approval to the plan, and Branch easily convinced Indian Commissioner W. P. Dole, who was an idealist and a man of peace. Dole seemed to think that a little good talk would turn the Sioux into idealists and men of peace.

The Pawnees had a good summer hunt and, if we may believe the agent, their crops were good also; in the fall of 1863, for the first time since they had come to the reservation, they were comfortably provided for. The white men at the agency were far from comfortable, for they were so frightened by the constant Sioux raids that the employees kept leaving and new men had to be found to take their places. The government farmer explained the crop failure as being due to lack of labor. The old agency buildings, practically all inherited from the Mormons, were falling to pieces because workmen could not be found to repair them. The only thing at Pawnee Agency that was in a robust condition was the payroll. No matter how little work was done, the costs continued to mount. But this did not interest the Pawnees. With the coming of autumn the Sioux had ceased to trouble them; they had large numbers of new horses (source unrecorded), and by trading these animals to the whites they obtained many needed articles. Trade was brisk at both the agency trading-house and the Kizkatus or Platt trading-house, just outside the reservation line. In October the Indian medicine-men put on a wonderful two-day festival of magic feats in the edge of the Pawnee village: a continuous performance and feast going on for two days and nights. The greatest feats were performed at night, either in the open air or inside the big earth-lodges, with only the flicker of flames in the firehole at the center of the floor to light the performers and the mass of intently watching Pawnees and white men. Among the watchers were army officers and noted scouts: the North brothers, Texas Jack, and his friend Buffalo Bill.

The Pawnees started on their winter hunt in October, 1863, and came home in March to prepare their patches of garden. Again they received no aid from the government farmer; indeed, this man and his helpers did nothing in 1864 further than to plant forty acres of corn so carelessly that nothing came up. The farmer's excuse was that Agent Lushbaugh had become so discouraged over the destruction wrought by the Sioux and drought in 1863 that he stated it was useless to put in a crop and gave orders that nothing should be done. He kept all the men on the payroll, however.

The Pawnees had used up their stores of corn, beans, and dried pumpkins and were destitute again. This spring was a sickly season, and many children died of diphtheria and measles. Mrs. Platt had left the school, which was now being conducted by Mr. J. B. Maxfield. He reported the school in bad condition. There was still no high picket fence to prevent children running away and to keep parents out. One little boy had been taken from school by his parents, and Mr. Maxfield wanted a ruling of the Indian Office which would make it clear that when a child was placed in school he became the property of the government and the parents ceased to have any control over their own child. Indeed, this teacher was a pioneer of the school of Indian educators which twenty years later was to turn every government Indian school into a kind of penal colony for kidnapped Indian children.

In June, 1864, Agent Lushbaugh went to Washington, to work for an appropriation by Congress to pay the expenses of his proposed peace council between the Pawnees and Sioux. Meanwhile the Pawnee women had planted their crops; but no rains fell during the entire spring, and in May the Sioux appeared and started their usual deviltry. The whites were more alarmed than the Pawnees, and on May 24 the frontier was thrown into wild excitement by a report that two thousand Yankton Sioux were coming down the Platte to attack Fort Kearney and begin a massacre of settlers. The Yanktons were all on their lands up in Dakota, with their agent loudly proclaiming their friendliness toward the whites. The real hostiles were now the Sioux, Cheyennes, and Arapahos in the country south of the Platte. They had been driven into hostility by the action of Colonel H. M. Chivington and his Colorado volunteer cavalry in the spring of 1864, but thus far they had not struck a blow in the Fort Kearney district. On June 28 a small war party attacked a number of hay-cutters on the Pawnee reservation (settlers who were illegally cutting hay on the Indian lands) killing three men and wounding four others. Most of the employees at the

Pawnee agency now fled down the Loup to the town of Columbus, where their wild talk spread fresh alarm among the settlers.

General S. R. Curtis, commanding the military department, considered this petty raid an excuse for telegraphing to the chief-of-staff in Washington; indeed, he constantly took up the time of General H. W. Halleck with such trivial Indian matters; and on the basis of an insane report that a thousand Minnesota Sioux were on the upper Platte, he demanded that he be given an additional thousand cavalry and a full battery of artillery to guard the frontier.

The Pawnees knew by June that they would have no crops. The drought was very severe, and in May swarms of grasshoppers settled on the corn patches. The tribe started for the buffalo range in June to obtain meat; but all along the Platte the troops were out, many of them men who did not know a Pawnee from a Sioux or Cheyenne and who were ready to shoot any Indian on sight; while in the buffalo range south of the Platte the Sioux, Cheyennes, Arapahos, and Kiowas were gathered, waiting for the Pawnees to appear. The latter tribe was in desperate need of food and persisted in the effort to hunt, but whenever they found buffalo and prepared for a surround they were attacked by the Sioux and their allies and forced to fight for their lives.

The Cheyennes had suffered most from Colonel Chivington's activities in April and May. They had had several warriors and some chiefs killed by the troops, and the young men were determined to strike back. They induced a few Sioux to join them, and after the buffalo hunt was ended, in mid-July, they made a great raid along the Denver road on the South Platte. Chivington had stripped the road of troops and marched them to the Arkansas to deal with a wholly imaginary Confederate invasion, and the Cheyenne warriors killed and burned and plundered at their will. They completely wrecked the stage line, burning stations and stores, blocking all travel on the great road. The troops were rushed up the Platte, only to find that the Indians had withdrawn; then, with the lower Platte almost stripped of protection, the hostiles struck there, again with complete success. The whites who had complained for years about the begging and minor misdeeds of the Pawnees now learned what real Indian depredations were like. The Sioux struck the Platte road west of Fort Kearney, capturing a wagon train, killing the teamsters, then raiding up and down the line. The Cheyennes attacked the Overland Stage line below Fort Kearney, burning every ranch and stage station between the fort and the little settlement of Meridian, at the mouth of the Big Sandy. This was the worst Indian raid in Nebraska history, the warriors burning nearly every ranch and stage station along a stretch of 300 miles of road, stopping all travel and causing the entire frontier population to stampede eastward toward the safety of the larger towns.

These great raids that struck terror into the hearts of the whites were really a boon to the Pawnee tribe. For thirty years the Pawnee chiefs had striven to induce the government to aid their people, who were being killed by the Sioux and Cheyennes; but as long as it was only the Pawnees who were suffering, the officials had shown little interest. Now General Curtis came rushing up from Kansas with a large force of troops to save the frontier; on reaching Fort Kearney he made a rapid trip north to the Pawnee agency, where (about August 20) he summoned all the sixteen recognized Pawnee chiefs to council and begged them to send their warriors with his troops to aid against the Sioux, Cheyennes, and other hostiles.

The Pawnees were filled with joy. Most of the men were eager to go with the troops, but General Curtis asked only a company of picked warriors. Joseph McFadden, a veteran of General Harney's fight with the Brulés on the Bluewater, now a clerk at the Pawnee agency trader's store, was given the temporary rank of captain, while young Frank North, another clerk at the store who spoke Pawnee fluently, was made a lieutenant. They got their picked Pawnee warriors as fast as they could write down the names and, about August 25, they set off with seventy-six Indians to join the troops at Fort Kearney. The Pawnees were jubilant as they marched southward toward their old hunting grounds on Republican Fork with this powerful force of soldiers; but their hopes of taking part in a big fight with their Sioux and Cheyenne enemies were not fulfilled, the hostiles having withdrawn before the slow-moving column reached the vicinity of their camps. In west Kansas the troops divided, General Curtis moving eastward toward Fort Riley, Brigadier-General R. B. Mitchell returning with the main body of troops to the Platte. Curtis took Frank North and two Pawnees with him as guides, and on the march he proposed that North on his return to the Pawnee reservation should enlist a company of Pawnees for regular service. After reaching Fort Riley Frank North started for the reservation to execute this commission. Meanwhile

Captain McFadden with over seventy Pawnees was scouting for General Mitchell along the Platte, but still the hostiles were not encountered; after accompanying Mitchell's column on a march westward beyond the forks of the Platte the Pawnees were ordered back to their reservation to be disbanded. This first company of Pawnee Scouts in 1864 rode their own ponies, the army providing them with arms. They wore cavalry jackets and hats or caps, so that the troops could distinguish them from hostile Indians. Their pay was to be twenty dollars a month, but Captain L. H. North was of opinion that they left the service without being paid.[117]

With the hostile tribes still raiding vigorously and the troops pursuing them, the Pawnees set out on their usual winter buffalo hunt in October, 1864, taking their women and children with them. They had to go. They had brought back little dried meat from their summer hunt; the drought and grasshoppers had destroyed their crops; and although Agent Lushbaugh had plenty of funds with which to pay a farmer and farm laborers for doing almost nothing, he had no money with which to buy food for his hungry Indians. Frank North had come back to the reservation before the tribe was ready for the winter hunt and had enlisted a picked body of young Pawnees for his new company of scouts. Being called to Omaha for a consultation, he left his men in camp near the little town of Columbus, but when he returned from Omaha he found that his Pawnees (who evidently took very lightly their regular enlistment as members of the U.S. army) had nearly all gone off on the winter hunt with the tribe. At this time Frank North's younger brother, Luther H. North, was home from his service with the Second Nebraska Cavalry against the Sioux of Dakota, and Frank now sent Luther and a Pawnee boy to chase the tribe up the Platte and, if necessary, south to Republican Fork with orders to bring back the strayaway scouts. Winter had set in with severe cold, and near Grand Island on the Platte Luther and his Pawnee were struck by a terrific blizzard during which they almost froze to death. But Luther North was determined to go on, and when the storm abated he and his Pawnee companion continued their ride. Luck was with them, for the blizzard had broken up the march of the Pawnee tribe toward Republican Fork, and now the Indians came drifting back to the Platte in small separate camps, striking the Overland Road at several points from near Fort Kearney on westward. Luther North went through the camps, enlisting the best of the young warriors for his brother's scout company, and presently he led a full compliment of Pawnees to the camp in which Captain Frank North was waiting.[118]

In January, 1865, the hostiles attacked the Overland Road above the forks of the Platte, burning all the stage stations and ranches, capturing wagon-trains, and destroying many miles of the Overland Telegraph line. They then moved their camps north to Powder River, leaving the lands south of the Platte clear of Sioux, Cheyennes, and Arapahos for the time being.

General Curtis, who was mainly responsible for the starting of this Indian war in the plains, had made a dismal failure of his campaign. He had struck no blow against the hostiles along the Platte, but they had raided where they pleased, had wrecked the great Overland Road, and had then moved northward with their camps overflowing with plunder. In the spring of 1865 a new commander was selected for the northern plains: Brigadier-General P. E. Connor, a westerner who had had some success in fighting Indians. The western newspapers spoke highly of Connor, who was reported to have a wonderful new plan of his own for protecting the roads from Indian raids, but when brought out into the light the general's plan proved to be nothing more surprising than a scheme for cavalry escorts for stage coaches and for arming and organizing the men of the wagon-trains so that they could protect themselves from Indian attacks. This plan had been tried in earlier years and had failed, but somehow the stage company officials and the public continued to have great faith in Connor. It was even reported that the Sioux would probably surrender without serious fighting when Connor took the field, and the general was said to have offered 2,000 Sioux (not yet caught) as laborers in the building of the proposed Union Pacific railway line up the Platte valley.

The Indian season opened with the coming up of new grass late in April. On May 5 the Sioux attacked a wagon-train and stole stock near Mullala's Station on the Platte; on May 12 and 13 they made attacks at Dan Smith's Station. The Indians then swung from the road west of Fort Kearney to points east, massacring a force of the Third U.S. Volunteers (Confederate prisoners who had enlisted to fight Indians and had been sent out unarmed, the road being considered perfectly safe), and destroying every stage station and ranch on the Blue from Buffalo to Elm Creek.[119]

Part of the Pawnee tribe, 355 persons, started on a buffalo hunt in May, taking what was considered the safe trail by way of the Little Blue. They were almost caught by the great raiding party of hostiles, and when the raid was over they were discovered in the vicinity by white troops. Their love for horseflesh nearly cost these Pawnees their lives. They had picked up on the prairie two mules and two horses; it was now found by the soldiers that the mules had belonged to the party of Confederates who had been murdered on May 18, the horses coming from two of the raided stage stations. The Pawnees were questioned very straightly. Their answers were frank; they denied injuring the whites in any way, and were finally permitted to go back to their reservation. There was such a clamor against the Pawnees that Colonel R. R. Livingston ordered an investigation. All Indian trails were scouted, and it was found that the Pawnees had told the truth concerning their movements. The whole tribe was then assembled at the agency, and military officers went thoroughly into every charge that had been brought against the Pawnees. In every instance the Indians were found to be innocent of the depredations charged against them.

This affair rather dimmed the hopes of the Pawnee chiefs that their tribe was now to join the whites in an alliance against the hostile Sioux and Cheyennes; for how could the Pawnees gain from a union with white men who were so ignorant that they could not tell a Sioux from a Pawnee and so suspicious that they always suspected that the Pawnees were raiding until charges were disproved? At this moment the Pawnees had eighty-seven picked warriors regularly enlisted and serving with the troops. This was the company of scouts Frank North had raised in the fall of 1864. With North as their captain, another white man as their lieutenant, and James Murie of the Skidi tribe as sergeant, this company of Pawnees was now in service on the Platte road. Later in the season they went against the hostiles with Connor's Powder River expedition; it would be no exaggeration to state that of the several thousands of troops employed, the Pawnee Scouts performed the best service. They found the trails, followed them, and located the hostile camps. They waylaid war parties of Cheyennes and Sioux coming home from raids on the stage line, attacked them, defeated them, and recovered most of the horses, mules, and other plunder in their possession. When the Arapaho village was attacked, it was the Pawnees who found the village and stampeded the Arapaho ponies. When Colonel Nelson Cole and Colonel Samuel Walker with their large columns of troops were in danger of complete destruction on Powder River, it was the Pawnees who found them and brought them the hope of succor.

The fine services rendered by the Pawnee Scouts in 1865-77 under white leadership causes one to wonder at the failures of the same Pawnees under their own chiefs. Something seems to have been wrong with Pawnee leadership. Their warriors were brave and enterprising enough; but sometime in the dim past (perhaps in the days when the mounted Padoucas had harried them mercilessly at the time when they had no horses of their own) the Pawnees seem to have picked up the idea that war meant horse-lifting, and as long as they were led by their own chiefs they could not break away from this theory. The Sioux would come down and kill one hundred Pawnees and carry off all the horses they could get. Instead of trying to strike back at the Sioux, the Pawnees would then send war parties south of the Arkansas to steal more horses from the Comanches and other tribes, only to have this fresh stock stolen by the Sioux almost immediately. Some Pawnees said that they could not fight the Sioux, who were too strong and too well armed. As for arms, whenever the Pawnees obtained a large number of new guns and a supply of ammunition, they nearly always sent some of their men south of the Arkansas to trade the larger portion of their new weapons to the Comanches and Kiowas for horses. Later Pawnee war parties would go south to steal horses from these same tribes; often the Pawnees were caught on the open plains, all afoot and armed mainly with bows, and were killed by mounted warriors, part of whom were armed with guns the Pawnees had traded to them. One must admit that there was something wrong with the Pawnee leaders who went through one disastrous experience after another and never learned that proper arms and a good reserve of ammunition were vital needs. Under the command of Frank North, his brother Luther North, and other white officers, these same Pawnee warriors—properly armed and led—were never defeated, and they won a number of handsome victories over their Sioux and Cheyenne enemies.

Agent Lushbaugh went to Washington again in the spring of 1865, presumably still seeking government funds with which to hold a Pawnee and Sioux peace council, but he found Congress a poor market for this scheme. On returning to the Pawnee reservation he was in a depressed mood. He informed the government farmer that it was no use to plant a crop. The Nebraska climate was too adverse for crop growing. He found a party of Kansa Indians visiting the Pawnees, and this seemed an excellent opportunity to test his ability as a peacemaker. He drew up a formal treaty of peace between the Pawnee and Kansa tribes, got the Indians together in council, and went through the ceremony of signing the chiefs' names and having

them touch the pen as an indication of their approval. This precious document he dispatched to the Indian Office in Washington,
with a full report of the proceedings. He also sent a copy of the
treaty and a friendly letter to the Kansa agent in Kansas, but
received no reply.

The Indian Office officials, regarding peace among the tribes as
a most important matter, were highly pleased with Agent Lushbaugh. They sent a copy of the treaty and a letter praising the
Pawnee agent's fine conduct to the Kansa agent. That gentleman
then sat down at his desk and penned a very frank and even bad-
tempered report to the Indian Office. He stated that in the winter
of 1864-65 part of his friendly Kansa Indians were hunting buffalo
in the plains when at night a party of Pawnees slipped into camp
and abstracted all the horses, leaving the Kansa folk afoot in the
heart of the winter plains. His Indians lost their horses, lost their
hunt and the supply of dried meat the hunt would have produced,
and very nearly perished of cold before they reached their own
reservation. In the spring of 1865 some boasting Otos told the
victims of this outrage that they had much influence with the
Pawnee chiefs, and that if some of the Kansa men who had lost
horses in this affair would come with them to the Pawnee reservation they were certain that all of the stolen horses could be recovered. The party on reaching the agency recognized nearly all of
the forty Kansa horses, but the Pawnees would not give them up.
The Pawnee agent then proposed a peace treaty, the Pawnees
offering to give six or seven of the stolen horses as peace gifts; the
Kansa warriors, who numbered only five or six men, felt that they
were practically being forced to sign the treaty. They signed, but
as they expressed it, they shook hands with the Pawnees "with the
tips of the fingers." They then went home and demanded justice,
a demand which their angry agent repeated in his report to the
Indian Office.[120]

Mr. Lushbaugh was removed in July, an Indian Office inspector
having found conditions at the Pawnee agency far from satisfactory.
The farming operations, which had cost so much money, had produced no results; the little school was still sheltered in a dilapidated
log shanty, and there was something queer about the new school,
which had been four years under construction, had cost a great
deal of money, and was so badly planned and built that while still
new it was hardly fit for occupancy. At this agency there were all
of the ugly rumors usual at agencies of the day: stories of secret
understandings between the agent, the employees, and the licensed

trader, and of underhanded dealings with contractors. The new agent, D. H. Wheeler, took charge July 10.

The Pawnees had gone on their summer hunt in June, this time under the escort of a company of cavalry to protect the people from the Sioux and from angry white settlers, many of whom still believed the Pawnees guilty of the raid on the Little Blue in May. They threatened to kill all Pawnees on sight. This was the best hunt the tribe had had in many years. Made safe from enemy attacks by the presence of the soldiers, they hunted buffalo and other game with great success, killing 1,600 animals and filling their camp with dried meat and skins. They went clear to the Arkansas and probably saw the Wichitas, who had been driven north during the Civil War and were living in destitution near the mouth of the Little Arkansas.

After fifty days of good hunting and happy wandering the Pawnees came home with great quantities of dried meat and skins to find the finest crops they had had in years awaiting harvest. The women set to work, drying corn, beans, and sliced pumpkin and storing them for winter use; the men loafed about, watching their new grandfather (Agent Wheeler) and the Indian superintendent, who was at the agency looking into the affairs of the late Agent Lushbaugh. In a council with the superintendent the chiefs asked that their annuities in future be paid to their agent in money, so that he might purchase wagons, cook stoves, and other articles they had more need for than they had for the blankets, Indian cloth, and similar articles which had been supplied to them in the past. In his printed report Agent Wheeler read into this request of the chiefs most promising signs of progress in civilization, and he suggested that the next step forward should be to set the authority of the chiefs aside and let the agent issue orders direct to the common Indians. The agent had not thought out this pleasing device for shifting all controls into his own hands. This scheme for breaking up the tribal organization and discarding the chiefs (like Mr. Lushbaugh's notion of making peace treaties between the tribes) was the product of an idea-mill run in Philadelphia by a group of Quakers and other high-thinkers, who knew nothing whatever about Indians but were offering the government without charge their best ideas for improving the Indian service. In 1865 the notion of helping the Indians forward by breaking the chiefs and destroying the tribal governments was new. It was not to be accepted as official policy for some years yet, but when it was adopted it broke the hearts of the Indians over a period of thirty years. If it in any manner accelerated their slow advance toward civilization, no one has yet demonstrated the fact. The Pawnees in 1865 had a fine set of chiefs, headed by the Grand Pawnee head-chief, Pitalesharo—called Old Peter by the whites who knew him best—a handsome, dignified, and friendly elderly man. Only by the employment of violent methods over a long period of years could the Pawnees of 1865 have been compelled to give up their chiefs and take orders from a white agent. Agent Wheeler must have known this. But, then, he was only writing a report that would make pleasant reading in Washington.

NOTES TO CHAPTER X

[115]Agent Lushbaugh's report for 1863; Pawnee depredations in Kansas, in *Official Records of the Union and Confederate Armies,* serial volume 32, p. 144.

[116]Judging from some outside evidence this seems to be correct. As for Agent Lushbaugh, he reported in writing about a bountiful harvest and then sat down and reported total crop failures.

[117]Bruce: *The Fighting Norths and Their Pawnee Scouts,* pp. 22-24.

[118]*Ibid.,* pp. 24-25.

[119]*Official Records of the Union and Confederate Armies,* serial volume 101, p. 261, p. 270, p. 274; serial volume 102, p. 514, p. 541. Samuel Bowles is authority for Connor's amazing offer of 2,000 Sioux as laborers on the Union Pacific line.

[120]*Annual Report of the Secretary of the Interior* for 1865, p. 568.

Brave Chief, Nesharu Rahikuts, Kitkehahki Pawnee, taken about 1858. (Pitt Rivers Museum, Oxford University)

Sky Chief (*at left*) with his three brothers and (*standing*) Baptiste Bayhylle, the interpreter. (Photograph by William H. Jackson, from BAE, Smithsonian Institution)

XI

In the Cage

WHAT HAD REALLY ENDED AGENT LUSHBAUGH'S RULE AT THE PAWNEE agency was his report that he had made a fine peace between his Indians and the Kansa tribe, and the disclosure by the angry Kansa agent that this alleged treaty was merely a cover-up for some horse-stealing operations Agent Lushbaugh's Indians had been engaged in. When Daniel H. Wheeler arrived at the Pawnee agency to take charge, one of his first acts was to summon the chiefs to council and inform them through the mixed-blood interpreter, Baptiste Bayhylle, that the Pawnees must at once take all the stolen Kansa horses to the Kansa reservation and restore them to their rightful owners. The agent then gave the chiefs a lecture. The Pawnees must stop stealing horses and settle down to work on their reservation. In future when they went on buffalo hunts, Bat Bayhylle or some reliable white man was to accompany them and keep a watch to see to it that no war parties or horse-lifting parties left their camp. The days of war and horse-stealing were now ended. As agent he expected a marked change for the better in the conduct of the Pawnees.

Just after this council Frank North (now a major in army rank) marched into the Pawnee agency at the head of his veteran Pawnee Scouts, nearly one hundred real warriors, laden with honors and loot, and nearly every man of them riding a fine horse taken from the Sioux, the Cheyennes, or the Arapahos during their campaign with the troops on distant Powder River. They had penetrated boldly into lands that no Pawnee had dared to venture into for the past two generations, and they had brought back Sioux and Chey-enne scalps as proof of their victories over those tribes. The Great Father in the East was pleased with their service, so pleased that he had given Major North the reward of a license to start a store at the Pawnee agency. This brightened the eyes of the Pawnees. Here

Pawnee scouts in 1869. (Western History Collections, University of Oklahoma Library)

was something real, something fine: not like the talk of their new agent, who wanted the Pawnee men to stop fighting and horse-lifting and go to work at dull drudgery.

In 1865-6 most of the Sioux and Cheyennes were wintering far away in the Powder River country, and the Pawnees had a good winter hunt on Republican Fork. They came home in the spring of 1866 with abundant supplies of meat and skins; and their content was increased in April by the appearance of an army officer who actually paid off the Pawnee Scouts. Getting paid for killing Sioux and Cheyennes was an almost incredible thing to the Pawnees; and if they were paid for going to war, why did their new grandfather, the agent, say that they must stop going to war, and scold them all the time even for little matters like horse-stealing? Attempting to explain all this to the Pawnees, Agent Wheeler failed dismally. It was useless to talk idealism to the chiefs and to tell them that the Sioux were their brothers, with whom they should smoke and make peace. In May the Sioux appeared. It was just a little raid, the Sioux slipping into the Pawnee village at night and getting away with eighteen horses; but it altered Agent Wheeler's idealistic views considerably. No Sioux had come within two miles of the house in which he was asleep; but when he heard of the affair the next morning he was excited. He telegraphed to the Indian superintendent at Omaha that he had had a close call; and he warned that if troops were not sent to guard the agency all the white employees would leave.

Part of the wild Cheyennes had now slipped back to their old haunts on the Republican Fork, and when the Pawnees set out on their summer hunt they took the Omaha tribe with them for safety. The Cheyennes made raids on the white settlers on the lower Republican; at first it was correctly reported that these were Cheyenne raids, but presently a report was spread that the Pawnees, Omahas, and Otos had made the raids. General W. F. Cloud of the Kansas militia was sent to Nebraska to demand that chiefs from the accused tribes should be sent by their agents to attend an investigation that the Kansas officials were planning to hold. Agent Wheeler reported that the Pawnees were on very friendly terms with all whites; that they had been accompanied on their hunt by Baptiste Bayhylle, a trustworthy and intelligent interpreter, and that he was convinced that they had committed no hostile acts while away from the reservation. He reported to Superintendent E. B. Taylor at Omaha who wired to Washington and was instructed not to send the chiefs to the Kansas meeting.

This affair proved very embarrassing to the Indian Office officials, who had just inaugurated the new Peace Policy with a clarion call for all highminded people and church groups to rally to the defense of the poor Indian, who was being abused, robbed, and hounded into hostility by the ruffian white population of the border. It was impossible for the Indian officials to refuse to cooperate in the Kansas governor's move for an open investigation of the charges against the Indians; yet the officials, both in Nebraska and at Washington, clearly regarded the Kansas move with great distrust. It was fairly evident at the time that the wild Cheyennes had made the raids; but the Pawnees and Omahas had money annuities, and if the Kansas men could build a case against these tribes they could file claims and collect damages. The unexpressed belief of the Indian Office was that the average Kansas frontiersman would swear himself black in the face to establish the guilt of the Pawnees and Omahas. They therefore made excuses, some of which were so badly constructed that they might well be termed falsehoods, and slipped out of the responsibility of sending any Pawnee or Omaha chiefs to Kansas. After seventy years the verdict must be that they acted wisely. After the year 1910 many Cheyennes admitted that their tribe made the raids in question, and most of the evidence produced against the Pawnees in 1866 bore the clear marks of falsification.[121]

The Indian Office was still upset over this Kansas affair when, in August, a white man came to Washington with nine Pawnees, some of whom he claimed were Pawnee Scouts who had never been paid for their services with the Powder River expedition. A little investigation disclosed that the man, who represented himself to be a government interpreter for the Pawnees, was a showman who had obtained a written permit from Agent Wheeler to take nine Pawnees on the road. Failing to make money in his regular line of trade, the gentleman had invented the plan of representing his Indians as Pawnee Scouts and trying to collect their pay. He vanished suddenly, and the Indian Office took charge of the Pawnees. The officials were so angry that they immediately ordered Agent Wheeler's dismissal, replacing him with an unknown man, John P. Becker, who took charge of the agency late in September, 1866.[122]

Mr. Wheeler's going was not regretted by the Pawnees. They had not found him congenial, and they did not trust him. This was demonstrated by an incident that occurred at this time. During the recent hunt the Skidis had hunted in a separate group. The other three Pawnee tribes found buffalo and killed so many that they hid some of the dried meat in caches on the Little Blue River. The Skidis found no buffalo, but on reaching the Little Blue, Crooked Hand, the famous Skidi warrior, found some caches, opened them, and distributed the meat to his hungry people. Later in the hunt the Skidis found buffalo, and they brought back considerable supplies of dried meat to the villages. Eagle Chief, the head of the Skidi tribe, then informed Pitalesharo, the head-chief, about the taking of the meat from the caches. The chiefs held a council, but could not agree on a settlement. The affair was serious, as the Kitkehahkis, whose caches had been broken open, demanded payment, while Crooked Hand absolutely refused to pay. He said that when the people were hungry any meat belonging to any Pawnees should be a free gift to the hungry. The chiefs never thought of laying the trouble before the agent; but presently they all rode off down Loup Fork, to consult Pani Leshar.[123]

Major Frank North and his brother, Captain L. H. North, were haymaking in a pasture near the little town of Columbus when the sixteen chiefs came riding down the road, "a mighty fine-looking lot of Indians," as Captain North said in later years. The chiefs came into the hayfield, sat down and smoked with Major North, then laid the knotty case before him, stating that his decision would be accepted by everyone concerned. There were many curious angles to the matter, the Skidis having put in counter-claims against the Kitkehahkis; but the Major brushed all that aside, stating that Crooked Hand admitted breaking into the caches and that he must pay for the dried meat he had taken. Back in the villages Crooked Hand was surrounded by a group of supporters, all armed and defying anyone to make them pay for that meat. Then the chiefs reached the embattled villages and announced that Pani Leshar had ruled that Crooked Hand should pay. The Skidi champion grew very thoughtful, grumbled a bit, shook his head, and then in silence put away his gun, his bow and arrows, his knife and tomahawk, and paid. If the government at this time had made Frank North agent for the Pawnees, with a free hand to use his own judgment in minor matters, he would have saved half of the annual expense, and the tribe would have been spared a great deal of misery and sorrow.

Agent Becker was a stopgap, and he remained with the Pawnees only through the winter of 1866-1867. In June he was replaced by Charles H. Whaley. This man had been the Pawnee farmer under agents Lushbaugh and Wheeler, when the government farm had been permitted to go to ruin, with the expense of its upkeep increasing year by year. During his brief reign, Agent Whaley increased the productiveness of the school farm by liberal expenditure of government money. The crops raised were supposed to be used in feeding the teachers and Pawnee children at the school, but this agent is stated to have sold the crops, failing to account for the money thus received.[124] These early Pawnee agents were perhaps no worse than the other Indian agents of the day, but that is not saying much in their favor. There were six Pawnee agents during the first ten years. Every one of these men sent in reports of progress and bright prospects for the future (if the necessary funds were provided); three of the six were dismissed after being caught in peculations; the other three were only suspected of shady dealings. Old Judge Gillis seems to have been the best of the six. He had physical courage, which the others seem to have lacked, and instead of hiding when the Sioux came, he went out with his revolvers and led the Pawnees to the attack. He did not fill his reports with high-sounding phrases about peace and progress, cribbed from the Quaker publications printed in Philadelphia, as the other agents did, while engaged in making money by underhanded methods. Of all these agents the three appointed by President Andrew Johnson were the worst. Too insignificant for other designation, they have been termed political wheel-horses, but horses is too large a word. The Pawnees admired horses; these agents were more like mice. After a decade of paper progress the Pawnees were just about in the condition they would have been in if they had never seen any of these agents, and the United States treasury was out some $400,000.

With their Sioux and Cheyenne enemies fleeing north to escape the troops, the Pawnees in 1865-6 did fairly well. They could now hunt in some security; they had plenty of meat and skins; crops were also good; but the happiness they had felt in early days when food was plenty was now spoiled by the constant nagging of their agents. Progress in civilization was being demanded by the Indian Office, and this was understood to mean that all Pawnee warriors must go to work farming, that all children must go to school, and that the old free life of wandering in the buffalo plains must be given up forever. The agents knew that such changes could not be suddenly made, but they had to make a showing in their reports; in order to do this they had to cajole or bully the chiefs into stating that they wanted plows and other farm implements. No one will ever know how many plows the government was induced to send to the tribe. In the early Forties enough plows were sent in one shipment to supply a white community of the size of the Pawnee tribe with this article for thirty years. Under the eyes of their agent the Pawnees traded these new plows to white men for any small articles that were offered, the agent failing to report this fact. In 1867 the tribe was no more ready to settle down to farming than it had been in 1840, but their agent was attempting to force the men to work by confining them to the reservation, and that little tract along the Loup was beginning to seem to the Pawnees a cage in which they were confined by the whites. Their love for wandering was as strong as ever, but if they left the reservation without a written pass from the agent they were pretty certain to find themselves in trouble with the whites.

When the Sioux and Cheyennes had gone north to Powder River in January, 1865, the Pawnees had hoped that their ancient hunting lands south of the Platte would be restored to them and that, freed from the attacks of enemies, they would be able to hunt buffalo in peace again, as they had done before the Cheyennes and Sioux had pressed into their lands early in the century. They did have three quiet hunts, but then, in 1866 and 1867, the government made peace with part of the Sioux and Cheyennes. The idealists in control of Indian policy at the time did not consider the interests of the friendly Pawnees in any way. They were determined to prove that the Sioux and Cheyennes were good, quiet people who would make no trouble if treated generously; and as soon as they had coaxed certain bands of these Indians into signing peace treaties they drew them down into the hunting grounds between the Platte and Arkansas, to get them away from the bad influence of their still hostile kinsmen, who were up on Powder River vigorously prosecuting their war against the whites.

The results of this policy of returning the "friendlies" to the lands south of the Platte were not long in making their appearance. In 1865 not a Sioux or Cheyenne raid had been made on the Pawnee reservation. In 1866 these raids were resumed, and troops had to be sent to protect the Pawnees and the white employees. With the Sioux and Cheyennes out of the way in 1866, the Union Pacific had been pushed westward almost to the forks of the Platte, passing along the southern border of the Pawnee reservation. There was no trouble until the Sioux and Cheyennes signed peace treaties and were permitted to return south; then Indian raids along the railroad became frequent. The government officials had no thought for the Pawnees, except when it needed their services. Early in the spring of 1867 General C. C. Augur asked Major Frank North to recruit a battalion of Pawnees, to help guard the workmen at the end-of-the-track camps on the Union Pacific; and although they were being attacked at home on their reservation by the Sioux, the Pawnees rushed to enlist. Major North made a record, filling four companies in a few hours, taking only the pick of the warriors.

At the end-of-the-track the Sioux and Cheyennes were enjoying themselves. Almost daily they appeared from the hills and rushed down on the graders and track-layers, killing a number of men and making off with every horse and mule they could get. They had found by experience that white soldiers were so slow that they could make a raid and get back to the hills before the cavalry could saddle and mount their horses. Then one day when the Sioux rushed out of the hills in reckless pride, singing and blowing war-whistles, they beheld a strange thing; the cavalry, instead of taking half an hour to get ready came out at once, advancing swiftly, and as they came the men began to undress. For a minute the air was full of flying cavalry hats, jackets, and other garments; and instead of a troop of cavalry the astonished Sioux found themselves facing Pawnee warriors, stripped naked for fighting. Equipped by the government, the Pawnees all had guns and pistols; but the guns were muzzle-loaders, and some of the men preferred to use their bows. They ran the Sioux toward the hills, recapturing from them a number of mules. The Pawnee mixed-blood, Bat Bayhylle, was using a bow. One Sioux had lost his horse and was running. Bayhylle made after him and shot him through the body. The Sioux grasped the arrow with both hands, pulled it through his body, fitted it to his own bowstring and actually hit and wounded Bayhylle with his own arrow. He then walked a few steps and fell dead. Later it was learned that he was the brother of the great Sioux chief Spotted Tail.[125]

These were great days for the Pawnee Scouts. In guarding the graders and track-layers they were for the first time meeting big white men—officials of the Union Pacific and generals of the army. Thousands of white men and thousands of horses and mules were working on the building of the railroad, and the Pawnee Scouts protected the workers until the line was pushed through the danger zone and on west into Wyoming. In June the Pawnee Scouts escorted General W. T. Sherman and his party from the end-of-the-track to Fort Laramie; on this march they had the good luck to run into a party of Arapahos who had raided an emigrant camp up on the North Platte. Coming south through the valley known as Cheyenne Pass, the Arapahos ran into Captain Luther H. North's scout company, which was far ahead of Major North's scouts, who were escorting General Sherman and his party. The Pawnees when they saw the Arapahos promptly started after them; in a lively chase of ten miles they killed four Arapahos and captured fifty-five horses.

Returning from the duty of escorting Sherman to Fort Laramie, the Pawnee Scouts, near the head of Lodge-Pole Creek between the forks of the Platte, came face to face with from 300 to 400 of their deadly enemies, the Sioux. The two parties halted, both bristling; then Nick Janis, a French trader and interpreter, rode forward from the Sioux ranks and spoke to Major Frank North, stating that he was conducting the Sioux to Fort Laramie to sign a peace treaty. North nodded and told him brusquely to move his Sioux to one side, off the way. Knowing well the pride of the Sioux, Janis shook his head. "By gar, Major, I dunno eef dey get out yo' road," he said; but when he went back to his Sioux he did persuade them to move, and the Pawnee Scouts, headed by Major North, rode proudly past them. Captain L. H. North, who told this story often, thought that if the Sioux had not had their women and children with them there would have been a big fight; as for the Pawnees, only the discipline they had learned under Major North kept them from going for the Sioux.[126]

Even after the Union Pacific track was laid the line was not safe from hostile Indians. Somehow Chief Turkey Leg of the Cheyennes had picked up a new trick; early in August, 1867, his band tore up the track four miles west of Plum Creek and derailed and plundered a freight train. Loading all their ponies with wonderful goods taken from the freight cars, the Cheyennes made off southward. Major North, with Captain James Murie's company of Pawnee Scouts, was ordered to the scene of this raid. The locality was the old Plum Point at which the Pawnees often camped in early times when they crossed the Platte here and started for their hunting grounds on Republican Fork. The old Plum Creek stage station was on the south side of the Platte, and there was a bridge here across Plum Creek. The Union Pacific line ran along the north bank of the Platte, and the railroad station of Plum Creek was on that side of the river. Major North and Captain Murie with their forty Pawnees were at the railroad station when Turkey Leg's Cheyennes again appeared on the south side of the river. They had come back with pack-horses to obtain another load of loot from the wrecked freight train; but the moment they made their appearance, North and Murie led the Pawnees across the wide Platte and advanced on the hostiles. The Pawnees had been rearmed with seven-shot Spencer carbines. With these splendid weapons they swept a superior force of Cheyennes off the field, pursuing them until after darkness fell. They killed at least seven warriors, captured fifteen women and children, thirty-five horses, and a large quantity of plunder which the Cheyennes had recently taken from the freight train.[127]

The Pawnees in this fight were Skidis. Thirty years before they would have selected one of their Cheyenne female captives and sacrificed her to Morning Star, but the Skidis had come a long distance over the hard trail toward civilization since 1837. They now cheerfully gave up their Cheyenne captives to be exchanged for two young white women, the Martin sisters, and three small white boys, who were captives in the Cheyenne camp on the Medicine Creek branch of Republican Fork.

Agent Whaley had learned the art of running the Pawnee agency while serving as farmer under Agent Lushbaugh, and on taking charge he at once proclaimed a new era of progress. The government farm, despite all the cost of pretended work on it, had been permitted to revert into a weed patch on which no crop had been grown in two years; but Whaley was for a vigorous farming campaign, with 3,000 new acres to be broken and planted. That is, he wrote to Washington for a large fund to be expended on such a program. Meanwhile the Pawnee women dug up with their hoes about one thousand acres in small patches, with no assistance from Mr. Whaley and his farming staff; this land the women planted by hand in their ancient and painstaking way. While they labored, Agent Whaley and his men and the male Pawnees busied themselves in preparations for the coming tribal buffalo hunt.

Much as he talked of progress, the new agent evidently had a bright eye on the main opportunities his position afforded. The weeks preceding the setting out of the tribe on one of its buffalo hunts was the time for heavy buying at the traders' stores, the Indians purchasing all that was needed to equip themselves for a hunt of some months' duration. At such periods it was the pleasant duty of the agent and his men to steer the Pawnees to the right store, that run by the licensed trader, in whose welfare the agent generally had a fatherly interest (an interest of perhaps twenty-five per cent). The two unlicensed traders, Lester W. Platt and D. W. Willard, had stores just outside the reservation line. As Platt and Willard had been among the Pawnees for many years and were well known and liked by the Indians, for weeks before the tribe set out on its buffalo hunt twice a year, the agent and his men worked full-time, trying to keep the Indians close herded and to induce them to buy only at the licensed trader's.

While Agent Whaley talked of progress Elvira Platt was making it, or so she believed. For years the kindly Christians in charge of Indian education had been demanding from the Indian Office a rule cutting off Indian school children completely from their families; they believed that only by such a severance of family ties could the children be quickly turned into imitation whites. Mrs. Platt, principal of the Pawnee school, now had such a rule in force; and although the parents were in the villages within sight of the school and the love between parents and children was deep and strong, no parent was permitted to visit the school. This was a boarding-school to which the children were taken while still small; there was no vacation liberty, and the children were to be kept closely confined and isolated from supposedly infectious contacts with their families until they were twenty. Mrs. Platt had a fervent faith that by such methods she was helping to build a new and nobler Indian race.

The Pawnees again in the summer of 1867 invited the Omahas to their reservation, and on July 29 the two tribes set off to hunt buffalo together for mutual protection. Just where they hunted is not known. The best hunting grounds, south of the Platte, were now swarming with Sioux and Cheyennes, and Custer's Seventh Cavalry was trailing these tribes. They had recently made peace; a peace that was not a peace; a peace in which the government thought only of protecting the new railroads, forgetting that it owed protection to the Pawnees, two hundred of whose picked warriors were serving in the Pawnee Scouts guarding the Union Pacific line. With the military denouncing the Sioux and Cheyennes as hostiles and the Indian Office officials describing them as friendly Indians who were being brutally mistreated by the army, the Sioux and Cheyennes had a happy time, alternately raiding, playing hide-and-seek with Custer, and running in to their new agency at the forks of the Platte to be petted and supplied with free rations, clothing, arms and ammunition. The Pawnees, who were really friendly, had to buy their own arms and ammunition and feed and clothe themselves, and whenever they went out to obtain buffalo meat and skins they had to fight Sioux and Cheyennes who were being supplied by the government with free arms and ammunition.

Despite the hostiles, the Pawnees had a good summer hunt, and coming home late in August found a fine crop awaiting harvest. The Poncas had had a crop failure, and on hearing the good news from the Pawnee reservation flocked down to visit the tribe whom in former years they had so persistently raided. The Pawnees gave these visitors a large part of their surplus corn. Part of the crop was traded to the whites for groceries and other supplies, and in October the Pawnees set out again to hunt buffalo. The Pawnee Scouts had fought valiantly this summer to protect the working parties along the railroad from Sioux and Cheyenne attacks, and now in the fall they were mustered out, their arms taken from them, and their tribe permitted to go hunting without protection. At the same moment the Sioux and Cheyennes came to North Platte on the Union Pacific and threatened to resume hostilities if not supplied with arms and ammunition. The peace commission that met these Indians in council gave in to their demands, excusing their own conduct by stating that buffalo were now so scarce that Indians could not kill them with bows. This was absolutely false, but the good men of the commission felt in conscience bound not to permit these Indians to go hungry for lack of arms and ammunition. In their report they stated with satisfaction that the Sioux and Cheyennes after leaving North Platte had a successful hunt on Republican Fork. What they did not state was that the Sioux and Cheyennes used up much of the ammunition supplied by the commission in attacks on the friendly Pawnees, who were prevented from hunting and had to return home without meat and greatly discouraged.

The fine crop of 1867 saw the Pawnees through the winter, and in the spring of 1868 the women set to work putting in a still larger crop. They were not hostile Indians, and so had to work for a living. The men were still warriors solely and would not help, but some of the chiefs had promised the agent that they would set the rest of the men an example by going to work with their wives in the corn patches. Not this year. Maybe next year, or the year after. Just now they were busy helping Major Frank North recruit 100 picked warriors to guard the Union Pacific line from the Sioux and Cheyennes, whom the government was preparing to bribe with an imposing mountain of gifts into signing yet another peace treaty.

In June the Pawnees received their little supply of annuities: blankets, knives, hatchets, and so on. They bought with their own money a small supply of ammunition, and in July set out to hunt. In May and June the great peace commission was at Fort Laramie, handing out free blankets, knives, hatchets, camp equipment, arms, and ammunition to any Sioux, Cheyenne, or Arapaho camp whose chiefs would touch the pen for the new peace treaty. Fully equipped with all they needed these Indians went to hunt buffalo south of the Platte. All was peace; but the military had their suspicions concerning the intentions of these Indians and sent Major North with two companies of Pawnee Scouts south of the Platte. North had some prominent eastern men with him, who had come on the scout in the hope of seeing an Indian fight. Near the Republican Fork the Pawnee tribe was found, trying to hunt buffalo. The chiefs complained of Sioux attacks, but no Sioux were to be seen. Major North with his scouts and the eastern men left the Pawnee village, but they had only gone a few miles when 500 Sioux warriors equipped with arms from the recent peace council appeared and made a fierce onset. The Pawnee Scouts got into a ravine and for five hours beat off the Sioux attacks. Meantime more of the hostiles had attacked the Pawnee village, which was on the march. The Pawnees pushed on, fighting as they went, and presently joined Major North, who promptly brought his men out of the ravine and prepared to assault the enemy with the aid of all the Pawnee warriors. The Sioux, however, drew off. The Pawnee Scouts went their way, under military orders; they had hardly gone when the Sioux came back and renewed their attacks on the Pawnee hunters. The same old tale. Every time the Pawnees started to hunt and became scattered over the prairie in little parties, killing buffalo, the Sioux appeared and either attacked the scattered hunters or the Pawnee camp, where the women, children, and old men were without protection. The Pawnees then had to leave the many buffalo they had killed and rush to camp, where they made a stand, then came out and drove the Sioux off. By the time the Pawnees got back to the buffalo they had killed, the meat was spoiled and had to be left for the wolves. Every day some Pawnees were cut off by the enemy and killed, but the Sioux would not fight a battle. Whenever the Pawnees got together and came out to fight, the enemy drew off, to return the next day and again attack the scattered parties of hunters or the unprotected camp.

The Pawnees gave up their hunt and went home. On the reservation they had left the largest crop they had ever put in; the weather had been perfect and they had expected a splendid harvest. They found the fields stripped bare and most of the trees leafless, for on August 3 incredible swarms of grasshoppers had settled over the agency lands, covering the ground in places two and three deep and destroying every growing thing. Agent Whaley reported casually that his Indians were entirely destitute and would probably suffer greatly. Any such report from a Sioux or Cheyenne agent would have brought train-loads of relief, but the Pawnees were given no assistance. They tightened their belts and waited patiently for the beginning of the winter hunt in October.

The Pawnees now had a bit of luck. The great peace treaty of 1868 had hidden away in it a provision that the Sioux and Cheyennes must leave the hunting grounds between the Platte and Arkansas, the old Pawnee lands on which these two tribes had intruded after the year 1820. This section of the treaty had not been drawn for the benefit of the Pawnees, whose interests did not in the least concern the peace-makers, but had been framed with the object of protecting the Union Pacific, the Kansas Pacific, and the white settlers from further annoyance at the hands of the Sioux and Cheyennes. The chiefs who signed this treaty seem to have been left in complete ignorance of its provisions. They had no inkling that their people were to be moved, the Sioux north of the Platte, the Cheyennes south of the Arkansas; and the peace commission (perhaps reluctant to spoil the good feeling engendered by the councils and the liberal handing out of gifts to these Indians) did not at once enforce this part of the treaty. Indeed, they encouraged the Sioux and Cheyennes to go hunting south of the Platte, where these Indians used the firearms given to them as part of the peace presents in attacks on the Pawnees, whom they drove out of the hunting grounds in July (1868). The peace commission remained unmoved. Pawnees did not count, but in August a band of Cheyennes, also armed with guns obtained as peace presents, swept down the Solomon Fork in the bloodiest raid the Kansas whites had ever suffered. General W. T. Sherman then acted. On September 7 he declared the Cheyennes and Arapahos hostile Indians and ordered the troops to begin operations against them; at about the same time Spotted Tail and the other Sioux chiefs were curtly informed that they were to remove their bands north of the Platte and go to the new Whetstone Agency on the Missouri in Dakota. Finding that the military meant what they said, the Sioux sullenly started north; most of the Cheyennes also withdrew; and when the Pawnees went on their winter hunt in October they found the country almost free of enemies. They had an excellent hunt, thus avoiding the starvation their agent had calmly predicted for them after the crop failure in August. The Sioux and Cheyennes had no need to worry over possible starvation, the government officials (always in dread of offending these troublesome Indians) having established huge depots of supplies near which the bands might encamp to be clothed and fed while they lived in carefree idleness.

These were the great days for the Sioux and Cheyennes. With the Indian policy controlled by idealists and humanitarians who were determined to rule by kindness alone, these Indians were paid to sign a treaty, then broke it, and were at once urged to accept more gifts, including arms and ammunition, for signing another treaty. Their chiefs were constantly meeting and counciling with generals, senators, cabinet members and other distinguished men, who made them great promises and gave them rich presents. Like all the other friendly tribes, the Pawnees were ignored. The Great Father did not send generals and cabinet members to visit them: they never saw a white man more distinguished than a simple Indian agent, and they received nothing further than the advice to go to work and earn their own living.

As the last hope of ever obtaining honest men to act as Indian agents, the government had decided that the tribes should be placed under the partial control of the churches, which were to select Indian superintendents and agents and were to be to a certain extent responsible for the conduct of these appointees. Under the new policy the tribes in Nebraska were turned over to the Hicksite sect of Quakers: Samuel M. Janney of this sect was made superintendent at Omaha, and Jacob M. Troth, also a Hicksite Friend, was appointed agent for the Pawnees. When this change was being accomplished, a committee of Friends wrote to Mrs. Elvira Platt, principal of the Pawnee school, asking her to inform the chiefs of the fact that the Friends were now to take charge of them. They wished the chiefs to be told that the Friends intended to help them and that this change would very greatly benefit the tribe. But the Pawnees had heard talk of this kind since 1820, coming from white men who always had the best of intentions. After listening in silence to Mrs. Platt's statement, they sat on, looking very grave but apparently puzzled as to what kind of answer they could send to these

new white friends. At last Lesharo Pitko (Twice-a-Chief) arose
and said with calm dignity: "We will wait and see what comes to
us." The chiefs then stood up and filed out of the room.[128]

Friend Troth was an honest and kindly man, who meant to help
in every way a Christian might; but he could not understand the
Pawnees, and he could not make them comprehend his view of life.
He regarded their ingrained love for wandering widely through the
plains as almost sinful, and wished to confine them straightly to
their reservation and put all the men to work. He had no patience
with men who wished to let dying Indian customs take a little time
for dying; he wished to end them at once. With the Sioux still
killing the Pawnees on their own reservation, he wished the Pawnees
to pledge themselves never to fight again; with their horses constantly being stolen by other tribes, he expected them to understand that stealing horses was a sin and a crime and must stop. If
the Pawnees were honest, kind, and forebearing, the other tribes
would reciprocate, and war and theft would end. A new brotherhood of peace was about to be accomplished. The Pawnee chiefs
listened and wondered.

The Pawnees had been on their reservation for ten years when
Friend Troth arrived: Sixth Month, First Day, 1869, as he wrote it
down in his report. During all those years the Pawnee agents had
reported steady progress in civilization, and they had expended
about half a million dollars for buildings, agriculture, education,
and so on. Yet Jacob Troth found the Pawnees little improved.
They were still very wild, still picking up a precarious living as their
forefathers had done, mainly by hunting and fighting. Most of the
thousands of horses in their hands had been stolen from other tribes;
war was still an all-absorbing interest; Christianity was almost unknown in the tribe, and after twenty-five years of education (the
first school having been established in the early Forties) not a Pawnee could write, and the great majority of the people knew no
English beyond a few choice phrases picked up from soldiers, bull-
whackers, and cowboys. The agency on which so much money had
been spent was in very bad condition. Most of the buildings were
only fit to be torn down, some of them ramshackle log huts taken
over from the Mormons in 1859, others cheap frames, badly constructed and in a terrible condition from neglect. The grist- and
saw-mill was out of order and would not run, although the government was going on paying out $3,840 a year for miller and engineer
salaries. Where the great sums spent on agriculture had gone was

a mystery. The farm, taken over from the Mormons in 1859, had shrunk in size and was now only 110 acres in a very bad state of cultivation despite the large staff of farm workers on the payroll. The Pawnee women dug and planted 1,200 acres by the same methods they had used since the beginning of Time. They had no help from the agency farmer and his staff. The large brick school was the only good building at the agency; but it had been badly planned, and although a large sum had been spent on its construction it was still hardly fit for use. Mrs. Platt, the head of the school, greeted the Quaker regime with joy. She was so weary of dishonest agents, who were enthusiastic in obtaining funds for education and later diverted most of the money to their own pockets. She had been begging them for years to build a high picket fence around her sanctuary, to keep Sioux war parties (and Pawnee parents) out. She now expected to get her fence, and also a quadrangle of low frame buildings to surround the brick school. Within these walls she would carefully confine all of the Pawnee children, some five hundred of them, and keep them isolated from their objectionable parents until she could turn them into good imitation white people. Troth heartily approved her plans and pledged himself to put them into operation.[129]

Most of the Sioux and Cheyennes had been cleared out of the lands south of the Platte in 1868, but in the spring of 1869 there were some camps of these Indians in that country, holding out in defiance of government orders. The military were preparing a campaign against these people, and General C. C. Augur sent Major Frank North to enlist a battalion of Pawnees for service with the troops. The Pawnees responded as they always did by almost tearing Major North limb from limb in their eagerness to have their names written down. General Augur now rewarded the tribe for its loyalty by requesting the Quakers to prevent the Pawnees going on a buffalo hunt, on the grounds that the troops might mistake them for hostile Sioux and Cheyennes. Instead of replying that any officer who did not know the Pawnees from the other tribes was not a fit person to lead troops in the field, the Quakers seized upon this excuse for forbidding the tribe to go hunting. The Quaker idea was that, if the Pawnee men were shut up on the reservation, sheer boredom might induce them to go to work. Any Pawnee child of eight years could have demonstrated the futility of this scheme.

While the Quakers were trying to keep the Pawnees cooped up on the reservation, a Pawnee man was murdered just outside the eastern boundary and Charles McMurty, a settler, was found murdered on an island in the Platte. Naturally, nothing was done about the dead Pawnee; but the white man's death caused great excitement, and a coroner's jury brought in a verdict that he had been murdered by Pawnees. The Quakers bullied the chiefs into giving up eight Pawnees, who admitted being on the island at about the time of McMurty's death, and one of these men, Yellow Sun, was put on trial for murder. In the past few months fourteen Pawnees had been murdered by white men, none of the cases being even investigated. The Quakers were all for justice being done, even if it was a very one-sided form of justice, but the Pawnee chiefs were not so pleased at seeing one of their men tried in a frontier court in which all the whites were prejudiced. Lesharo Pitko, who took his responsibilities as chief seriously, attended the trial and listened for hours to Baptiste Bayhylle's translation of the evidence. It was clearly going badly for Yellow Sun. The chief, seeing that his side was losing, at last got to his feet and said to the astonished judge, Baptiste translating for him: "My father, you have lost one man; recently I have lost fourteen. Let us call it even and let this boy Yellow Sun go." The end of the story is buried in the forgotten past. Neither Captain L. H. North nor William E. Walton, who was licensed trader among the Pawnees at this time, could recall the fate of Yellow Sun.

The Pawnees were heartbroken over the refusal of the authorities to permit them to carry on their ancient custom of hunting buffalo. The prediction that the idle men would go to work was not fulfilled. A few, mostly boys who had been trained in the school, cut a little hay; a few others, who had wagons, worked in the fields to the extent of driving to the corn patches and letting the women load the wagons with corn and vegetables, then driving to the Indian village and there letting the women unload the wagons. The rest of the men did nothing. Fortunately the tribe had an excellent crop. They were not Sioux, and unquestionably if, after being prevented from hunting, their crop had failed the officials would have let them starve. The chiefs insisted on going on a winter hunt, soothing Agent Troth by letting him order plows, wagons, and harness with their annuity money, instead of guns, pistols, knives, and other lethal weapons, which they really needed more, as long as the Sioux were about. They had an excellent hunt, no Sioux or Cheyennes being sighted, and came home with great quantities of dried meat, robes, and furs.

The Pawnee Scouts had a very active season, taking the field in
the winter of 1868-9 to aid the troops in searching for hostile camps
in the lands south of the Platte, guarding the Union Pacific line in
the spring, and in summer joining General E. A. Carr's expedition
against the Tall Bull band of Cheyennes. Trailing this band, the
Pawnees found their camp at Summit Springs near the South Platte;
and shortly after noon of July 11 the camp of eighty-five lodges
was charged by fifty Pawnees and two hundred cavalry, Major Frank
North of the Pawnees riding into the camp ahead of all others. In
a hard fight the camp and all its contents were captured; fifty-two
Cheyennes, including Chief Tall Bull, were killed; fifteen women
and children were captured; 418 horses taken, mainly by the Pawnees; and a white woman captive was rescued. The Pawnees later
took part in the pursuit of Tall Bull's band in the lands north of
the Platte, but the fugitives moved at such speed that the troops
never came within sight of them.

The Indian war was now over; the Pawnee Scouts were mustered
out of service, and (forgotten by all the friends they had made in
the army) the Pawnees were left under the absolute control of
Quakers who were under the delusion that the best way in which
they could aid the tribe was to destroy the age-old customs and habits
of the Pawnees as swiftly as possible. Up to this time the chiefs
had carefully concealed from Agent Troth the fact that parties of
Pawnees were still slipping away from the reservation, mainly to
steal horses. Troth did not understand Indians; but his Pawnees
understood him and kept their horse-lifting operations very carefully
concealed; but in the winter of 1869-70 a party of Pawnee warriors
concluded a deal in Cheyenne horses on such a scale that the matter
simply could not be concealed.

To go back a few years: Big Spotted Horse (*Asawuki ladaho*),
the Kitkehahki boy who in 1852 had killed the Cheyenne warrior
clad in the Spanish coat-of-mail, had now grown up to be very
proficient in the Pawnee art of abstracting desirable horses from
enemy camps. He was constantly engaged in this work; he had good
success, and he might have prospered greatly, if he had been as
expert at gambling as he was at horse-lifting. As it was, he lost at
various Pawnee gambling games most of the horses he had risked
his life to obtain, and (reduced to a breech-clout and moccasins
by his losses) he would then set out to go two or three hundred
miles on foot in quest of more horseflesh. In 1867 he joined his
friend Lone Chief and a few others in a most dangerous attempt to

steal horses from the watchful Osages. The men came home with thirty head. In 1868 Big Spotted Horse seems to have gone off with Lone Chief again, on a trip that took them clear down to Red River, where they rediscovered the Wichitas, those southern cousins of the Pawnees.

These men came home from Red River in March, 1869, just at the time when the Pawnees were finding out that Quaker rule was dictatorship and were not liking it at all. Presently Agent Troth refused permission for the tribe to go on a summer buffalo hunt, so that the men would have to remain where they were and (theoretically) go to work at farming; but now Lone Chief and Big Spotted Horse began to talk of the wonders of the Wichita country: a kind of Indian paradise in which men could still be men and could fight, hunt buffalo, and steal horses whenever they chose with no Quakers about to refuse them permission. All this was unknown to Agent Troth and his employees; they did not even find out that anything unusual was happening when Lone Chief and his friend got three hundred Pawnees to join them and slipped away from the reservation, heading for Red River. They visited the Wichitas, made peace with the Kiowas and Comanches, and came north to rejoin the Pawnees in the autumn. Agent Troth never learned of this astonishing performance, and he imagined that he knew everything his Indians were doing.[130]

When the tribe set out on its winter hunt in October, 1869, Big Spotted Horse got a party together and went south of the Arkansas River again. There he led his men to a camp of seventy-five lodges of Cheyennes—a very dangerous place for a little party of Pawnees, all afoot; yet, under cover of darkness, Big Spotted Horse led his men into the Cheyenne camp, where they cut loose all the best horses that were tied in front of the lodges. They then rounded up the general herd of loose animals and got away with six hundred head. All that night the Pawnees drove hard toward the north, frequently changing the horses they rode and keeping the herd going at top speed. When they got across the Arkansas they felt safer; the Cheyennes would not follow them here, but white frontiersmen might see them and try to take their captured herd, so they traveled north along obscure trails, moving cautiously. This trip was made in the coldest part of winter, and in southwest Nebraska the party ran into a great blizzard and had to lie out in the wind and snow for three days and nights. Some of the men had fingers and toes so badly frozen that they fell off, but they clung tenaciously to their captured herd.

The arrival of this party in the Pawnee villages was an event of such proportions that it could not be concealed, and Agent Troth now for the first time became aware of the existence of an Indian called Big Spotted Horse. He also heard about the stolen horses and grew highly indignant. According to Captain L. H. North the agent now summoned Big Spotted Horse to his office and through the interpreter, Bayhylle, he solemnly informed the big Pawnee that he was the greatest horse-thief in the entire world. Thinking that his grandfather (the agent) was paying him a mighty fine compliment, Big Spotted Horse came forward to shake hands, but Bayhylle shouted at him to stand back and began an elaborate oration in Pawnee, trying to explain that when a Quaker called you a great horse-thief he meant that you were . . . well, a bad boy. Big Spotted Horse just could not believe it; but when Agent Troth, through the interpreter, ordered him and his friends to start at once with the stolen herd and return the animals to their rightful owners, the Pawnee began to realize that something was wrong. Questioning Bayhylle earnestly, he obtained a glimmering of the truth. Their grandfather, the agent, was wrong in his head. The poor fellow was suffering from a delusion that stealing horses from enemies was bad. His idea of making all good again was for the Pawnees to take the horses back to the Cheyennes, who would then put their arms around the Pawnees and say: "What good boys you are! Come right in for a nice hot cup of coffee." Knowing very well that if he and his comrades ventured near the Cheyenne camp with the stolen animals they would be promptly filled with Cheyenne bullets and arrows and then cut to pieces and their separated limbs left on the prairie for the wolves, Big Spotted Horse said *"No!"* several times in a loud tone and walked out of the office.

The wrathful Quaker called all the chiefs to council, and after making many threats, hardly in conformity with the kindly ways of Friends, bullied them into giving up Big Spotted Horse and five of his fellow criminals who were turned over to the military and confined in the guardhouse at Fort Omaha.

This affair for the moment convinced Agent Troth that the bright reports he had heard of Pawnee progress in civilization were much exaggerated. Even the chiefs would not cooperate in returning the stolen horses to their owners, an act of common honesty. No one would even tell him from what tribe the animals had been lifted. After writing to several agents to inquire if their Indians had lost a herd of 600 horses, and getting no answer from these agents, he called another council of chiefs and demanded that they should return the horses at once to their rightful owners. The chiefs demurred. It was not too cold to bring stolen horses to the Pawnee agency, but much too cold to take them back home. Why, the warriors might freeze their fingers and toes! Their grandfather, the agent, must be patient. In the spring when the weather was warm the chiefs would have another talk with him.

That was a hard February and March; many horses died of exposure and hunger; and a strange thing was noted, for whenever the chiefs informed Agent Troth of the taking-off of another lot of animals, the deaths were always in the stolen herd. The Pawnee horses seemed surprisingly healthy, but perhaps the stolen animals were not used to the rigorous northern climate. White horse-thieves were also busy on the reservation and the Sioux made their customary stealthy visits, carrying off a considerable number of horses; here again the Pawnee herds were miraculously spared and only animals from the stolen herd were taken. By June there were few of the stolen animals left, and those such scrubs that no Sioux or white horse-thief (or Pawnee) would look at them. The chiefs decided it was time to have another talk with their grandfather, the agent. Agent Troth was quite pleased with their honest offer to return the stolen animals, but he was not so pleased when informed that the Pawnee men must be paid and paid well for taking the animals south and that they would not go farther than Fort Harker in west Kansas, where they would leave the animals for the Cheyennes to claim. Nothing would induce any of the Pawnees to accept the agent's Christian project to have them go right into the Cheyenne camp, shake hands, and become brothers. They simply lacked faith. Moreover, they even refused to go to Fort Harker unless a responsible white man went along to protect them from the Kansas settlers. Agent Troth unwillingly accepted the terms, and early in July eight Pawnees, led by Captain L. H. North, set out for Fort Harker with thirty or forty scrubs (all that was left of the herd of 600 Cheyenne horses). One night in Kansas their camp was suddenly surrounded by a mob of armed white men. It was only the presence of Captain North and his bold stand that kept the whites from attacking the Pawnees under the pretext that they were hostile Indians.

Big Spotted Horse and his comrades spent several months in the guardhouse at Fort Omaha, but the quarters were comfortable, food plenty, and some of the soldiers and officers were friendly. There were poker games. Then, late in the spring, a judge looked up the law and found that there was no statute under which Indians could be prosecuted for stealing from Indians, and the six Pawnees were released with due apologies. They took the Union Pacific train for home, planning what they would do with the wealth of Cheyenne horses which even the white men now admitted belonged to them, but when they reached the Pawnee villages and heard that their horses were all gone they were stunned.

Big Spotted Horse presently recovered sufficiently to talk, and as he talked he grew angry, and before long he was the maddest Indian in the two Americas. That Quaker . . . . Who now was the horse-thief, the very big horse-thief? The angry Pawnee denounced Quakers and white men in all their classes and categories as meddlers and trouble-makers and thieves; he declared that Nebraska had become a land only fit for squaws and the kind of Pawnees who would let a Quaker who did not know one end of a gun from the other order them about. Then this unreconstructed warrior shook the dust of the hateful little reservation from his moccasins and set off for Red River, for the land of the Wichitas, where men were still men.

NOTES TO CHAPTER XI

[121]This Kansas trouble is dealt with in the *Annual Report of the Secretary of the Interior*, 1866, p. 222.

[122]*Report of the Commissioner of Indian Affairs* for 1866, p. 44. The Indian Office now went into the show business, and as long as these Pawnees were detained in Washington they were kept busy performing war dances before groups of prominent persons, including the dowager queen of Hawaii.

[123]Pani Leshar: Pawnee Chief. The scouts gave Frank North this title of honor in the field, after a success over the hostiles.

[124]These assertions were made by Elvira Platt in an official report as head of the Pawnee school. She stated that the Indian children went hungry while the agent sold for his own benefit the crops these children had helped to raise.

[125]Information from Captain L. H. North; Bruce: *The Fighting Norths*, p. 26. Bayhylle at this time was a sergeant in the Pawnee Scouts.

[126]North information; Bruce, pp. 27-9.

[127]North information; Bruce, p. 26, p. 30.

[128]Mr. William E. Walton, who was made licensed trader for the Pawnees when the Quakers took charge, informs me that Benjamin Hollowell, a Quaker educator, headmaster of the academy at Alexandria, Virginia, and a personal friend of President Grant, was consulted by the President and ad-

vised the appointment of Janney, Troth, and the other Hicksite Quakers, who were put in charge of the Nebraska tribes. Mr. Walton states that Jacob Troth, the Pawnee agent, was a native of Accotink, Virginia, a personal friend of Hollowell, an honest and honorable man, but a visionary with a head filled with impractical theories.

[129]Mrs. Platt's report, in *Report of the Secretary of the Interior* for 1869, p. 749. The effects of the Platt system of educating the Pawnee youth away from their own people were becoming apparent by 1869. A few boys and girls who had gone through the school were now grown up and some were married. They had no home and no people; the educators had spoiled them for life among the Pawnees; the whites would not accept them. A few boys solved their problem and outraged Elvira Platt's high ideals by enlisting in the Pawnee Scouts, reinstating themselves with their own people by becoming good warriors, and quickly reverting to what the educators scornfully termed *Indianism*.

[130]Grinnell: *Pawnee Hero Stories*, pp. 46 *et seq*. The author has additional information from Captain L. H. North, who knew Lone Chief and Big Spotted Horse well.

XII

Blown Away Southward

MOST OF THE PAWNEES STILL HOPED THAT THEY COULD CONTINUE TO live mainly by hunting and wandering in the plains and when their enemies, the Cheyennes and Sioux, were removed from the lands between the Platte and Arkansas rivers by the government in 1868-9 this hope was strengthened. But in truth there was no chance whatever that the old free life of the tribe could be maintained for any number of years. The hostile Indians had gone, but the new railroads were now bringing in thousands of white families; the log and sod dwellings of these settlers were springing up in every part of Nebraska and Kansas. The buffalo herds were being systematically destroyed by parties of white hunters, armed with the best modern rifles, and at every way-station along the railroads huge quantities of buffalo hides were stacked up, waiting for shipment. Even the most stubborn-minded of the Pawnees had to admit that the buffalo would not last many more years, and with the herds destroyed the tribe could no longer support itself by hunting.

In 1870 the Pawnees were in dire need of wise leadership and government assistance; but at this period there was little hope that the government could be of any use in aiding the tribe, for the Indian Office was under the control of visionaries whose object seemed to be to uproot tribes like the Pawnees and by some magic to suddenly metamorphise them into self-supporting Christian farmers. After thirty years of government effort to encourage farming, in 1870 the best farms on the Pawnee reservation were of about three acres in extent, the average Pawnee family farming less than one acre. Most of the men were immovably opposed to working with their hands, and even if the government was foolish enough to attempt to force the Pawnee men to work, the Quakers were hardly the proper persons to inaugurate a policy of coercion.

303

Some of the Pawnee chiefs had the right idea, and in 1870 they went into the corn patches and attempted to help the women by plowing. To substitute the horse and plow for the ancient method of digging the soil by hand was true advancement, and although the chiefs made a sad display of themselves as plowmen, they did win over some of the Pawnee men who began to try their hand at helping their women to grow crops. But Agent Troth was merely impatient with all this. He desired a sudden and overwhelming change that would turn all the Pawnee men almost overnight into farmers who could compete with their white neighbors. The Indians were growing old-time squaw corn (not a marketable crop), beans, squashes, and other vegetables. They ate everything they grew, and by tripling their little acreage of these crops they could at least feed themselves; but Troth was eagerly demanding that they should give up growing corn and vegetables and go in suddenly for wheat farming, which they knew nothing about, on a large commercial scale. Even this was not enough to satisfy this Quaker meddler in other people's lives. He demanded that the Indian villages should be broken up and that the Indians should scatter out over the reservation, each family on a large farm. And this at a time when the Sioux were still raiding the Pawnee reservation. In the spring of 1870 these raiders killed five Pawnee men and a woman within sight of Troth's office windows, and they would have killed a great many more if the people had not been living in their villages, where they could keep together and defend themselves.

The Quaker superintendent of Indians, Samuel M. Janney, who was in charge of all the Nebraska tribes, was even more determined than Friend Troth to force the Indians suddenly into self-support through farming. His plans embraced the breaking up of the Pawnee, Omaha, and Oto tribes, the placing of each family on a farm of its own, and the providing of plows, horses, harness, wagons, and other farming needs for each family. As the government would not supply the funds necessary for the carrying out of this revolution, Friend Janney proposed that Congress should pass an act providing for the sale of part of the lands on the already too small Nebraska reservations, and with the money thus obtained he would equip each Indian family with the means for beginning farming on a commercial basis. That these Indians would suddenly leap from farming on a scale of one acre for each family to farming quarter-sections of land, this Quaker theorist had not a trace of doubt.

William E. Walton, the licensed trader at the agency in Troth's time, had much to say in later years concerning this agent's impracticable schemes. The saw- and grist-mill, built by the government in 1859, had been an expense, but of no help whatever to the Pawnees. With an engineer and laborer for the mill always on the payroll, the machinery was out of repair most of the time; when it did work practically all the men and teams employed at the agency were kept busy hauling wood to keep the engine going. Wood was scarce on Loup Fork. This nonsensical performance robbed the Indians of fuel they badly needed and kept all the men at the agency at work, cutting and hauling wood. During ten years not one agent or superintendent had the honesty to report that this mill was a toy and a wicked waste of money; that the Pawnees, living in earth-lodges, had no need for lumber; that they had never grown a bushel of wheat; that their corn was mainly cut when green and dried like old-time sweet corn, so that a grist-mill was of no utility whatever. But Troth, visioning all the Pawnee men suddenly going to work at wheat-farming, considered the mill most important, and in 1870 he proposed to convert it to a water-mill at an estimated cost of $3,700. The Indian Office officials, who welcomed any wild-cat plan that was labeled *Progress,* heartily approved of Troth's mill dam, but funds were the difficulty. The government, which was spending millions to feed and clothe the Sioux in idleness, had no money with which to aid the self-supporting Pawnees, but in the end the sum required was filched from the tiny Pawnee annuity money. The idealists saw nothing wrong in this; they were just disregarding the law with the good intention of aiding the Pawnees. Agent Troth now built a dam in Beaver Creek, over the protest of local white men, who warned him that it would not hold. The angry stream took the dam out twice, but even then Troth would not give up. He made proposals for rebuilding the dam on a new plan, asking for further funds; but, instead of money, an inspector was sent to Pawnee Agency, and on his report Troth was removed from office.

The Pawnees, who had been almost destroyed by the Sioux and other enemies in the period 1840-1860, now in 1870 were threatened with disaster which was being prepared by well-meaning and kindly Christians who were incapable of understanding Indians, but still had the hardihood to accept office and to make decisions that affected the lives of tens of thousands of people. Most of these Indian officials were pacifists who held ingrained opinions that kind treat-

ment would tame the wildest Indians and make them amenable to
reason.

It had cost the whites hundreds of lives and millions of dollars
to uproot the Sioux from the lands on and south of the Platte and
drive them north to their new reservation in Dakota; but this task
had been finished in 1869, and both the whites and Pawnees in
Nebraska imagined that they were now done with the Sioux and the
terror that tribe had created. Then, in 1871, the officials permitted
Red Cloud to bring several thousand wild Sioux to a new agency
on the North Platte, thus breaking the government's word that no
Sioux would ever come back to the Platte. Spotted Tail was now
given part of what he demanded: the right to leave the Missouri
River and locate at an agency in northwest Nebraska. These changes
had just been made when the Sioux assumed the attitude that all
lands north of the Platte belonged to them, and they announced
that they would fight the moment any white men came north of the
river. Fearing trouble with the Sioux, the officials in Washington
ordered the wagon trains that were hauling free supplies to Spotted
Tail's Indians not to cross north of the Platte. The wagons were
held in camp, piling up thousands of dollars in demurrage charges
against the government for every day they were delayed. To get out
of this dilemma without resorting to the dreadful expedient of sending troops to escort the trains and daring the Sioux to attack them,
the alarmed officials ordered the wagons to go to Red Cloud's agency
on the Platte and unload there. They then gave Spotted Tail the
temporary privilege of coming to the Platte for his supplies, but
giving in to the Sioux was a dangerous practice. Spotted Tail—
realizing from their vacillation that the Indian Office men were in
a fright—promptly defied all authority, and, taking his own bands
and part of Red Cloud's, he boldly crossed the Platte and went
down to Republican Fork for an extended buffalo hunt. Instead
of sending troops at once to drive these Sioux north of the Platte
again, the weak officials began to worry, fearing that the Sioux might
not find enough game to feed their large camps, and plans were
discussed for sending free rations to these defiant Indians.

When Red Cloud was on his way home from Washington in the
fall of 1870, Superintendent Janney buttonholed him on the streets
of Omaha and begged him to make peace with the Pawnees. The
great Oglala warrior replied that he could do nothing about such
a matter without consulting his people. He never consulted them.
Janney then wrote to Spotted Tail at the Whetstone Agency in

Dakota and begged him to make peace between the Sioux and Pawnees, but no reply was received from the Brulé chief. These Quakers persisted in regarding the ancient and deep-rooted hate of the Sioux for the Pawnees as a little misunderstanding that a friendly talk would put an end to.

Except for the Sioux raids in the spring, 1870 was a quiet year among the Pawnees. The Pawnee Scouts were in the field, patroling the railroad line, but they saw no fighting. The Union Pacific officials, in acknowledgment of the great service the Pawnee Scouts had rendered in guarding the working parties while the road was being constructed, had given orders that all Pawnees should ride free along the line in Nebraska. Some of the Pawnees were having a lovely time, riding on the cars, visiting with fine white people from the East, getting free meals at the stations, selling beadwork, bows and arrows. Agent Troth was annoyed. He wished to keep all the Indians on the reservation, where in his view they should work every day, and he did his best to have the free rides abolished.

Superintendent Janney had kept after Spotted Tail in the matter of peace between the Brulés and the Pawnees. Spotted Tail took a full year to reply, and then stated that his Brulés would not make peace with the Pawnees because the other Teton Sioux tribes would be angry if they did. Almost at the moment that this notice was received from the Brulé chief, a war party of his men came down on the Pawnee agency, killing three Pawnee women and two boys who had recently graduated from the school. These boys lost their lives simply and solely because they had been taught in school that it was wicked to carry arms.

The Pawnees had a good summer hunt, plenty of buffalo, and not a Sioux or Cheyenne to trouble them. It was a drought year, yet on reaching home the Pawnees found a fine corn crop in their patches, while the agent, who was telling them constantly that they would never get anywhere until they went to growing wheat, had lost all his wheat and oats.

Troth was at any rate improving the agency. He had put all of the old buildings in fine shape and built several new ones. At last, after ten years of longing, Mrs. Platt had the high picket fence around her boarding-school; Troth had even painted the fence white, and he had built at the Indian villages a big, comfortable day-school, where a woman teacher was instructing fifty of the children. The Quakers were supplying clothing for the school children; they had also sent out a matron to live in the Indian villages and care for the sick and aged. For the first time the Pawnees left some children and aged people in their villages when they went hunting in the winter of 1871-1872. There was little danger of a Sioux attack in winter, and the Quakers were caring for the children and old people. This was a hard winter, with great storms and deep snow, and the tribe had poor hunting. The people came home late in the winter, very hungry and destitute, and Agent Troth distributed among them some potatoes that had been grown by the Pawnee boys at the farm-school. No appeal for aid was made; the Pawnees tightened their belts and got along somehow. At this time the Sioux, who were threatening war and doing all they could to make trouble, were being fed lavishly. The government in 1871 paid for Sioux beef $1,314,000, and about the same sum was being expended for Sioux bacon, mess pork, flour, sugar, and coffee. The blankets for the Sioux cost $236,000 in 1871, and these Indians, living in absolute idleness, were also receiving free canvas for tipis, free camp equipment, and free tobacco. The Pawnees had nothing from the government except a $30,000 annuity (about $10 for each person) paid for lands they had given up; and, lean year or fat year, the same humanitarians who were so solicitous for the welfare of the fierce and ungrateful Sioux, left the Pawnees to shift for themselves.

Friend Janney had now left the office of Indian superintendent at Omaha, and Barclay White, another Quaker, had taken his place. Barclay White was a shrewd and energetic man. He at once made arrangements with the military headquarters in Omaha to receive telegraphic warning of raiding parties reported as leaving the Sioux agencies, and these reports he passed on by telegraph to the Pawnee agent. Very early in the spring of 1872 he was informed by the military that a Sioux war party was on its way to attack the Pawnee villages. These warriors, however, had set out too early in the season; there was no grass for their ponies, and not caring to walk 200 or 300 miles, they presently turned back. Two companies of United States cavalry were then sent to the upper waters of Loup Fork, where they intercepted and drove off a war party of seventy Sioux headed toward the Pawnee reservation.

The railroads were still bringing in great numbers of white homesteaders, and in 1872 the whites began to take up prairie lands to the west and north of the Pawnee reservation, forming a kind of barrier against future Sioux attacks. The military were planning a post in this new district to deal with Sioux war parties; it began to appear that with a few more years of watchfulness the ancient menace of Sioux attacks would be ended.

Most of the homesteaders who were thronging into the country were from the East and did not have the suspicion, or even hatred, toward all Indians that had been characteristic of the old frontier population. These people got along well with the Pawnees. There were still men in Nebraska who were ready to shoot Indians on the slightest pretext. Barclay White reported that recently a friendly chief had been killed by one of these men who had then boasted of his deed and induced the local editor to print an account of it. The state authorities had taken no action. But there were many signs that such wanton killings would not be tolerated much longer, and on the whole the prospects for friendly relations between the Pawnees and their white neighbors were growing brighter every year. The old demand for removal of the tribe from Nebraska had died out, and nearly everyone seemed satisfied that the Pawnees should remain where they were permanently. There were, however, two dangers to be guarded against: the Sioux, and that class of Indian Office officials who were ready to uproot a tribe at any moment if they imagined that they could benefit the Indians in that way.

The Sioux who had defied the government and gone hunting on the Republican Fork in the summer of 1871 were not punished in any way. Having broken the treaty and defied the authorities, these Sioux were not only permitted to go on another hunt south of the Platte early in the winter but the government agent actually aided the Indians, providing them with extra rations and clothing to lessen their hardships while on the hunt. Meantime the friendly Pawnees had difficulty in obtaining permission to go hunting and had to provide their own needs, the government failing to aid them in any manner. This was the winter when Grand Duke Alexis of Russia came to Nebraska for a buffalo hunt with the Indians, and General Sheridan detailed General Custer to arrange for the hunt and other entertainments. Custer, with his love for dramatics, put on a fine spectacle, with the aid of W. F. Cody and Spotted Tail. This chief brought five hundred picked Sioux warriors in all their glory to go on the hunt with the Russian visitor. The Pawnees, as always, were ignored. They were hunting to obtain food for their families, fearful that with the Sioux swarming in the hunting grounds they would be attacked; but they had the Omaha tribe with them, and somehow these friendly Indians managed to make a fair hunt.

The Quakers had succeeded in ending the buffalo hunts of the

Ponca tribe. This little tribe had come to the Pawnee reservation
in the summer of 1871 and accompanied the Pawnees on a buffalo
hunt, but it was their last. In the spring of 1872 the Quakers for-
bade the Pawnee hunt. The chiefs appealed to generals Sheridan
and Ord and obtained their permission for the tribal hunt. Pitalesharo, the head-chief of the Grand Pawnees, led this hunt. In the
Pawnee camp were two young Yale men, George Bird Grinnell and
his classmate, James H. Russell of Kentucky. Baptiste Bayhylle and
Texas Jack (J. B. Omohundro) [131] were with the Pawnees as trail-
agents with authority from Agent Troth to prevent horse-stealing
parties from leaving the camp.

The Pawnee hunters left the reservation on June 8. On the
10th, Congress passed the bill which the Quakers were pressing,
authorizing the sale of 50,000 acres of Pawnee land lying south of
Loup Fork to obtain funds to defray the expense of placing each
Pawnee family on a separate farm. The Quakers were so eager to
complete this transaction that Friend Troth was sent to chase his
Indians out along their hunting trail to obtain the approval of the
chiefs. He caught up with the Indians near Grand Island, called
a hasty council, and induced the chiefs to touch the pen while he
wrote down their names. How did he do it? The Pawnees did not
like the "agreement" which had been concocted by the Quakers
alone, and many of the chiefs feared that this scheme for putting
each Pawnee family on a separate farm would end in the Sioux
coming down and killing most of the scattered families.

The Pawnees had a fair hunt. The Sioux were south of the
Platte, but fortunately they did not have the opportunity to make
an attack in force. A small Sioux war party found the Pawnee camp
and almost succeeded in stampeding the whole Pawnee horse herd.
White buffalo hunters prevented the Pawnees from having a good
hunt. These professional hide-hunters were scattered in small parties
all over the country near the buffalo herds; on several occasions
when the Pawnees had located a large herd, had taken hours to
make a cautious approach, and had the herd almost surrounded,
white hunters rushed in, firing with repeating-rifles, and frightened
the herd into wild flight. These white men did not care for much
meat, and they at times gave the Pawnees the carcasses after strip-
ping off the hides; but this was a slight compensation for the loss
of the great quantities of meat that a successful surround produced.
Some of the white hunters were among the roughest characters on
the frontier, and more than once parties of these men threatened

to attack the Pawnees for coming into the hunting grounds and allegedly hindering their operations. This was one reason why Texas Jack had been employed to accompany the Pawnees. He could handle the worst of these white hunters.

When Agent Troth was removed another Quaker, William Burgess, took his place. Burgess and his wife had formerly run a seminary for Quaker children in Pennsylvania, and soon after reaching the Pawnee agency he removed Elvira Platt and placed his wife on the payroll as head of the Indian school. He continued the crusade Troth had conducted, to induce the Pawnees to give up hunting and try wheat-growing as a method for earning a living. None of the Quakers had the slightest realization that it was impossible for people who from the earliest times had obtained only a fraction of their food from crops to give up hunting and become at once successful farmers. The Pawnee chiefs had no faith in the optimistic schemes of these whites; but the Quakers were in complete control of the tribe, and by exerting every form of pressure Agent Burgess obtained a promise from some of the chiefs to give up hunting. About one fourth of the tribe insisted on going hunting, and by stubbornly sticking to it they in the end won a grudging consent from their agent.

These Quaker visionaries were still clinging to their plan for a peace between the Sioux and Pawnees; and just as the Pawnee hunters were leaving for the buffalo plains in early July, Agent Burgess sent some of the chiefs with Baptiste Bayhylle to Fort McPherson, near the forks of the Platte, to meet the Sioux chiefs and smoke the peace pipe. The officers at the fort had been instructed in advance to do all in their power to bring the Sioux chiefs in; messages were sent both to the chiefs and to the Sioux agents, but not one Sioux turned up for the peace-making. The Pawnee chiefs came home, wondering if Quakers ever faced a simple truth, such as this, that the Sioux did not desire peace.

Sky Chief (*Tirawahut lashar*), one of the best chiefs the Pawnees had, was selected by the Indians to lead the buffalo hunt in July, 1873, and Agent Burgess picked John W. Williamson to go along as trail-agent to keep the Pawnees in order and to protect them from white men and, if possible, from the Sioux. Williamson, an employee at the agency, was very popular among the Pawnees. A handsome young man, with long wavy brown hair falling to his shoulders, the Pawnees gave him the name of *Bukskariwi* (Curly Head), but at times they called him *Chaikstaka laket* (Whiteman

Leader). He had with him on this hunt another young white man, L. B. Platt, the son of Lester and Elvira Platt, who had been brought up among the Pawnees. Other leaders on this hunt were Fighting Bear (*Koruksa tapuk*)[132] and Sun Chief (*Sakuru lashar*), the latter being the heir (nephew apparently, not son) of Pitalesharo, the head-chief of the Grand Pawnees.[133] Williamson in his later report gave the number of hunters as 250 men, 100 women, 50 children, all mounted, and with 100 extra horses to carry packs of dried buffalo meat and hides.

Going south from near Grand Island on the Platte, this party killed fifty-five buffalo at the point where they struck Republican Fork. This was in the middle of July. Crossing over to Beaver Creek, they had fine hunting, killing 400 buffalo and obtaining all the meat and hides. They then turned westward up the Beaver, where they met white hunters who told them that there were Sioux in that direction. Turning to the southwest to avoid this danger, the Pawnees hunted on Sappa Creek, but found few buffalo. In a council it was decided that the white hunters had invented the story of the presence of Sioux to keep the Pawnees out of good hunting grounds. Turning northward the party went to Driftwood Creek and killed 200 buffalo; they then went on north to the Republican. Here on August 4 white hunters warned them of a large force of Sioux not far away to the north. Williamson advised a retirement down the Republican to a grove of timber, a good defensive position. Fighting Bear angrily accused him of cowardice, declaring that no Sioux sign had been seen, that the white hunters had made up their story to prevent the Pawnees obtaining more buffalo, and that even if there were some Sioux about, the Pawnees had whipped the Sioux often enough in the past and could do it again. Williamson replied that they had come out to hunt buffalo and were not properly armed to fight Sioux. There was a fierce argument. In the end, instead of taking the safe trail homeward down the south bank of the river, the Pawnees crossed north of the Republican, and on August 5 went up a ravine and came out on the plains west of Frenchman's Fork, where they found bands of buffalo quietly feeding. The camp moved on; the warriors pursued the buffalo, killing many of them. The Pawnees were skinning and cutting up the buffalo when a band of about one hundred mounted Sioux charged over a bluff and came down on them. Sky Chief was shot and scalped while engaged in skinning a buffalo, and several other men were killed. At sight of the enemy, the men who were with the moving camp rushed the women and children and the pack horses loaded down with the dried meat and hides from nearly 800 buffalo to the shelter of the ravine. Williamson came out to parley, but the Sioux fired on him and drove him back. Young Platt found himself surrounded and had his revolver taken from him. (The Sioux had strict orders from their chiefs not to kill a white man.)

Pursued by the enemy, the Pawnee hunters made for the ravine, and presently gathered sufficient force to come out and fight. They held the Sioux off for about an hour; then suddenly the prairie was alive with mounted Sioux, from 800 to 1,000 Oglala and Brulé warriors riding into view and charging in on the Pawnees from three directions. One look at the advancing hordes, and the Pawnee warriors made a rush for the ravine, but the place was a death trap, and they began cutting the packs from the extra horses to provide mounts for the women and children. The Sioux were already on them, riding down into the ravine and also along its western and eastern sides, raining bullets and arrows down on their victims. In the few moments before the Pawnees could mount, thirty-nine women, ten children, and a number of men were shot down. The survivors fled in panic, the Sioux pursuing them for three miles down the ravine, out into the Republican valley, and down the valley eastward. During a ten-mile chase most of the fugitives managed to cross south of the river. The Sioux were preparing to go after them when a bugle rang out and a troop of the Third Cavalry led by Major Russell appeared from a belt of timber on the north side of the river. At sight of the troops the Sioux made for the hills, and presently the last groups of their warriors had vanished.

Major Russell had learned that the Sioux were planning an attack, and he had made a hard march to intercept them, but he was too late. He now tried to coax the Pawnees north of the river, but they would not cross. The women and children were wailing and screaming, and most of the men had lost their courage. Young Platt crossed and led the troops to the ravine. The place was a charnel, dead Pawnee women and children lying among dead horses and broken camp equipment; the Sioux had stripped, scalped, and mutilated the dead, and they had gathered many lodge poles, piled dead bodies on them, and burned them.

They had carried off eleven women and children, about one hundred horses, the packs of dried meat and hides from 800 buffalo, and a great quantity of arms, saddles, camp equipment, and other plunder. After examining the scene of massacre, the troops withdrew leaving the dead Pawnees to the wolves.[134]

John Williamson took the wounded Pawnees on horses and in pole-drags to Plum Creek, now Lexington, on the Union Pacific, where he had the wounds dressed by a surgeon. The rest of the Pawnee hunters made their way to Elm Creek, where they were put in box cars and sent down the line to Silver Creek, the nearest station to the Pawnee agency. The wounded had arrived ahead of them. When these survivors of the massacre reached the Pawnee villages, the sound of mourning was heart-breaking. Agent Burgess collected all of the information he could and concluded that thirty-nine women, ten children, and twenty men had been killed, a total of sixty-nine dead. The men who witnessed the burial of the dead in the ravine on August 24 counted sixty-five bodies, but some Pawnees had been killed far from the ravine; some of the wounded, trying to escape, had died on the prairie. John Williamson may have been correct when he made his written report on August 12, estimating the dead at about one hundred. In later life he put the figure up to 156. About 1875 J. B. Dunbar obtained from the Pawnees the names of eighty-six persons who they asserted had been killed or had died of wounds received in this butchery.

The Sioux who had perpetrated this deed of blood were from Red Cloud and Spotted Tail agencies. They had no need for buffalo, being well fed by the government, their main object in going hunting being to escape for a season from the boredom of reservation life. They had come south of the Platte in two great camps with the permission of their agents, who had sent two incompetent trail-agents along to keep the Indians out of mischief. With the Oglalas was old Antoine Janis, a French fur-trader who had lived among the Sioux so many years that he thought like a Sioux and was much astonished at the outcry over the killing of the Pawnees. Stephen S. Estes was trail-agent for the Brulés, a nonentity who had no control over the Indians and who attempted to clear his own skirts by laying the blame for the massacre at the door of the military officers; then finding that view hardly tenable, shifted all of the responsibility for the affair to 'Toine Janis. Estes also attempted to inculpate the Pawnees, claiming that the Stinking Water was a boundary between Pawnee and Sioux hunting grounds and that by going north of this stream the Pawnees invited attack. There was no such dividing-line recognized by any Indians, and the

Pawnees did not come north of the point indicated; their camp was forty miles from the Sioux camps, and the Sioux deliberately sought an opportunity for making an attack, planned it, and executed it with no serious opposition from their trail-agents.

The trail-agents' reports placed the Oglala camp (mainly Kiyuksa Sioux headed by Chief Little Wound) on Whiteman's (Frenchman's) Fork and the Brulé camp on Stinking Water, one ride from the Oglalas. Janis reported that scouts sent from his Oglala camp discovered the Pawnees on August 1, far south of Republican Fork and still farther south of Estes' imaginary boundary line. Little Wound, on receiving the report of his scouts, asked Janis if Agent Saville had given him orders to prevent an attack on the Pawnees. Janis said no. The chief said that the agent had warned him strictly not to attack whites, or the Pawnees *on their reservation*, but that nothing had been said about an attack on Pawnees in the hunting grounds. To this Sioux opinion as to the legality of the coming operations, Janis made no objection; he quietly watched the Oglalas don their fighting finery, arm, and ride off to seek the Pawnees. In the so-called battle that ensued two of his Oglalas were slightly wounded, but Estes had one of his Brulés killed and two or three mortally wounded. The Oglalas brought back to their camp three Pawnee women and four children; the Brulés captured one woman, two girls, and one boy.

The humanitarians in charge of Indian affairs, whose policy of giving in to the Sioux was the prime cause of this massacre, expressed the greatest abhorrence of the deed, asked Congress for the paltry sum of $9,000 to recompense the Pawnees, and stated that under no circumstances would the Sioux be permitted to go hunting again. The Sioux went hunting that same winter, with the consent of their agents. In 1874 the Sioux not only went hunting, they were also regularly supplied with rations from a special base on the railroad at Julesburg, established by the government to make certain that the hunters did not suffer from want of food.[135]

This disaster in the hunting field shook the Pawnee tribe like a great explosion, and the people whom the Quakers had recently reported happy and contented burst forth in bitter complaints against their lot. The old hatred of being cooped up on the reservation flared out anew. They would never be permitted to hunt or wander again. The Sioux, who did not need the meat, would go hunting, but the Pawnees would be ordered to stay at home and live on their crops. How could they do that? At the very moment that the news of the massacre was received, hordes of grasshoppers and Colorado potato beetles were devouring their crops. The forthcoming sale of part of the reservation angered the Indians, and they had had trouble recently with white settlers whom they had caught cutting timber and hay on Pawnee land.

Big Spotted Horse had shaken the dust of the reservation from his robe after being released from prison for stealing 600 Cheyenne horses, and he had gone to live with the Wichitas in southern Indian Territory. Coming home in 1872, he joined his friend Lone Chief and some others in talking over a project for the removal of the Pawnees to Indian Territory. These men were not chiefs; they had little standing in the tribe and were afraid to come out in the open and face the chiefs, who would certainly oppose their scheme. Then in August, 1873, came the massacre, and the Pawnees were so demoralized that many of them were criticizing the chiefs. Lone Chief, Big Spotted Horse, and their friends now boldly called a council, made the proposal that the Pawnees should escape from all their trouble by moving south, and backed up this proposal by making it known that the Wichita chiefs in council had sent a formal invitation for the Pawnees to come and live with them.

Led by the head-chief, Pitalesharo, the Pawnees denounced these men, and the council broke up in wild confusion. The chiefs had a strong case. The Wichitas, now reduced to 280 people, had no land of their own but were squatting on land which the government by treaty had recognized as the property of other tribes. The Pawnees had a good reservation, and if they remained on it they would soon be prosperous again. Three hundred Pawnees had gone south in 1870 to visit the Wichitas and had become very ill with chills and fever, some dying and many others being ill for a year or more after their return to Nebraska. The men who were talking removal were unreliable, and some of their statements were untruthful.

But these men had acted at the exact moment when discontent among the people had reached its highest point. They had the great advantange of proposing immediate action to people who were burning to act. Within a few weeks after the massacre they had won over two-thirds of the tribe, and with this following they left the reservation and started south. They had gone about fifty miles when Indian soldiers sent by the chiefs overtook them and ordered them to return. The people encamped, and their leaders, Lone Chief and Big Spotted Horse of the Kitkehahkis, and Leading Chief (Frank White) [136] of the Chauis, went back to the agency with the soldiers. The Pawnees later asserted that the leaders on reaching the agency had a talk with Agent Burgess and gave him presents—bribed him—and that he then gave them a pass permitting them to go to Indian Territory. One cannot credit this. Burgess was an upright and honorable man, and his friend Barclay White, the Quaker superintendent at Omaha, reporting immediately after these events, stated that the Pawnees who went south did so without permission, following men who had no standing in the tribe and who were misleading the people.

We have only to look at the next actions of these men to see that this was true. On returning to camp they secretly consulted their closest friends, and the families in this group then sent their horses away from camp and concealed the animals. They then spread the word that their horses had been stolen; when the rest of the people obeyed the order and started back to the reservation these thirty lodges remained in camp on the excuse that they could not move until they found their animals. The main body of Pawnees was hardly out of sight before the stay-behinds got their horses out of hiding, packed their belongings, and set out for the Wichita agency. When they reached that place the agent there reported their arrival and asked the Indian Office for instructions. He stated that these Pawnees had left their reservation in Nebraska without permission of their agent. To this report the Indian Office officials made the significant reply that since these Pawnees had made the journey to the Wichita agency they should be permitted to remain there, as it was expected that in the coming year the whole Pawnee tribe would be removed to Indian Territory. This leaves no question as to who it was that decided to remove the tribe south; for at the time this letter was written at the Indian Office the Pawnee chiefs were united in opposition to removal, and the Quaker agent and Quaker superintendent of Indian affairs in Nebraska were working out plans for the rapid improvement of the tribe on its Nebraska reservation. It was the visionaries at the Indian Office who wrecked those plans.

An official report states that on July 5, 1874, the Pawnees held a council and asked the government officials to remove the tribe to Indian Territory, because the grasshoppers were again destroying their crops. This meager report does not hint at the fierce factional fight that was going on in the tribe, nor at the part the government officials were taking in this struggle. Examining other evidence, we find that the Pawnees had come through the winter of 1873-4 with some aid from the government, beef being issued at the agency for the first time in Pawnee history. This ration of meat pleased the common Indians, but some of the chiefs feared that the free beef was a bribe to win support for some official scheme. The Quakers in control of the tribe were cheerful, stating that the Pawnees were beginning to recover from the demoralization caused by the massacre of August, 1873, and that a good crop in 1874 would finally cure the feeling of discontent among the Indians. Here it is apparent that the Quakers had no thought of removing the tribe to Indian Territory. The whole of their plan was to concentrate on a bountiful crop in 1874; once more they induced the chiefs in council to agree that $10,000 should be taken from the tribe's little annuity fund to be expended on farming equipment. The agent plowed 350 acres, to add to the 1,000 acres the Indians already had under cultivation, and by unremitting pressure many of the Indian men were induced for the first time to aid the women in the fieldwork. But, being what they were, the Quakers could not understand the Pawnees. They now undid most of the work they had accomplished toward improving the morale of the tribe by forbidding the Pawnees to go on a summer buffalo hunt. Moreover, they had put all the eggs into one basket; all depended on a good crop, and in early July the grasshoppers appeared and began to devour the crops.

Frank White and his friend Big Spotted Horse still had quite a following, whose one desire was to go to Indian Territory. These two leaders of the removal project had brought home to Nebraska a formal invitation from the Wichita chiefs for the Pawnees to come south and live with their tribe. Considering that the Wichitas, reduced to a handful of people, were living on a small tract of land borrowed from other tribes and that they were in no condition to take care of several thousand destitute Pawnees, this invitation from the Wichitas did not impress the Pawnee chiefs in the least. But Frank White and Big Spotted Horse were loud in their praise of the southern country. It was a fine wild land, where the Pawnees could go back to their old way of life, freed from the control of white men. Moreover, some of the tribes in Indian Territory had promised to give the Pawnees hundreds of horses if they came there to live, and this offer of horses won over many Pawnees to the idea of removal. The order forbidding a summer buffalo hunt played straight into the hands of the removal party, whose leaders circulated briskly among the groups of angry Pawnees, spreading the word that in Indian Territory the tribe would be free to hunt whenever it chose to do so. They failed to add that game in the Territory was just about exterminated and that a very few years more would see the death of the last buffalo. When the grasshoppers appeared in early July, Frank White and Big Spotted Horse took immediate advantage of this indication of the coming crop destruction. Barclay White now came to the agency again, and on July 5 Frank White, Big Spotted Horse, and their followers asked for a council and informed the Quaker official that the people wished to remove to Indian Territory because of the destruction of their corn by grasshoppers. The chiefs promptly denounced these men as persons of no importance in the tribe who were deceiving the people.

It seemed as if all the gods were at work trying to destroy the Pawnees. The Quakers, like all the other liberals who were then interesting themselves in Indian affairs, had adopted a new policy of what they termed democracy which was based on the fine-sounding theory that the chiefs, supposedly tyrants, must be disregarded and the common Indians taught to think and act for themselves. Barclay White knew that the common Pawnees were not competent to deal with important tribal affairs and that legally no agreement with the Pawnees could be made without the full consent of the chiefs in council; but he now ignored the bitter opposition of the chiefs, took a rough count among the common Indians, and announced that as a majority seemed to favor removal to Indian Territory he would so report to the officials in Washington.

The Pawnees who were for removal now set to work tearing down the Indian villages, on the excuse that they had to sell the timbers to obtain money for food, but the real object was to commit the tribe irrevocably to removal by destroying the dwellings. The Quakers now gave up their pretense of control over the situation and reported to Washington the disaster to the crops, stating that if the Pawnees remained where they were they would have to be fed at government expense during the coming winter. The inference one would naturally draw from such a statement was that by removal to Indian Territory the Pawnees would not require assistance; but in truth the cost of assisting the tribe in the Territory, due to poor transportation facilities, would be greater; the tribe would give up its well-improved farmland in Nebraska for unbroken wild land in the Territory, which would much retard any effort on the part of the Indians to regain self-support through agriculture; finally, the Pawnees, by abandoning their villages in Nebraska, would make it obligatory for the officials to rehouse the Indians in their new location at great expense.

The Quakers had now passed the Pawnee problem on to the Indian Office, and they were promptly notified that a member of the Board of Indian Commissioners was coming to the Pawnee agency to deal with the situation. This gentleman, B. Rush Roberts, a Quaker, picked up the Indian superintendent, Barclay White, at Omaha, and the two came to the agency and ordered Agent Burgess to call a council. When the Indians assembled these Quakers made the bland announcement that the Great Father, having learned that the Pawnees desired to remove to Indian Territory, had sent Friend Roberts out with a paper for the chiefs to approve: the usual form of miscalled agreement, drawn up in Washington without any consultation with the Indians concerned, and to be signed by the chiefs without the altering of a single word, if they wished to avoid the danger of displeasing the Great Father. Barclay White now spoke fervently of the friendship of the Quakers for the Pawnees, and in the name of tribal welfare he urged the chiefs to place their mark of approval on this paper at once.

This sudden demand for removal from a quite unexpected direction left the Pawnee chiefs stunned. They sat in silence for a long while; then a tall and dignified Skidi, Lone Chief, arose and going forward stood for a time staring fixedly at the three Quakers in grim-faced silence. When he spoke it was to denounce all white men. He said that when the Pawnees had signed the old treaties, giving up nearly all their lands, the government had pledged its word that this little reservation should be the home of the tribe forever. Their fathers and grandfathers were buried in this ground, and the Skidis would never give up their old home to go to a strange land in the south. Pitalesharo, the head-chief, now expressed his opposition to removal in strong terms, and another chief stated that his heart was filled with sorrow that the Great Father could not help the Pawnees where they had always lived, but wished to tear them from their old home and help them in a new land far away.

The Quakers now spoke. They said that they were the true friends of the Pawnees and had come to help them, but that it was no longer possible for the tribe to prosper in Nebraska, for even if the Sioux menace could be removed the trouble caused by the white settlers would increase from year to year. In effect, the Quakers, having received their orders from Washington, were going back on their own recent conclusions that the trouble with the Sioux and the lesser trouble with the white settlers would soon end and the Pawnees would then be happy in Nebraska. The pressure now put on the chiefs was more than any Indians could bear, and one by one they gave in. But they were not convinced; over their hearts lay a black foreboding that between the efforts of the Christian Quakers and the pagans Big Spotted Horse and Lone Chief, their tribe was being enticed toward destruction. If the government had not put all its power back of this project the chiefs would have held out against it.

The Quakers, now actively leading in the removal plan, induced the Pawnees to send part of their people to the Wichita Agency in the autumn of 1874. Most of this first group of migrants are said to have been Skidis, and they marched all the great distance from Loup Fork to Red River on the Texas frontier, the government apparently failing to assist their movement in any manner. Most of the children and old people were left on the reservation in Nebraska, with part of the tribe remaining to protect and care for them during the winter. The Pawnees who made the march south were placed under the control of John W. Williamson as trail-agent, but Pitalesharo the head-chief accompanied the column. He was still bitterly opposed to removal. As he was fording Loup Fork on horseback in the midst of a throng of Pawnees on the first day's march southward he was shot in the leg and was taken back to the agency by his friends. Some said that his pistol had gone off accidentally, others that he had shot himself so that he might be buried in the land of his fathers on the Loup. It was even whispered that the whites had instigated the shooting because the chief continued his opposition to removal. At the agency the old man refused to permit the amputation of his mangled leg, and within a few days he was at rest in the Grand Pawnee burial-ground on the hill south of the Loup.

The Pawnee column moved southward very slowly, making frequent halts to hunt, or simply to remain in camp for an all-day quarrel. Factional feuds, mainly over the question of removal, constantly blazed anew, but in February, 1875, Williamson brought his column safely to the Wichita Agency. Here they found a camp of 360 Pawnees who had been induced by Big Spotted Horse and Lone Chief to come south with them in 1874 without official permission. This pioneering group had had a good time on Red River, but they had not progressed in civilization by Quaker standards. They had joined the Wichitas in planting some corn, only to have it consumed when the wild Kiowas came on a visit and turned their ponies into the corn patches. Next the Kiowas, Comanches, and Cheyennes had revolted against the government and started a war, the Pawnees watching with much pleasure while the Kiowas and United States cavalry engaged in battle at the Wichita Agency, an engagement which had ended in more injury to the frightened Wichitas than to either of the contending parties. Big Spotted Horse had acquired quite a herd of new horses, some said from the Cheyennes, but there was a suspicion that he had been visiting the horse herds of certain Texas cow camps. He was very pleased with himself, but the Pawnee chiefs were not pleased with him, and he carefully avoided their society. The tribe was now put on rations and settled down in their tipi camp to await the arrival of their agent from Nebraska, who was to help the chiefs select the site for the new Pawnee agency.[187]

NOTES TO CHAPTER XII

[131]Texas Jack and his partner, J. W. Carver, were professional hunters who saw a great deal of the Pawnees from about 1868 on. They had a hunting camp on the Medicine Creek branch of the Republican in the Pawnee hunting grounds. In 1874 Jack took the Earl of Dunraven on a hunt in western Nebraska. From 1873 on, in winter, Jack and his friend W. F. Cody played the leading roles in Ned Buntline's melodrama, *The Scouts of the Plains,* in New York, wearing buckskin costumes made by Pawnee women.

[132]Head-chief of the Pitahauerats, born about 1800. A brave man, but not a wise leader.

[133]Captain L. H. North knew Sun Chief well and was certain that he was the nephew, not the son, of Pitalesharo. The Pawnees counted descent in the female line, and there is no record of a chief being succeeded by his son. *Sukuru* is the sacred name of the sun.

[134]This account of the massacre follows in the main John Williamson's contemporary report, republished in *Nebraska History Magazine,* v. XVI, number 3.

[135]*Report of an Investigation at Red Cloud Agency;* Washington, 1875, p. 481.

[136]*Liharisu lashar.* Captain North translated this name as Traveling Chief. Frank White was a warrior, a former Pawnee Scout, an orator, and (as Captain North put it) a progressive, whatever that might mean among the Pawnees of the Seventies. Grinnell, in *Pawnee Hero Stories,* records that when the tribe was on the winter hunt, 1872-3, the Sioux stole so many horses in the camp that the Pawnees cried out bitterly. Frank White and Big Spotted Horse took immediate advantage of this discontent and urged the people to come with them to the Wichita country. Getting few recruits, these men went down to Red River and induced the Wichita chiefs in

council to send a formal invitation to the Pawnees to join them. Coming home to Nebraska just before the massacre of August, 1873, they made use of the Wichita invitation, telling the Pawnees that here was the best way out of all their troubles.

[137]Both Grinnell and Dunbar made bitter but not very specific charges that the Pawnee removal was caused by an organized movement among the Nebraska settlers to get rid of the tribe whose lands had greatly increased in value since the coming of the railroad. A careful search in contemporary Nebraska records fails to disclose any organized effort to bring about the removal of the tribe to Indian Territory. There were some settlers near the reservation who made threats and talked of getting rid of the Indians, but Agent Burgess and Barclay White knew all these men and were confident of their ability to stop their trouble-making. It was in Washington that full advantage was taken of the trouble the Pawnees were in to press for removal, and in the face of this policy shift at the Indian Office the Quakers had to co-operate or give up and hand in their resignations. Being idealists, they stayed, shifting their attitude to conform with the new policy which was made by idealists of their own sort: men who saw nothing wrong in uprooting Indian tribes on a wild theory that removal to Indian Territory would benefit them. The bad effects of removal on the Pawnees did not deter them from going straight on with the removal of one northern tribe after another to the Territory. Commissioner of Indian Affairs John Q. Smith took a leading part in these removals, especially interesting himself in a mad scheme for removing 20,000 warlike and unconquered Sioux, an act that would have brought on the greatest Indian war in our history. The fact is that Grinnell and Dunbar listened to the heartbroken and angry talk of many Pawnees who were too simple to see as far as Washington or to look as high as the head of the Indian Office for the cause of their troubles. They talked of the white settlers who had made threats and committed some acts of violence; these men, they said, had caused the removal of the tribe. But this was not true, although these Pawnees certainly believed that it was.

Eagle Chief (?). (Western History Collections, University of Oklahoma Library)

Baptiste Bayhylle, almost one hundred years old when this picture was taken by Prettyman in 1885 in Indian Territory. (From *Indian Territory: A Frontier Photographic Record*, by W. S. Prettyman and Robert E. Cunningham, Norman, 1957)

A Pawnee Indian camp, 1889, seventy miles south of Arkansas City. "The Pawnees continued the ancient method of curing hides even after the buffalo were gone from Indian Territory. This is a cowhide being readied for moccasins and other leather-work." (From *Indian Territory: A Frontier Photographic Record*, by W. S. Prettyman and Robert E. Cunningham, Norman, 1957)

"These Pawnees are pictured on tour with Pawnee Bill's Wild West Show about 1890. Prettyman's photograph was made when the two Bills, Pawnee and Buffalo, had competing shows on the road." (From *Indian Territory: A Frontier Photographic Record*, by W. S. Prettyman and Robert E. Cunningham, Norman, 1957)

War Chief of the Pawnees poses with William Pollock and Ralph
Weeks. (From *Indian Territory: A Frontier Photographic Record*, by
W. S. Prettyman and Robert E. Cunningham, Norman, 1957)

XIII

On Black Bear Creek

LEAVING THE PAWNEE CHILDREN AND A FEW OF THE OLDER INDIANS
on the reservation in Nebraska, the Quaker agent William Burgess,
and his son Harry E. Burgess, went south by rail in November, 1874,
to select the new home for the tribe. Seeking advice from the
Southern Indian Superintendent, a Quaker, Burgess was led to favor
a fine tract of land immediately west of the Arkansas River and
north of the Cimarron as a home for the Pawnees. These Quakers
knew nothing and cared nothing about Indian history, and they
were completely ignorant of the fact that the lands they had selected
were those on which three of the Pawnee tribes had lived from
about 1685 to 1735. There is no evidence that the Pawnees had
any memory of this older home of their people. After driving the
Pawnees, Iscanis, and Wichitas from these lands, the Osages had
claimed the country; but through treaties the lands had passed into
the possession of the Cherokees, Creeks, and Seminoles. The greater
part of the new Pawnee reservation was land lying within the
famous Cherokee Outlet or Cherokee Strip; a little land in the
southern part of the reservation was claimed by the Creeks and
Seminoles. The new reservation contained about 391,000 acres, and
was slightly larger than the Pawnee reservation in Nebraska.[138]

After examining these lands, Agent Burgess went to the Wichita
agency in December, 1874, to meet the Pawnees; but the main camp
of the Indians did not arrive from Nebraska until late in February.
They had had a slow march, being encumbered by great quantity
of personal belongings, and they had been held in camp many days
by winter storms. On their arrival Burgess induced the Indians to
accept the lands he had selected for them. They agreed with little
heart, for most of the people were already disillusioned about this
southern country, and homesick for Nebraska. The tales their

329

fathers had told concerning this land in the south did not seem to fit what they had seen with their own eyes, and they had heard many things from the Pawnees who had come south in 1873 and had now been a year with the Wichitas. This once mighty tribe, the Wichitas, was now in 1874 a tiny remnant of some 250 poor people living on bad beef issued to them by an Indian agent, for there had been a drought in the south as well as in Nebraska and the Wichitas had lost all their crop. Of the other Caddoan tribes with which the Pawnees had associated between 1650 and 1750, the formerly powerful Tawakonis were now reduced to 140 people, the Iscanis and Kichais to 100 each, and the Wacos to 125. The great tribes of kinsmen that the Pawnees had for generations talked about with such respect had disappeared, leaving these little groups of poor people as their only representatives.

For some years the humanitarians at the Indian Office had been accustomed to spend lavishly on their plans for hastening Indian progress in civilization, and they had gone into the scheme for improving the condition of the Pawnees by removing them to Indian Territory with the full expectation that Congress would provide the necessary credits. But Congress had now adjourned without voting money to aid the Pawnees; it had not even approved the sale of the Pawnee lands in Nebraska, thereby making Pawnee money available for the resettlement of the tribe on its new reservation. This money crisis shocked the officials at the Indian Office into a sudden realization that they had got themselves (and the Pawnees) into a very bad position by deciding to hurry the tribe off to Indian Territory while the people were destitute, disheartened, and could be maneuvered into giving up their home in Nebraska on the promise of better things in the south. The officials now forgot that Agent Burgess' presence in Indian Territory was imperatively required, to see to it that his Indians moved promptly to the new reservation and put in a crop. They telegraphed for Burgess to come to Washington for a conference, and he dropped everything and went. For a time it seemed that the officials would have to tear ›up their great plan for improving the Pawnees and order the Indians to march back to their reservation in Nebraska: a dreadful thing to happen, an event that would probably bring on a congressional investigation into the uprooting of the Pawnees. The Board of Indian Commissioners, that stronghold of the church and humanitarian groups interested in improving the condition of the Indians, was now appealed to; and with the approval and support of this powerful body the Indian Office decided to go into debt to carry out the Pawnee plan, and to trust to the generosity of Congress to pay off the debts next year, either with government or with Pawnee money.

The Pawnee plan was a costly one, and the officials stubbornly refused to alter it in any way to save part of the expense. The country was in the grip of the great depression of 1873-1879, and when the Indian Office attempted to purchase supplies for the Pawnees on credit, it met with little success. A second-hand saw-and-grist mill was finally obtained from a firm that was willing to take a chance that Congress might pay the bill in two or three years; some agricultural implements and tools were obtained in the same way, and Agent Burgess managed to induce a number of men to enter his employ on terms of board and lodging, plus a promise that Congress would be asked to add a money wage at the next session.

Because of these delays, the Pawnees did not reach their new lands until the end of June, too late to put in a crop. Thus the first results of the officials' high-minded attempt to improve the tribe were that a people who in Nebraska had been self-supporting were thrown into poverty and had to be fed by the government. The Indians (at least the women) were eager to work, but the plan made in Washington stood in their way. They wanted to build new earth-lodge villages; but such villages were regarded by the officials as relics of barbarism, blocking the way toward progress, and Agent Burgess was reminded time and again by the Indian Office that the heart of the great plan was to break up the old village organization and put each family into a neat frame or log house on its own little farm. Burgess was extremely busy, putting up vitally necessary storehouses and other agency buildings; he had neither men nor money for building Indian homes, and the Pawnees could not do this work, for they knew only the method for constructing earth-lodges. Thus the persistent efforts of the Indian Office to break up the Pawnee custom of living in earth-lodge communities resulted in the tribe settling down near the new agency in communities of canvas tipis. The people had lost most of their comfortable cowskin tipis in the Sioux attack of 1873. The canvas tipis with which they had been supplied were neither comfortable nor healthful; and here the people were on Black Bear Creek in four camps, one for each Pawnee tribe, living like blanket Indians in perfect idleness, and like blanket Indians being fed and clothed at government expense. No improvement was possible this year, and probably not for several years to come. The plan did not permit the Indians to help themselves in their own way, and the officials who insisted that the plan should not be altered did not have the funds necessary to aid the people according to plan.

The 500 Pawnees on the Nebraska reservation put in crops in the spring of 1875, to feed themselves and the children who were still attending the government schools. They had a good crop, and if the whole tribe had been here at home they would not have had to be fed at government expense. There were so few Pawnees in the old villages now that they needed protection, and a company of U.S. infantry was stationed at the agency. Early in the morning on August 23 the wife of Eagle Chief, the Skidi head-chief, left the lodge to examine some sweet corn she was drying, and on approaching her corn patch she was shot dead by lurking enemies—some said that they were Sioux, others that they were white horsethieves disguised as Indians. Soon after this the troops were withdrawn; and on September 30 a band of fourteen men, dressed as Indians, made a bold attempt to stampede the whole Pawnee horse herd. Foiled in this by the boys who were guarding the animals, the raiders killed one of the boys within sight of the agency and made their escape. This was the last attack on the old reservation.

Late in the fall this last contingent of the tribe started on their long march to Indian Territory. Part of the Skidis had maintained stubbornly that they would never leave their old home, but the officials had made it impossible for this little group to remain. Agent Burgess had come north to lead these Indians to the new reservation; as they had among them most of the children of the tribe and many very old and infirm people, he bought twelve wagons and teams to transport part of the people and their belongings. Some of the Pawnees had their own wagons, and a few had good carriages or buggies. A herd of cattle was taken along, and beef and rations were issued to the Indians once a week. On issue days there was feasting; by the middle of the week all the food was gone, and the Pawnees had to send out foraging parties to obtain aid from white settlers along the line of march. At Manhattan, Kansas, in a district which had belonged to the Pawnees or their Caddoan kindred in Coronado's time, this last group of the retreating tribe performed war dances before throngs of staring white people and obtained some food.

Striking southward from Junction City, they passed through what our romancers term the Kingdom of Quivira: a rich region which the Caddoans had held from ancient times until on into the 18th century. Crossing the line into Indian Territory, the Pawnees came among their old enemies, the Kansa, who had been removed from their home in Kansas. Here across the Arkansas River toward the west were the lands where the Pawnee and Jumano villages had stood in the 18th century, when the French had come up the river to supply these villages with guns and trade goods; but the Pawnees who now stared across the river from their camp of canvas tents had no memory of these earth-lodge towns in which their own ancestors had dwelt. Going on through ancient Pawnee lands, now held by the Osages, the people camped on Buck Creek; and here the chiefs went up on a hill and looked across the Arkansas River into the new Pawnee reservation. The next day the people crossed the river at the Pawnee ferry and followed a new road southward to the agency on Black Bear Creek. The land was pleasant prairie country, covered by a rich growth of wild grasses, marked here and there by groves and belts of timber. In the distance toward the south rose the blue and misty hills that bordered the Cimarron and Arkansas. Along one side of the road where it approached Black Bear Creek was a row of new log buildings extending in a straight line for about one mile: the new Pawnee agency. Near the agency and along the stream they found their tribe encamped in four groups of canvas tipis.

It was in November, 1875, that this last party arrived from Nebraska. The Indians were already suffering severely from chills and fever. Experienced men would have expected this. It always happened when northern Indians were brought into the Territory; but the officials in Washington seemed to be always taken by surprise when their latest victims torn from northern homes reached the south and all fell sick. The condition of the Pawnees was aggravated by scanty and improper food, and still more by the fact that the officials refused to permit these Indians to provide comfortable native dwellings for the use of their families. By the middle of the winter half the tribe was down with chills and fever and the death list was growing daily. The Indian Office had no money, and it took the necessary funds from the little Pawnee annuity to build a rude hospital to shelter the sick.

On reaching their new reservation the Pawnees had been visited by their ancient enemies, the Osages, and that tribe had proposed peace, which the Pawnees gladly accepted. The Osages then arranged a peace between the Pawnees and Cheyennes. This pleased the Quakers very much; but when presently the Osages began to send war parties into the Pawnee reservation to steal horses, the Quakers were a little shocked, and the Pawnees were filled with wrath. They wanted to go after the Osages with a sharp stick, but the most that Agent Burgess would permit was for authorized Pawnee police to arrest any Osages caught in the act of stealing horses and to escort them off the reservation, with a warning not to return. Naturally, the Osages came back for more horses; white horsethieves made their appearance, and the Pawnees, strictly forbidden to make reprisals, saw bankruptcy staring them in the face. They were losing all their horses.[189]

Nearly all of the Pawnees were now living in perfect idleness. A few of the men were employed in driving wagons, for every pound of supplies had to be brought over the new road from the railroad town of Coffeyville in Kansas, about one hundred miles away. Many of the Pawnees had agreed to come to Indian Territory mainly because they were promised permission to go on buffalo hunts; but it was now found that herds of buffalo were few and were very far toward the west, the native tribes and white hide-hunters having killed off most of the herds. In the winter of 1875-1876 Burgess gave permission for some of the Pawnees to go hunting, but this party found little game and returned home sadly disappointed. They tried again in the following summer, but with the same result.

The people were so hungry and so eager to hunt that the chiefs kept young warriors stationed at Fort Reno, 100 miles west of the Pawnee agency, to report promptly if herds of buffalo appeared in that district, the only one in which the Pawnees were permitted to hunt. On one occasion two Pawnee buffalo scouts at Fort Reno, White Eagle (David Gillingham) and Dog Chief (Simon Adams) went on foot, running most of the way, from the post to the Pawnee agency, 96 miles, between early morning and evening on the same day, to report the presence of buffalo.

During the years 1875 and 1876, while the Indian Office was making great efforts to induce Congress to sanction its experiment on the Pawnees and pay off the debts it had incurred, someone suppressed the truth as to the condition of the tribe in Indian Territory. From a casual reading of the official report all seemed to be well with the tribe. Burgess reported considerable sickness in the winter, followed by general good health in the summer of 1876. This was a very mild description of the situation. Nearly every Pawnee family had lost one or more members from chills and fever, and most of the living were sick. The people had the custom of drinking river water, and the new water aggravated their illness. Burgess reported nice progress—the people were working hard; they had put in a good crop. He did not state that they had planted only one-fifth of the acreage they had had in Nebraska. The people were still in camps of canvas tipis, and the officials far away in Washington were still so determined that there should be no more earth-lodges that they made the plan for wooden farmhouses a provision in the bill to aid the Pawnees, which they introduced in the session of Congress in 1876.

During this bad time George Bird Grinnell and John B. Dunbar came to visit the Pawnees, and both of these keen observers were shocked by the deterioration in the tribe. Grinnell stated that the Indians were very miserable and sick, that they had lost a great many people; the living were listless and longed to return to Nebraska. He referred to the bad agents the tribe had at this time, and although he named no names it is apparent that he meant William Burgess and the new Quaker, Charles Searing, who succeeded him in 1877. How far these agents were at fault is difficult to determine. They were executing orders from Washington and attempting to carry out a plan for a model Indian community, which was not to be altered in any way.

Big Spotted Horse, who in 1873 had talked so many of the Pawnees into favoring removal, was now the most unpopular man in the tribe. The Pawnees made his life so unbearable that he finally applied to the agent for transfer to the Wichita agency, and when this favor was refused he ran away. Some time later news trickled back to the Pawnee reservation that the Kitkehahki brave had been caught by Texas cowboys while he was taking liberties with their horse herd, and that they had shot him and left his body on the prairie. This was well. Big Spotted Horse did not have it in him to become a good reservation Indian; he had always desired such a death, and to be left on the prairie for his brothers, the wolves.[140]

The government had now involved itself in a war with the Sioux, and the military, finding the Sioux more of a handful than had been foreseen, remembered the Pawnees and sent Major Frank North and his brother to seek recruits in Indian Territory. The Norths came by stage from Coffeyville, Kansas, reaching the Pawnee agency about midnight and finding quarters in the agency farmer's house. In some way the news that Pani Leshar had come to enlist scouts got out, and scores of Pawnees came and sat on the ground around the house all night, to be the first to have their names put down in the roll.

The Norths found the tribe terribly changed for the worse; but the old fighting spirit was still very much alive. The agent's stone office building was turned into a recruiting place, but it would not hold the hundreds of warriors who were clamoring to be taken, and the meeting was adjourned to the open fields. Major North got his one hundred men as fast as he could write the names down, and there were still twice that number clamoring to be taken. One old man pleaded with Major North to take his boy named Arikarard (Antlers) who was only fifteen. He said that they need not give the boy any pay, and if the rolls were completed, could not Pani Leshar take the boy along as his personal servant? Major North finally gave in, and this Pawnee boy, later known as Rush Roberts, distinguished himself in the bitter fighting at Dull Knife's Cheyenne village in the following winter. When the scouts started in wagons for Coffeyville, on the railroad one hundred miles from the agency, they were accompanied by over one hundred Pawnee boys, mostly afoot, who followed them the whole distance, hoping that Major North could find a way to take them with him. At Coffeyville guards had to be set to prevent these young Pawnees from stowing away on the train and going with the scouts.

The summer campaign against the Sioux was ended before the Pawnees reached Nebraska. They were sent to Sidney Barracks near the forks of the Platte, where they were given horses and arms. After some preliminary marches to get the men and horses into condition, they were ordered to Red Cloud Agency in the middle of October; but on reaching the Niobrara River Major North received orders to join Colonel R. S. Mackenzie's cavalry force in the Chadron Creek district. Red Cloud and Red Leaf had left their agency and gone to join Swift Bear on Chadron Creek, and Mackenzie had marched from Camp Robinson near Red Cloud Agency with the object of forcing the Sioux to return to the agency. This was to be accomplished without a fight if possible. Marching all night after an all day march to the Niobrara, Major North made the junction with the cavalry before dawn on October 23. As more than half of the Pawnees had been given poor horses, he had brought on this march only forty-two men. Mackenzie had eight troops of cavalry; and despite the fact that the Sioux were supposed to be very much on the alert, this large force approached their camps without being discovered. Captain L. H. North was sent with half the Pawnees to help the cavalry deal with Red Leaf. Before day dawned the Pawnees charged into the Sioux camps followed by the cavalry and stampeded all the Sioux ponies, leaving the rudely awakened Sioux to decide whether they would obey Mackenzie's orders or attempt to fight on foot against a superior force of cavalry and mounted Pawnees. They gave up without firing a shot and were marched off to Camp Robinson, where the sullen Red Cloud and his friend Red Leaf were put in the guardhouse. Mackenzie was so pleased with the neat work of the Pawnees in this affair that he permitted each Pawnee to select a pony for himself from the seven hundred head they had taken from the Sioux.

In November General Crook collected a large force at Fort Fetterman on the North Platte, west of Fort Laramie, with the object of making a winter campaign against the Sioux and Cheyennes. When the Pawnees joined this force they found that they were for the time being the allies of their old enemies, the Shoshonis and Sioux; for Crook had small forces of scouts from both these tribes. The Pawnees got on well with the Shoshonis; but with the Sioux, headed by the proud Three Bears, it was a different story. Crook had practically forced the Sioux to serve as scouts, and they were in a nasty humor. On the march from the Platte to Powder River the Sioux spent most of their time in jeering at the Pawnees and insulting them, and on several occasions Major North had a hard time to hold his Pawnees down. They wanted to fight.

The Northern Cheyennes, led by Dull Knife and Little Wolf, had hidden their winter camp in the canyon of the Red Fork of Powder River; but Crook's scouts found this village of 173 tipis, and on November 25 after a hard night march the cavalry, led by the Pawnees, charged into the village. The object was the usual one of getting the enemy pony herd and destroying the village; but the Cheyennes, driven suddenly from their tipis, took refuge in strong positions among the rocks, opening such a severe fire into their own village that the troops had to be drawn back. Fighting continued all through the day, but the troops could neither get into the village nor drive the Cheyennes from their stronghold in the rocks. About noon the Shoshoni Scouts advanced into the village; but they could not hold their position and had to come back. Three Bears of the Sioux then made a boasting talk and led his men forward, but they soon had enough of it and came back. Captain L. H. North now begged his brother to permit him to go into the village with just one Pawnee, and after some discussion the Major assented. Captain North selected one of his Pawnee sergeants, Peter Headman, and by making a very cautious advance they got into the village and attempted to stampede the Cheyenne horses; but these animals had been subjected to every form of violent alarm for many hours and simply would not run when North and his Pawnee attempted to start them by waving blankets and yelling. The Cheyenne shots were hitting in every part of the village, and one by one the Cheyenne ponies were being shot down. North and his Pawnee finally got the herd bunched up and started, and once on the run they kept going. Colonel Mackenzie was so pleased with this feat that he gave the whole herd of Cheyenne ponies to the Pawnees. Later in the day the entire force of Pawnees made their way into the village where, on orders, they set to work destroying the Cheyenne property. Despite the heavy fire still coming into the village, the Pawnees made coffee and dined on dried buffalo meat, the first food they had eaten in twenty-four hours.

General Crook, after the destruction of the Cheyenne village, started his troops toward the Belle Fourche, on a report from the scouts that hostile Sioux camps were in that direction; but this turned out to be incorrect, and the fight at the Cheyenne village was the last one that the Pawnee Scouts ever had. After a horrible march in bitter weather the command returned to Fort Fetterman, December 29, and the campaign was ended. The Pawnees with part of the cavalry now marched to Fort Laramie; and continuing their movement from that post, the Indians reached their original quarters at Sidney Barracks, January 20. On the 21st the two North brothers sat down and wrote twenty-seven pages of letters for their Pawnees, telling the people at home about the fight at the Cheyenne village, the bravery of this Pawnee and that, and the ponies and other trophies captured.

In April, 1877, General P. H. Sheridan ordered that the Pawnee Scouts should be mustered out of service at Sidney Barracks, the men being given the choice of transportation home by rail, of leaving their captured ponies behind, or of marching home with their ponies. Major North thought that the Pawnees had earned transportation by rail for both themselves and their ponies, but the General refused to alter his view; the scouts therefore set out for home, taking their 250 ponies with them. They had begged Major North and his brother to accompany them as a protection from rough frontier white men, who might attempt to attack or rob them, and this the Norths agreed to. This last force of Pawnees to leave Nebraska marched from Sidney Barracks to Julesburg on the South Platte, going on south through Cottonwood Canyon, on to Medicine Creek and across the branches of Kansas River to the town of Great Bend on the Arkansas. Here Major North went down with malaria; his brother Luther remained to nurse him, and the Pawnees crossed the Arkansas and went on south to the Pawnee agency.[141]

The scheme for removal of the Pawnee tribe to Indian Territory, which the officials at the Indian Office had decided on in 1873 and had executed in the two following years, was finally approved by Congress on April 10, 1876. This bill, drawn by the Indian Office officials, authorized the expenditure of $300,000 for the removal of the tribe from Nebraska and its settlement on the new reservation in Indian Territory. The men who prepared this legislation took every possible advantage of the helpless position of the Pawnees to try the mad experiment of breaking an Indian tribe suddenly to pieces, placing each family on a 160 acre farm, and forcing the Indians swiftly from the hunter stage into the position of farmers competent to compete on equal terms with white men. These Christian idealists at the Indian Office had already brought the tribe to the verge of ruin. But the officials seemed blind to the truth, and in 1876 they were just as determined as in 1873 to execute their Pawnee plans without the altering of a single feature in the program.

What they had done to the Pawnees was seen by the North brothers when they came to the agency in the summer of 1876 to recruit a company of scouts. The Norths knew the Pawnees better than any official ever could; they had lived with them for years, spoke their language, and knew nearly everyone in the tribe by name. They found nearly all the Pawnees sick, mostly with chills and fever and lung complaints. These Indians who had been industrious and had supported themselves in Nebraska were living in complete idleness, partly forced on them by the impracticable schemes of the Indian Office, partly due to the people having lost heart completely. They were living in tattered and very dirty canvas tents, because the Indian Office idealists wanted model farmhouses and would accept nothing else. The people had little food and evidently had been half-starved ever since coming south. They had no clothing, most of the Indians, young and old, having nothing beyond thin cotton sheets, which they draped about their naked bodies. All their great herd of horses and mules had disappeared, stolen by Indian and white thieves. They had sold or traded all their weapons to obtain a little more food; an involuntary act of disarmament that had delighted the Quaker pacifists who were in charge of the tribe but had completed the heartbreak of this warrior people. There was no school, and the death rate among the Pawnees, particularly the children, was a shocking thing.

In the printed reports the officials had managed to write around all of the conditions here described and to present a hopeful view of the tribe's condition. Only by going beyond these reports and noting the observations of disinterested men (George Bird Grinnell, John B. Dunbar, and the North brothers) can we glimpse the grim truth; but the Christian planners at the Indian Office failed to suppress one item of evidence. In their own tables of statistics one may find the tell-tale figures on Pawnee population: 1872, 2,447; 1876, 2,026; 1879, 1,440. Very few of these deaths were from age; they were nearly all caused by sickness, the direct outcome of the model plan to help the tribe by removing it to Indian Territory.[142]

On May 16, 1877, William Burgess was replaced by another Quaker, Charles H. Searing of New York. The Pawnees had now been on the new reservation for a full two years, surely a sufficient period for completing the model plan for settling each family on a farm of its own; yet Searing found two-thirds of the tribe still camped in tattered canvas tipis at the agency. The other third, flying in the face of official opposition, had built themselves comfortable earth-lodges, and Burgess had evidently failed to report this fact to the Washington office, where earth-lodges were as red rags to a bull. The agent had built ten log houses for chiefs and headmen at the agency; the Skidis, always the most enterprising group, had left the agency and built an earth-lodge village for themselves about two miles to the northeast. The Grand Pawnees and Kitkehahkis were encamped on Black Bear Creek near the agency, the Pitahauerats having a camp of their own some three miles toward the southeast. Land had been set aside for the Grand Pawnees and Kitkehahkis eight or ten miles west of the agency; but nothing would induce them to go there. Agent Burgess had made very few improvements. His own office was a small stone building of good construction, but the rest of the agency buildings were of cottonwood logs with roofs of cottonwood shingles. Very little planting had been done by the Indians thus far. In 1877 the white employees had broken 650 acres in four tracts, one for each Pawnee tribe. This land was to be used by those Indians who decided to live in village communities. The plowed land was not planted. Poverty, sickness, deaths in every family, and the system of free rations, had thoroughly demoralized the tribe. Even the women, always noted as hard workers, did little now; the men spent most of their time gambling for trifling stakes. The idealists at the Indian Office in Washington knew the situation, although they did not dwell on it in their optimistic annual reports, and they had seen to it that Agent Searing should have a whip to wield against any Pawnee who refused to work when ordered to do so. The office had inserted in the Pawnee bill of April 10, 1876, a provision that Pawnees who did not work might be cut off the annuity rolls. This meant that the Pawnee and his family would be left to go naked and to do without many necessaries of life which were included in the annuity issues. But the Pawnees were too disheartened to care much whether they went naked or not.

In the later seventies and early eighties the ever-turning wheel of Indian policy had completed another revolution. The Quakers, Episcopalians, Presbyterians, and other church bodies which a decade before had joyfully accepted President Grant's proposal that they should nominate members of their own church bodies for appointment as Indian agents, had now burnt their fingers so often that they gladly relinquished this control over the appointment of agents and limited their operations to the making of Indian policy. Holding an annual meeting in Washington for this purpose, these well-meaning dabblers in Indian affairs, like the designers of ladies' bonnets, seemed unhappy if they could not invent new policy models every twelvemonth. In the early seventies they had advanced the theory that the Pawnees would progress rapidly if uprooted from Nebraska soil and removed to Indian Territory, far from the bad influence of white settlers; but now, in the early eighties, they reversed this theory and forced on the government a new policy based on the theory that only by daily contacts with whites could the Indians be inoculated with a desire to progress. Without a blush the Indian Office, which had removed the Pawnees from Nebraska solely to get them away from the proximity of white settlers, now put pressure on the chiefs to induce them to agree that the new Pawnee reservation should be opened to white settlement.

The Christians and idealists had come a long way from their original stand of kindness and forbearance toward their Indian brothers and were openly advocating the employment of force to compel progress. Determined to make the Indians work and work hard, these Christians, who denounced control of the tribes by the army as a brutal proposal, made up their minds to cut off from free government rations any family whose male members failed to work satisfactorily. It was a plan to starve the Indians into progressing; but to cover its nakedness with a gloss of Christian righteousness, the inventors of the project went into the New Testament and brought out a text attributed to Saint Paul: *He who will not work shall not eat*. They did not find that Saint Paul had said a word to the effect that women and little children should not eat, but simply used the text as a justification for starving entire Indian families.[143]

In 1882 the Pawnee rations were suddenly stopped. Fortunately the tribe had a good corn crop that year; but—being Indians—most of the families invited their friends to feasts and also gave away a large part of their corn and dried vegetables. There was much suffering that winter, and the only assistance obtained from the government was a series of severe lectures from the new agent who told the hungry Indians roughly that he hoped they had now learned their lesson and would husband their surplus food in future. After eighty additional years of lectures and hardship, there are plenty of Indians today who have not yet learned that simple Christian lesson: *Waste not want not*.

With all the pressure the agents had brought to bear on the Pawnees, only fifty-five families had been induced to settle on separate farms by 1882. The tribe had now lost all their horses to Indian and white thieves; they had eight mules in the entire tribe, and the farm work was little more than gardening by the ancient hand method, women doing most of the work. Hundreds of thousands of acres of land lying unused were an irresistible temptation to the whites and, forgetting that if the Pawnees were to progress they must use their land, the officials gave in to the demands of white cattlemen and leased huge blocks of the reservation. True, an attempt had been made to put the Pawnees into cattle growing; but the cattle had been issued to the tribe at the moment when rations were cut off, and nearly all of the eighty stock cattle had been killed and eaten by hungry Indians. In 1883, 150,000 acres of the 283,020 in the reservation were leased for three years to cattlemen at an annual rental of three cents an acre, and the more inert of the Pawnees settled down to live in complete idleness on lease and annuity money, paid once in six months. It was a pittance; but the Pawnees had learned since coming to Indian Territory how to live on almost nothing. One may say that they were too lazy to work or that they were bewildered by new conditions and really could not make a living; but with government rations stopped they did manage to live. There were some families that were doing fairly well; they usually had corn, vegetables, and even meat, and by tribal custom they were expected to share with their poorer neighbors. Such were the results of the well-meant Christian effort to force this tribe to adopt suddenly the white man's way of life.

Those families that had made some progress had much to complain about. The leasing system had filled the reservation with cattle belonging to the whites, and at first the herds got into the Pawnee fields, and the hungry Indians had to watch while the animals devoured their crops. Even after the Indian Office compelled the cattlemen to fence off their range, the situation of the more advanced Indian families was very trying. They had built good frame houses, which they had painted and furnished: quite unlike the log cabins with no furniture that most Indians called homes. These Pawnees had bought with their own money some horses and farm machinery, and the Indian Office reported with pride that the tribe was seventy-five per cent self-supporting; but in 1887 a severe drought wrought such devastation that even the hard-bitten Indian Office officials of the day decided to resume the issuing of free rations and clothing. A period of violently fluctuating economic conditions was thus instituted. In 1888 rations were stopped, presently to be resumed, to be stopped and resumed again.

No one will ever know what sufferings the Pawnees had to endure during this transition period, between 1874 and 1890. In 1883 their agency was combined with the Ponca and Oto agencies, and only a clerk resided among the Pawnees. This man had practically the powers of life and death over the Indians. He could do great harm or great good, according to his nature. In the early eighties Captain Rees Pickering was in charge; after 1885 M. L. McKenzie was clerk for the Pawnees. The Indian police took orders from this clerk; but the Pawnees were surprisingly law-abiding, and the duties of the policemen were almost entirely taken up with pursuing and capturing Pawnee children who had run away from school. The prison system at the Pawnee boarding-school seems to have been thoroughly established by 1883; the children were little less than prisoners, and their parents were generally carefully excluded from the school precincts. In order more effectively to separate the children from their families, the practice of shipping them off to Carlisle and other distant schools had come into vogue, and in 1884 thirty-two Pawnee children were sent into this kind of exile. In the spring of 1887 measles broke out at the Pawnee boarding-school, and to avoid having to care for the sufferers the agent ordered the clerk who was in charge among the Pawnees to "kick the children out." This order was obeyed; and of eighty-five children affected, between thirty and forty died from lack of care. Now and again an affair of this kind threw a lurid light on what was happening among the Pawnees; but as a rule all minor acts of oppression were hidden behind a screen of nicely written official reports. With the old heavy loss from enemy attacks completely removed, the Pawnee population dropped from 2,026 in 1876 to 804 in 1890, and despite the attempts of the officials to make it appear that this loss was unavoidable, the result of hereditary diseases and pulmonary complaints, it was apparent that nearly all the deaths were due to the weakening effects of lack of food, clothing, and proper shelter.

In each of the four Pawnee tribes there were nonprogressive groups who insisted on keeping up the old type of village life to which the agents so strongly objected. These people lived in earth-lodges; but year after year the number of earth-lodges dwindled as new families moved to their own farms and established themselves in log or frame houses. The Pawnee houses were real. Among most of the tribes a house was four log walls and a clay floor, an empty shell without comfort and very unhealthy. The Pawnees finished their houses inside and furnished them comfortably, and Grinnell in 1889 reported that the reservation was dotted with neat farm-houses, barns, and granaries, many of which would have done credit to a New England homestead.

The Pawnees had achieved this success by their own efforts, start-ing without horses or proper tools, and with the majority of the tribe undernourished and sick. As late as 1887 950 Pawnees were treated by the agency physician in one year for various forms of fever. The agents by this date were reporting that most of the sickness in the tribe was lung trouble and hereditary. How strange that this taint had never been observed in Nebraska, and that among the Pawnee school children in Indian Territory, who were properly sheltered, clothed, and fed, there was no trace of lung complaints. One agency physician, who did not regard it as one of his duties to shield the Indian Office officials from the blame for removing this northern tribe to the south, reported nearly one thousand cases of fever and one case of consumption. The worst was over by 1885; but fever continued to be the great enemy, and the birth rate was still lagging behind the rate of deaths.

One of the things that had broken the hearts of the Pawnees was the theft of all their horses soon after they came south in 1874, and one of the first things they did after getting on their feet was to begin buying horses and mules. In 1884 they had a few horses and eight mules; in 1886 they had 184 horses and mules, 159 head of cattle, 100 hogs, and many chickens. In 1888 the tribe owned 1,525 horses and mules, 500 cattle, 1,000 hogs, and 3,000 chickens. They had 2,560 acres under cultivation (twice the acreage they had had in Nebraska) and raised 60,000 bushels of corn, besides great quantities of vegetables and some wheat and oats. In this year the ration system was finally abolished. Nearly all the people were now on their own farms, living in comfortable houses in the midst of fields, which they had neatly fenced in.

Some contemporary observers remarked that this advance of the Pawnees demonstrated the wisdom of the plan to remove the tribe to Indian Territory; a curious view, surely. Had the planners expected the loss of nearly half the people in the tribe through sickness as a preliminary step toward prosperity, and had they counted on the theft of all the Pawnee horses and mules as another means for elevating the position of these Indians? It should be obvious that in Nebraska, where the climate suited them and where their horses and other property would have been much safer than in Indian Territory, the Pawnees would have done better.

The tribe might have done very well now if it had not been for the insidious leasing system which the Indian Office, with its curious aptitude for defeating its own aims by thoughtless actions, had set up in the Pawnee reservation. The officials insisted that the Indians must work; but it permitted the leasing of Indian lands, and the moment the lease money began to come in many Pawnees sat down, to live in idleness. They had worked to prevent the starvation of their families, but now they were gentlemen rent collectors, and why should they work? The agent lectured them on the loss of self-respect that would surely overtake any man who did not work honestly, but such talk was alien and repugnant to the Pawnee philosophy of life. They could idle away their time and retain their self-respect very comfortably, and this they proceeded to demonstrate. Only the Indian Office men were unhappy. They could no longer report progress in civilization and an annual increase in acreage planted and crops garnered by Pawnees.

In 1889 the condition of the Pawnees was good, except in the view of those intolerant persons who expected Indians to give up suddenly all of their old customs and become replicas of New England white farmers in a single generation. The people were comfortable, and each six months, when lease money and annuity money was paid at the agency, there was a grand outburst of feasting and gambling. The Pawnees were split into two opposing factions, as most tribes of the day were, and the progressives and non-progressives took opposing sides on any question that was agitating the people, thus producing factional fights that added much happiness to life on the reservation. The Skidis were progressive; two-thirds of them spoke English, dressed like whites, furnished their houses like whites, had buggies, mowing machines, and reapers. But the other three tribes were non-progressive, clinging to the Pawnee language and customs; and among them only the boys and girls who had returned from off-the-reservation schools wore white people's clothing. The Pitahauerats were the least progressive of all. For twenty years the agents had hammered at the authority of the chiefs, reporting that these men were the worst influence in the tribe; yet when a court of Indian offenses was formed in 1889 the agent found that the men who were most respected and looked up to by the Pawnees were the chiefs, and whether he liked it or not he had to select as judges of the court Sun Chief, head-chief of the Grand Pawnees, Eagle Chief, the old Skidi head-chief, and Brave Chief, the head-chief of the Kitkehahkis. This after twenty years of crusading, to break up the tribal organization and free the common Indian from the alleged tryranny of the chiefs! These judges were the very type of men the agents had been denouncing since 1868; they were all non-progressive, none of them spoke English or wore white clothing, and yet they were the men above all others that the Pawnees, progressive and non-progressive, loved and respected. They made excellent judges, their court proving a model in fairness, good sense, and decorum. These judges made their own code of laws for the reservation, framed purely along Pawnee ideas of right and wrong. In their first year they decided twenty-four cases, four estate cases, ten adjustment of debts among Indians, three cases of the burning of Indian property by Indians, four cases of drinking, and three divorces. Of real crime there was none. Some of the pupils returning from eastern schools set up as lawyers, and, as the Pawnees took naturally to litigation, they did well.

Fifteen years after the Pawnees had been torn from their reservation in Nebraska and removed to Indian Territory with the sole object of isolating the people forever from the evil effects of contact with white populations, the Territory of Oklahoma was formed and the whites came up to the very boundary line of the Pawnee reservation. Some came even farther. Within two years of the opening of the new lands the Pawnees had over half of their horses and mules stolen and were suffering much from white depredations on their timber lands. These first troubles were soon righted. In 1893 the Pawnees all became citizens and their surplus lands were opened to settlement, the Indians becoming a part of a civilized community. The good results for the Pawnees that had been predicted by the Indian Office officials failed to materialize. Care had been taken to settle each Indian family in advance on a good farm before the reservation lands were opened to the whites; the lands remaining were then settled on by white families. There still were many settlers who desired land, and a considerable number of the Pawnees, families that had been working their own farms, succumbed to temptation, rented their land to white men, and moved to the "village" (the agency, now the town of Pawnee) to enjoy a life of idleness. They did not realize that idleness sooner or later means poverty; they sold what they had, little by little, and then discovered when too late that the rent money they received from their white tenants was just about enough to keep life in their bodies. Somehow, money did not stick to Pawnee fingers; but as the years passed the town of Pawnee had an ever-growing number of white tenant farmers who had made comfortable sums out of rented Pawnee lands and had now retired to comfortable and well-provided homes in town.

When a Pawnee died his land was sold and the proceeds divided among the heirs, who promptly spent the money. Such windfalls were frequent at first, providing happy periods of plenty for many Indian families; but new heirs had a way of bobbing up after estates had been liquidated, demanding their share; and presently land titles from Pawnee Indians acquired a bad reputation; fifty per cent of such titles were under a cloud, and loan companies refused to touch them. The whites complained bitterly, and the Pawnees found money to live on harder and harder to obtain. In 1901 the whites got up a petition to the government, asking that half of the remaining Pawnee lands should be sold, and complaining of the burden this great tract of non-taxable Indian land imposed on the white community. The government took no action.

The makers of Indian policy in Washington were now showing an ever increasing desire to shift the responsibility for caring for Indians to the local authorities, and when the Pawnee boarding-school was burned down at night in 1904 the children were placed in the public school. The schoolboard presently petitioned the government for some assistance, stating that these Indian children came from tax free families that contributed nothing to the support of the schools, and that the government should pay something to help out. The Indian Office replied that the public spirited citizens of Pawnee, Oklahoma, should be proud to assist these Indian children in obtaining a free education, and regretted that the United States government could not assist.

In 1917 the Pawnees went to war, fifty-six men, mainly young married men who were legally exempt, entering the service. Eighteen got as far as France; one was killed in action, and one died from the effects of poison gas. In the second World War the Pawnees took their full share, their men fighting in lands that their ancestors had never heard of, in Africa, Italy, France, Germany, and in the islands of the distant South Seas. Today (in 1950) they are again being called into the armed services.

The Pawnees remained in general very poor until 1933, when the Roosevelt administration began pouring out funds of every kind for their assistance. The Pawnee tribe, moribund for so many years, has been officially revived in a quaint new form, with a constitution and by-laws, and they have a corporate charter and a Pawnee Business Association. What the final result of these experiments may be the future must disclose; but unquestionably the Pawnees since 1933 were better cared for than ever before, and their number has steadily increased.

NOTES TO CHAPTER XIII

[138]The boundary of the reservation as originally set by the Indian Office followed the channels of the Arkansas and Cimarron rivers with a western line along longitude 97°; but by act of Congress, April 10, 1876, the west line was altered to echelon along the township lines, as may be seen on any large Oklahoma map, the present Pawnee County having the same boundaries as the Pawnee reservation of 1876.

[139]The Quakers were very happy over the Osage peace offers—the dawn of a new day, the beginning of brotherhood between Pawnees and Osages.

White men taken in by an ancient and simple Indian trick! The Pawnees reserved judgment but gave the thing a trial. Osage peace parties kept coming to visit, each party receiving handsome gifts, including horses, from the Pawnees. Then the time came when the Pawnees could spare no more horses as peace gifts, and the Osages promptly started stealing what horses were left in the Pawnee herd. As the Quakers, persisting in their quest for peace, refused to permit the Pawnees to retaliate and steal Osage horses, within a year the Pawnees lost every horse and mule they had brought from Nebraska.

[140]Information from Captain L. H. North.

[141]This brief account of the last campaign of the scouts is based on Captain L. H. North's narrative. See also Grinnell: *Two Great Scouts,* and Bruce: *The Fighting Norths and the Pawnee Scouts.*

[142]The authority here is mainly the manuscript narrative of the North brothers' visit to the Pawnees in 1876, in the Nebraska Historical Society library.

[143]Ration-cutting as an incentive to work was being experimented with while the Pawnees were still in Nebraska, and it later became a fixed government policy. Christian idealists and humanitarians proposed the use of this starvation method to force the Indians to progress rapidly.

Appendix A

The Padoucas

During the past twenty years archeologists have found in the high plains of eastern Colorado and Wyoming and in the plains and sand hills of western Nebraska a surprising number of Indian camp sites or village ruins that date back to the late prehistoric and forward into the early historic period. Dr. E. B. Renaud, then of the University of Denver, in his Archeological Survey of the High Western Plains catalogued and described an impressive number of such camp sites, while in western Nebraska A. T. Hill of the Nebraska State Historical Museum did the pioneer work and then actually excavated some of the sites, obtaining valuable data on the way of life of these early plains-dwellers. Because the first sites in Nebraska were found on that pleasant little sand hills stream which has been wrongly named the Dismal River, this type of Indian remains has been termed Dismal River culture. Its principal characteristics are the making of rude pottery, the use of roasting-pits (evidently outdoor ones) instead of fireplaces for cooking purposes, and the late date of the remains, indicated by finds of glass beads and bits of metal. In Chase County, Nebraska, on the Stinkingwater, a northern branch of Republican Fork, Mr. Hill found and excavated a village of the Dismal River type which covered some seventy-five acres and was as extensive as the largest Pawnee villages of the early historic period. Here some post ends were dug up, and on being subjected to the tree-ring method of finding dates it was found that the trees from which these posts were cut had stopped growing in the first decade of the 18th century. A similar date was obtained from the tree-rings in another site a little farther to the southwest, in Dundy County. Mr. Hill and his assistant, George Metcalf, tentatively identified these ruins as former villages of the Padouca Indians, and from the historian's viewpoint there can be no question that this identifi-

cation is correct and that all the so-called Dismal River culture sites
in western Nebraska are Padouca remains, and that probably the
camp sites in western Kansas, eastern Colorado, and Wyoming, containing pottery similar to the Dismal River type, are also Padouca.

Early in the 19th century, after the Padoucas as a powerful nation
holding the western high plains were gone, this tribe was identified
as Comanches; and every writer who has mentioned the Padoucas
up to the present, except Dr. George Bird Grinnell and the present
writer, has followed the lead of the earlier authors and termed the
Padoucas Comanches. When this new Dismal River type of early
culture was discovered Dr. W. D. Strong was struck by the fact that
these remains must be those of the Padoucas. He believed the
Comanches were the Padoucas, but after an intensive search he
could find no evidence that the Comanches had ever made pottery
or cultivated crops; and since these village ruins were filled with
broken pottery of local manufacture and clear evidence of the growing of crops, Dr. Strong dropped his effort to identify these Indian
remains as Comanche and left it there.

But why leave it there? These sites are in exactly the localities
in which both the French and the Indian information placed the
main groups of Padoucas. The account of Spanish Louisiana in
1785 moreover terms a south branch of Loup Fork (either Dismal
River or a nearby stream) the River of the Pados or Padoucas, and
it was here that the Dismal River culture was first noted. It was
here on the Dismal that the Omahas told Mackay in 1795 that the
Padoucas had a fort, and here A. T. Hill found remains of what
seem to have been extensive settlements of the Dismal River type.
Moreover, this Dismal River type extends down into western Kansas;
there the Padoucas were still holding out in strength as late as 1725.
Here in Scott County, western Kansas, there are some Pueblo Indian
remains mingled in a site of Dismal River culture, and for fifty
years past our scholars have agreed that these are the remains of an
Apache rancheria at which some runaway Pueblos from New Mexico
took refuge, remaining for some years. But, even with such evidence
before them, most of the ethnologists still believed that the Padoucas were Comanches.

Leaving out the Comanches, who made their first appearance in
the plains near New Mexico about the year 1700, who never made
pottery or planted maize or other crops, how could the great Padouca
nation of the period 1670-1750 be anything else except plains
Apaches? Some of these Apaches—the Gataka or Prairie-Apaches—

were in northern Nebraska or even as far north as southern Dakota at the period 1673-83 and were then trading with the Arikaras, a trade which they kept up until after the year 1800. Dr. A. B. Thomas, from Spanish evidence, has concluded that bands of Apaches were living near the forks of the Platte in the early 18th century, and Dr. E. B. Renaud's catalogue of camp sites in that district supports such a view. Indeed, all down the plains, from near the Black Hills of Dakota to the head of Red River on the Texas border, the Apaches were holding the lands, as the Spanish records indicate, at the very period when the French always spoke of those western plains as the home of the mighty Padoucas.

There is not space here for a lengthy discussion of this problem. The main points for the identification of the Padoucas as Apaches are these: the Padoucas made pottery and grew some crops; the Apaches did the same; the Comanches and all their Shoshonean kindred did not make pottery or cultivate crops. When Villasur set out from New Mexico to go to the Pawnees in 1720 he took a force of Apaches with him (either Jicarillas or Carlanas); yet when he met disaster in the eastern plains all the Indians on or near the Missouri reported to the French traders that this Spanish officer had brought a force of Padoucas with him. The French now sent Bourg-mont up Kansas River to visit and make peace with the Padoucas; when he reached the grand village of the Padoucas, evidently a little to the west of the present town of Salina, he found that these Indians grew crops and lived in some form of semi-permanent lodges. They were therefore not Comanches. His description of them tallies with the Spanish descriptions of the Apaches. In 1774 the French trader Gaignard was trading in the Tawehash or Pawnee villages on upper Red River. He and his men had had many personal contacts with the Comanches, Padoucas, and Apaches, and in all his reports he uses the names Apache and Padouca as synonyms. To clinch the matter, an unnamed Frenchman on Red River, about the date 1720, made a report, printed in Margry, volume VI, page 236, in which he speaks of the Indians who are "known to the Spaniards as Apaches, and to us [the French] as Padoucas."

This problem as to the identity of the Padoucas is not one to be decided by quoting men who wrote between 1806 and 1840, when the Padouca power had vanished. What value is there in these late statements when compared with the information of Frenchmen who lived in daily contact with Padoucas and Comanches? These Frenchmen traded with these tribes; they bought and sold Padouca slaves, and their evidence was that the Padoucas were Apaches.

As for the name Padouca, it may be of Siouan origin, but it might be a word of Pawnee origin. In Pawnee *patu* means *blood* and also *enemy;* and the French often wrote Padouca as Pado or Padou.

Appendix B

Pawnee stream-names

Some of these names were collected by Dr. M. R. Gilmore about the years 1910-1915; some come from Captain L. H. North, who learned them from the Pawnees as early as 1860; others are from modern Pawnee informants. In some instances all these sources of information agree on the names; at other times they differ.

Missouri River: *Kiz paruks ti*: Wonderful River.

Platte River: *Kiz katuz*: Flat Water, Shallow Water.

Niobrara River: *Kiz kakis*: Swift River.

Keyapaha River: *Ra kiz katit hiburu*: Big Black River.[1]

Elkhorn River: *Kisita* (*Kizu,* river, *sita,* up-stream).

Wahoo Creek: *Kipistat kizu*: Dogwood River.

Maple Creek: *Rakizu kizu*: Wood Water or Wood River.

Salt Creek (southern branch of lower Platte): *Kait Kizu*: Salt Water.

Shell Creek: *Ska perus kizu*: Shell River.

Loup Fork: *Its kuddi*: Many Wild Potatoes.

Cedar River, branch of Loup: *Kitta pa to ut*: Canebrake.[2]

Beaver Creek, branch of the Loup: *Kiz perra ha tus*: Sandburr River.[3]

Big Blue River, Nebraska: *Urutu kaku*: Muddy Water.

Little Blue River: *Uruzta reyus*: Blue Mud.

Republican Fork: *Ki ra ru ta*: Filthy Water (defiled by buffalo herds).[4]

---

[1]*Katis*: black; *hiburu*: big. Note the name for Smoky Hill River.

[2]This stream was called Cedar and Willow Creek. But why Canebrake?

[3]George H. Roberts of the Skidis says the name for this stream was *Kituks kitsu*: Beaver Stream. Captain North agrees.

[4]*Kizu*, water; *raruta*, it is filthy.

Beaver Creek, branch of Republican Fork: *Kittux kitsu*: Beaver Stream.

Prairie-dog Creek, branch of Republican: *Uskuts*: Prairie-dog.

Solomon's Fork of Kansas River: *Kitsa we cha ku*: Fountain-by-a-Stream.[5]

Smoky Hill Fork: *Rahota katit hiburu*: Big Black Forest.[6]

Arkansas River: *Kits ka*: Longest River (running eastward).[7]

Salt Fork of Arkansas: *Kiz pahuti hoddi*: Little Red River.

Cimarron River: *Kait*: Salt.

North Canadian River: *Ki ra ru ta*: Muddy.[8]

South Canadian River: *Kiz pahut*: Red River.

Black Bear Creek (on present Pawnee lands): *Koruks katit kiysu*: Black Bear Water.

Appendix C

White men among the Pawnees before 1850

Chouteau, Auguste and *Pierre*. These important St. Louis traders are said to have been trading on the Platte and among the Pawnees as early as 1762.

Gervais, Joseph. Trader among the Nebraska Pawnees before 1800; took the chiefs to Santa Fé for councils in 1803 and 1804.

Pappan, Joseph. Came to St. Louis in 1770, and became active in the Pawnee trade. His half-Pawnee daughter, Emily, married Lucien Fontenelle.

Pappan, A. L. Son or brother of Joseph. A trader among the Pawnees and interpreter for them at the St. Louis treaty, 1818.

---

[5]This name refers to the sacred spring, now called Wakonda Spring. The name looks like a garbled form of the old Pawnee name for the spring: *Kits a wits uk*.

[6]This name refers to the Big Timbers in the upper valley of the Smoky Hill, a favorite spot for winter-camps.

[7]This may be correct; but most of the tribes, from at least as far back as the early 18th century, called the Arkansas in Kansas and Colorado Flint or Flint-knife River. The Pawnee warriors were organized into Knife-Lance societies that seem to date back to the 18th or even the 17th century, and the knife-lance was *kitsita*, which is not very different from the name given above for Arkansas River. The lanceheads were originally made of flint.

[8]This name is the same as the one for Republican Fork. The old-time Pawnees certainly did not call both these important streams by the same name.

Pappan, LaForce. Son of Joseph. Trader among the Pawnees in 1819. He married a Pawnee girl and his daughter married Henry Fontenelle.

Gonore, J. T. A trader among the Pawnees. He interpreted for the chiefs at St. Louis, 1818.

Julien, S. Traded among Pawnees; interpreter at St. Louis, 1818.

Semino or *Semineau.* Traded among the Pawnees; a Pappan employee in 1819.

Bijeau, Joseph. Trader among the Pawnees, 1819; went with Major Long's expedition.

Ledoux, ... Trader among the Pawnees in 1819-20; went with Major Long.

Malboeuf, Etienne. Trader and interpreter for the Pawnees c. 1821.

Simoneau (same as *Semino?*), *Charles.* Interpreter for the Kitkehahki Pawnees, 1821.

Birdair, Michael. French trader; was interpreter for the Skidis "and Pawnees" in 1821.

Manitou (nickname). An old French trader among the Pawnees who was go-between for the Spanish officials in 1800-6 in their Pawnee negotiations.

LaBarge, Joseph. Trader in the Skidi village, 1832-3.

LaChapelle, ... Trader among the Arikaras on the Upper Missouri; had an Arikara wife. When that tribe came to Nebraska in the early 1830's LaChapelle came with them and was nearly lynched at Bellevue by enraged traders in revenge for whites killed by the Arikaras. The whites did lynch Garreau, a mixed-blood Arikara, in the woods near Bellevue. LaChapelle remained among the Pawnees, where Charles A. Murray found him in 1835, living with two Kitkehahki wives. The Pawnees called him *I-sha-pa,* which was their pronunciation of LaChapelle.

Bayhylle (also *Bayhille, Behale*), *Baptiste.* An intelligent and brave Pawnee mixed-blood whose father was a Mexican and mother a Pawnee. He could not write, but was a trusted government interpreter and agency employee from about 1860 on. He was a Pawnee Scout in 1867, and he went to Indian Territory with the tribe in 1874 or 1875.

Vasquez, Barony. Traded among the Pawnees before he went with the Pike expedition in 1806.

Dorio (*Dorion?*). Mentioned by Charles A. Murray as a trader among the Kitkehahkis before 1819. He was a French mixed-blood.

Gantt, Captain. He traded among the Pawnees after 1825, and in

1835 he acted as Colonel Henry Dodge's messenger to the Skidis and Arikaras, whose confidence he had gained.

O'Fallon, John. Early U.S. Indian agent and fur-trader; active in Pawnee affairs.

Dougherty, Henry. Another early agent who dealt with the Pawnees.

Pilcher, Joshua. Another early fur-trader and Indian agent who had dealings with the Pawnees.

Appendix D

Miscellaneous notes

Chiefs. It is very difficult for a writer to keep in mind that among the Pawnees, who counted descent in the female line, the rule was that a chief could not be succeeded by his son. Yet this was clearly the situation. A nephew, the son of the dead chief's *wife's* sister, usually succeeded. Thus Pitalesharo, the last head-chief of the Grand Pawnees in Nebraska, who died of a wound in 1874, was succeeded by a nephew, Sun Chief. Names were often hereditary in families, and it is interesting to note that the Grand Pawnees had a chief named Sun Chief in 1825. Curly Chief of the Kitkehah-kis went to Indian Territory with the tribe in 1874 and died there. He was succeeded by an heir in the female line; but in later years his grandson became chief of the Kitkehahkis, not by right of descent from his grandfather Curly Chief but through the female right of his mother, Curly Chief's daughter.

Chiefs and priests. The chiefs were hereditary keepers of the village sacred bundles, but these bundles could not be used without the consent of the priests, who kept the sacred rituals. Thus the chiefs kept the tools needed for the sacred ceremonies, but the priests alone knew how to use these tools and had the right to use them. The priests undoubtedly exerted very great power in the villages, on the tribal hunts, and in war. The women could not plant their crops or harvest them without the ceremonial assistance of the priests; and at every important moment of life, from babyhood to old age, the Pawnee had to consult the priests and pay for their services. Compared with such tribes as the Sioux, Comanches, and Kiowas, the Pawnees were certainly a priest-ridden people, and this does not seem to have worked to their advantage.

Caddoans and Iroquois. A strange development of recent years has been the repeated references of archeologists and linguists to the supposed early connection of the Pawnees and other Caddoan tribes with the Iroquois and their Cherokee kinsmen. Pawnee pottery and stonework of the late prehistoric period is said to be surprisingly similar to early Iroquois material, and the linguists have found many links between the Iroquoian and Caddoan languages. Sixty years ago Gatchet recorded what he regarded as traditional evidence of a Pawnee, Wichita, and Caddo migration at a very early date from the northeast. Here we have hints that in the prehistoric period the Iroquois, Cherokees, Pawnees, and other Caddoan tribes may have lived in a single group, perhaps in the region east of the Mississippi and south of the Ohio; but up to the present time there is not sufficient evidence of this to form more than a vague surmise as to the location of these tribes before the year 1450.

Clans. On November 17, 1763, the Caballero Macarti reported to the Spanish authorities that the Grand Caddos were divided into four families or tribes (really clans) called Beaver, Otter, Wolf and *Leon* (Panther). In the 19th century ethnologists obtained a fuller list of Caddo clans; but it is obvious that this increase in the number of clans was due to the incorporation of many tribal remnants into the Caddo tribe, these surviving groups of formerly strong tribes bringing into the Caddo organization new clan names. Among the Pawnees these clan groups with animal and bird names were unknown. The Skidi Pawnee clans bore the names of ancient villages which were in existence at the time of Closed Man's coming; and in this Pawnee tribe the animal and bird names belonged to the societies of doctors or priests. Among the Arikaras the same animal and bird names belonged to the men's age-group brotherhoods, which seem to have had no connection with a clan system.

Caddoan stock. This linguistic stock might have been named for the Pawnees, the most important surviving tribe of the stock, if J. W. Powell in naming the stock had not used an alphabetical list of the tribes. He thus came on the name Caddo before reaching Pawnee and called the stock Caddoan. It is an interesting fact that the relationship of the tribes in this stock, established by Powell and others on linguistic grounds late in the 19th century, has been confirmed by a document written by a Spanish priest in east Texas about the year 1716. This document, printed in Harrington, page 273, was not considered important enough to merit translation into English; yet here we have the statement that the Caddoan Indians of east Texas regarded the tribes as far north as the Missouri River in the Dakota country, including the Arikaras, as not only kindred but as actual members of a single nation. This more than confirms the widest claims made by our ethnologists on linguistic evidence.

The knife-lance. The Pawnee warriors belonged to brotherhoods known as knife-lance societies. These organizations seem to point back to a time when the tribe had no horses and the principal weapon in war was a small lance that could be used by footmen. The DeSoto narratives refer to the Caddoan warriors' attack on foot with lances ("sharpened sticks"), and the archeologists have found in prehistoric Caddoan village ruins two types of flint points, which they term arrowheads and lanceheads. Again, when the Pawnees destroyed the Villasur expedition in 1720 they are stated to have charged into the Spanish camp on foot armed with *lancias*. There does not appear to be any record of the use of small lances for fighting on foot among the Pawnees after 1720; yet all the warriors continued to be members of knife-lance societies, each society having a knife-lance of peculiar decoration and special name.

The Salines. These salines in the Oklahoma plains were of great importance to the Caddoan Indians, both as sources of salt and as hunting fields, because of the attraction of the buffalo and other game to these salt deposits. The Grand Saline or Great Salt Plain lay between the Nescatunga (Salt Fork of Arkansas River) and the Cimarron, west of the meridian 99°. The Rock Saline was northwest of the Grand Saline from which it was seventy-five miles distant. It was an eerie place: a level flat of hard red earth surrounded by fantastic naked hills of red clay and gypsum. A salt spring flowed out of the base of a tremendous red hill, forming a small salt stream, and other salt springs were dotted about the flat. Here there was a huge red cedar which Texier states "the Pawnees worship fervently," to which they brought gifts and made sacrifices. In dry seasons the flat land at the Rock Saline was one mass of thick rock salt, which the Indians broke up and carried away on their horses. After they had driven the Caddoan tribes away from the Arkansas River in southern Kansas and northern Oklahoma, late in the 18th century, the Osages fell heir to these salines, from which they attempted to bar other tribes; but the Pawnees and even occasional parties of Arikaras from Dakota, continued to come south for salt, while the Comanches and other plains tribes disputed the Osage claims to the salines. A late record of a Pawnee visit to the Rock Saline is to be found in the Kilian notebooks, number six,

p. 33. Here a Kansas pioneer records that in 1861 he was hunting with other men on Spillman Creek when fourteen Pawnees visited their camp with stolen Mexican horses, some of the animals loaded with rock salt from the saline near the Cimarron. These Pawnees stated that they had been away from home for eight months.

Skidi star chart. This very old star map, made on a piece of animal skin, is reproduced in the *National Geographic Magazine,* July, 1944, page 195, where Dr. M. W. Stirling remarks that from astronomical evidence the chart dates back to the time of Columbus. From the historical viewpoint, it may be added, this chart dates to the time of Closed Man, for it shows his Four Directions villages in the west as four large stars.

Human sacrifice. Dr. Clark Wissler suggests that this Skidi Pawnee practice was drawn from Aztec origins; but where are the connecting links between the Aztecs and Skidis? No other tribe in the plains had this peculiar custom except the Arikaras, who are said to have abandoned sacrifices soon after their first contacts with the white traders. The Skidi ceremony of sacrifice had some similarities with customs noted among the Caddoans of east Texas by the Spaniards after 1690; but these southern practices were termed cannibalism. Father Casanas found cannibalism being practiced openly among the Caddoan tribes of Texas, and his description of the frame of poles to which the victim was bound reminds one of the similar frame used by the Skidis in their human sacrifices. Casanas termed this frame a *cross,* and so also did the Frenchman Penicault in 1714. Cannibalism among the southern Caddoans was clearly not simple man-eating, but was a form of sun worship, whereas the Skidi sacrifice was a rite of star worship. Just as the Skidis turned the victim to face Morning Star, the Texas Indians turned theirs to face the rising sun; then late in the day they turned the victim to face the setting sun. In Texas priests were in charge during the torturing, killing, and cutting up of the victim, and they portioned out the flesh to the different families, whose women took it away and cooked it. Among the Skidis there were no traces of cannibalism, and the indications of that custom found by archeologists along the Missouri River in eastern Nebraska and western Iowa lie outside the Skidi territory. Dr. Wedel found human bones on the floor of a temple in the Quivira area in Kansas, and here again we have a hint of Caddoan Indians practicing human sacrifice both as a religious rite and for the purpose of eating the victims' flesh. Our ethnologists have usually attempted to gloss over or hide

these plain indications of cannibalism among our Indians at an
early period; but it becomes clearer every year that several of the
Caddoan tribes were cannibals, as were also the Iroquois, who are
supposed to be distant kinsmen of the Caddoans.

Big Spotted Horse. Captain L. H. North used to speak of this
warrior as a Pawnee progressive; perhaps because he did things
and, having done them, went elsewhere and left innocent persons
to pay for what he had done. This Pawnee was six feet two inches
tall in his moccasins—a big, good-natured fellow, always laughing
and joking, when not fighting. As a progressive he disapproved
violently of Quakers and all white men who preached against fighting and horse-lifting. In both these arts he was an adept; but being
an inveterate gambler, he lost in Pawnee games and white man's
poker most of the horses and other valuables he gained by risking
his life on the warpath. Whenever he came home with a good haul
of enemy horses, he gave some of the animals away, gambled the
rest, and became a poor man again. He was very fond of his wife
and child, and unlike the other Pawnee men he was not ashamed
to exhibit his fondness in public. He helped his wife with her
fieldwork and openly and shamelessly carried the baby; but no man
dared to make the usual jeering remarks that greeted any Pawnee
who was caught doing squaw work. Captain North stated that Big
Spotted Horse was a scout in Captain S. E. Cushing's Pawnee company about the year 1870, but he did not serve in the Pawnee Scouts
in other years. He is said to have served with the Indian scouts led
by Captain R. H. Pratt in Indian Territory in 1874, in the fighting
against the Kiowas and other hostiles.

Sharitarish. Note the Pawnee name of the mixed-blood interpreter Baptiste Bayhylle: *Lashar shereterik*: Chief-the-Great-Spirit-
Shines-On. The second part of this name resembles Sharitarish. The
Hon. Charles A. Murry who spent part of the summer of 1835 in
the lodge of Sharitarish seems to mean (p. 206, London edition of
1900) that the medicine-man told him that Sharitarish was the son
of a famous chief named Bear-Who-Walks-in-the-Night.

Little Kitkehahkis. This was the name of a band and village on
Loup Fork in the first half of the 19th century. Lesser and Weltfish
state that in recent years the Pawnees informed them that this band
split off from the main Kitkehahki village "not more than three
generations ago" to follow a new chief named Curly Chief. Here we
have another example of modern Indian memory. Curly Chief was
the man who led this band when it went to Indian Territory in

1874, and the band had led a separate existence probably even before Curly Chief was born.

Pitahauerat. Frank North said in 1870 that this name meant Down-the-Stream, which on the Platte and Loup meant east: Eastern Village. Lesser and Weltfish carefully dissected the word and gave its meaning as "man who goes east." This has as faint a trace of historical sense as most of these modern explanations of Caddoan tribal names, whether the explanation comes from the Indians themselves or from linguists. The French traders habitually called the Pitahauerats *Tapage Pawnees,* which the Americans translated into *Noisy Pawnees.* In the Pawnee Hako ceremony *rata* means *screaming,* *pita* means a *man;* and for all we know some French trader with a smattering of the Pawnee language may have guessed that these two words were the origin of the name Pitahauerat, which he built into Screamers or Tapages. The Pitahauerat second band was called Kawarakis, which seems to refer to horses, *kawara* (Caddoan pronunciation of Spanish *caballo?)* meaning *horse* and *kish* meaning *people.* In Pawnee *horse* is *arosha,* but in Arikara it is *kawarusha,* and we have the statements of many old Pawnees that the Kawarakis folk "spoke like Arikaras." It is quite possible that they were Arikaras, for whenever disaster overtook that tribe, as when the Sioux drove them from their villages in 1794-5, some group of Arikaras usually went south, to live with the Pawnees.

Eagle Chief and Ter-ra-re-cox. The family of *Ter-ra-re-cox* (they claim this is a very old Pawnee name meaning *Warcry*) had a paper dated 1869 which described this man as *the Soldier of the Skeedee Pawnees,* a rank which we might term that of war chief. Ter-ra-re-cox had made a fine reputation among the Skidis; he was very popular, and seemingly not above taking advantage of that fact; for, according to the statements of the Pawnee trader, Walton, in the early 1870's this chief was making a hard push to have old Eagle Chief thrown out of his position of head-chief, to which rank Ter-ra-re-cox wished to be promoted. Here we have a curious sidelight on the statements of the Pawnees that their head-chiefs were selected on strict rules of hereditary right, and that ambitious warriors could not win to such rank. Yet Ter-ra-re-cox nearly did. He had a great following among the Skidi warriors, and he was making up to the government officials and traders in such a manner that he had the old head-chief terribly worried. When Walton was going to Washington on business in 1873 Eagle Chief came to him privately and begged him most earnestly to see President Grant and inform him of the trouble that Ter-ra-re-cox was stirring up among the Skidis. Walton thought that President Grant had enough of his own political troubles to deal with and should not be bothered over Skidi Pawnee politics; but while in Washington he did go to the Indian Office and put old Eagle Chief's case before the officials in as strong a manner as possible. He was given an impressive document which stated that Eagle Chief was the recognized head-chief of the Skidis, a good and loyal man, who would be officially supported in his position as long as he remained loyal. On receiving this document from Walton, Eagle Chief was very happy. He thought all his troubles were ended; but the very next year he lost his reputation for loyalty when he opposed with all his strength the government plan to remove the tribe to Indian Territory. Ter-ra-re-cox at once renewed his efforts to oust the old chief, and he and his numerous followers were probably responsible for the surprising shift of opinion among the Skidis, who in 1873 bitterly opposed removal to Indian Territory, but in 1874 swung to the opposite view. Most of the Pawnees who went to the Territory in 1874 were Skidis; but on reaching the south they fell sick, lost all their horses and became terribly discouraged. They began to tell each other that their troubles were caused by their foolish desertion of their good old leader, Eagle Chief; they blamed Ter-ra-re-cox and his friends for having misled them; and now they turned against these men and once more accepted Eagle Chief as their natural leader. When in 1889 the government formed a court of Indian justice among the Pawnees, it was found that Eagle Chief was the most respected and loved man among the Skidis, and he was made judge of the court as representative of that tribe.

Grass-lodges in Nebraska. North of the Platte, in the district near the town of Schuyler, there are extensive remains of Pawnee villages of early date, in which there seem to be no traces of earth-lodge ruins, and some archeologists have suggested that the Indians here must have lived in some form of semi-permanent dwellings, such as grass-lodges, the traces of which would soon disappear after they fell in ruins. One objection has been made to such a theory, and that is that we have had no record of the use of the southern type of grass-lodges by the Pawnees of Nebraska. But I have found such a record. In the spring of 1813 a party of fur-traders led by Robert Stuart was coming down the Platte from the Rocky Mountains. They crossed to the south bank of the Platte a few miles west of Plum Creek, in the district in which the Pawnees usually encamped for many days before starting on their buffalo hunt in western Kansas. Here the Stuart party found a heavy trail and the remains of a very large Indian encampment, and in this camp they found a "straw hut" or grass-lodge with three Indian women living in it, who stated that they were Pawnees. Here we have the proof that the Pawnees did construct grass-lodges in Nebraska and were continuing to do so as late as 1813—not in their permanent villages, where they used earth-lodges, but on their hunting expeditions, when they expected to remain in one camp for a considerable time and wished to have a comfortable dwelling. Such grass-lodges must have lasted for years, if repaired each season.

The Pawnee massacre of 1873. Dr. Carver, the showman, was putting out some publicity for his show in 1926, in which he recounted his feats of marksmanship when, in 1873, he had a match with another buffalo-hunter named Buffalo Curley, Carver winning the match by killing 160 buffaloes in a single run. This match was run "in the winter of 1873," on Frenchman's Fork, in the very district in which the Sioux massacred the Pawnee hunters on August 5, 1873. The Carver account states that a great number of white buffalo-hunters, a troop of cavalry and several officers and their wives from Fort McPherson on the Platte, and a large gathering of Sioux and Pawnees had assembled to watch the match, and that the whites had much trouble in preventing a fight between the Sioux and Pawnees. Carver continues that the Sioux were so angry that "they registered an oath that if ever the Pawnees came into the country again they would scalp the whole lot. True to this threat, the next summer the Sioux surprised the Pawnees and killed 350 of them in this same country, only a few miles from where this great [buffalo-killing] championship was decided." If this tale is true, the government officials had plenty of warning of the bloody intentions of the Sioux, and it was criminal carelessness on the part of these officials that caused the disaster to the Pawnees. The Sioux were being bountifully fed on free government beef, flour, and other provisions. They went buffalo hunting for pleasure, and in the hope of a still greater pleasure—the opportunity to kill a few hundred friendly Pawnees.

Appendix E

Tables of Population

These figures on Pawnee population are the best available. They exhibit a steady and dreadful loss in population from 1675 to 1905, and then a slow increase. About 1700 the Pawnees seem to have been divided into Skidi Pawnees 22 villages, Arikaras 10 villages, Black Pawnees and Panis Piques about 13 villages. Up to 1845 Indian agents, fur-traders, and missionaries rated all Pawnees over 10 years as adults; but the age has been increased from time to time until today (1950) we find scientifically trained welfare workers referring to Pawnee girls of 20 as children.

PAWNEE POPULATION

Date	Villages	Lodges	Men	Women	Children	Total	Authorities and remarks
1675	40+						French reports.
1719	45						LaHarpe. Includes Arikaras.
1764			3,700				Col. Bouquet. Panis Blancs, 2,000 men; Panis Piques, 1,700.
1804	4		700				Gazetteer of Western Continent. Nebraska Pawnees only.
1806	3		1,993	2,170	2,060	6,223	Lieut. Z .M. Pike.
1811	2		1,300			5,000	Missouri Gazette, Apr. 25, 1811.
1820	4	330				6,500	Edwin James. Reliable.
1824			2,000				Agent O'Fallon.
1825	3		2,050			10,250	Col. Henry Atkinson.
1829	3					8,000	Sec. of War. Panis Pique, 4,000; total Pawnees, 12,000.
1833						10,000	George Catlin.
1834						11,000	Official report.
1834						8,000	Missionary report. Reliable.
1836						12,500	Official.
1836	4	270				10,000	Missionary report.
1840	6	270	1,449	2,185	2,808	6,244	Missionary Report. First actual count.
1846						12,500	Agent's report. Same number every year.
1847			1,200			8,400	Missionary estimate. Number of warriors in 1848.
1850					1,200	5,000?	Agent's report: "4,000 to 5,000." 1,234 died of cholera in '49.
1856						4,686	Agent.
1860						4,000	Nebraska settlers' estimate.

Date	Villages	Lodges	Men	Women	Children	Total	Authorities and remarks
1861						3,416	Agent.
1862						3,414	Agent. Actual count.
1864						3,350	
1865						2,800	Number on annuity roll.
1866						2,750	
1867						2,935	
1868						2,831	Male, 1,218; female, 1,613.
1869						2,398	
1870						3,000	George Bird Grinnell. Estimate.
1871						2,364	
1872			509	876	1,062	2,447	Gain in year, 83.
1874						1,788	In Nebraska, others Ind. Ter.
1875						2,276	First census of tribe in Ind. Ter. Male, 866; female, 1,160.
1876						2,026	In Ind. Ter.
1879						1,440	800 deaths in first five years in Ind. Ter.
1881						1,250	Children, 384.
1886						998	Births, 28; deaths, 77.
1888						869	
1890						804	Male, 380; female, 424; school children, 124.
1900						650	
1905						646	
1910						653	
1915						679	
1920						731	
1925						809	
1928						835	Male, 410; female, 425. Adults, 420; minors, 425.
1930						844	
1934						906	
1936						957	Adults, 468; minors, 491.
1938						977	Males, 494; females, 483.
1940						1,017	Males, 516; females, 501.

POPULATION BY TRIBES

Date	Villages	Men	Women	Children	Total	Lodges	Authorities and remarks
				Grand Pawnees			
1700	3?						Three sacred bundles.
1770	1						
1804	1	280			1,000		Lewis and Clark. Too low.
1806	1	1,000	1,120	1,000	3,120		Lieut. Z. M. Pike.
1820	1				2,000	100	Edwin James. Families, 500.
1825	1	1,100			5,500		Col. Henry Atkinson.
1840	1	330	563	888	1,781	84	Missionaries. Actual count. Boys under 10, 416; girls under 10, 472.
1862					903		Counted by agent.
1872		140	254	365	759		Counted by agent.
1939					200		Pawnee estimate.
				Skidis			
1650	22						French reports; Pawnee tradition.
1686	17						Father Douay.
1701	12						French map, said to date 1701.
1717	9						French report.
1723	8						Renaudiere.
1750		900					Father Vivier. Say 4,000 population.
1806	1?	480	500	500	1,485		Pike.
1820	1				3,500	145	Edwin James. Reliable. Families, 900.
1822						120	J. Morse.
1825		700			3,500		Col. Henry Atkinson.
1834						70	John Dunbar. Reliable.
1840	1	469	598	839	1,906	64	Counted by missionaries. Boys under 10, 367; girls under 10, 472.
1862	1				1,166		Counted by agent.
1872	1	154	232	244	630		Counted by agent.
1938					450		Pawnee estimate.
				Kitkehahkis			
1700	2?						Two bands and two sacred bundles.
1804	1	300			1400		Lewis and Clark.
1806	1	500	550	560	1,618	44	Pike.
1820	1				1,000	50	Edwin James. Families, 250.
1825		250			1,250		Col. Henry Atkinson.

Date	Villages	Men	Women	Children	Total	Lodges	Authorities and remarks
1840	3?	404	709	810	1,923	81	Counted by missionaries. Boys under 10, 371; girls under 10, 439.
1862					784		Counted by agent.
1872		124	208	218	550		Counted by agent.
1938					250		Pawnee estimate.

Pitahauerats

Date	Villages	Men	Women	Children	Total	Lodges	Authorities and remarks
1700	2						Two bands and two sacred bundles?
1832							Up to this date the Pitahauerats were counted as Grand Pawnees.
1833					1,000		John T. Irving.
1840	1	246	315	271	832	41	Counted by missionaries. Boys under 10, 134; girls under 10, 137.
1862					561		Counted by agent.
1872		91	182	235	508		Counted by agent.
1938					100		Pawnee estimate.

Index